MAKEOVER

from **WITHIN**

MAKEOVER *from* WITHIN

Lessons in Hardship, Acceptance, and Self-Discovery

TY HUNTER

with

EILA MELL

CHRONICLE BOOKS

SAN FRANCISCO

Library of Congress Cataloging-in-Publication Data

Name: Hunter, Ty, author.
Title: Makeover from within / Ty Hunter.
Description: San Francisco, California : Chronicle Books LLC, [2022]
Identifiers: LCCN 2022008157 | ISBN 9781797217529 (hardcover)
Subjects: LCSH: Hunter, Ty. | Fashion designers--United States--Biography.
  | Image consultants--United States--Biography. | African American
  fashion designers--Biography.
Classification: LCC TT505.H86 A3 2022 | DDC 746.9/2092
  [B]--dc23/eng/20220223
LC record available at https://lccn.loc.gov/2022008157

ISBN: 978-1-7972-1752-9

Manufactured in China.

Packaged by Christopher Navratil
Developmental edit by Susan Lauzau
Designed by Tim Palin Creative

10 9 8 7 6 5 4 3 2 1

Chronicle Books LLC
680 Second Street
San Francisco, CA 94107
www.chroniclebooks.com

For my creators,
my mom and my dad—
and for my creation, my daughter.
You are my inspiration
and my motivation.
I love you.

Contents

My Brother, Ty Hunter
by Beyoncé

We were looking for a stylist, but we ended up with a new member of our family, and I ended up with the brother I have always wanted.

Ty Hunter came into our lives to add to the sartorial splendor of Destiny's Child, and to essentially help my mother, Tina Knowles-Lawson, who was designing, sewing, and creating original looks for us for all appearances as well as touring.

My mother used everything in her skills and imagination to create costumes and a matching wardrobe for the group on a small budget, as designer after designer turned her down when she requested clothes for the group. She had to pivot because they made it clear they were not interested in dressing us. But she also knew she needed help and could not continue doing it all on her own.

She first met Ty at a clothing store in Houston, Texas, in 1999. He had recently moved from Austin after deciding that he no longer wanted a career in the medical field. More than his love and understanding of fashion, it was his humility and kindness that drew my mother in. She promised him she would get him out of that store, and she did. His first styling credit was for our "Survivor" video, and he has made it a point to help others the way my mother helped him.

When he became my stylist, Ty knew that I was more interested in clothes that fit and not who designed them. He focused on finding true talent and introduced

On a break from shooting the "Bonnie & Clyde" video

me to emerging designers. In doing so, he paid it forward, giving others an opportunity to create original designs while building their careers.

Ty is a beautiful human who sees beauty, style, and grace in everyone. Every single day I am reminded of what my mother first saw, a kind, passionate, hard worker with the biggest heart.

He is also incredibly patient. Imagine your first job is to style three young women who are evolving right before your eyes, changing their minds constantly about what works and what doesn't—but he never lost his cool. His hard work and diligence have paid off, as he has become one of the most respected fashion stylists working today while building relationships with every fashion house, iconic and emerging.

Ty knows styling, from draping to understanding the perfect silhouettes and choosing the right fabric for that instantly iconic look. He also knows how to make a statement with less. When we discussed the wardrobe for the "Crazy in Love" video, Ty and my mother knew instantly that less is more. A white tank top, denim shorts, and red shoes. Nothing else. To this day, he still says that was his favorite moment.

I could pull out a thousand memorable looks that we have created for red carpets, photo shoots, and performances, from the Met Gala to the VMAs, but what stays with me the most are the endless conversations we have had about life, love, and the importance of family.

That Ty would name this book *Makeover from Within* not only says everything about the genuine person he is, but it reminds me of something my mother has always said, that "external beauty is fleeting, but beauty from within never fades."

Readers of this book are about to go on a beautiful journey with my friend, my confidant, my brother, Ty Hunter.

INTRODUCTION

We're all Easter eggs, and everybody is trying to make the shell beautiful. That's the society we live in. In reality, the yolk is the most vital part. What's inside is what feeds us and helps us push forward. So many people think, "Once I get this thing or achieve that goal, get this guy, look a certain way, have the right house or car, I've arrived." But you arrived when you were born. I arrived on August 20, 1972. I have everything I need to be happy—and so do you.

I started on social media to keep in touch with friends and family. The first photo I posted was in a fabric store with Miss Tina Knowles. I just took a picture of spools of fabric. Gradually, my posts moved from photos to motivational quotes, and the overwhelming response to the thoughts I shared (some mine and some borrowed wisdom from others) made me realize I wasn't alone. I'd be on a tour with Beyoncé and people would come up to me to say how much they loved my page, and how it helped them get through a difficult time in their life. I could have easily kept posting fashion but I was interested in a bigger picture. I wanted my social media presence to be about mental health and helping people cope with their everyday. I used yellow to bring light to the darkness that can live on the internet, and I called my page "Ty's Yellow Pages."

Navigating this world can be difficult, and pushing yourself day to day is a process. My community helps me see what people are going through, and supporting them keeps me going, keeps me real. I've had people say my words helped them when they were suicidal or that my posts steadied them through a divorce. That made me realize my platform is bigger than me. I want to keep that upbeat flow going. It's easy to put out negativity, but I choose what I want to receive, which is positivity and blessings. So that's what I put out.

And that's what I choose to put out in my life too. As a stylist, I make sure people look good on the outside. That is part of my job. But I also make sure my clients feel good about themselves. I help them love themselves and overcome what they view as problem areas on their bodies. I get them to a place where they see fashion as fun and don't take it so seriously. Maybe you feel like you want to work on your body. Fine. Change is worthwhile if you're strengthening something you truly think needs improvement. But that effort doesn't mean you're not beautiful and perfect right now. You need to get to that place of self-love. Once you are happy in your skin, work on the shell all you want. But start your makeover from within. Keep your main focus on the real you, on your heart and soul.

I'm happy with myself now, but my self-assurance was hard-won. And as I listened to you all—friends, family, and followers—I realized I had more to share than social media could encompass. This book was a way for me to go deeper into my experiences and share what I've learned in a way that lets you see the whole spectrum of my life—the sadness and misfortunes and heartbreaks along with the triumphs and joys. I want you to know the beautiful, generous people who have cared for and encouraged me and also the folks who did me wrong. And I want you to see how I dealt with it all—my mistakes, triumphs, hard work, and lucky breaks. There's such richness in our experiences if we learn to look at them as opportunities for growth rather than as things that just happen to us.

There are going to be good days and bad days, but I know I can survive those bad days and surmount the difficult things. I don't have to be afraid, because whatever comes my way, I can handle it. And you can too. That's what tough times show us. And the people who love us are going to be right there with us in our dark hours, just as we will be there for them. We need to treasure those loved ones and continue nourishing that vital part of ourselves that understands we are perfect just as we are. And we need to have faith that bright days will always come again.

PART I

Becoming Ty

ONE

The Women Who Shaped Me

Women have always been my comfort zone. All my life, women have allowed me to be myself in a wholehearted way that didn't come naturally to most of the men I knew growing up in Texas. And I was surrounded by strong, independent women! These women wanted to know my opinion on things. My stamp of approval mattered to them. And theirs mattered to me. Their care and attention has always made me feel important, special, loved. It has shaped me into who I am.

When I was little, I never wanted to be apart from my mom. We depended on each other. She had me when she was only nineteen, and in a way, we grew up together. She'd left my dad soon after finding out he had gotten another woman pregnant (with my lovely sister, Sonya). So she was alone. But she was never really alone.

At first, when I was a baby, my mom and I lived with my grandmother, who stepped in to help raise me. My mother called my grandmother Mama and my grandma called her Connie, so I called my grandmother Mama and my mother Connie, too. I didn't stop that till about junior high. I saw my grandmother as the authority figure, in charge of both my mom and me, though my mom didn't see it that way. Mom was clearly my parent, but she was always my friend too. Even now, that's my girl.

Above: My godmother, Ethel, my great-grandmother, Mama Bea, and my grandmother, Georgia

When I was two or three years old, my godmother, Ethel, and my mom got an apartment together. Ethel and my mother have been like sisters ever since they were girls. Both had four brothers and were the only daughters, so they needed each other; they craved that feminine energy, and that's what they gave each other.

Ethel has always been in my life; she's a second mother to me. She helped take care of me, and she is the one I turned to if I needed help with something practical. Ethel knows about almost everything, and what she doesn't know, she's going to find out. She worked for the comptroller's office in Texas and we relied on her, on her strength and levelheadedness. She did our taxes growing up, and she gave us legal guidance. She understood how to handle life situations. But she could be a lot of fun too. Sometimes I would watch Ethel and Mom get ready to go out at night. They seemed so glamorous and grown up. Looking back, I realize they were only in their twenties! Mom and Ethel adored Natalie Cole, and whatever Natalie did, they would do. They had wigs, and they'd put their real hair in the front and blend it into the wig to look like Ms. Cole. They'd make updos, with knots and braids, just like Natalie Cole used to wear on her TV specials and in the Posner hair product commercials you'd see every time you watched *Soul Train*. She was a beautiful fixture in my life.

I especially loved helping Mom choose her outfits for those evenings out, and I was mesmerized as I watched her put on makeup and do her hair. Her transformation from nine-to-five hospital worker into beautiful young woman going out on the town captivated me. She would model different clothes and jewelry and ask me what looked best on her, and I felt so special that she took my suggestions. My mom showed me early on that when you feel confident about the way you look, you feel better about yourself.

On the nights Mom and Ethel went out clubbing, they would drop me off at my great-grandmother's house. I called her Mama Bea, and she was my everything. I just loved being around her. I'd sit for hours and listen to her talk to her friends—she was so funny and spicy. There were a lot of kids who lived right by her, and I would run around and play with them, so I always had a lot of fun at her house. When it was time for bed, she would lay all these handmade quilts and big blankets out on the living room floor. She would fold them up so thick that it felt like I was laying on a mattress. That was before there were blow-up mattresses! She made me so comfortable that I never had a problem falling asleep there. In the morning, Mama Bea made golden hot water cornbread cakes in an

Every woman is a queen. Remind them daily because this world can make them forget.

My mother, Connie, a new mom at nineteen

iron skillet. She'd add a pat of butter and sprinkle sugar on top, simple things that were just so good.

Mama Bea never changed, even as she got older. She had no filter. If someone spoke Spanish around her, she thought they were talking about her. We would tell her, "Mama Bea, those people are not talking about you. They're talking about canned goods. That has nothing to do with you." She was ready to fight at the drop of a dime. She was just a funny, little, skinny lady (I look a lot like her) who kept us laughing all the time.

Once my friend Damon came with me to her house. Damon had dreads, which in Texas was a rare thing. I had always wanted locks, and my hair was in this growing phase; I had just started twisting my fro a little bit. Mama Bea said, "I hope you don't think you're going to grow those things in your head like your friend. I hate them things. They look unclean. I don't like them."

"Mama Bea, I want my hair like that," I told her.

She said, "I don't like them and your friend looks crazy."

"Which friend?" I asked. "The one right here?" I opened the door to the living room, where Damon was sitting. She said to him, "Well, baby, they look good on you. But Ty . . . his head is too long and they just won't look right on him."

Mama Bea was the only person who would get in the car with me when I got my driver's license. Everybody else said I couldn't drive. She and I would just roll. I'd go pick her up and we would go to garage sales, thrifting all day, just having the best time. That woman gave me so much love.

Mama Bea may have spoiled me a little, but she had been very strict when she was raising my grandmother. She was so worried about her children going down the wrong path in life that she didn't allow them to do anything. When Grandma finally moved out of the house, she went wild partying and living it up. She eventually settled down, and she promised herself she wouldn't do to her kids what Mama Bea had done to her. She kept that promise. My uncles had a lot of freedom, and could pretty much do what they wanted. My mom had more restrictions than the boys, but she could still date and live her life.

Mom adopted the same parenting philosophy her mother had. She'd been raised with a sense of independence and she wanted to pass the same kind of freedom on to me. She wanted me to be safe, so I was supposed to let her know where I was, but other

Mama Bea always reminded me of Flo from the TV show Alice: "Kiss my grits!"

than that I was allowed to explore. I'd go out early and be gone all day. That's back when you could be on your bike and not come home until 10 p.m. and nobody thought anything of it.

The independence my mother gave me allowed me to not lose my mind when I got older. I never really rebelled the way some of my friends did. I didn't have to. They would cut up and do crazy stuff, but because I had such freedom I could keep myself in check. They would make some risky plan but I wouldn't go along—I couldn't do that to my mom.

I could talk to my mom about anything and everything, and that helped me stay out of a lot of trouble. She didn't make anything seem too tempting, like, "This is the cookie jar, now don't go in it." Her attitude was, "This is the cookie jar—go in it, but don't eat too much." If you tell someone they can't do something, you create curiosity. My mom's way of thinking was a blessing, and it kept me on the straight and narrow.

A night on the town for Ethel, Mom, and my cousin Dee Maxwell

As I grew, I liked being with Mama Bea and my grandma and her friends more and more. I liked talking to them and I loved their wisdom and old stories. I have an old soul, and I could relate to the way older folks talked about the past. When I went to church, I preferred to sit in the pew with older people, where I'd get a good nap and candy. Older people keep it real and don't sugarcoat or hold anything back—and why should they?

In our family, the older women were always the center. My grandmother was our rock. She was the one who gathered the family together; if she was going to be somewhere, then we knew that certain cousins and friends would be there too. And she was *my* rock. She was there to help take care of me, from the time I was a baby.

Clockwise from top: Mom with me and my little brother, Cedric—the original Willis and Arnold from Diff'rent Strokes; high school portrait of Mom; Mom on her twenty-fifth birthday. By the end of the night, her top would be covered with money—people pinned bills to her as a birthday present.

Grandma was always cooking for every holiday and every party to make sure everybody came together. When she passed away, you could see those connections start to slowly trickle away. But you could also see some links continuing. When I was younger, Mom was too busy working to do much cooking but my grandmother was smart enough to teach her how to prepare some of her signature dishes. I thank my mom for learning how to make my grandmother's stuffing and Mama Bea's sweet potato pie. Now she cooks these family favorites exactly like her mom and grandmother did, and it's like having a little bit of them back. Priceless.

When my grandmother died, we found out that she had already made arrangements and paid for her funeral. The family also found letters she had written to each of her kids telling them how she felt. She wrote those letters way before she got sick because she wanted to make sure everyone knew what they meant to her. It was beautiful the way she took care of everyone, even after she was gone. I plan to do the same.

All my life, these amazing women have given me honesty, loyalty, support, and trust. They've been there for me, regardless of what I'm going through. I know they're not going to judge me. They've shown me that it's okay to be completely myself. To be black, to be gay, to be sensitive. Because of these women, I have an understanding of and compassion for humanity. To this day, I need to have feminine energy around me. Women keep me balanced. They remind me to stay grounded. They remind me to hold my shape.

Celebrating with my grandmother at my brother's wedding

Take the time to learn from the elders in your family. You won't always have that opportunity and there may be a day when you're sorry you didn't.

Mom and my grandmother, Georgia

Ty's Takeaways

> Ask for help from loved ones you trust and care about. It's not weak to ask for help or communicate your problems—the people you confide in will appreciate that you chose them. Showing your vulnerability and helping each other through difficult times brings you closer. Trust is hard to build, so when you find someone you can trust, hang on to them. These are the people who will stay with you forever.

> Take a little time to reflect on the people in your life who have shaped you, then go and thank them—write a personal note, call them on the phone, or take them out to lunch. We're all influenced by the people around us, so show gratitude to the loved ones who've made you the person you are today.

> Make memories with your loved ones and cherish every moment you have together. At any given moment, God could ask them to come home, so spend your time with family in a way that will leave you with no regrets. Build lasting memories; so many people relate that they are sorry they didn't record their loved ones' stories, take more pictures, ask questions about their past, or save voicemail messages. It takes less than five minutes to check on someone and let them know you care.

Four generations of the women I love

TWO

The Day My Life Changed

My dad loved me. I always knew that.

He was there for me all my life, even though we didn't live together, for the most part. But he was always a phone call away. A few times a week he'd come around the house to pick me up and we'd spend time together. He and my mom had a complicated relationship—they were on and off for years. When I was four, they got back together for a time. That reunion resulted in my brother, Cedric. At times, I couldn't even tell if they were together or not.

They called it quits for good by the time I was about eleven. I knew what a family was supposed to look like. My cousins all had a father and a mother who lived together, and so did the families I saw in movies and on TV. My situation was different. I watched my mom bust her ass to make sure we had all we needed and much of what we wanted, which gave me so much respect for her. Life for my mom was harder without my dad, but in a lot of ways, I felt

My handsome dad at fifty—he always looked younger than his age.

more comfortable when he wasn't there. I was more reserved in front of my dad. I could whine to Mom and get what I wanted, but Dad wasn't having that. He could be fun but was stricter than my mom. With Mom, I felt free to be myself. I could sit with my legs crossed in front of her, but not my dad. Boys aren't supposed to cross their legs. I had to watch myself when Dad was there.

At least once or twice a week, Dad would take Cedric and me out to eat. That was exciting! Mom cooked—or at least she heated up food for us at home. She wasn't a good cook when I was little, though she got better later, when she had more time to perfect old family favorites. My dad would give us what we liked—fast food, comfort food.

Three amigos: me, Dad, and my brother, Cedric

I loved to go for pizza with him at a place in Austin called Mr. Gatti's Pizza. Mr. Gatti's had a projector that played old black-and-white TV shows like *The Little Rascals* on a movie screen. It was so cool because it felt like being at the movies. Even as an adult, when I was back in Austin I would make sure to go to Mr. Gatti's with my family. My dad also took us to Dan's Hamburgers, where they have the best milkshakes to this day. We went to drive-in movies, Six Flags, SeaWorld. Once, he even took the whole family on a guided tour of a cave. It was so special to be there with my mom and dad and my brother. I had never been inside a cave before, and that day showed me another part of the earth, a part with areas that were narrow and scary, unlike anything I'd seen before. I loved hearing the guide talk about the history of the cave. It was a beautiful experience, and my dad got a lot of cool points for taking us there. Years later, when I was working with Beyoncé, we ended up shooting a House of Deréon campaign in a cave, and it took me right back to that special time with my dad.

Dad and I were very different. My father was obsessed with sports, and that is something I couldn't get into. He tried to interest me for a long time, though. A couple of times, he bought us tickets for the Super Bowl. These tickets were not cheap! Most boys my age would have jumped at the chance to go, but not me.

At the game, I asked him for money to go to the concession stand and I walked the whole arena, just people-watching. I did not want to sit and watch no game! That was so boring. Give me the halftime show, give me the mascot. I was cool with those things, but the actual game? No. I would watch people and imagine who they were, what they did. I'd see someone and think, "Her name is Yolanda and she's a parent with three kids." I would put together scenarios of what I thought people's lives were like. I got so good at it that sometimes I would ask people their names and I had guessed right!

As I got older, when my dad took me on day trips to Houston to go to ball games, I would duck out without him knowing. We'd be with my uncle or a friend of his, and I'd ask my dad what time he thought the night was going to end. I'd tell him I was going to the car to get something, then I'd meet friends and we'd go to the mall or ride around. They'd drop me off after an hour or two, and I'd go back and sit with my dad. He finally stopped inviting me.

Cedric and my dad were on more solid turf because Cedric was into sports too. It was a natural bond and gave them something easy to talk about, a way to communicate. Their relationship became very strong, and I was happy about that. That's what my dad wanted.

I didn't think Dad loved me any less than he loved Cedric, but all he did was watch sports all day, every day. Even much later, when he was in the hospital, he'd watch any game that was on. Dad lived and breathed sports, and even though we could not connect on that level, we loved each other and built our own relationship.

I only really got to know my dad as a person, not just as a parent, at the end of his life. In his final months, as I sat at his bedside, he opened up in a way he had never done before.

New Orleans

Don't leave anythin[g]
You never know if t[he]
conversation will b[e]

Art contest winner

Tyrone Hunter of Pearce Junior High won first prize from Les Patrons, a support group for Para- mount Theater, anis entry in the junior high divi- sion in an art contest based on the play *Cyrano*.

Winning first place for my painting of Cyrano de Bergerac in the district- wide junior high contest

When I learned about my dad, I learned about myself. After he passed away, I was cleaning out his things and was shocked to find a drawer full of amazing pen-and-ink drawings he had done. I had no idea he was an artist—I had been artistic, too.

My brother and my dad had such a beautiful relationship because of their shared love of sports, and my dad and I could have connected over our love of art; I grieve this missed opportunity. If I had known that my dad loved art the way I did, I would have felt much more connected to him. I actually stopped doing art, something I regret now; seeing my dad's creative side would have let me feel free to thrive in those areas.

Until those final days of his life, I never knew Dad played the saxophone and was in a rock band either. I always wanted to play an instrument, but I didn't have the motivation to follow through. Knowing that was a gift he had would have lit a fire under me, and maybe I'd have pursued music more seriously. I always wanted to please my father and make him proud.

If I had known we had these shared interests, it would have meant a lot to me. Discovering my dad's creativity made me feel more in tune with him. It showed me where my talents come from—that was a gift he gave me. I sometimes wonder why he never shared these interests with me. Possibly, his own father wasn't interested and discouraged

Witnessing Diana Ross's talent and creative flair up close changed me forever.

his talents, or perhaps he didn't feel art and music were masculine, and he wanted us both to get along in a world where doing what's expected makes life easier in many ways.

Dad may have wished I liked football and basketball and baseball. He may not have understood how to nurture my creative impulses. But when I was eleven years old, he did something for me that changed my life. I even remember the exact date: September 10, 1983. Diana Ross came to the Frank Erwin Center in Austin, and my dad took me to see her concert.

At the concert, I stood in awe watching Diana Ross perform. The stage was round and in the middle of the floor. This was my first live concert and my first time seeing that kind of spectacle. I didn't know a stage could be on the ground—I'd seen concerts on TV, and they always showed a traditional proscenium stage. The show felt like something special even before it started.

Diana Ross did her costume changes onstage, and the costumes were all made to break down into other looks. It was such an exciting visual experience. She had on this huge gown for "I'm Coming Out," then the gown broke down to a suit, then a bodysuit that got cut up while she was singing "Muscles." That gown had layers and layers. I was so intrigued by this transformation of fashion. I had never seen anything like it. The changes happened so quickly, and I remember feathers and furs and all this fabulosity happening right there in front of me. This was something fresh.

I wanted more, more, more, and she gave me everything I wanted. The performance had special impact coming from a Black woman. I didn't grow up seeing a lot of beautiful and fashionable Black women on my TV set. I had Thelma from *Good Times* and Dee from *What's Happening!!* but they weren't in that Diana Ross realm. I finally saw the same kind of allure on TV years later when Diahann Carroll joined *Dynasty* as Dominique Deveraux. In my eyes, Diana Ross was the epitome of glamour, and I became a huge fan.

That day, I got my first glimpse of how a live show and fashion and music could come together, and I never forgot it. I had always been fascinated with creating looks, and my interest only intensified after that. Diana Ross showed me a world; she gave me a sense of the possibilities.

There are no rehearsals for life, so live as if the spotlight is on you.

I knew I needed to learn everything I could about fashion and the magnificent displays you could create using clothes and accessories. I began to dream and absorb all I could from fashion magazines, billboards, anywhere I saw people dressing with style. I would emulate the looks as best I could through thrifting, giving everything my own spin.

That concert was one of the best things my father and I ever did together. I knew he was doing it because he thought it would make me happy. He was stepping outside his comfort zone. His willingness to put himself out there for me told me he thought I was special. That night I knew, even though I wasn't ever going to be the son who would captain the team or even just hang out and watch the game with him, he accepted me for me. He saw who I was, and he loved me for it.

Ty's Takeaways

> If you're a parent, show your kids who you are. Had I known my dad was artistic and creative like me, I would have grown up feeling less different from others, and probably would have felt even closer to my father. Kids strive to please their parents. Knowing you share a passion gives them so much pride.

> I saw the effort my dad made to do things I liked. People notice when you go the extra mile to make them happy. Doing something for someone else is much more rewarding than always thinking about yourself. Experiencing something new with someone you love is an opportunity for growth, both personally and in that relationship.

> Support loved ones in their dreams and goals. Give them as much fuel as you can so they can fly high. Watching others soar will feed your soul almost as much as succeeding in your own goals!

> Don't envy the relationship between others in your life. Instead, look for your own way to bond. Cedric and my dad spoke the language of sports, which was beyond me, but I loved that the two of them had a way to connect. I didn't try to fit into that type of relationship, which would have felt false.

> Seeing that Diana Ross concert with my father awakened something in me. I didn't know how it would manifest, but that experience became part of who I am at my core. Never forget the things that make you who you are. Even if you're not currently in a position to pursue your passions full time, always work on the things that feed your soul in some way that is meaningful to you.

Opposite: My dad played saxophone in his high school band. He was a music lover, so I'm not surprised he drew musicians with their instruments. I was so inspired to learn he was an amazing artist.

THREE

When I Became Cool

was not a cool kid. I was always the teacher's pet: a skinny, smart kid with good grades and a huge fro. But I was also the class clown so I had a lot of friends, though these were not the popular kids. Starting in third grade, I would bring my teachers presents. I'd give them anything but an apple—that was the thing people in cartoons did. Instead, I would take them pears, tangerines, grapes.

I stood apart from the other kids, especially the boys, in other ways, too. The other kids, and even some adults, told me that I was "feminine" or "gay." I didn't know what that was. I was just being me. I wasn't happy sitting at a football game—I'd rather have been shopping, and I didn't hide it.

I also loved playing with dolls. We didn't have any at home since it was just my brother and me, and dolls for young boys was not a thing back then. At least not in Austin, Texas. But when my mom took me to the babysitter's house, the sitter, Deborah, would let me play with her doll collection in a separate room,

I was mad at my mom that day and refused to smile. Such a mischievous kid.

Easter Sunday circa 1979—I could have flown away with that collar!

away from the other kids. I adored dressing the dolls and doing their hair, making them look glamorous. I'd cut up socks and make dresses out of them. Boy toys were so boring! All the boys did was shoot guns and play with LEGOs. I wanted to create things and make them pretty. I loved hair and I loved clothes.

Deborah went on to become a well-known artist. Coincidentally, Beyoncé has one of her portraits. When I first connected with Deborah on social media, she didn't remember me, but when I told her where I lived, she knew. She only watched me a handful of times, but she had a big impact on me. She allowed me to indulge my imagination and create glam looks for hours at a time. She didn't judge me, even though I was out of step with the other boys, and that time at her house gave me a sense of ease and the freedom to explore my creative side.

My journey to cool started in junior high. Eighth grade was when my sense of style kicked in on a whole other level. I began wearing glasses (I'm blind as a bat), and I always chose funky eyeglasses. I had a really good Jheri curl. This was the time of Michael Jackson's "Thriller"—I was definitely influenced by his style, the leather jackets and the Jheri curl. I had this little flavor, but I was still a nerd.

In tenth grade, I started hangin' with my cousin Aundoy, who was very popular. He was older than me and didn't even go to my school. He would pick me up in his Jeep at lunch break. I would hang out with him at college parties. It got to the point where the kids at my school were just wearing me out—now that I was hanging out with older kids, I didn't have patience for my classmates' immaturity. They were home playing Atari and I was out dancing and going to Kappa parties at UT.

The only thing I got good grades in was art. Classes like photography, I'm passing. Spanish was so bad I would cheat my ass off. I wouldn't bother to write notes on my hand, I would have my whole fucking book out in my lap. That's how bold I was. I got caught cheating, but because I was so audacious my teacher let me finish the test. I still failed. At this point, I was going to school just to be cute. I didn't like anything. I went from straight-A junior high student to barely making it in high school.

When I was around fifteen or so, I transitioned my passion for styling dolls to the girls and women in my family. My cousins Teri and Naudia would come to my house, and the first thing we'd do was go into the bathroom so I could do their hair. It was so exciting to make over real people I loved. Later, when I worked in retail, I would dress and style mannequins in much the same way I put together looks for the people I knew.

When I style a person, I first get to know them a little bit and learn their insecurities about their body. The goal is to eventually get them past that lack of confidence. If someone doesn't like their legs, we can do funky hosiery at first. I get them to a point where they have confidence about their so-called problem areas. We're born without clothes; our first outfit is our skin. We have to learn to be comfortable in that. I also want the person I'm styling to be a part of the process. I could just give them look #37 from Givenchy, but at the end of the day, they are building their own brand and they have to feel 100 percent their best in what they're wearing.

Posing with friends for the Bronner Bros. hair show in Atlanta

A person with style doesn't follow trends. They set them.

I'd always played with clothes and jewelry, and as I got older, I loved going to garage sales and shopping in vintage stores. Back in the '80s, if you wore hand-me-downs or clothes from Goodwill, people would tease you. But because I knew how to put a look together and make it my own, nobody even knew my clothing and accessories were secondhand. The details didn't matter; people just saw a unique and cohesive look. Fashion is not about how much things cost; it's about self-expression. It's about how you put pieces together, how you make a look yours. I love vintage shopping because there are so many beautiful things in this world, and fashion can live as long as you put life into it. Things that were once special to someone else can now be special to me. I like items with a sense of history, and when I thrift, I imagine who the items could have belonged to and the lives those people led.

High school was about style. I wore baggy rayon shirts and pants, big glasses, and a high top fade. I was so skinny that I would wear two pairs of shorts under my pants and an extra shirt. Instead of a backpack, I often carried a briefcase, for a little flair. I was starting to get attention. Girls who used to think of me as a brother were now talking to me in a different way.

And most of my friends were girls—I related to them better and we were interested in the same things. It was that comfort zone that ricocheted from being around the women in my family. But I was close to four guys: Cedric, Braylon, Octavius, and Jeremy. I would dress them all and do everybody's hair. I found this bleach kit that had stencils, and I made three hearts in my hair and dyed them blond. It became my thing. My guy friends wanted it too, so we all had these platinum-blond hearts in our heads.

We danced all the time and became a dance group behind this rapper in Austin. We'd save our money and buy matching shirts. These guys loved me for me. People started to recognize that I would always give them fashion; it was part of my DNA. I won best dressed at school, even with no budget. So many people were asking me to dress them, even guys on the football team. Some kids paid me to go school shopping with them, and classmates started dressing like me.

*Left: High top waves in 1990
Above: Rocking my favorite polka dots*

47

People said I looked like Will Smith from *The Fresh Prince of Bel-Air*—I had that kind of vibe. When I let my hair grow really tall, I started to get Kid from Kid 'n Play. I had blond in my high top fade, and people sometimes mistook me for him. I loved the way Big Daddy Kane dressed, but Kwamé was the one I loved most because he wore polka dots all the time. I was obsessed with polka dots. They seemed so rebellious, so against the grain. It was rare that you saw people in polka dots, so they stood out. Whenever I saw polka-dotted clothes or accessories, I had to have them. I got my first polka-dot shirt at the Gap—it was expensive back then, around $30. Men's fashion in the hip-hop community started to go from oversized looks and jogging suits to clean, polished looks. The risk takers in fashion were really coming from hip-hop, and I felt very comfortable with that updated look.

Jordache, Girbaud, Calvin Klein, and Gloria Vanderbilt jeans were the hot thing. My mom usually couldn't afford those but every now and then she would splurge and I'd get something with a designer label. I would never pair those designer jeans with a trendy shirt. That's what everybody did. Instead, I dressed them down. Labels and luxury are great, and I've always done unusual things with them. I would stack diamond bracelets with rubber ones. I'd pair a Gucci shirt with jeans or a suit with my raggedy All-Star shoes. I always put my stamp on what I wore. My flashy has never been just flashy. I'd wear old Converse with a tux or diamonds with a T-shirt and jeans long before that kind of mixing was an accepted thing. I've always thought high-low was the coolest way to pair things.

Family members were my first clients. Here, I'm cutting my Uncle Jim's hair.

I had to stay on point, but my mom didn't have money to get us haircuts all the time so I saved up until I was able to purchase a pair of clippers. I started practicing on Ethel's sons and my little cousin. During this era, the late 1980s, there was a popular haircut that was a straight line across the front and the same length on the sides and back—they called it the chili bowl. The good thing was, you didn't have to fade it in. The fade was hard to learn, but the chili bowl I could do.

I started cutting my own hair, and that's really how I learned. When I went to the barbershop, I would watch what they did and learn technique. The barbershop was next door to a beauty shop called Golden Touch. My friends and I would hang out at the barbershop and then go next door and talk to the girls at the salon. All the girls went to get their hair done. These two shops were the place to be. Black hair was art back then. There were all these designs and colors and sprays, the French rolls, the crimps. Guys had high top fades and even finger waves. Men experimented with their hair back then. Think Kris Kross, Kid 'n Play.

It was a party every day at Golden Touch—they had liquor in the back at closing time. Sometimes they would cook; other times people would bring food in. I became friends with the people who worked there, and they asked me to be their model. I wasn't afraid to let them do whatever avant-garde hairstyles they wanted to try. I was always bold with my style, and I hated, hated to blend.

All the guys I hung out with were straight, but they started to care a lot about their clothes and hair, more than was usual for men of color in the '80s in the South. My hair was blond, and they asked me to dye their hair blond too. I wore colored contacts, and they started to wear them too. They started to take on my style. The football coach in our high school told me to stay away from his players because they were becoming pretty boys. He worried they were more into their looks than the game.

I became known for doing hair, and I learned to do weaves, color, perms. I was good at doing designs. I picked up a lot about doing women's hair from spending so much time at Golden Touch, and word spread. Everyone in my family stopped going to the beauty shop and just came to my house. My mom's friends all came to me. Mama Bea wanted to be in on it, so I did her wigs. The drug dealers would arrive at my house at 11 p.m. before they went out because they wanted to look fresh. I began making really good money.

> # A true fashionista doesn't care what anyone thinks. Their opinion is the only one that matters.

My early modeling days in Houston, Texas. I decided I'd rather assist the agents and scout models than be one!

I understood the value of what I could do beyond the money I could make. I saw how changes outside could lead to changes inside. One girl I went to school with got teased a lot. I was intrigued by her because she was super smart. You could see she was insecure but she didn't let that stop her from participating in class. The teacher would sometimes tell her that he wasn't going to call on her because other people needed to participate too. I saw that she had potential to grow her confidence, so I started to talk to her. She was a sweet person and I wanted her inner beauty to shine. It took her a while to warm up; she was very guarded. She finally trusted me enough to let me make her over. I did her hair, and I went thrifting and found some stuff for her. I only spent around $10 but her new look changed everything for her. She saw herself in a different way.

She eventually went back to her old look but she carried herself differently. The experience gave her new confidence. People who get makeovers sometimes go back to their former way of dressing but they're never quite the same. Once they see their potential, they always have that confidence, even if they choose to focus on their dress only for special occasions. But their outward transformation unlocks something inside, and they carry themselves differently.

For me, being cool meant finding my own way of being; it meant learning who I was as a person and what I had to give. I was lucky because I found my passion early, even though the road wasn't always easy. I was a young Black man in the South who liked clothes, hair, and jewelry. My way of fitting in was not fitting in, and I learned to be good with that. I became cool.

> Be yourself. If you lose anything on the journey to your authentic self, it wasn't meant to be with you in the first place. I have genuine guy friends who have never given a fuck about how masculine I am. They allow me to be my true self without judgment. They love me for my heart and my soul. A lot of times, people see you better than you see yourself. Pray for the day you see the great in you that other people see.

> Don't let other people's views of you define who you are. The important opinion is yours: how you feel about yourself is what matters. Listening to your encouraging inner voice is the only way to build confidence and get to that place of self-love.

> Take pride in your appearance but don't obsess about the outer shell. You want to look for a balance that lets you be the best you can be, body and soul. Taking good care of your body is part of honoring your truest self, but you need to take just as much care of your mind and spirit.

> It's okay to pamper yourself! Choose your indulgences from a place of self-love. Once a month, set aside a day just for you. Get your hair done, go for a mani-pedi, get lunch with friends, or do whatever it is that makes your soul sing.

FOUR

I Fell a Couple Times But I Ain't Never Laid There

My mom worked so hard to give my brother and me a comfortable middle-class life. Meanwhile, when I was a teenager we liked going to the Southside, where my cousins Darrell and Michael lived and which, in the judgment of the time, was a "bad" part of town. The whole flavor of the neighborhood was exciting. There was always something going on there, and it seemed rowdier and more alive than the neighborhood where I lived. I liked to hang out at Darrell and Michael's house because there I could explore and do grown-up stuff. There was drinking, sex, staying up all night—things that did not happen at my house. I didn't take part in everything, but I learned about the good and the bad of that wilder way of life. At home, I was going to choir rehearsals and Bible school. My cousins were around my age— we were all teenagers then—but they lived on the edge more than I did.

It was the early '90s, and in Austin at that time there was an all-white area, around Sixth Street, where you could see live bands and people would walk around drinking beer. The area had that whole Texas college-town vibe of loud country music and rock bands. If you wanted to listen to R&B and hip-hop, you went to the Black parts of town. That's where you got the jazz, the blues, the R&B, the hip-hop. There wasn't a place where you could enjoy the whole mix.

Things were pretty segregated in Austin then. I'd watch TV and see cities like New York that had people of different cultures living and working together, and I was in awe. It

I graduated from high school at age seventeen, unsure of my next steps.

wasn't until later in my life, when I started to work with people from all different backgrounds, that I realized how much I had missed out on. I fell in love with all these different cultures, with their foods and customs, and their different ways of looking at the world.

Austin has changed since my growing-up years. It's a more diverse place now. SXSW brought so many people to the city. Tesla recently moved its headquarters from Silicon Valley to Austin. It is no longer unusual to see people of different backgrounds together.

After high school, I wanted to be out all the time. I was very social—I loved to dance and just have fun. Plus, I loved getting dressed to go out. That was the best part! I could be cute and dance and mingle. I loved networking. Going out was our social media back then! When I was twenty, my cousin helped me get a job at a company that made heart valves. When we passed FDA approval, the company decided to throw an appreciation party, so they rented out a clubhouse in an apartment building. That was perfect because the party venue was just up the hill from a club where my friends and I hung out. We could go to the party and then sneak off to the club later.

The company party was five days before my twenty-first birthday, and my coworkers gave me a cake and sang "Happy Birthday." They gave me a card with money inside and a cassette tape of Lenny Kravitz's "It Ain't Over 'til It's Over," my favorite song. When it started to get late, my coworker Carl and I went down the hill to the club. We were just going to stay for about an hour and then go back to the company party.

Everybody at this particular club would hang out in the parking lot, playing music loud in their cars, so you didn't need to spend much time inside. The parking lot was better than inside! In Austin, there were little cliques. One group would all buy small trucks, outfit the trucks with speakers and neon lights, and airbrush a name on the truck. Other people would get Impalas and trick them out. This parking lot was a parade of cars from different parts of Austin. When Carl and I got to the club, just about every person who made me happy was there. I was overjoyed. I joked to Carl, "This must be my last day on earth because I'm so happy to see everybody."

I had to use the restroom, so I went inside. The line was super long and it was just after 1 a.m., time to go back to the company party, so I decided to go behind the building and piss. As I started back around the building to find Carl, two guys came up to me with guns and put them up to my head. All I remember was that they were Black men. The taller one was my complexion and the shorter one was dark complected. They said, "Where's it at, motherfucker? Give us the shit."

I didn't know what they were talking about. I was wearing gold necklaces, and I started trying to give them everything I had of any value. They pushed me into the brick wall. What scared me most was that I wasn't scared. Everything was happening so fast. I thought I was about to die because these guns were up to my head, but then a sense of calm ran through my body. I went into a zone of peace. I really thought this was the end for me, and I accepted that I was going to die. As I looked around, all I saw was a big dumpster and trash on the ground. There was a strong smell of piss. I didn't want my vessel, my shell, to be discovered in that place.

I took off running. I didn't run straight, either. I ran to the left, to the right, to the left, in a zigzag. I don't know how I got that courage. Everything was blurry and yet so sharp. I was focused, but at the same time, it felt like a dream. I heard *pow, pow, pow.* I kept running, and then I fell. I just felt heat and a sensation of being pushed to the ground. The guys ran to their car and tried to hit me with the car on their way out but missed. I got back up and started walking. I didn't even know I'd been shot.

I looked down and saw blood all over my clothes. I yelled for Carl, who saw my blood-soaked clothes and threw my whole body over his shoulder. He ran to the nearest apartment building, laid me under a tree in the middle of the complex, and started knocking on every door. It was after one in the morning, but finally someone answered a door. I'll never forget the heavyset older man who came out wearing boxers and no shirt. He had a kid in diapers and another kid trailing him. The man came over to me, looked at my wounds, and went inside. He came back with belts and tied them around my thigh.

In this part of town, the ambulance took a while to get there. People were looking over their balconies at me lying under the tree. A lot of the neighbors came outside, and some were crying. The ambulance finally came, and they cut all my clothes off. I was butt-ass naked, lying there with all these people looking at me. I had a feeling of fear and composure at the same time, and the odd mix of emotions was so unfamiliar it scared me. Even when the men approached me with guns, I was calm. I think that saved my life because it allowed me to think clearly and helped me get away from the shooters. I believed then and I believe now that a higher power and angels above were protecting me and guiding me.

In those moments on the ground, bleeding, I felt violated, not only from the attack but from the literal exposure—I was lying there naked in front of nearly every person I knew. People who'd been at the club had gathered around as the paramedics worked. I didn't know if I was going to survive. I was vulnerable and was also thinking, "Why me?" I did not want to go out like that. There were so many things I wanted to do in my life. I thought of my mom and how devastated she would be.

The ambulance took me to Brackenridge Hospital, where my mom worked as a unit clerk and my grandmother worked as a nurse. The staff there called my mom. They only told her I was shot—they did not say whether I was alive or dead. My grandmother was already there when I arrived and she was able to put Mom at ease.

I had borrowed my cousin Ron's pants that night. They were baggy, olive-green pants he'd bought at Oaktree. I had on a white shirt with tans, browns, and greens in it. The pattern was leafy, and those pants were perfect with it. Ron didn't normally lend things, but he did that night. I used to wear boxer shorts, but I didn't like the way the print showed through the pants, so that night I wore briefs. It's God's grace that I did. I was shot with a nine millimeter, but they tried to hollow-point the bullet. They did it wrong, which is why it didn't shatter in my leg. One of the bullets went into my thigh and stopped in my muscle tissue. The other went through my thigh; it grazed my testicles but they were somewhat protected, held close to my body by the briefs. That's how fashion saved my life, literally!

Removing the bullet by going in and cutting muscle tissue would have caused more damage, so doctors left it in my thigh, knowing my body would eventually reject the foreign object and push it out. I had to go through whirlpool treatment and therapy but, just like they said, one day I felt a hard knot on my thigh. It was the bullet surfacing. Doctors were then able to cut the bullet out easily with a scalpel. Because my testicles had been opened by the grazing bullet, I was told I might never have kids, a scary thought at age twenty-one. At one point I was in danger of developing gangrene, and we worried my leg might have to be amputated.

I turned twenty-one in the hospital and went home the next day. Every other day, I went back for treatments for my leg. They would sit me in a metal tub in what smelled like bleach water, which kept the wounds clean and prevented infection. If the leg wound had any yellow around it, they would take a scalpel and carve it out. My testicles had to heal on their own, with no stitches but a little help from some medicated cream. I'd put the white cream on a maxi pad and wrap the "wings" around my underwear.

It was two or three months before I could start to walk again. I thank the Lord that the bullet didn't touch any bone. I was in a wheelchair, then progressed to a walker, then to a cane. I had to learn how to walk again. Feeling helpless was hard; I was such an independent person. Having to rely on other people was one of the most difficult parts of the whole experience. But I had no choice. I understood I needed the help and I was grateful for my mom, my grandmother, my girlfriend, Draya, and all those in my life who could give it.

I didn't understand why this horrific thing had happened to me. Nobody did. My friends were walking around with guns looking for the guys who shot me. I didn't know what to tell them. I hadn't focused on their faces. I just knew one guy was tall and light complected and the other was short and dark. I received death threats at the hospital, and the feeling of being hunted while I was injured was terrifying. People would call and say they were going to fuck me up. I have no idea why.

Mental healing influences physical healing. You have to change your mindset to become whole again.

The word on the street was that I'd been shot as part of an initiation; the order was to shoot this guy who was a local drug dealer. Did I look like that guy? Not really. But we had the same kind of swag and style. We were both light skinned. So the guys thought I was him.

I was nervous because the shooters were still out there, and I didn't know if they were going to try to finish the job. The police investigated but never arrested anyone. I developed a fear of being in large, crowded places. I, who'd always loved being out and about, didn't want to go anywhere. In the back of my mind was always the fear that those guys could hurt me again. Whenever I saw two men together, especially if one was tall and one was dark, my heart raced. This sense of paralysis lasted for more than a year, until I finally was too weary to keep up that level of anxiety.

Getting shot was a wake-up call. In my teens and early twenties, I used to go to clubs and crowded spots where shootouts happened every weekend. There was nowhere else to go, so you would go out and just pray. After the shooting, I knew I could not continue to go to places where this kind of violence kept happening. I didn't want to keep putting my life at risk. I came to understand that you can be a good person, but bad can still find you, and putting yourself in risky situations raises the chances of trouble.

I had a moment, after I was shot, when I cultivated more white friends. I started to go to more college parties. I listened to more rock 'n' roll. I opened up my tastes, in part because I was afraid to go to the places where I used to go. I found myself hanging out on Sixth Street instead. I felt more at ease not being around my people at this moment because I did not want to run into two men who looked like the ones who shot me. I felt at home with my white friends; they had good energy. Most of all, they gave me a space where I didn't have to face the fear I felt from the shooting.

Then I had another wake-up call. During this time after the shooting, I was allowing my fear to cut me off from my own people. I am a Black man, and I had to get over the fear that any two Black guys together might be out to get me. How could I feel that way? I have a brother, cousins, uncles, friends, all of them Black men I love who are nothing like the guys who shot me. That was something I wrestled with. I understood on a rational level that you can't avoid a whole culture because of something that happened to you and that one bad person doesn't represent an entire race or culture. You don't throw away a dozen eggs because one is cracked. Yet it took time for me to get over the visceral fear I felt. I think that happens a lot, and has a lot to do with racism and self-hate. I realized that my fear, based on a singular personal experience, had been amplified by cultural currents that associate Black men with criminal behavior. So I was conflicted, both afraid for my safety and awash with love for my people. I couldn't, and didn't want to, avoid my race—that would be denying my DNA, my family, my culture. It took some time and deep reflection, but I came to see it wasn't Black men I was afraid of, it was the actions of two humans who had threatened me. That was the perspective I had to hold on to.

But I did eventually realize that I couldn't live in fear. One day I just got tired of running from the unknown. I had to start living my life again. There was talk that one of the guys who'd targeted me was in jail, so that helped. But my near miss changed me forever in some respects. It taught me to become more aware of my surroundings, and to this day, when I go to an event or a club, I find out where all the exits are. Anything can happen at any time, and it's good to have a plan.

Never underestimate the healing power of a positive mindset and a good attitude.

I also resolved to stay away from situations where I was likely to encounter problems but not to avoid my whole community. And the truth is, I hadn't done anything to invite trouble. My brush with death showed me that no matter how good a person you are, anything can happen. When it's your time, it's your time. "It Ain't Over 'til It's Over"— the Lenny Kravitz song that had always been dear to me and had been gifted to me that very night—underlined that it wasn't my time. That song became a sort of anthem for me. I was put on this earth for something bigger. God gave me another chance, and I had to dig deep inside myself and figure out what I was meant to do.

When I was recovering, I had a lot of time to think about what I'd lost and what I could have lost. I also had a lot of time to think about the gifts I had in my life, chief among them my family and friends. They are the ones who got me through that time. My family made it a point to check in on me. They took me to whirlpool treatments and to my physical therapy appointments. Because my grandmother was a nurse, she regularly checked my wounds to make sure they were healing properly.

More than anything, getting shot mended the relationship with my brother. We had been in a rough patch for a long time. My mom had forced me to take him with me everywhere I went, so I thought of him as a burden and spent most of my time trying to get away from him. But he came into my hospital room crying, and he said some really beautiful things. He told me he loved me. I put away my resentment and recognized the gift I had in Cedric. On that day, he truly became my brother.

It seems funny to say I am thankful that I got shot. But in a way, I am. That experience, traumatic as it was, helped me look at life from a different perspective. I'd always thought that being a good person was enough. But I had to look around me, too—to be in tune with what else was going on in my surroundings, and be smart about where I spent my time and with whom. As I recovered, I refocused my energy. Instead of partying every weekend, I worked on getting my life in order, and I spent time with the people I loved. Even though I was down, I never just laid there. I got up—and I keep getting up.

Don't let your hopes and dreams be derailed by physical challenges. It's easy to give up, but there are so many victories ahead. Keep pushing!

Above: With Cedric at his wedding in 2006
Right: Full of food and love at Thanksgiving, right after dinner at Grandma's house

Ty's Takeaways

> Find the courage and strength to keep going. Don't give up. I could have become a hermit who lived in darkness. Because I didn't die the night I was shot, I knew I was on this earth for a reason. Not everyone has a revelation through some difficult or violent event the way I did. Sometimes the dawning is slower and gentler. But everyone has a reason for being here; everyone's life has value—never forget that.

> Nothing lasts forever—not good times and not bad times. People sometimes run away from the bad times (dependence on drugs or alcohol, unhappy relationships). The key is to go through the experience, then learn from it. Dark times give you what you need to become who you were meant to be.

Faith can get you through anything. I was in serious danger of losing my leg and was told I probably couldn't have children. You have to be able to see sunshine in any dark time. Learn to visualize the better outcome; say what you desire out loud. Feed the light. The higher powers control all those things. We just have to stay on the ride and not jump off—it ain't over 'til it's over.

Rocking my ServedFresh with Passion
collection in Austin, Christmas 2018

FIVE
Crushed

I had my first crush when I was in the third grade. Janet was this beautiful girl with long hair like Sade. My friend Jason was her "boyfriend," and he had me write his notes to her and draw pictures for her. I was basically a modern-day elementary school Cyrano.

One day I stole a butterfly necklace from my mom's jewelry box. Then I found a gift box on the ground, and I painted flowers on it and put the necklace inside, then gave it to my friend to give to Janet. She was so happy. I was shy and didn't have the courage to speak to her, so she never knew how I felt. But I was happy to see her happy.

When I was a kid, we'd pass notes that said, "Do you like me? Yes. No." There'd be checkboxes next to the yes and no. I got a lot of checkmarks in those "yes" boxes back in the day! But not from her. One day she asked Jason to walk her home, and he invited me to come along. I missed my bus on purpose just so I could walk with them. I wanted to see where she lived. As time went on, I think she started to like me too, but she was with him. I remember her so vividly. And I remember that feeling of butterflies you get when you like someone. It's so exciting when it happens for the first time, but that thrill of a relationship's beginning is a feeling that never gets old.

The next time I felt those butterfly wings fluttering I was sixteen and at summer school. Draya looked like Halle Berry; her hair was done real nice and she had on biker shorts. That was the look back then—like in the movie *Boomerang*. She was my first real girlfriend. We would stay on the phone all night. I'd take the phone into the bathroom and close the door so we could have privacy. I'd be in all these weird positions with my legs straight up on the wall, twirling the cord. She was in the band at the rival school. I'd go to the game, run over to her side, and then run back to my side before I got killed. I didn't go to my prom, but I took her to hers.

We were in love, and our relationship got serious—our families met and became intertwined. Even though I was a hot-and-bothered kid, with temptations all around, I wanted to learn fidelity to my partner and to fight urges to fool around with other girls. Draya and I decided to save ourselves for each other.

When you're young, you have all sorts of ideas about your future and about what your life and your relationships will be like. You dream and you think you are safe in your plans. But sometimes your plans are spoiled—and sometimes you learn that your friends are not who you thought they were.

Karen, who was a year behind me in school, was like my sister. We met when I was fifteen, and we just connected. One of my friends had a thing for her and was always flirting with her, and I would tease her about that. We joked a lot—I knew how to make her laugh, and I liked feeling clever. In high school, she was a sexy dresser, and she was considered a little fast for her age. I knew Karen wasn't a virgin—she liked to tell me about her sexual exploits when we were in high school. And though a lot of my guy friends liked her, she and I were strictly in the friend zone. So it was a bit freaky when she started flirting with me. At first I thought she was joking, but then I realized she really liked me, which felt all wrong.

One night when I was twenty-one, Karen called and asked me to pick her up late at the laundromat. She was there with Rochelle, a bully, and Jessica, a shorter, light-skinned girl with braces who I thought was cute. They were the only three people at the laundromat at that hour. I helped them get their stuff together, and one of them asked me for my car keys so they could put their stuff in the car. But then they locked the door to the laundromat.

At this point in my life, I was very skinny. Rochelle and Karen were big and voluptuous. Though they were a year younger than me, they were taller and heavier than I was. They pushed me inside the laundromat's restroom and one of them blocked the door. They told me I wasn't getting my keys back and pulled my pants down. I was pushing them away, but there were three of them. Before I knew it, I was on the ground in the pitch-black restroom. One girl was holding me down and another was at the door. I was a virgin; Draya and I were waiting, planning to have our first sexual experience together. Even though I didn't want this, my body couldn't help but respond. Karen got on top of me and started riding me. Afterward, I put my clothes on and told them they were crazy, and what they did was messed up. I felt crushed by what they did, and I felt dirty and disgusted. For most guys, losing their virginity is a highlight in their life. For me, it was nasty. I drove Karen home as planned. She was in a flirty mood, but I was repulsed by her. I couldn't be friends with her anymore. I never spoke to her again and I tried to wipe that night from my mind.

I never told anybody this story until years later when I told some guy friends, who thought what happened to me was a good thing. They said I was lucky. But I was not lucky. It was a horrible, twisted introduction to something that was supposed to be beautiful and loving. I was in a relationship and was saving myself for my girlfriend, who was also a virgin. I had been waiting for this special moment of intimacy with the person I loved, and instead I lost my

> **Don't allow the darkness of the past to block the light of the future.**

virginity to that nastiness. I felt defeated. And my friends did not understand. From that point, I never talked about it. I never told my girlfriend, then or ever. If I had been a girl and those who assaulted me had been three men, the reaction of my friends would likely have been very different.

I truly believe that everything you do in the dark comes out in the light. I'm proud of the sexual assault survivors who are standing up for themselves. Until recently, I didn't feel like the people I've confided in have understood why my assault was upsetting to me. This is especially true of my straight male friends, who tended to see what happened in terms of a joke or as a stroke of luck. But to me, sex is an intimate moment that I want to spend with a person I choose, one I have feelings for and care about. When you are sexually assaulted, woman or man, another person is taking that choice from you, and that's wrong. But our culture glorifies situations like mine because the assumption is that men are always pursuing sex and women are more reluctant, so if a woman pushes herself on a man, he should be grateful. This kind of thinking creates a fear that when you tell your story, people won't understand. They'll believe you should be happy that it happened. That's part of what makes a lot of men stay quiet about being raped.

I never told Draya about what had happened to me. I felt dirty. As a man, I didn't feel like I could be a victim, and I didn't believe I'd get the nurturing or support I needed. So I chose to stay silent, but that only made me cold and distrustful of others. I didn't want to lose Draya, and I just wanted to forget everything and wipe the slate clean. But I discovered that those wounds stay fresh for a long time if they are not attended to, and that damage haunted me for years.

After the assault, I started having a lot of one-night stands with women. Draya and I had started fighting and we often took long breaks from each other, so I found myself free to pursue other women. But I did not allow my heart to get involved in any relationship. I felt hollow. I wasn't me. I'm sure this was a reaction to being assaulted by Karen and her friends, though I didn't think too deeply about it at the time. I felt powerless and angry; I became another person.

I was mean to girls (except for Draya, who I trusted, but even with her I wasn't my best), and I hung out with knucklehead guys who did girls wrong, and that helped me feel like I wasn't so bad, like I wasn't the only one behaving this way. I felt like I had been wronged, so I no longer cared who I hurt. It was an awful time in my life.

You don't have to become what hurt you.

I started to have terrible luck. And when bad things happened, I would see the faces of people I had hurt. One time, I started a fire when I was cooking french fries. I burned my whole hand putting it out, and as I did that, I visualized girls I'd done wrong. I had several car accidents, and pictured girls I'd treated badly. This was karma at work, and I had to wake the fuck up. I realized I wasn't that person, that guy who was careless with people's feelings. I was acting mean and selfish because I wasn't living my truth. When you become an actor in your own life, you learn what it is to keep living a lie. When your lies get exposed, you're in a very dark and uncomfortable place. I was unhappy, so I made other people unhappy. I had to go off by myself and figure things out.

I started to do things alone. I would go to this park in Austin called Mount Bonnell to sit and think. I felt like I was drowning, and my solitary time in nature gave me a way out of those feelings that had me trapped. As I spent more time reflecting, I realized my friends were not the right crowd for me. I was not living my truth. These guys were all straight. You couldn't even have a girlfriend without getting teased. You'd be called whipped. Drug dealing, drinking, living a materialistic life—these things were glorified. That wasn't me. I had shaved my head and gained weight. I had to escape that body and that mindset and find my truth.

There was no happiness to be found in the random affairs I was having. I had plenty of sex but no love. Only time alone let me be still enough and quiet enough to consider what love meant to me. I was hurting people who loved me, and I didn't like that feeling.

I had to recapture that thrill I'd felt when I first saw Janet, when I met Draya—I had to look for the innocence and joy that relationships can bring and learn to trust in love again. Karen and her crew had taken something from me and I couldn't change what happened. But I could change the way I reacted. I could change my thoughts and my actions. Once I stepped away from negative influences and confronted the hurt and shame of my assault, the positive energy started to flow again. I understood that I couldn't expect to be happy if I was making other people miserable. Karma is real, folks. What you put out into the world is what you get back.

Ty's Takeaways

> Being hurt is not an excuse to hurt others. I thought that by keeping my assault a secret, I was protecting myself from the further hurt and humiliation of people's judgment. It took me a while to realize that if I had shared my story, I would have had much more support than misunderstanding. Nothing sweet comes from bitterness, and causing pain to a person who genuinely cares about you ultimately wounds you both.

> Learn how to love being alone. When I started traveling by myself, going to dinner alone, seeing movies solo, I built my confidence and became more self-aware. Love your own company, and invite into your life the people who enhance your experiences.

> The company you keep matters. If you spend time with people who do not share your core values, you will eventually find yourself in situations where you're not comfortable. You don't have to agree with your friends about everything, but a shared belief about right and wrong is important. I'm not proud of my actions when I was hanging around a group of people who viewed life much differently than I did. It wasn't until I broke away from the group that I really felt like myself again.

> It's okay to take a break when you need one. Be available to support your family and friends, but if you get to a point where you've lost yourself, you need to step away. Spending time alone can help reset your mind and spirit so that you can move securely into the next chapter of your story.

Rocking prints at the Annual Veuve Clicquot Polo Classic

SIX

Yanked from the Closet

Before I ever had a gay experience, I was labeled gay. Though I was well liked in school, there were kids who would bully me, and the word *gay*, a slur at that time, was regularly flung at me. Being Black but light complected means you're often called a pretty boy, gay. Many lighter-skinned Black men didn't want to be known as either of those things, so they intentionally stayed a little scruffy. My cousins could have been models, but to avoid those stereotypes they acted more like bad boys and didn't pay much attention to grooming.

As I got older, the gay label began to bother me and I fought it. I went from just being myself to learning the mannerisms associated with masculinity, mimicking what masculinity is supposed to look like. In this one way, I wanted to blend. When it came to fashion, though, I gave what I wanted because it made me feel good. It didn't matter if I had on the gayest of gay outfits. I would wear my hair bone straight and parted down the middle, in a black bob, and other girly-ass hairstyles. There was nothing gayer back then than a light-skinned Black man with a blond bob. But I knew the balance, and I knew how to tone things down. If my hair was in a blond straight bob, I would wear Timberlands and wide-leg jeans. If I had boy hair, I could wear more feminine looks. I tried to make sure that masculinity was the top focus to avoid the gay stigma.

I moved to Houston in the mid '90s but I would occasionally go back to Austin to visit. On one of these trips home, I had my first sexual experience with a man. His name was Aaron, and he was the older brother of my best friend, Jeremy. I'd spent a lot of time with Jeremy when we were in high school, so I got to know Aaron and the rest of the family too. I was intrigued by Aaron's "I don't give a shit" attitude. He thought outside the box; he wore his hair different and dressed different. People talked about him, but he was still very popular.

A few years after high school, when I was visiting Austin, I spent the night at Jeremy's house. Aaron was still living there, and the only spare bed was in his room, so that's where I stayed. Alone in that room with Aaron, my heart beat so fast. The curiosity and sexual tension were killing me, and I finally made a move. He responded, and that night we ended up sharing a bed. Being with a man felt natural, which is what made the fear kick in. Every influence in my life to this point—my church, my family, my friends, my schoolmates—had led me to believe that being gay was bad. What did these feelings of mine mean for me? I told myself that I was just experimenting—and even though my experiments were with Aaron, that didn't mean I was gay. I went into fight mode so I didn't "become" gay. As much as I could, I fought those feelings. There was no way I could be gay.

I got spiritual and became more involved in church. I would go on Saturday and Sunday, and I sang in the choir. What I didn't know was that there were many other gay men hiding in church. No one talked about it. We were all just trying to stay close to God, and perhaps atone for what felt to us like the sin of being gay.

One of the church regulars contracted AIDS and wrote a letter outing other church members. That letter was the source of much gossip as members speculated about their fellow churchgoers. I was shocked, and that disclosure made me realize a lot of people struggled with being gay. At the time, influenced by the messages I absorbed from the wider culture around me, I actually believed that being gay was a disease. And then along came AIDS, which claimed the lives of so many gay men. Seeing my friends die made me determined to cleanse my thoughts and not become a statistic.

Despite my pledge to stay on the straight path, I found that difficult to do. When I started fooling around with Aaron, I was still seeing my girlfriend, Draya, but we were having problems. So I "experimented" again. My cousin had a party at his house. His wife, I later learned, told her best gay friend, Mason, that she thought I was gay and that we would be cute together. Mason looked a lot like me, though he was white. All night at the party, people kept saying we looked alike. He and I talked all night. At one point in the evening, I looked at him and he looked at me, and the attraction was undeniable. It scared me because this roomful of people became just him and me. It was the first time I could see myself in a relationship with a man. But I fought that feeling; I pretended it wasn't happening. We were talking, but at the same time I was thinking, "I have to get out of here."

When it was time to leave the party, one of my cousins asked for a ride. And then I was asked to give Mason a ride home, too. I told two of my friends that they had to come with us. I didn't want to be in the car alone with Mason. On the way home, someone suggested we stop by SXSW, the new media and music festival. This was in the very early days of SXSW, maybe the second year. It took place in this little club in Austin and featured some rock bands, some rap.

It cost $20 to get in, which was a lot of money back then, at least to me. There were only two hours left, so I suggested some of us check it out to see if it was worth it. I parked the car and everyone got out except Mason, who was in the front with me. As we sat in the car talking, it started to rain really hard. There were no cell phones yet; it was the time of two-way pagers. He and I waited there, knowing the others were not going to come back until the rain slowed. At one point in our conversation I looked away, and Mason put his hand on my thigh. My heart started beating super fast. I said, "Take your hand off of me. It's cool and all, but I'm not like that." He said he was sorry, but that he was very attracted to me. I said, "Don't worry, but just don't touch me." We sat there awkwardly until my friends finally came back and said it wasn't worth going in. I went out of the way to take Mason home first.

About three days later I got a call from my cousin's wife, who asked if Mason had left his wallet in my car. I found it under the seat and I ended up driving it to him the next day. When I got to his house, a girl opened the door. Kathy was Mason's best friend, and she was playing loud music and cooking. She told me I was cute, pulled me into the house, and insisted I stay for fajitas. When Mason finally came out, I gave him his wallet. I stayed for a margarita and a fajita, but that was it.

Not long after, I ran into Mason at a club. He asked me for a ride home, and I agreed. This ride was different. Before I knew it, we were kissing in front of his house.

Our relationship built from there. I would see him after work at least three or four times a week. My shift at the heart valve company was from 3:30 p.m. to midnight, Monday through Friday. He would have dinner ready when I got to his house, along with a hot bath sprinkled with rose petals. He'd give me massages. Mason was a very romantic person, and I really got to experiment with a side of myself I was just discovering. Being with Mason at his house was a getaway, but I wouldn't go out in public with him. It worked out pretty well for me, though, since I got off work at midnight. The only places open were IHOP and Taco Cabana, so mostly he would cook.

I felt like I was living two lives. My church viewed being gay as a sin, and those teachings echoed as my relationship with Mason deepened. I didn't want to be thought of as a bad person, I didn't want to hurt my family or friends, and I certainly didn't want to go to hell. But I also felt that what I had learned could not be true. I believe that God made me who I am. I knew I was a good person, but I was very afraid that the people I cared about wouldn't accept me. I had heard horror stories about coming out. Some were disowned by their families; they were harassed and called names. I remembered the way fellow church members had been treated when they were outed. I didn't want my family to have a black cloud of shame over them, so I continued to keep my secret.

My relationship with Mason was deeply romantic but we also built a friendship. He gave me a place to be myself and talk about what I was going through and the space to work through it all. His house became a home away from home. I didn't spend the whole night there—I'd stay until about 3 a.m. We had a good time together, and he began to introduce me to his friends. I was always worried they might know someone I knew and I'd be found out. I never felt safe about that.

Draya and I, by this time, were on a break after a huge fight. Our romantic relationship was pretty much over, but we still loved each other. Because we lived in different cities and saw each other only on her breaks from school, it was hard to keep our connection strong and hold everything together. Mason and I saw each other steadily for a few months during the time Draya and I were on a break. He learned my daily routine and became friends with some of the people around me, though I didn't know about that—he was already friends with my cousin's wife. Then he started to show up at places I went to and I became uncomfortable. I felt like he wanted the world to know we were together, but that was not what I wanted our relationship to be. I just wasn't at that place. I was very much DL, very hidden. I tried talking with Mason about my feelings, but he didn't understand why I was upset. He was so open and free with his identity as a gay man that he couldn't relate to where I was at that time in my life. Today, I look back and admire his courage and the way he lived. I envy the freedom that gave him.

I was confused as hell and didn't know what direction to go. I had passion with women, but I was never fully comfortable with them sexually. In private, I'd curl their hair and they'd straighten mine. But in public, I felt like I had to watch my mannerisms so they didn't have to be embarrassed by people telling them their boyfriend was gay, something that had happened more than once. I grew up around mostly women, so I knew how to talk with them—I'd tell them if their shoes were cute or their hair looked great. Most guys didn't say shit like that. (I think that is bullshit. Men should let women know they're paying attention to them.)

With Mason, I felt completely free. I could just be me, and that was a massive weight off my shoulders. We spent our time almost exclusively at home, so I never had to worry about what the outside world thought.

> **Coming out is something you have to do at your own pace. Speaking your truth is freeing, but you should come out when you feel like it will make your life better, not to make others happy.**

After I had been dating Mason for about three months, Draya called. She said, "We did it! I'm pregnant." I had been told I likely couldn't have kids, so this was amazing news. Draya is an incredible woman and I wanted to be an awesome father, so I knew I had to end things with Mason. I wanted to be in my child's life, and I felt like I had to fix my relationship with Draya. I meant to give my child that life I didn't have, with a mother and a father in a family home.

Being a gay father didn't make sense to me at that point. That wasn't something you saw on TV or really anywhere. I didn't know any openly gay people, let alone fathers. And I could not walk away from my child and my child's mother.

I took Draya's pregnancy as a sign that being with Mason was wrong, and I told him I was sorry but I had to end our relationship because I had a child on the way. He said, "I hear what you're saying, but I don't think you're going anywhere." He was very calm.

Draya moved back to Austin from New Jersey, where she had been going to college, to have our baby, and she stayed with my mom and me at first. I was in full-on father-to-be mode. I went to Lamaze classes with Draya. We researched having a water birth. Draya considered all the options. We watched parenting tapes and went shopping for baby clothes and gear. I helped her prepare the nursery. I was so happy. I prayed to God that we would have a girl. I didn't think I'd know how to raise a son because I wasn't what society considered a real boy. I was into fashion and hair, not the typical masculine things. Today, I know I would have been a great father to a son, but at the time I worried about it.

You wasn't cool if you didn't know how to shoot pool.

Then one day I got a page from a mysterious phone number. It was Mason. He said, "You better come to my house after work tonight or I'm going to call your fucking baby's mom and your mom and tell them you're gay and you're fucking me." I called my mom to tell her I'd be taking overtime and would be late getting home.

When I got to Mason's place, he went off. He said, "You can't just come in and out of my life and think this is okay." I told him, "I'm sorry it happened this way, and you have every reason to feel the way you do. But this happened and I want to be a great father. Please be understanding." He said, "No. Fuck that. We're going to be together." He pressured me—blackmailed me, really—to see him at least twice a week. I was so stressed out. On top of this, I was working full time. I was preparing for a new baby. I was trying to hide Mason.

Draya began to mention this mysterious friend of mine, Chris, who started calling the house. She'd say, "I talked to your friend Chris today. Can you believe that his girlfriend stood him up after he made a meal for her? That bitch." Mason was using a fake name and telling her about his girlfriend, but he was really talking about me. I came home so stressed every day, thinking, "This is the day it all falls apart."

He became friends with the receptionist who worked at the heart valve company. Every Friday there was a rose on my car. I would go out of town, to Dallas or Houston, and I would still find that rose on my car. When I was sick, my mom would open the door and say, "Baby, you got these girls so crazy over you." He would leave serving trays at my front door with medicine, Campbell's soup with a bowl and spoon, orange juice. My two lives were colliding.

I wasn't sleeping and was nervous as fuck. I was fighting with Draya. I couldn't even totally focus on her because I was also fighting my own demons. I was tired. I was skinny as fuck. I had homeboys and friends who wanted to hang out and party, but everywhere I went, Mason was there, so I stopped going out. It all became too much, and ending my life began to seem like the solution. I didn't like having to spend time with him. We'd be having sex and I was so miserable I wanted to kill him.

When I got to the point where I thought seriously about signing out, I realized that I loved living. I knew what I had to do. Mason called me at my job because I wasn't calling him back, and said, "You better come see me tonight, you motherfucker." I said, "You know what, Mason? Call whoever you need to call and tell whoever you need to tell. I cannot live like this anymore. If you need phone numbers, let me know." I hung up and I felt light, even though I knew there was going to be a war. I felt a great release, because I'd accepted whatever repercussions would come. I had to get that weight off me. It was stripping me of my character. I didn't have a spark anymore. I no longer knew the person I was looking at in the mirror.

It was raining when I got off work at midnight. I went to my car to find my windshield and all my windows broken out. I got towels from the trunk, cleaned the glass and water off my seat, and drove home. I woke up my mom. She was frantic, scared to see me soaking wet and miserable. I said, "I have a lot of stuff going on. I don't know if I'm gay. I messed with this guy and he is stalking me now. I don't know what to do. I'm sorry." I just started crying. She held me and said, "Don't worry about this. I love you." My phone rang. It was Draya, almost nine months along now, and she was with Mason. She said, "How could you do this to me? You probably gave me AIDS." She told me I wasn't going to see my child. Mason said, "How could you hurt me?" Between them, they called me every bad name under the sun. It was a mess.

The next morning my mom told me, "We will get through this. Just promise me you won't tell your dad and your brother." I didn't want anybody to know, so that was fine with me. I went to work and learned that Mason had told some of the people there. The woman I sat next to was my closest friend in the company. I was her child's godfather. She started crying and said, "I let you keep my son." My heart fell to the ground. Did she think that because I was gay, I was a pedophile? Nothing could be further from the truth, and her ignorance was like a nail in my soul.

When Mason finally cooled off and called again, I said, "Mason, I'm sorry for the way this ended up. If you ever loved me even a little bit, please just leave me alone. I cannot take anything else. Please." He hung up the phone and never called me again.

Not long after my last conversation with Mason, Draya called. She had watched an *Oprah* show about gay people and now saw things differently. We were going to be co-parents, she told me. Our relationship was a roller coaster. Sometimes we got along, and other times we wanted to kill each other, a pattern that would continue for years.

There's a whole
world out there
when you open
those closet doors!

Everywhere I went in Austin, people were talking about me. The word was out: I was gay Tyrone who got a girl pregnant. People were judging me, and I could sense the whispers, the pointing fingers. It started to not feel like home anymore. I didn't feel comfortable going to the mall or any of my other favorite spots.

You can hurt people when you're in the middle of trying to find out who you are, when you're looking for your true self. Even if you do it unintentionally, you hurt them. You have to own up to your faults and accept your true self. God knows my heart and my intentions. This was a very hard, dark, and grimy time. But what seems like the worst thing that can happen may really be just getting you where you're supposed to be—to your true self. I had to go through that turmoil and get called out and be put through all of that misery to be who I am today, to be unapologetically me. I don't have to live a lie. I can be myself. Once I got the stamp of approval from the people I cared most about, I didn't give a shit about anybody else.

Years later, when I was in Asia on tour with Destiny's Child, I got a message saying I needed to call Kathy, Mason's friend. I had heard a year or two earlier that Mason wasn't doing well; he was abusing drugs and had become a prostitute. When I spoke with Kathy, she told me Mason was in hospice in Florida, where he lived with his boyfriend. He had AIDS. My heart sank. I asked if I could talk to him. She made arrangements for me to call the following day. When I called, Mason's boyfriend answered. He said, "You're the Tyrone that I could never amount to. Mason really loved you." He told me he would bring the phone to Mason, but that he couldn't talk. He could only hear me. I told Mason, "I just want to say I am so sorry for how everything happened with us, and I want to personally thank you for all the things that happened between us. Even the stuff that we both considered bad, because if you hadn't done what you did, I would not have been able to live my truth and be who I am today. I just want to say I'm sorry and thank you so much. And I love you and I pray that you get through this." He could only mumble. You could hear him crying a little bit. I hung up the phone and I cried.

Three days later, as everybody was singing "Happy Birthday" to me, I got another message to call Kathy. She told me that Mason passed away that day. I started hysterically laughing and crying at the same time. That motherfucker still got the best of me. He died on my birthday! He taught me how to be romantic and to allow myself to be vulnerable. Through my relationship with him, I learned that I could reject the standards of masculinity I saw around me. True masculinity is me being the man I am.

Getting through the hard stuff was a lot of work, painful work, but I'm at a point in my life where I'm happy. I'm comfortable with my sexuality. I'm fulfilled living life as a single man. Yet I'd also be happy to share my life with someone special. Love is an adventure that is always worth taking.

Family photo with Mom, Cedric, and my Jheri curl

Ty's Takeaways

> You're going to unintentionally hurt people as you search for your true self. Anyone you lose along the way isn't supposed to be in your life. Finding your authentic self may not be easy, but it's going to be worth it. Everyone comes into your life for a reason and a season. People who don't support you being you—the real you—don't deserve your company.

> Sometimes we get into dark places, troubled situations where we feel we can never be happy again. But there is a light at the end of that tunnel. Keep pushing through the hard stuff and you will reach that light. I'm living proof. So much can change in a short time. Better is around the corner, so stay patient and continue to believe.

> Live your life for yourself, not for others. We try to please other people, but it's important to please yourself first. When I wasn't me, I felt evil, and I hate that I was ever that vicious person. I behaved that way because I wasn't living my truth, and I was desperately unhappy.

> Own your faults and mistakes. Clean up your messes, then learn to love yourself unconditionally. It's important to acknowledge any hurt you may have caused or mistake you may have made, but forgive yourself and ask for forgiveness from others. Don't forget about the people you may have hurt, even if it wasn't intentional. I made it a point to reach out and make amends with as many as I possibly could. Forgiveness is a beautiful thing.

SEVEN

My Greatest Treazure

Early in elementary school I discovered the phrase *treasure hunter*, and I was fascinated by the idea. What better way to spend your time than looking for hidden treasure? I decided right then that if I ever had a daughter I would treasure her, and that would be her name.

In 1994, I was dating my girlfriend Draya, though we were off and on. I had a good job with the heart valve company and she was in college. Every holiday, she would come home from school to visit or I would go see her, and we were thinking about the future.

Draya had always wanted kids, and I did too. And I knew I wanted to have mine while I was young. At my high school graduation, I'd seen a friend of mine standing with two older people. I knew her grandparents were coming to town for graduation, so I went up to them and asked how their flight was. They didn't know what I was talking about, and my friend explained that they were her parents. That made an impression on me. It solidified my sense that I wanted to be a young father who could grow with my kid. I hoped to have a relationship with my child like my mother and I had.

Draya and I were only in our early twenties when we decided to stop using condoms. After about two years, she announced we were going to have a baby. I was thrilled

Above: Trezure

Celebrating Christmas with my Trezure circa 1997

(especially since my gunshot wound had left me unsure I'd be able to father children), but I was also scared. I was experimenting with gay relationships and was terrified of being exposed.

Back then, being gay and being a parent didn't go together—at least, there weren't visible models of what good gay parents looked like. In the midst of so much happiness, fear took over. If the world wouldn't accept me as a gay parent, how would my child? I didn't want to hand a burden down to my child; I didn't want people to tease her or make her feel like she had to protect me. I was afraid she might hate me.

When Draya found out I was gay during her pregnancy, our already tumultuous relationship got even rockier. I didn't know how I would fit into my child's life—or whether I'd have to fight to have any role at all.

Trezure's birth was a beautiful experience, yet it was also a deeply uncomfortable one for me. We had arranged a labor room with a sitting area, including a couch and a TV, so Draya could have her family there. It was mostly her family in the room. And me. Everyone had just found out I was gay, and they were not happy with me. I painted on a smile but my emotions were whipping around. I was excited, knowing my daughter was about to come into the world, but I was also surrounded by people who wanted to beat my ass. My feelings of guilt and shame hung over me. I never meant to hurt Draya—I was just figuring out who I was—but she was hurt all the same.

The labor room was chaotic, swirling with intense emotions, until the moment Trezure was born. At that point, all my discomfort melted away and was replaced by a sensation of warmth. I felt connected to my daughter immediately. I felt like her parent. I thought, "Here is this person who is a part of me." She was so beautiful, and I felt special, proud, and indescribably happy. As I cut the umbilical cord and she took her first breaths in this world, I resolved to do everything in my power to be the best parent I was capable of being. It was time to get my life in order, to grow and become an adult. Now I had someone depending on me.

I never fully understood how deeply my parents loved me until I became a parent and felt that same love for my daughter.

When Trezure was an infant, my coming out was very fresh, and Draya needed time and space to become comfortable with the situation. I understood and was respectful of her need, but it meant that I didn't get to see Trezure as much as I would have liked. Draya's mother watched Trezure sometimes, and she allowed me to come see my daughter even if Draya and I were avoiding each other at the time. She acted as a mediator, helping us co-parent in a way that let us work through our anger and pain instead of hurting our daughter. She stood by Draya, of course, but I appreciated that she understood I needed to be a part of my child's life.

Draya and I had to deal with the transition out of romantic coupledom and into amicable co-parenthood, which was not easy. We were young and dumb and just trying to figure things out. At times, we were selfish, and that affected Trezure. Draya and I would fight, and then sometimes I couldn't see Trezure for a while. I would see her whenever Draya decided to make it happen. We didn't have email or texts or cell phones always on, only pagers and landlines, and it could be hard to get in touch. Not knowing when I was going to see Trezure was very stressful, and I needed some stability. Eventually, I decided to get a formal visitation and child support agreement from the court so I had a legal right to see my child.

A look into your child's eyes is motivation to keep pushing yourself to be what they need.

Trezure and I had a lot of fun and silly times together. I sometimes miss her being small. She's my most beautiful creation.

When we appeared in court, I was on one side of the courtroom and Draya was on the other with her mom and my daughter. Trezure was crying for me to hold her. The court fight came at a low point in my relationship with Draya and her family, and they told the judge they didn't want Trezure around me anymore. I thank God for that judge. She said, "I can tell by the way that child is crying for her father that he's a good dad. Whatever goes on in the bedroom on your side or his side is nobody else's business." I got my visitation rights.

I was so relieved to be able to see my daughter and build a relationship with her that wasn't wholly dependent

TREZURE 4 yrs old 06/19/99
Fathers Day!

At the park in Houston, Texas

on my relationship with her mom. But there were still obstacles. As my styling career took off I traveled more, and I couldn't always be there with my daughter. Draya was with Trezure most of the time, taking good care of her. I wanted to do my share and make sure Trezure was always provided for, whether or not I was getting along with her mother and whether or not I was there in person, so I paid all of their bills until my daughter turned twenty-two. People used to ask me why I did that. Nobody understood. In the beginning, it was partly guilt about how things turned out; I couldn't give my daughter a traditional family, and I wasn't always there physically. But if Draya didn't have a roof over her head, then my daughter didn't have a roof over her head either. When I was on the road working, I had to know that my daughter would be okay. Whatever that cost, it was worth it.

As a baby, Trezure was a little ball of joy. I loved holding her, and I wanted to protect her always. I get nervous holding other people's kids, especially newborns, but it was different with my daughter. I never had any fear with her. We played all the time, and watching Trezure grow and become her own person was a miracle to me. As she got older, she became a big ham; she loved having her picture taken and giving concerts. And I loved just being with her.

Trezure was always independent. She'd come up with adventures for us to go on when we spent time together. It was always catch-up time because I was away so much. We would do fun things like go salsa dancing on the pier or go to the beach and play volleyball, see movies, have picnics, go shopping—whatever she wanted to do. Even as a little girl, Trezure felt confident enough to speak her mind. When she was

Pops and Trezure, home for the holidays

six, I was on tour and out of town for her birthday. She let me know she was unhappy that I missed her party. She wasn't afraid to tell me the truth, and I had to deal with it. I was devastated when she cried on the phone. I went out that night and got her name tattooed on my back.

Eventually, Draya and I got to a place where we could co-parent the way I always hoped we could. Draya and I agreed that we would never spank Trezure. Instead of physical discipline, we would have meetings. We let her tell us what we needed to work on. But then we would also tell her the areas where her behavior needed improvement. That worked for us. We allowed her to grow and become her own individual. Sometimes I would stay in the guest room at Draya and Trezure's house when I was in town. They would cook for me, and the three of us would do things together. There was even a time when we all lived together in Houston, for about two years, along with my boyfriend, Ted. Trezure and Draya and Ted and I were a good team. We adults took turns picking Trezure up from school, and together we created a stable family. Trezure had that extra love in the house. Our arrangement might have seemed weird to the outside world, but for us it was perfect.

In that time we lived together, Trezure and I grew even closer. I got to wake up and see my daughter and be there when she went to bed. I got to see the little daily routines, like brushing teeth, eating cereal, loading the backpack for school, doing math homework—all the things you miss when you're not a parent who lives with his child. I'd have loved to preserve our arrangement, but when Draya's grandmother passed away, she and Trezure moved back to Austin.

From the day my daughter was born, I dreaded telling her I was gay. I knew that time would come; I just didn't know when. She came to me when she was six or seven and said, "Dad, you could get any boyfriend. You're so cute." I guess she figured it out, seeing Ted and me together and sharing a bedroom. That was such a healing moment for me. The two people who meant the most to me—my mom and my daughter—accepted me and loved me. That gave me the extra piece of armor I needed to feel complete and strong. I had been haunted by the fear of having to tell her I was gay,

and I was finally able to let that go. All I
had worried about turned out to be no
big deal for her. That's really when my
truth started.

After that declaration, Trezure put
together an outfit for me to go out in. I
put that little outfit on, and it was a mess!
But I gained a sense of freedom and
didn't care what anyone else thought:
Trezure had given me her approval.

I liked to bring Trezure around my
flamboyant gay friends. It brought out
a little sassiness in her. They taught
her the latest gay lingo and would
get her acting silly. It was just a sweet
break from her everyday life. She never
showed any hesitation in accepting me
for who I was, and she was open with her friends about me too. Once, I took her and her
friends to get their nails done, and her friends told her, "Your dad is so cool. We wish
our dad was gay."

My biggest regret as a dad is that I missed a lot of moments with Trezure. She grew up
in the years before FaceTime and Zoom, and though we talked on the phone, I missed
seeing her smile and watching her as she told me about her day. I'm blessed that she
grew up to be understanding, but it was hard for her that I had to miss holidays and
special occasions. When she was about twenty, she got a styling job on the film *Carter
High* and she began to appreciate what it was like for me all those years. It meant a
lot that she told me that, that she recognized how consuming the job could be and

forgave me for not being around. I always carried so much guilt for missing out on experiences with her, so to hear that she understood the sacrifice I made to provide for her was so satisfying.

Being a father taught me what authentic, unconditional love is. I learned to put my child's needs ahead of my own and that the world is bigger than me. Even now that we are both adults, my daughter shows me so much patience, and I continue to thank her for teaching me how to be a great parent. When you're a parent, you have responsibilities and someone who depends on you. After Trezure was born, I no longer had the option to be selfish. When I found myself in a dark place, knowing I was responsible for this beautiful child kept me going. I could have no idea, all those decades ago when I first grew obsessed with searching out treasure, what a cherished part of life my daughter would become.

A father is a daughter's first male role model. Wrap her in love and teach her how to love herself so she learns to say yes to healthy relationships and no to harmful ones.

Ty's Takeaways

> Do your best to build and maintain positive, nurturing relationships. Stay away from drama as much as possible. Sometimes life is as hard as you make it. No one has a remote control that switches your moods: no one can make you happy, mad, or sad. You're in control of your life, so focus on cultivating a healthy mindset day after day.

> Put out what you want to receive. When you put out goodness, it comes back in abundance. It may not come back on your timetable, but it always comes back, and at the perfect time.

Reality sometimes means you can't live with the people you love. Keep your bond strong by making up for lost time whenever you can, and be sure family and friends understand you would rather be with them than away. Let loved ones know that you treasure them and that part of loving them is taking care of their needs. Find ways to stay connected when you cannot be with them physically (video chats, texts, notes, fill-in journals), and when you do spend time together, be fully present.

> Be true to yourself, and don't hide your authentic self from those closest to you. That does not mean behaving inappropriately or crossing good boundaries—it means letting people know who you are and what is important to you. Though I had dreaded Trezure learning I was gay, I was free to be my best self once that was out in the open and I knew she accepted me. Trust that your people will love you for yourself.

Fun times with Trezure

PART II

Finding My Destiny

EIGHT

A Path To Purpose

would have liked to study fashion. Putting together looks was something I loved and excelled at, but I never thought I could make a career doing what I loved. It didn't seem practical. And I thought any job associated with fashion would make me look gay. When I graduated from high school, that was a truth I was still running from. I didn't know what to do with my life, and as for so many kids, college was the default. I had friends heading to college, friends going into the military, friends who were getting jobs. I wanted to explore life outside my hometown of Austin, I just didn't know what was out there. So, out-of-town college it was. Since my cousin Larry was at the Art Institute of Dallas, I thought that would be a good place for me. I applied and was accepted into the music business program.

I didn't do well. The music business was not my passion. I didn't like the foundation courses, and when I finally got behind the mixing board to create, I wasn't happy there either. I preferred my lunch breaks with a friend, where we sketched fashion and looked at different textiles.

Even if I didn't care for school, the move from Austin to Dallas was a good change for me. I took an apartment with two roommates and dipped my feet in the water of adulthood. My mom paid for everything, so I was by no means an adult, but I gained some independence.

After a year, college seemed a waste of money. I was just at school to dress up and be cool and meet people, so I dropped out and moved back to Austin, not knowing what my next move would be.

Cousins and friends in my situation went into the military. My brother enlisted in the US Navy. Service was something of a tradition in my family—all my uncles served in the military. But they came back with these harrowing stories, and one suffered from terrible PTSD. I knew the military was not for me—I have my own sense of discipline, but I'm not regimented in the way the army or navy requires; I would have quit on day one.

College and military service were out but I had to find something to do. The job my cousin got me making heart valves was a good job with benefits, making more money than I'd ever made before. I figured I'd give it a try. It was a grown-up job, and I was ready for it, although I knew at some point that no matter how good the money was, I would need something that involved more creativity.

I was one of the youngest people working at the company. Other employees would tell me about their dreams and what they had wanted to be before they started working there. One of my coworkers was an older man who worked all the time. He never took days off and he came in on holidays. If anyone couldn't make it to work, he would fill in for them. He did this in order to save up a lot of money. He and I used to talk, and he'd tell me about the things he wanted to do when he retired. When that day finally came, we had a going-away party for him and sent him off with our well-wishes. That man died three days later.

My coworker's untimely death and the stories of lost ambitions

Know that you're only failing if you're not learning from your mistakes. Don't let wrong steps be wasted: they can teach you as much as—or maybe more than—the things that go just the way you planned.

motivated me to hang on to my own dreams. I didn't want to be telling some junior employee years later what my dreams had been. I couldn't see working there year after year just to have a steady paycheck. I wanted to do other things. I would rather fail than not have tried at all.

The job making heart valves may not have fulfilled my every life goal, but it was a place of growth for me and I was happy there. Then one night, as I was getting ready to go to a club with my best friend, I noticed a scar on his chest. I asked him about it and was shocked when he told me he had a heart valve. Of course I knew I was making heart valves for people, but the fact that my best friend had one changed everything for me. I started to take a very long time to do the work because I needed to be sure everything was absolutely perfect. It hit me that I was making something that people relied on to keep breathing, to keep living. Had I been constructing them carefully enough? Was I moving too quickly? I wasn't sure. I started working more slowly to make sure everything was precisely as it should be. I could not afford to make any mistakes.

Before I knew about my friend, I went to work every day thinking about money and production numbers. When my mindset shifted, and I thought about how fragile life can be and how people depended on this device I was responsible for, I became exceedingly cautious and my production numbers dropped dramatically. The quality of my work was good, as it had been before, but now my productivity was down. I started to get pressure to keep those numbers up, and something had to give. The place I had loved going to had become a place I dreaded.

The company offered family leave for up to three months, and I requested the time. I told my boss I was having family problems and wanted some time off. He said, "Ty, you know we love you. Your job will be here. Take your time. I hope everything is okay with your family."

Everything in life seemed so precarious. People were depending on me (me, a twenty-three-year-old!) to make heart valves. I was unbelievably stressed. I'd been shot and still felt sometimes like I had to look over my shoulder. I'd been yanked out of the closet and was struggling to figure out my relationships—I was now known around my hometown as the gay guy who got a girl pregnant. The AIDS crisis was at a high point, and being Black and gay felt like a heavy weight. The fear and stigma around AIDS, portrayed as primarily a gay disease at that time, only intensified the homophobia that already existed. All my life, I'd dealt with racism; layering on homophobia only increased the number of people giving me problems. It all felt like too much.

To reclaim my sense of myself, I had to get away—not only for myself but for my family. This time away, I decided, would be either a short break or a life-changing experience. I really didn't know which.

I asked my cousin in Houston if I could stay with him for a month. I will never forget telling my mom I was moving. She said, "You can't lose this job. You make good money. This is a good job." I said, "Mom, I don't want to be like you and work all my life at a job where I'm not happy. I know you were a single parent, and you had no choice. I want to step out on faith and take a chance. If it doesn't work, I can come back. I don't want to look back and wish I had taken a risk."

> **Those who love us sometimes hold us back without meaning to. Growth can be painful. It can be scary for our family, just like it's scary for us.**

Though my mom was unhappy that I was taking leave, my grandmother, who lived with us at the time, said, "You go ahead and live your life. Your mom is going to be okay." It was hard to move out and move on, but I had to in order to grow up. My mother did everything for Cedric and me. We never had to worry about anything. When I moved to Houston, my goal was to not contact Mom for anything. Up until that point, anything I needed she would get, whatever she had to do.

I packed my car and drove to Houston. With every mile, I felt the weight dropping off me. Houston was a bigger city, and no one knew me there. I could reinvent myself, away from the gossip and drama that followed me around Austin. I started to go out and meet people and to learn about the gay culture. I got to know the city. Houston was a blend of cultures, much more of a melting pot than Austin. That city made me feel alive, like there was a place for me.

Fun night with my angel, Nicole, who looked out for me in my early days in Houston

My first month in Houston, I partied my ass off. The first good friend I made was a drag queen named Nicole. I fell in love with Nicole because she had such a motherly presence. She gave me home. She was very protective of me since I was so new to the gay scene. If someone tried to talk to me, she'd tell him to go away. If I thought someone was cute, she'd say, "He ain't shit."

During those early days in Houston, when I didn't have money, Nicole would get me groceries. They were illegal groceries—she would write a hot check! But I was a kid and she fed me. I could go to her house and stay all day. There were others she took care of, too, trans girls and drag queens. They performed at the gay clubs. It was fun to watch them rehearse and get dressed to go out. I went from staring through a microscope for hours on end to hanging with these vibrant people, all doing their own thing, and I didn't want to go back. I had to figure out a way to stay in Houston.

One day I was at T.J. Maxx looking for something to wear. They were hiring and I applied. I started as a cashier, but before long I was moved to visuals in the home goods section. I hated it! I would create a beautiful display, with pillows and candles and other luxe items, but it wouldn't last an hour—customers could shop the displays and they'd grab all the pieces I'd arranged so lovingly. My nice display would be a mess. But I needed the job. I was a new parent, and I had to provide for my child. I needed a second job to make ends meet, so I worked at OfficeMax when my shift at T.J. Maxx was over. The two stores were on the same strip, just four doors from each other, so I ran from one retail job to another just trying to make my life work.

Back in the day, the big mall in Texas was the Houston Galleria. With three connecting mall spaces, the place was enormous. It had all the high-end stores, Fendi, Louis Vuitton, Gucci, Dior, Christian Louboutin. It had an ice skating rink in the center and the best food court ever. The Galleria was the spot to be every weekend—people would dress up to go there. They'd travel from all over to shop at that mall.

One day, wandering in the Galleria, I walked into a store I'd never seen before called Bui Yah Kah, run by Vietnamese siblings by the name of Bui. Bob Marley was playing, and the store was decked out with palm trees and a waterfall—there was just a vibe. They sold Billabong and other surf brands, but they also carried inexpensive dresses and skirts with high side slits like the ones Aaliyah and Monica wore. Girls could spend $10 and go out and be cute. Even though the clothes were inexpensive, you could tell by the lining and the stitching and the weight of the fabric that they were good quality. One of the brothers working on the floor that day said to me, "I like your vibe. You're cool; you should work here." I was thrilled! I started the next day.

I did well at Bui Yah Kah and was meeting a lot of people, so I left OfficeMax and then T.J. Maxx to work there full time. I fell in love with the Bui family, and they became an instant family to me. They made me a store manager, though that did not work out. I found being a manager stressful—I'm too nice! I just let people do whatever the fuck they wanted—it wasn't in my DNA to tell them no. If they wanted time off, I'd work a whole shift by myself rather than make them come in. I was lenient when people were tardy. I was very laid back and understanding. I felt that if you let people work in a way that makes them comfortable, they'll give you their best effort. That philosophy was successful because the store's numbers did go up when people worked with me, but I wasn't happy in that position. It looked on paper like I was a good manager, but it took too much out of me.

While managing people was hard for me, I discovered other talents that came to me easily. When things were slow at the store, I would redo the displays rather than sit around. The brothers decided they wanted me to just do visuals for all six of their Houston-area stores. This was a great thing for me. I wasn't on any schedule, and they gave me complete creative freedom. I was good with the visuals and the displays as well as working hands-on with the clothes themselves. Not only did I dress the mannequins, but I was also still selling and styling customers. I had a few regulars who only shopped with me, and I slowly started to build my client book during that time.

One day when I was at Bui Yah Kah, Miss Tina Knowles walked in. The song "No, No, No" was getting heavy play on the radio at the time. Destiny's Child were hometown girls, so you best believe in Houston their songs were on the radio all the time. They hadn't gone global yet but they were getting big. Very big.

I knew who Miss Tina was because I had just watched Destiny's Child on *MTV Cribs* and they showed the house, which Tina Knowles had designed. I thought she was amazing—she turned Beyoncé's room into a genie's bottle! She also made clothes for Destiny's Child, which impressed me even more.

Miss Tina and I just connected. My mom was four hours away, and Miss Tina gave me a motherly energy I loved. A month or two later, I met Michelle Williams and also Farrah Franklin, who was in the group at the time, and I got to know them. Eventually, Kelly Rowland

At Beautycon in LA—Miss Tina was a speaker and I was there to show support.

started to come to the store, and she and I became friendly too. Solange was a little kid then! I got to know all of them, except Beyoncé. I would help Miss Tina whenever she came to the store. Eventually, I got her phone number, and when things came in I thought she'd like, pieces that would work for the group, I would let her know.

After about four years at Bui Yah Kah, I moved to bebe, which, at the time, was *the* store. Girls everywhere were walking around in rhinestone bebe T-shirts—we couldn't keep them in stock. I soon became one of bebe's top salespeople—I made so much money there because I was honest. Customers knew I wouldn't tell them something looked good just to make a sale. I developed a loyal clientele, and I basically styled them. I would put aside pieces for them to try on that they would not normally have given a second look. Sometimes they would buy a piece from another store and come in to get advice on what to pair it with. Women would come in asking for me, and if I wasn't there, they'd come back when I was. It wasn't uncommon for me to have customers in every dressing room. I was a natural salesperson, and my clients trusted me to make them look their best.

At the store, I developed a system that smoothed things for me and made everybody else happy too. As a thank-you, I would buy the cashiers lunch. We salespeople got paid commissions, but the cashiers were paid hourly and didn't have that opportunity to make more money. I thought it was only right to balance things out a little. If another salesperson didn't have a lot of sales, I would give them some of mine. I didn't mind letting my colleagues take credit for sales I made because it created a better workplace if everybody did well. We were all working together to make the store an awesome place for customers, and I wanted everyone to know I was a team player.

At bebe, I also learned not to judge people by the way they looked. Rich people don't flaunt rich. You had to know fashion to know if something was expensive or not. I could see someone in flip-flops and know the brand was Yves Saint Laurent, even though there was no logo. The other salespeople would run up to customers who were wearing head-to-toe Versace and spend hours with them, only to have them leave the store without buying anything. I'd help the lady in the T-shirt and cutoff shorts who would spend $2,000. I also had low returns because people were happy with the items I helped them choose.

My popularity around Houston rose from working at bebe. Celebrities would come in and become my clients. It got to the point where I'd go to a club and the DJ would announce, "We got Ty Hunter from bebe in the house." It was hilarious. But that's how big bebe was.

I was happy: I had a boyfriend, I was living in Houston, and I was the top salesperson at bebe, making good money. It was a fun job, and all was good in my world.

Then one day the music video director Joseph Kahn came into the store. I knew he'd directed Janet Jackson's "Doesn't Really Matter" video, since I'd recently watched a *Making the Video* episode about it.

To understand my excitement about seeing Joseph Kahn, you have to understand how obsessed with Janet Jackson I was. Every time she came on TV, I was pinned to the screen. When her concert tour came to my area, I'd drive to her hotel to look for her. I'd look for her at the airport in the private jet area. I'd try to win concert tickets on radio giveaways. René, her ex, used to let me go up to the front at her concerts. I didn't know him, but every performer likes to have the most excited fans in the front. Seeing their fans hyped up helps them give a good show. Beyoncé would do that too. There's a section set aside for these super enthusiastic fans like I was. René could see how much I loved Janet Jackson. I stood out at those concerts because everyone else was wearing "Rhythm Nation" black and I would be in a white suit with shoulder pads from Oaktree. Once, when Draya was pregnant and we had an argument, she went into my room and ripped down all my Janet Jackson posters. I was a

Ethel; my other mother, Miss Tina; Mom; and me at the Essence Festival

grown-ass man, too old to have Janet Jackson posters on my bedroom walls, but that's how much I loved her.

The "Doesn't Really Matter" video was amazing to me because it was set in a futuristic Japanese city, and I was really into Japanese culture, especially the fashion. In the video, Janet danced in these great wide-leg jeans, which were Japanese-inspired. I was so happy because I wore them too, but this was a different style for her and I was excited to see her wearing them. She had this Japanese razor-cut hair. It was just a dope video.

I told Joseph Kahn I had seen the video and how impressed I was by him. He thanked me and asked if I worked there. I told him yes, and he answered, "You're wasting your life away." And out he went.

This was a wake-up call. It was the heart valve company all over again. I couldn't stop hearing his words in my head, and this place I had loved became a place I dreaded going.

Soon after my encounter with Joseph Kahn, all the women of Destiny's Child walked into bebe together. MTV was following them, shooting a video chronicling a day in the life of Destiny's Child. Each girl said hello and gave me a hug—Miss Tina too. She gave me a look because she didn't realize

I already knew Kelly, Michelle, and Farrah. I had met everyone except Beyoncé. I walked into the back, where Beyoncé was looking at shirts, and she said, in her deep, raspy voice, "Are you Ty? I heard a lot of good stuff about you." As they were leaving, Miss Tina said, "I'm going to get you out of here one day." It was too outrageous a thought to believe at the time.

Though I was working hard, I had no car and no money. My boyfriend at the time had given our car to his drug dealer. I was paying not only my bills but all of Draya and Trezure's bills too. To get to work, I had to either catch the bus or ride my bike. About a month or two after Miss Tina made that promise to me, I had a day off. I was depressed and decided to call her to see if she needed help. She asked if I could meet her at Hymie's. Hymie Zelaya was the tailor who made the wardrobe for Destiny's Child; he brought her illustrations to life.

At this time, I only had $30 to my name because, in addition to giving up our car, my boyfriend had cleaned out my bank account. In order to get to Hymie's I had to catch a cab, which cost $15, half of all the money I had in the world. But I did it, and that's when things really started to happen for me. After that first day, Miss Tina told me she was willing to give me a try and see if working with the group was something I would like.

Playing around with the girls at MTV's Total Request Live (TRL)

I went to work for Miss Tina the next day. I told my manager at bebe I'd been offered a job working with Miss Tina, and she realized what an opportunity it was—she told me I should get out of there and not come back.

As one of my first assignments, Miss Tina and I went shopping to create the looks for the "Survivor" video. There was camouflage everywhere. We had army surplus to the surplus! At the time, retailers were offering bonus tracks on CDs exclusive to their stores, and Destiny's Child had such a deal with Target for "Survivor." We were preparing to shoot a commercial for Target's bonus track when I got a look at the call sheet. The director of the commercial was Joseph Kahn. I couldn't wait to tell him that a month earlier his comment had lit a fire under me. The next morning I tapped Joseph on the shoulder. He recognized me! I told him that because of what he'd said, I was now working for Destiny's Child. He said, "I knew it!" He changed my life with just one sentence.

After the "Survivor" video, I went back to Austin to visit my mom. She hugged me and said, "I'm proud of you and I'm glad you didn't listen to me." She loved me so much that she couldn't stand the idea I might make a big mistake. The thought of me on my own in Houston, at first without even a job, terrified her. She'd worked her whole life to have stability, and she worried about me risking mine.

But if I hadn't taken risks, I would not have left college; I would not have left the heart valve company or T.J. Maxx or bebe. I would not have met Miss Tina. All along the way, I let myself be guided by intuition and I took chances. My success was due to my willingness to venture out, in part, but it was also due to being good at what I do. It

If you have an opportunity, take it. Follow your dreams; don't just wish they'd come true. Don't go to bed thinking, "Woulda, coulda, shoulda."

Another amazing DC-3 concert with outfits designed by Miss Tina for the Destiny Fulfilled *World Tour*

came because I worked hard to help other people be their best. I showed up at every job and hustled my ass off, whether that job was setting up displays or helping customers or clients find the right outfit. I never looked down on anyone, and I considered us all a team, dedicated to making a good experience for the customer. It took a while, but that philosophy and hard work led me to a career I could only have dreamed of when I was a skinny eleven-year-old dazzled by Diana Ross.

Ty's Takeaways

> Every step you take is a step further along your path. Even if that step ultimately does not take you where you want to go, if you are learning along the way, you are getting closer. Don't discount the false steps—discovering what you don't want helps you discover what you *do*.

> Standing up to ignorance in the world can make you strong. But if you don't find support—either internal or from others in your life—it can tear you up, and you start believing the negative things people say about you. The key is to not allow other people to tell you who you are—you have to *know* who you are; you get to *say* who you are.

> Go out and find your passion and your purpose. Things you think of as a hobby, things you love to do, things you daydream about—those can be your bread and butter. Even if it's not your full-time work, keep doing what feeds your soul, and you will get to that place of happiness. I had a friend who worked on Wall Street but whose passion was in the gym. That friend eventually became a personal trainer and was much happier as a result. I left jobs where I was making good money but was unhappy. I could not have imagined that my passion for thrifting, dressing friends, and dressing windows would lead to a career that so fulfills me.

> Choose collaboration over competition. Making others look good helps you look good. Most work involves a team effort, and projects thrive when everyone is pulling together and is given what they need to contribute their best. Recognizing others and being generous puts out good energy that always comes back to you. Help others when you can. You never know when you'll need that hand to come around and help you.

NINE

Meeting My Destiny

Working with Miss Tina was the most intensive fashion program I could have asked for. I was thrown straight into the fire. There was no warm-up, no practice period, no baby steps. Right away, we got started styling the group for the Grammys and the "Survivor" video, two extremely high-profile projects. I wanted to prove myself so badly that I worked flat out.

I was like a sponge, absorbing everything Miss Tina could teach me. She'd come up with an idea and sketch the outfits, sometimes on the back of an envelope, then we would go over them together—she let me have a lot of input. We'd go out and source fabrics, get all the trims, buttons, and rhinestones, pick out the prints. Not long after, we'd be at Hymie's, watching him bring the outfits to life. In those early months, I was in student mode, just learning everything I could and taking it all in.

I started in 2000, and there was no Google, no Style.com. Cell phones had only recently been introduced, so we had no smartphones. We didn't have access to all the information and resources we have now. Miss Tina and I would buy the special editions of magazines that featured collections from the fashion shows. *L'Officiel* and others published them a few times a year. These editions were very expensive—we'd spend hundreds of dollars on them—but they were invaluable. She and I would cut out photos and create inspiration boards. I learned about a lot of designers from those magazines. I was from Texas; I was used to having just the mall for inspiration, so this was a whole new world. The magazines showed me fashion from abroad before I ever hit a fashion show, before I even knew what Fashion Week was.

We knew what we wanted for Destiny's Child, but at first we didn't have as many options as we would later. In the early days, designer showrooms didn't let us pull from them—Destiny's Child hadn't yet reached the level of celebrity where top designers

Kelly, Beyoncé, and Michelle, ultra chic in blue camo. I used to have to rhinestone and glitter these looks!

were vying for their attention. Not having access to designer looks didn't matter, though, because Miss Tina was able to create beautiful clothes conceived just for the girls. A lot of young women at the time were into the tomboy look, with baggy clothes and overalls; TLC and Aaliyah went for this style. Miss Tina always wanted Destiny's Child to represent old Hollywood glamour, like a young Supremes.

Miss Tina showed me how to take inexpensive fabric and make it look like a million dollars by changing buttons or zippers. Little details make such a difference. I learned that and so much more from her—working with Miss Tina and Destiny's Child gave me the perfect opportunity to practice my craft and experiment with fashion while surrounded by people who cared about me and wanted me to succeed. I made the shoes Beyoncé wore in the "Check on It" video by cutting up a tennis shoe and taking the platform heel off another shoe. Then I bought a BAPE shoe and asked Hymie what type of glue to use to bring my vision to life. I took my time deconstructing and reassembling the pieces, staying up all night to work on the boots for the next day's shoot. I had to pray because we shot earlier than expected and the boots didn't have enough drying time. But they stayed together!

I joke that a lot of the things I do are bootleg because I know how to work with nothing. Once, I accidentally left Kelly's skirt for a concert on the private plane. In the venue's dressing room were a curtain and a tablecloth that were close to the right color, so Miss Tina and I took fabric from them to make a skirt. I got good at working under pressure. There have been times when a zipper popped during a concert and Beyoncé would just sing from wherever she was standing while I went onstage and fixed it right there in front of thousands of people. I don't have stage fright anymore!

I learned from Miss Tina how to stay steady when the unexpected happens and find a solution instead of panicking and running away. That is among the most valuable life skills you can cultivate, no matter what you choose to do.

Early in my time with Destiny's Child, the girls were just starting to hit, so they were in demand. They had back-to-back hits with "Survivor" and "Independent Women," and everyone wanted them. They did TV shows, awards shows in different countries, radio shows. In the beginning, we did really small tours at small venues, including colleges. While the work was constant, we also had so many fun moments growing and learning together. The girls were so silly. They'd sing almost everything; they would make up songs on the spot. Keeping that lightness is important when you are building something. That life can be intense, so laughter is key, along with the steady belief that what you are doing is leading somewhere good. We were ready to see as many blessings come in as possible because they worked so hard for it.

The girls would be on the tour bus praying and reading scripture. They were very grounded. They didn't even go out. You'd see them at awards shows dressed up, and then you didn't see them anymore until the next thing. I, on the other hand, would go out to clubs unless one of them stayed in my room watching movies or something like that. Once in a while, I'd go out with the dancers, but mostly I'd meet up with a friend if one was local or just go out by myself to explore the different cities and countries.

Spending so much time together made the Destiny's Child team super close. When we were on the road, the group often rented a place so everyone on tour could hang out together. We'd sometimes all stay in the same hotel, but not always, and the common space gave us the opportunity to get together and relax out of the spotlight. Some tours lasted two years, so these gatherings kept us connected as our own family—and it made life on the road a lot easier, especially for those of us who weren't used to it. We went from country Texas people to world travelers as Destiny's Child became America's hottest girl group.

You need pressure to create a diamond—so keep it light, press on, and shine!

People can sometimes pit women against one another, but Beyoncé, Kelly, and Michelle didn't operate like that. They had a system that worked, where everyone made sure that the others were happy; it was a true sisterhood. If one girl wasn't done with her hair, the others would come and help curl it. They understood that the whole package had to look right; it wasn't about any one of them.

And those girls in Destiny's Child treated me like their big brother. They invited me to pretty much everything they did, including Christmas. Miss Tina felt like a second mother to me, and being with her and the girls made being away from my own family a little easier. One year, Beyoncé, Kelly, and Michelle put their money together for my birthday and bought me a diamond ring. That ring became my favorite—it was the first thing they bought for me. Another time, they paid for me to go to Miami for my birthday.

In my second year working with Miss Tina, I still didn't have a car, so I was going to rent one to drive from Houston to Austin to see my mom. It was Christmas Eve and I had a four-hour drive ahead of me, so I was trying to get on the road. Miss Tina asked me to go with her to pick out a car for her nephew before I left. She said she didn't feel like driving and needed my eye. I was mad because I don't like driving at night, and it was a long drive. But I took her to look for a car. She wanted to get him an SUV, and she asked if I thought he would like the car we were looking at. I thought, "It's a free car! He's going to like it!" I texted my mom to tell her I was going to be late. We finally found this green Mercury Mountaineer and we went inside the dealership. She double-checked with me to see if I thought he'd like it. I said he would. She was doing the paperwork and the salesman asked her nephew's name. She said, "Actually, it's for my son right here. Ty, you fill out the rest. This is a Christmas gift from me and Beyoncé." They bought me a car!

I loved the car and the jewelry and the trip, of course, but the biggest gift wasn't material. I can never be grateful enough that Miss Tina, and later Beyoncé, provided me with a consistent flow of work. I'd see my fellow stylists out looking for work, going through dry spells, but I was able to create a life and feed my daughter thanks to these amazing women. The outside world saw us as celebrities and stylist, but we were truly a family. Celebrity styling is a competitive business, and I'd watch my peers get replaced at the drop of a hat. You couldn't even be sick or send an intern. The next thing you know, the intern is the stylist. I never had to worry about that. Maybe it's a Texas thing—we're really strong on loyalty. Once you break faith with me, it's a wrap. Beyoncé told me, "If no one ever sees us together, it's because you left. You will always be my brother."

When I was working with Destiny's Child, I was so busy I didn't realize how special an opportunity I had. Only later, when I had time to stop and reflect, did I truly appreciate the blessings I've been given in my career. Though all of us on the Destiny's Child team

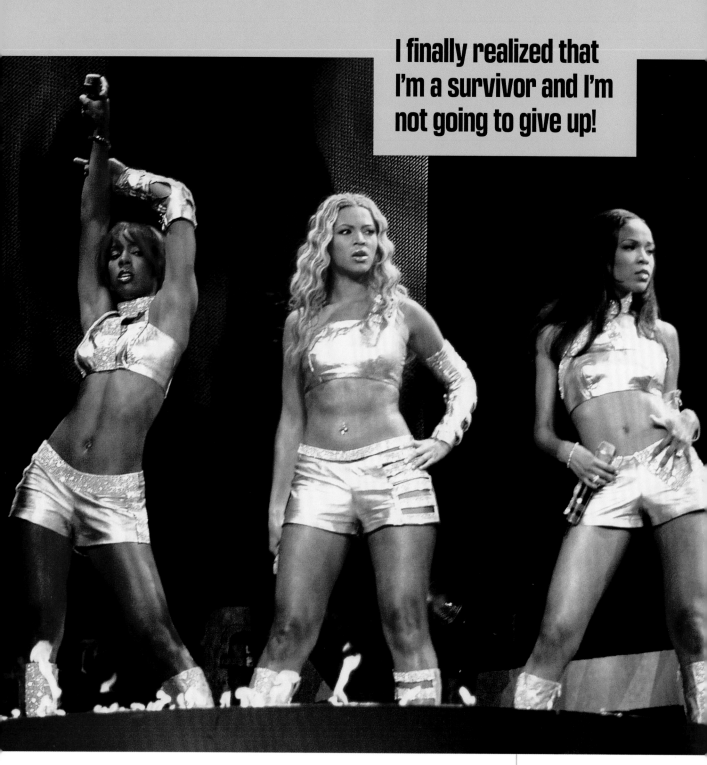

I finally realized that I'm a survivor and I'm not going to give up!

The girls on fire in Miss Tina's gold lamé designs for the Destiny's Child World Tour

worked very hard, we also had great privilege, and we appreciated that. We worked every day: we'd do a video one day and fly to the other side of the country for an awards show the next. We did red carpet appearances, photo shoots, hosting gigs. I was dressing not only Destiny's Child but also the dancers, usually about ten, so there was a lot of wardrobe.

I traveled a lot, helping to style the group, and I visited parts of the country and the world I'd never seen and met celebrities I'd only glimpsed on TV. I met Michael Jackson and Prince at the Grammys, and though I was starstruck inside, I never showed it. That was one of the reasons Miss Tina felt comfortable with me. I felt like I deserved to be in any room. We're all human. I never saw celebrities as being better than anyone else (except Janet Jackson!).

Travel was a privilege I came to appreciate. I didn't get my first passport until I was with Destiny's Child, when I was twenty-seven. The first time I had my passport stamped was when I flew to Berlin with the girls for a promo tour. My first foreign city, Berlin will always have a special place in my heart. It had an energy that felt so different from home, and I was intrigued by everything I saw. I'd stay out all night just walking around. If our car pickup was at nine in the morning, I would walk into the hotel at seven. Whenever I had a day off, I would explore. I went to bars and restaurants and clubs. I once went to a gay club, and when I went looking for the restroom, I quickly learned that the club had a sex dungeon, which was apparently not that rare. That woke me up!

Leaving the United States showed me there was a whole world out there I knew little about. That first trip left me hungry and ready to travel and stamp my passport. And I did! I'm on my fourth passport now—I was fortunate to get a chance to see how alike the world's people are in many ways. At heart, most of us want the same things: safety, love, health, respect. One day we were in Japan, doing that country's version of *TRL*. Nobody spoke English but people on the street all piled up at the window. The girls were doing the show and the song "Survivor" came on. All the people started singing along. It was the most beautiful moment. These people didn't speak English, but they were singing the verses so clearly. It made me look at that song in a different way. The "Survivor" lyrics have always resonated with me because it was the first video I did with Destiny's Child and it came at a time when I was learning to survive my doubts and fears. That message of endurance is one I relate to, and I could see in the faces of those Japanese fans that they related too.

When I first joined the Destiny's Child team, I'd been afraid to leave the country, but seeing up close so many examples of our common humanity changed me. I wanted to go as many places as possible and discover new foods and cultures and ways of looking at the world. Other people in my family mostly didn't have an opportunity to travel—the few who did went because they were in the military. I felt like I was this simple kid from Texas who happened upon this amazing, expanding experience, and I was thankful for it. When I came home, I had the fresh perspective that only stepping outside your own comfortable surroundings can bring.

When Destiny's Child took breaks and after the group's run, I did the girls' solo projects. I was there for all my sisters. Even though it was a lot of work to style them and their dancers, it never felt difficult. They were my sisters; you just support your family.

Michelle had the first solo project, recording a gospel album. Then Kelly did an album; she had a song called "Stole," which was serious and deep. Next came Solange, who was around sixteen at the time; I did her album, music videos, photo shoots, and tour. And then Beyoncé came out with "Crazy in Love." I put her in the bodysuit with the fur shawl; there was fire in the background and she was with Jay, dancing and on the ground. That was the moment she turned into a woman. I went to the trailer and cried a little bit. I felt like my baby sister was growing up.

I transitioned to styling Beyoncé primarily, and I was with her for fifteen years (with a couple of little detours). Beyoncé and I are similar in so many ways. She's like the female version of me, and I'm the male version of her. Sometimes we communicate with just a look. I can stand at the front of the stage and gesture to her, and she'll know exactly what I mean. We're both very humble. Despite her song "Diva," she is not a diva, at least not in the negative sense people mean when they use the word. She and I are just country folk from Texas who believe in loyalty and treat everyone the same. The person you're looking down on today could be the same one you're looking up at tomorrow. Beyoncé acknowledges everyone, from the person at the front desk to the housekeeper. A lot of celebrities don't do that. She's very sweet, reserved, and funny. I'm like that too, in certain ways. People think I'm shy and quiet; in reality, I'm very loud and funny, but only a close few experience that side of me.

Closed mouths don't get fe so speak up until you're fu

Destiny's Child sparkling in Dolce & Gabbana at the 2005 World Music Awards in LA

Ty's Takeaways

> You get what you give. Hard work and perseverance pay off. Keep your faith and put in the work, and things will happen. The outcome may not be exactly what you expect, but it'll be what you need. And it could be more than you ever imagined.

> Teamwork makes the dream work. When you're styling celebrities, hair, makeup, and fashion all go together. If any one of those elements isn't right, the misfire reflects on the whole team as well as on the client. This is true of almost every field of work you can think of! So learn to work well with others and accept constructive criticism if you want to succeed.

> Use your voice to advocate for yourself. No one can know what you need to feel happy and fulfilled if you don't tell them. Keeping thoughts about your needs to yourself is a recipe for resentment and dissatisfaction. The people in your life are more willing to help than you may even realize. After all, they want you to be happy!

> A healthy workplace is essential to your own well-being and satisfaction—often, you spend more time with coworkers than you do with friends and family. Set the example you want others to follow. When trust builds over time, you may find that the people you work with become a second family.

> Never feel like a celebrity—or anyone!—is better than you are; we all have different gifts. God created you, just like he created the people you idolize.

TEN

Partners in Style

Like most people who care passionately about their work, I like to do everything myself. And like most people who care passionately about their work, I figured out eventually that I needed other people's help to grow and thrive.

Miss Tina and I were doing everything for all three girls—the hair, the styling, the shopping, and the designing, with help from Hymie. The looks for a red carpet event or a two-hour concert can take weeks to plan, but that length of time was luxurious. I never had that much time because the girls were so busy, so we were run ragged and realized we needed more help. My mind is clearer and I can be more creative when I don't have to worry about FedExing. But you're taking a chance when you add people to a team that's already great, and you have to be sure you are bringing in people you can trust. We worked with truly dedicated and talented people over the years, and I learned that having a supportive, hardworking team in place helps me be a better stylist. At first, Miss Tina and I worked with just Hymie; later, we added Timothy White, a tailor. Timothy is a hands-on person, so in addition to the tailoring, he shopped for fabric, went to FedEx, and generally did whatever the situation called for.

Raquel Smith came after that, and she was a huge asset. Destiny's Child was growing in popularity, with more and more appearances and shoots scheduled, and the workload was becoming too much for us to manage ourselves, so we brought Raquel onto the team as an assistant. She had been an intern for House of Deréon, Beyoncé and Miss

Tina's ready-to-wear fashion line, so we knew she was a hard worker, and we liked that she was trustworthy and not starstruck. Raquel could do everything from lifting heavy bags to styling. She proved herself, and there came a point when I was no longer comfortable calling her my assistant. She became my styling partner.

Beyoncé steps out wearing Roberto Cavalli at the launch for her fragrance, Pulse.

Members of the Destiny's Child styling team aren't the only design professionals who helped further my career. Certain fashion designers and stylists were unbelievably generous with their time, talent, and advice, and working with them has been among the greatest honors of my life.

The girls were actually wearing designer clothes before we were invited to work with any designers; we were just purchasing the garments. As they got bigger, the top names in the fashion world began to seek them out. Building relationships with designers was one of the most exciting parts of my job. I loved going into showrooms and taking whatever I wanted! It's such a privilege to walk into a showroom and touch these luxurious clothes that no one has ever worn. Seeing high-end garments straight off the runway in person made me feel like I was stepping into the pages of those fashion magazines Miss Tina and I used to cut up for inspiration.

The first designers to allow Miss Tina and me to pull looks for Destiny's Child were Roberto Cavalli, Giorgio Armani, and Alberta Ferretti. Being allied with those houses was a big deal. Roberto Cavalli was one of my favorites because anyone wearing his clothes stood out from the crowd—his cuts and choices of prints were so rock star.

To me, Giorgio Armani is the god of fashion. He basically invented red carpet dressing, and when you think of timeless elegance and luxury, Armani is the man.

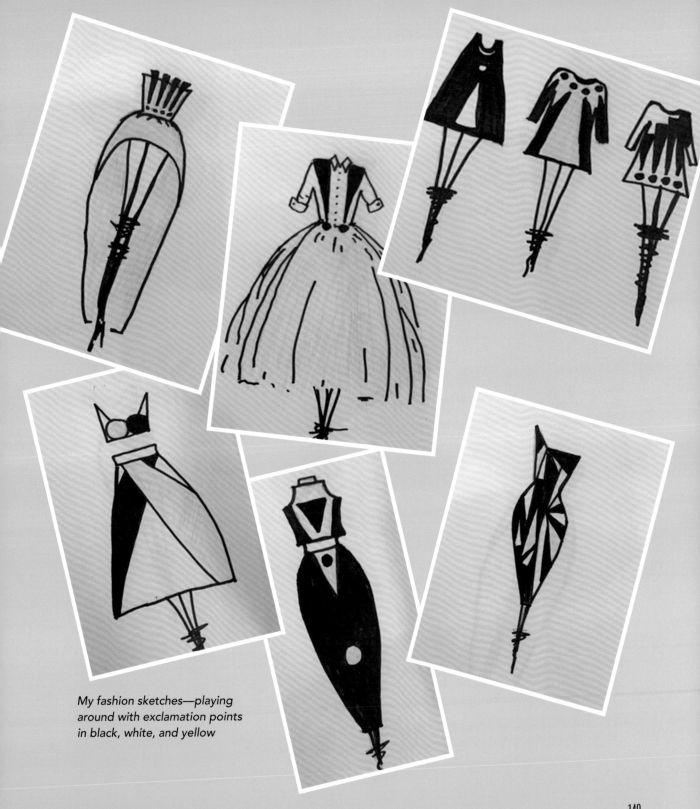

My fashion sketches—playing around with exclamation points in black, white, and yellow

Before I even knew what fashion was, I knew who he was, so meeting him was very meaningful to me. He doesn't speak much English, so he had a translator when I met him. He's very warm, and I was in awe. He took Beyoncé, Miss Tina, and me to his headquarters, and I was so inspired to see how this one person built a huge empire. In addition to his multitude of fashion lines, he has lines of accessories, cosmetics, and home furnishings, and owns restaurants and hotels. His name was cut into the grass at the airport in Milan! Giorgio Armani gives off a sense of power and strength, and for him to be so chill and humble and a ball of light was a revelation.

To move forward, you have to pay it forward.

Meeting the designers in person helps you get a feel for their art and the choices they made for their collections. I'm an energy person, so I like to meet the designers, whether they're at the top of the field already or just starting out. If someone doesn't seem like a good person, I don't want to use them. Why would I help someone who's nasty to others when there's a good person just starting out in his Brooklyn apartment? He is hustling, trying to achieve his dreams. I'd rather help that person. I always tried to be that person, too, the one who was hustling but not stepping on anyone else to get where I was going.

Two important things I've learned in my career are that relationships are critical and that being generous with your time and knowledge pays off. Not only does it pay off in pushing your career forward, it's just a better feeling to be a good person and not petty or vindictive. I always tried to give people the benefit of the doubt and extend a little grace to those who needed it. And I valued the people who reached out and helped me.

Two stylists were so generous to me when I was starting out. Having seasoned stylists in my corner meant a lot. People in the world of celebrity fashion can be ruthless, so when you come across bighearted folks, you learn to treasure them.

I met the first, Freddie Leiba, when he styled Beyoncé for *InStyle* magazine. After that, he would contact me whenever he visited showrooms and saw pieces that looked right for her. At that time, a lot of stylists in LA were like hoarders. They would pull whatever they thought was hot even if their clients couldn't fit into it, just so nobody else could wear it. New York stylists weren't like that so much because it wasn't as competitive a business there. Red carpet fashion was exploding in LA, brought about largely by Joan Rivers, whose red carpet coverage was key in bringing designers' names to the public's attention. Dressing celebrities for events and awards shows, most of which happened in LA, became big business, and didn't always bring out the best in everybody.

Freddie was my unofficial mentor—I had his phone number and could call him for anything. I was intrigued by his poise and his presence. I'd go to shoots and see other stylists who were nasty and talking to interns like they were nothing, but Freddie was always well mannered and kind, yet he kept everything moving. He was so calm, and we shared that same low-key demeanor. Freddie has an elegant presence. When he styles something, it is polished and regal. He showed me that you can be humble and still be well respected in this business. You don't always have to be promoting yourself. He influenced many of my decisions, both fashion-wise and on a personal level—his impact on my style choices and philosophy of work was huge.

The other stylist who guided me was Phillip Bloch. Anybody who knows Phillip knows he's a party all by himself. I first met him at a club, and I would often see him out. We later connected on the set of Beyoncé's *Carmen*-inspired Pepsi commercial—he was one of the stylists. Of course, I already knew his work. He was probably the first celebrity stylist, and I respected his craft. Seeing how down-to-earth and cool he is made me love his work even more. Like Freddie, Phillip would contact me if he saw things that looked like Beyoncé. He connected me to designer Elie Saab, and I built a great working relationship with Elie too. Phillip gave me good, strong advice about being in the entertainment business, which can be cutthroat. He was so open and helpful, making sure I knew everything I needed to know so I wouldn't be surprised in any situation. I respected him because most stylists want their clients to be the only one to shine, but Phillip understood there's room for everyone.

Stylists with profiles like Freddie Leiba and Phillip Bloch didn't have to help me, but they extended a hand when I needed it and I'll never forget their kindness and generosity. Because of them, I help other designers along the way. That's the way it should be. It doesn't take anything away from you if someone else succeeds too.

It's important to help those people you really believe in. I'd sometimes get criticized for dressing someone in a new designer. But everybody's favorite designer started somewhere. I learned from Beyoncé, "If it's hot, why not?" A piece doesn't have to be

Partnering with Raquel Smith was so rewarding— our shoot for the stylist edition of Level Twentyone magazine reflected the fun we brought to our work!

from a known designer or an expensive label to be good. I met a young designer named Queera Wang, and I dressed Billy Porter in Queera's work. Queera Wang took $2,000 and did a whole collection that looked like it cost a million dollars. It's not about labels; it's about craftsmanship and talent.

I made it a point to go to Fashion Week two years in a row wearing outfits that cost no more than $25 a day. I still landed at the top of several best-dressed lists. It's not about the budget. Standing your ground and not caring what people think are most important. All that matters is that you and your client are happy, because you're not going to be able to please everyone.

Trust is a big part of working in fashion and styling. You have to be able to rely on the people you are working with, the designers and jewelers, and they have to know you are going to take care of the items they loan you. A couture gown can cost anywhere from a couple of thousand to more than ten thousand dollars, but jewelry is a whole other level. A small diamond pendant can cost several million. Normally, when you pull diamonds, you need to have a guard on site with you. There's so much red tape involved. But I was able to build a bond with premier jeweler Lorraine Schwartz, and that trusting relationship allowed me to do my job without any stress. Once we established that connection, I wouldn't use other diamond jewelers, and we became good friends. I spent seven Thanksgivings with Lorraine. Other jewelry designers would offer to pay me to use their pieces, but I wouldn't do it because of my loyalty to Lorraine.

At the Polo Classic, wearing a women's blazer from Woolworths in South Africa. The rest of the look, including shoes, came from a thrift store and cost less than $25.

Being willing to work with people and to step back when it makes sense is part of my personal philosophy. It can be cool to see what other stylists do with your clients, and because the women in Destiny's Child were like family to me, I never felt threatened when someone else styled them. Magazines often want their own team to handle styling for their shoots, and I liked to see the shake-ups that a new stylist might create. I loved it when B. Åkerlund put Bey in camouflage and green hair for the "Superpower" video. If I had come to Beyoncé with that, she'd probably have said, "Ty, get out my face." Working with a different stylist allowed her to break out of her zone and try new things.

I truly believe what's meant for me is going to be mine, so I never felt threatened or competitive with my peers. There's room for everybody. I love to see other people's creativity. It's fascinating to see how different people style the same outfit, and I'm always rooting for my colleagues to succeed.

Ty's Takeaways

> When you're happy with the way you look, it shows. We're not born with clothes on. Your first outfit is your skin. Once you get right in that outfit, nothing else matters, because you know who you are. Knowing who you are gives you the confidence you need to get through life. It gives you protection against negativity. You can't be shook.

> Give to others. Reach back and pull someone else up. When you bless someone, blessings come your way. I believe so strongly in helping others bypass the difficulties I went through. It's rare to find someone whose talent and heart align; when you do, take a chance on them.

Collaborations can unlock a layer of creativity you never realized you had. Surround yourself with people who inspire you to level up and grow. It's not possible to know everything, so if you are going to elevate yourself, you have to be open to what you can learn from others.

Your best work comes when you have a team you can trust. Knowing you have one another's back lets you build together and raise your game. But before others will trust you, you have to trust yourself. Confidence starts from within.

Know that you don't have to carry all the weight yourself. I used to do everything myself and was afraid to rely on other people. But once I found someone I could trust, my work processes became smoother and less stressful. I realized how important it is to have another creative eye and opinion.

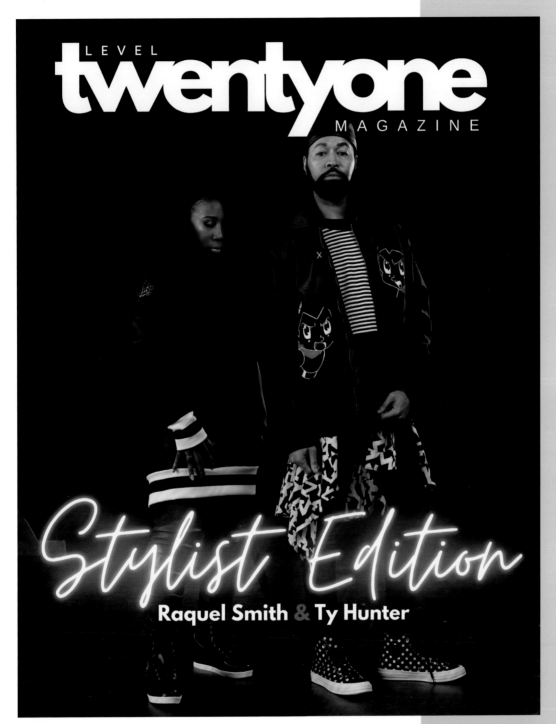

Raquel and me on the cover of Level Twentyone magazine's stylist edition

ELEVEN

When the President Tells You It's Time to Change

It was my honor to stand with President Barack Obama at the 40/40 Club in New York City.

Sometimes you are moving through your life and things are going pretty well, and then lightning strikes. Which is not always a bad thing.

In September 2012, Jay-Z and Beyoncé hosted a fundraiser for Barack Obama's reelection campaign at their 40/40 Club in New York City. It was an intimate event, with only about a hundred guests, and everyone was allowed to take a picture with Obama. Raquel Smith and I were there because we dressed Bey, so I didn't expect to get a picture. To our surprise, we were called over. The woman escorting us didn't know we had met the president a few times before, and she reintroduced us. President Obama said, "Man, you guys do a great job. You're Beyoncé's stylists. Where do you go from there?"

That moment played over and over in my head. It reminded me of the awakening I had when I found out my friend had a heart valve and of Joseph Kahn's words to me when I was working at bebe. That feeling hit me again. It was another wake-your-ass-up moment. I was in a good space with my family. I wasn't living paycheck to paycheck like a lot of my stylist peers. But the president's words reminded me to look at the bigger picture and not just at what was happening at that moment. You can get comfortable in a given situation, whether it's good or bad. I had been making good money at the heart valve company and everything was great. But I had that little feeling of doubt. And you know what? The heart valve company was sold a few times and operations moved. If I had stayed, my job would have disappeared. And bebe stores ended up closing when the company decided to sell online only. So even though working for Beyoncé is the best job anyone could have, there were other things I wanted to do. It was time to look to other goals. It was time for the next chapter of my life.

Not long after my moment of revelation with Obama, I did the On the Run Tour with Beyoncé and Jay, followed by a video with Beyoncé and Coldplay. After that, I had about three months off. I had never been off that long in all my time working with Beyoncé. By this time, I had started designing a line of shirts with a company called ServedFresh and was also working on a technology-based project. I was glad for the time off so I could focus on my own projects, including the design work, as well as on speaking engagements and hosting jobs. I'd never had time to do that kind of stuff before.

I had missed my daughter's twenty-first birthday because I was in LA working on the Coldplay shoot, and the time off gave me a chance to think about my life and

I know I am not doing everything on my own—I have guidance from a higher power. You may think missing a flight or going home to get a forgotten item is a bad thing, but I see it as protection. Who knows what your higher power helped you avoid?

I loved the graphic black-and-white costumes we did for Beyoncé and Jay's On the Run Tour.

what I wanted to do with the rest of it. Soon after, I told Bey I needed to leave. She told me I was a star and she knew this day would come. She said, "I'm here for you and I'm going to support you." Leaving was the hardest thing for me, but our relationship grew even closer after I left. To this day, we are there for each other. Outside of my family, my love and comfort and safety are with Beyoncé and her family. I have peace when I'm with them. We trust one another completely. It wasn't just styling. Beyoncé wasn't my paycheck; she was my sister. Every move I made was for her greatness and happiness.

Me and B—break time on the "Emotion" video

Leaving my job as Beyoncé's stylist and going out on my own were not easy transitions. It was scary because I was off payroll for the first time in years. I went from traveling nonstop to being at home figuring out what was next.

To make things more complicated, a story in the media made it seem like I got fired, and that became the word on the street. I didn't allow the gossip to bother me, but some showrooms and designers started treating me differently, and that was a big wake-up call. I learned that some people only care about you when you can do something for them; they don't really care about you. The genuine people hung in there, and I lost the ones who were only there for my connection to Beyoncé and that world. It was a humbling experience, and I had moments of doubt and depression. But even in my darkest hour, I believed better things were coming. I got through the bad times by asking myself what I was supposed to learn and figuring how to get out of them.

Instead of living in the past or second-guessing my choice, I dedicated time to other projects. I started sketching and spent more time writing in my journal. I had been on a train moving full speed ahead, and now I had gotten off at my stop. I needed to decide what direction to go from there. I spent more time with my family and found fulfillment in that. I could finally be there for all the birthdays and weddings as well as the everyday get-togethers.

Leaving the comfort of my steady gig was a sink-or-swim moment for me, and I was sometimes scared of drowning. A lot of people thought I made the wrong decision, but I believed that this slow time was what my soul needed. It took me a while to kick myself out of the dark. You have to go through the storm, but at the same time it's important to give yourself an expiration date. You may not feel better by the time that date comes around, but that just means you need to feel those emotions and learn to live with them. I've learned that if I'm going through something, I'm not going to drink alcohol or do anything that might alter my brain and prevent me from really feeling the pain or fear or unhappiness. The problem will still be there when I stop drinking or whatever. And maybe I'll have added a thorny vice to deal with. You have to face your problems. That's what helps you grow.

> # The dark times we get through make the next ones that much easier to overcome. We lose our way when we run from the dark.

Miss Lawrence, who gave me words of encouragement when I needed them most

When the phone case I'd designed was ready to launch, I wanted to give it to some people as a gift. I didn't send it to Beyoncé and the rest of the girls right away because I felt it would be too easy to hand them the phone case and have them promote it. I wanted to prove to myself that I could have a successful product launch on my own. I made a list of people to gift, and the first person on it was Blake Lively. I added some other names and ended with Miss Lawrence. As soon as I wrote his name down, he called me for the first time ever. He said, "Babe, I just want you to know I'm so proud of you. I see what you're doing." I immediately started crying. I told him that no one knew, but I had just quit my job with Beyoncé two days earlier to focus on other things. He said, "Baby, you can only run in place for so long. You're going to be fine. Run, baby, run." I cried my ass off.

I poured myself a glass of wine and sat out on the patio at my friend Rena's, where I was staying in Boca Raton. As soon as I sat down, Blake Lively called me. She was with someone who wanted to give a poncho to me and Beyoncé. Blake Lively's was the first name I wrote down and Miss Lawrence's was the last. I took that set of phone calls as a sign that God was telling me He would have me from the beginning to the end, and everything would be fine. From that moment, I truly accepted that the move I made was the right one, and everything just started happening.

The week after those calls from Blake Lively and Miss Lawrence, I got a phone call from Mike Muse, the Millennial Entrepreneur Champion with President Obama's My Brother's Keeper initiative, asking me to be a part of that effort. Obama launched MBK to help address the opportunity gap that exists for young men of color, and MBK partnered with the Small Business Administration to highlight hands-on experience across a range of businesses. He chose seven Black men, each of us at the top of our chosen field, to tell our stories in a series of summits as a way to encourage our community.

As part of the initiative, we did a media campaign that included interviews and talk show appearances as well as speaking engagements at places like the Apollo. We each had a different story, and it was electrifying to have men from all different backgrounds come together. I was a Black gay man in fashion, one man was a personal trainer, another

I am deserving of all the good that has come to me. Nothing bad lasts forever, so prepare for the good.

worked in politics. We had all worked to help and impact others, and we all told our stories in a transparent way. We didn't polish up our backgrounds to make them look pretty. The audiences heard our experiences, complete with all the dirt and grit. We let people in on the bad times in our lives and how we overcame them.

Being among the seven men chosen to participate in My Brother's Keeper was a highlight of my life. And working for Barack Obama? It didn't get better than that. To be part of something so positive and to be associated with Obama was extraordinary. The president was the one who had given me the impetus to strike out on my own, and being invited to share my story as part of his initiative let me know that I was destined to do more than style people, as much as I loved my work. On that campaign, I got to connect with an audience and share my life stories in a way that could support other people, and that was a truly powerful feeling.

Three months after I stopped working with Beyoncé full time, she asked me to dress her for the Met Gala. I'd never considered my departure a permanent break, so I was glad to know she felt the same way. I was just working on other things, and Beyoncé knew I was forever there if she needed me. When I appeared on the red carpet with her at the 2016 Met Gala, it shook the industry up because of all the rumors that I'd been fired. I continued to dress her for certain occasions, and that confused everyone. No matter what, I will always be there for Beyoncé and for all the girls whenever they need me.

When my shirts with ServedFresh came out, I wanted to launch them without relying on early promotion from Beyoncé and the girls, just as I had with my phone case. I just posted a picture of the shirts on Instagram, and right after I posted, Naomi Campbell contacted me and asked if I would send her a shirt. Naomi *is* fashion, and I'm forever grateful for her stamp of approval. *Vogue*, Yahoo, and tons of magazines started contacting me and doing stories. The media have supported my projects in a wonderful way. I believe that putting out positivity and being good to people brings the love back to you.

Opposite: Beyoncé, stunning in a custom latex Givenchy gown at the Met Gala in 2016

Top: My SIX:02 collection was inspired by diversity
Bottom: Naomi Campbell, rocking my first design with ServedFresh

The next period in my life was a time of intense creativity and reinvention, and I was never lacking for projects and partners. Some partners approached me, and other opportunities I searched out. In 2017, Foot Locker asked me to design a collection for their SIX:02 line, a performance fitness apparel and athletic shoe brand for women. SIX:02 carried only Beyoncé, Rihanna, and Kylie Jenner at the time, so it was amazing to be included among those names. My picture was featured on billboards in Times Square, one block away from the office where I used to work with Beyoncé's production company, Parkwood Entertainment. I never thought I'd have billboards in Times Square and on Thirty-Fourth Street. That wasn't part of my plan. I just wanted to put out a line!

After the SIX:02 collection launched, I met a designer named YounHee Park at the Concept Korea fashion show during New York Fashion Week. I fell in love with her line, Greedilous. YounHee herself is a ball of love. We immediately became brother and sister. She doesn't speak any English and I don't speak any Korean, but we found a way to communicate. We can be together for hours and it just works. She wanted to do a collaboration, so I designed the bags for her fashion show for two seasons.

Later, Hyundai contacted me to do a clothing line. I knew this would be a perfect opportunity to bring in YounHee. We had a show at the Soho House in LA for a capsule collection that was never intended to be sold. It got a lot of press, and BTS was part of the campaign, which brought the collection a lot of attention. People who don't speak the same language can still come together to create something beautiful. We communicated through fashion and love for each other.

Even as I continued with my design projects, I became increasingly interested in connecting with people and connecting people to one another. A lot of this interest came out of my work with My Brother's Keeper—it had sparked in me a desire to keep engaging with people on many different levels. My Brother's Keeper brought me to the Apollo to speak to audiences, and the energy of the crowd was exciting. I grew up watching *Showtime at the Apollo*, so to stand on that stage and talk about my life was special. I felt the history of the theater as I stood there, and I was honored to be on the same stage where great Black musicians from Ella Fitzgerald to James Brown to Smokey Robinson to Diana Ross and the Supremes had appeared.

But speaking from a stage to an audience is only one way to communicate, and it's not the most personal way to reach people. I was interested in exploring some other avenues. When I met Claire Sulmers, founder of the popular website Fashion Bomb Daily, we connected right away; she gave me instant warmth. We did an interview together during Fashion Week, and it was like we already knew each other. After the interview, we walked down the block to get noodles. That's where we really bonded. To see a sister in fashion who was Black, with dreads, impressed me and showed me she was genuine. Claire was not trying to look like anyone else.

Around that time, 2016, Legendary Damon and I were getting ready to start a series of brunches called No Basics Brunch. We knew we needed some female energy with us, and I thought of Claire. The

Korean designer YounHee and I became fast friends, united by fashion if not by language.

167

Claire and me, dressed for our cocktail events

brunches were an opportunity for people to get dressed up (that's where the "No Basics" comes in!), have cocktails, and connect. We'd invite a different host and DJ each week. It became a big event. Claire would come up with themes like stripes, or polka dots, or Versace, and she and Damon and I would dress accordingly. We did these brunches in the summer in Harlem, and it was always a good time. That lasted for two years.

Then Claire asked me to do a series of talks with her called Cocktails with Claire. We had guests like stylist and fashion designer Patricia Field and makeup artist and creative director Jay Manuel. We would all have our moments where we would tell a story, and then we'd do a Q&A with the audience. The more I did those talks, the more comfortable I became in front of the mic. The more I told my story, the freer and more alive I felt. When that series finished, I started another with Raquel Smith, who had become my styling partner with Beyoncé. In these talks, I stressed that life is not always easy or beautiful. You can be up one minute and down the next, but your hard work and dedication will pay off eventually and your investment will feel good. When I talk to people, I sometimes feel that a higher power takes over and allows me to give people what they need at that time. And it's scary because it's the same thing I need at that moment.

Motivational speaking gave me so much fulfillment, and I was always happy to find opportunities to do more. Soho House, a members' club, invited me to do a series of talks at all of their locations in the United States. At one of those talks, I got in front of the crowd and the whole audience was white men in suits. I didn't know if they would relate to me, but I told myself to just go out there and tell my story and be my authentic self. I don't sugarcoat anything. When I talk, you get the rawness and the realness.

People often get nervous in front of a crowd or a camera because they feel they have to act a certain way. They end up talking and acting in a way they wouldn't normally. When I learned to let go of that expectation and just be me, I was able to speak in front of thousands of people. When you share your story, others want to open up and tell their own stories. You learn so much that way. There is nothing like being in a room with people. Communicating with a person on social media can make you feel like you know them, but you're only seeing one dimension. When you finally meet that person, it's the most beautiful thing.

In the days after I left my job with Beyoncé, there were definitely dark times. I was lost and didn't know what would come next. But getting quiet and being patient and listening to my inner voice were transformational. The victories that came out of those dark times are so bright. I struggled out of my comfort zone to enter new territory. It wasn't necessarily a safe place, but it was intriguing and it led me to learn more about myself. I would never have accomplished that had I stayed. "Where do you go from there?" President Obama asked me that day at the 40/40 Club fundraiser. His words have echoed through my head over the last years, and I've learned that you don't need to always have an answer, but you need to keep asking the question.

Ty's Takeaways

> Don't get too comfortable. Anything can happen. You always need a backup plan. That's true with everything—work, relationships, finances. Giving too much of ourselves to anything is a risk—what happens if it goes away? Are you still complete? It's hard to let go, but you have to be mentally and physically prepared for disruption, even in good times. Nothing lasts forever, good or bad.

> When gossip is swirling around you, sometimes it's better to be quiet. Let people think what they think and judge how they judge. Those battles are not yours to fight. You don't have to prove who you are. Let your work and your actions do the talking, and allow time to heal your wounds. To do otherwise is a waste of energy.

> You can't run from fear; you have to go through it. The goal is to cope in the darkness so you can get to the light. Greatness lies on the other side of fear. When you reach that other side, you'll have that armor to face the next battle of insecurity and fear.

> Keep going and never stop growing. Time is precious when you have dreams and goals. You will know when the moment is right— you'll feel it in your gut. Don't deny the universe when it speaks through your inner voice. I believe prayer changes things, but you also have to put in the work to get what you want. Every day is a fresh opportunity to fulfill your dreams.

> Success is all the sweeter for having embraced the discomfort that lies outside your comfort zone. Sometimes you have to break out of that zone and live with uneasiness and pain to get to that place of triumph. But don't mistake healthy growing pains for true dissatisfaction; if your sleep is uneasy and you dread going to work, it's time for a change. Take an hour each day to visualize where you see yourself, then do research and make a plan to get there. Eventually, you'll be educated and aware of what you need and want in your career.

t the Essence Festival in New Orleans with Ethel and Mom. They came to support me and see me spea

PART III

Being Ty

TWELVE

Facing Race

BLACK PRIDE

self - Identity for Blacks

unity of all my brothers and sisters

Endurance of all Blacks

Dad's art; he made this piece in high school.

Every summer when I was growing up, I visited my Uncle Curtis in San Jose, California. He had many friends of many different races, and I loved the mix of people I met there—being around such diversity enlightened me. I liked going to Uncle Curtis's because it was so different from what I was used to, and I felt free.

It was during one of these summers, when I was twelve years old, that I first experienced blatant racism. Some redheaded white kid asked me, in the ugliest way possible, "What are you doing here, n@#$*%?" I was stunned. No one had ever said that word to me before. What did he mean, what was I doing there? I was on vacation. This was not supposed to happen on vacation. I told my uncle and he talked to the kid's brother. Eventually, everyone just walked away. But the experience left me heartbroken and angry, degraded by the way I had been treated. I couldn't understand why it happened.

Fast-forward to my late twenties. I was driving to visit my grandmother and had Trezure in the car with me. She was only six years old. A cop pulled us over for no good reason. He claimed I made an illegal turn, but I had been going straight. This happened in one of the small towns where my mom told me to always drive the speed limit and be careful of my driving etiquette. In Texas (as elsewhere), some towns are known for racist or discriminatory behavior. Growing up Black, you just know that when you go to certain areas, you go the speed limit and do everything perfectly because if you get pulled over, the authorities will harass you.

The officer gave me the third degree and then, in front of my daughter, made me get out of the car and lie on the concrete while he patted me down. He searched me to the point that I felt violated. Then he searched my car. Trezure was crying the entire time. Of course he didn't find anything. I had given him no reason to think I was perpetrating some sort of crime. He did not care about the emotional damage he was inflicting on us. I'd seen such displays on TV and had read about them in the news, but had not had direct experience of so much aggression from an officer. It took me right back to that ugly moment with the white kid in San Jose. Black people deal with racism every day, but often it's subtle. It hurts and it takes its toll, and we've been excusing it for way too long. But this felt dangerous in a different way; it was in-your-face, daring me to not comply.

Trezure and I both wound up crying for the rest of our trip. I felt so helpless. This injustice, this insult, was at the hands of a police officer, a person who was supposed to make us feel safe, not threatened. And I had no recourse; I just had to take it. As a Black person, if you speak up, you are accused of being radical and causing problems. You can either suck it up or fight back, which often escalates the situation. I did not want my mom to get that call telling her I'd been killed or taken to jail because I spoke up. Nor did I want my daughter to witness that, though I couldn't stop her from the inescapable realization of what it's like to be Black in America.

Moments like those with the white boy and the police officer, along with the thousands of small indignities and abuses we endure as Black Americans, made the emergence of a charismatic Black man as front-runner for the Democratic presidential nomination all the sweeter. A Black president was something you never thought would happen—the idea seemed so far-fetched that Chris Rock made a movie in 2003 called *Head of State*, in which he runs for and wins the presidency.

A Black man as president is something we never even put in our dream-a-dex, so I was glued to coverage of the 2008 presidential election. For the first time in my life, I felt like I was a part of the democratic process and that the winner mattered to my life. There was someone I felt represented me. To see that dream become a reality as Barack Obama won

This moment opened up a doorway to higher possibilities, and being in the room was a highlight of my life.

Watching your heroes soar can help you claim your own piece of the sky.

the election was an empowering moment for people of color. At that moment, we knew we could do and be anything. Obama gave so many people hope.

Being with Beyoncé when she sang "At Last" at Barack Obama's inaugural ball brought me such profound joy, which was deepened by the impact his election had on Black culture. I cried so much as Barack and Michelle Obama started their first dance as president and first lady.

Beyoncé was so busy leading up to that evening (she went to the inauguration) that we didn't even have time for a fitting. I showed up to the area where tents were set up as dressing rooms for the ball. I brought about twenty-five dresses and hung them from the ceiling because they didn't have a rolling rack. The dress we chose was elegant and timeless—a sleeveless champagne satin gown with a rhinestone appliqué, designed by Elie Saab. I didn't want anything too trendy. When she put on that gown, we knew it was just right—it was a fairy-tale moment. We did the fitting right there, and thankfully we didn't need any alterations. I walked her to the stage and stood at the foot of the stage when she sang.

Having a Black president made me feel so proud. Barack Obama was our superhero. When Beyoncé came off the stage, we held each other and cried. It was a powerful moment, and we needed it so much. Being part of that day and witnessing history was one of the most momentous things that has ever happened to me.

During the eight years Obama was in office, I felt a greater sense of unity in our country. I always say nothing lasts forever, good or bad. When it was time for Obama to leave office, no one knew what was to come, but watching this era come to an end was bittersweet.

I'm so grateful I had the opportunity to meet Barack Obama.

Sadly, some of the days ahead were bleak ones. George Floyd's murder was the catalyst for a fresh look at the ways race affects how we see one another, for both me and a majority of Americans. Because it happened during the pandemic, people had a lot of time to focus on and think about the killing and the dynamic that contributed to it. The world was shut down; there was no place to go. Every day, on every TV channel, you'd see the video play and hear stories about it. I'd go on social media to get a break but found so much ignorance there. Things became very divided, and people posted a lot of comments without researching the facts. I found it very hard to deal with the injustice. That murder, captured so courageously on cell phone video, was a very dark and painful episode, and I felt it deeply.

Even though protests were happening right in front of my door in downtown LA, I couldn't be out there on the front lines. At the time, my mom had cancer. I wanted to be out there demonstrating, but I couldn't take a chance on being exposed to COVID-19 and spreading it to her. I hunkered down in my apartment. I'd keep my curtains closed because outside my window was a show, with gunshots and cops launching smoke bombs. I divided my house in half and stayed in the front part because the whole back of my condo was windows. Anybody could throw something. I turned my whole place into a little studio.

But I had to do something, so I started reading Black history. I learned so much about myself during that time. I studied, and I discovered so many things about the history of Black people I'd never learned in school. It was empowering to find out all the things Black people created, about the many Black innovators I'd never known: Garrett Morgan invented the three-position traffic signal; George T. Sampson created the first automatic clothes dryer; John Purdy patented improvements to the folding chair; Thomas Elkins was responsible for the "chamber commode," which incorporated a flushing toilet into other furnishings; Frederick McKinley Jones invented refrigerated trucks. I also learned about things that were stolen from us. In many neighborhoods Black people had built, their land was taken away and their property destroyed. We don't have that history laid out for us. We learn about a few icons in school, like Martin Luther King Jr., Harriet Tubman, and Rosa Parks, but we don't learn about the breadth and depth of the contributions Black people have made. It was energizing to do my own research and fill in those gaps, and I wished I had known as a kid there were so many role models for me. I would have felt empowered knowing my people were so accomplished and had created so many things that the world uses daily.

I used my social media platform to spread the knowledge I gained. I lost followers and got a lot of hate, but I also got a lot of people telling me that my posts started conversations in their households. One such comment came from someone I knew was racist, and that was enough to let me know I was going in the right direction. I want my page to be a place people can go for enlightenment and positivity or to just get away from the chaos of the world.

Loss and protest helped shift the world.

There's so much history that's not taught in schools. Take time to learn the hidden stories few people know.

The events that led to the 2020 protests are certainly dark moments in our history, but they have given people the opportunity to speak up and be heard in ways they hadn't been before. People are fighting for their rights, for equality and justice. It made me teary-eyed to see all different cultures and people all over the country and all over the world stand together for my people as the Black Lives Matter movement gained strength, and to know we don't have to fight alone. That moment felt different. For the first time, I felt at my core what the words "We the People" really mean.

Ty's Takeaways

> Stand up for what you believe in. Fighting for equal rights today makes the world better for future generations. Pray for the day when no one is judged by the color of their skin.

> Learn your history so you can feel more complete. School taught me a tiny fraction of the information that was available. Investigate and learn the highs and lows of your ancestors' accomplishments. When you educate yourself, you can educate others. Know the history of your culture so you can pass that information on and break the cycle of hate.

> Race is a sensitive subject, but it must be discussed openly if we are ever to break generational bigotry. During the BLM protests, I received many comments from people who thanked me for opening up the topic for discussion, which allowed them to start important conversations about racism in their homes. It was rewarding to see positivity coming from that dark time.

THIRTEEN

Removing Chairs from the Table

Out with Dad—he was sick at the time and I took him to his favorite restaurant in Austin.

My mom has always kept bad news from me

My mom has always kept bad news from me because she doesn't want me to worry. I think a lot of parents are like that. They are used to caring for us, and they aren't ready for the tables to turn. But tables turn whether you are ready or not, and being in the dark made things even worse when I eventually learned the truth.

In 2018, I was getting ready to go to an event for luxury leather goods brand MCM when my mom called. She tried to play down her news, but she had stage 4 breast cancer. Instead of going to the event, I went to the airport and caught a flight to Austin. Mom had a doctor's appointment the next day, and that's when I heard the full report about her illness. She'd been secretive about her health in an effort to protect me—that's why the cancer had advanced so far before I heard anything about it. Right away, I knew I had to stay positive because if I were to break, she would break too. I knew I had to tell her that we were going to fight this. I had to summon all my strength because I'm a very sensitive man and it felt like this news was destroying me inside. But my determination lent my mom the strength she needed to handle the situation.

Mom's cancer opened my eyes about a lot of things: health, life, love. A loved one's illness can make you reevaluate your whole existence. She is my superhero, and there's this Kryptonite weakening her; it felt like there was nothing I could do about it. But that didn't stop me from trying. Being a vegan, I thought we should change my mom's

Ty's Takeaways

> Death is a part of life. Make memories with your loved ones while you have them with you. Give them your time because tomorrow isn't promised. Put things in perspective and really line up what's important to you. We're all running and trying to succeed, trying to get known, trying to make money, but are we living in the moment?

> When the people in your life need you, be there for them. Parents, grandparents, family friends, and maybe even siblings or spouses can grow frail or ill, and it can be easy to stay away or bury yourself in the busyness of your own life. Do your part. Step in and help however you can—not only because they need it, but because that act will reward you. Doing good makes you feel good.

> Let others know who you are. They might be more accepting than you think. But you also need to let people move at their own pace and prepare yourself that they might need time. Coming out can be such an emotional roller coaster—it's important to get that weight off your chest, but you have to be ready for the ride.

> It's never easy to lose a loved one. Although I miss my father, I feel even closer to him now than I did when he was alive. I believe his spirit guides me through life. For me, keeping my dad's photos and videos on my phone helped—I could see him whenever I wanted. I also wear two of his rings to keep him close to me. For others, writing down memories or going to places where you spent time together might be healing. You don't always have to visit a gravesite to connect with those who have passed—I feel a person's spirit is closer in places you enjoyed together. Celebrate their life to help heal from their death.

Christmas with Mom and Dad

EPILOGUE

I was having a very low moment when I moved to LA in 2020. I had just lost my dad, my mom had stage 4 breast cancer, COVID-19 was spreading, incidents of racism were surging as Black Lives Matter protests rose, and I wasn't working. I finally built up the courage to visit my boyfriend, who was riding out the pandemic in another state. The day after I got there, he came home late, and I found out he had been cheating the whole time we were apart. Though it was 2 a.m., I left and went straight to the airport, where I bought a ticket to Austin to see my mom. My boyfriend and I had been together for five years, and I thought of him as my family. I was devastated.

The day after I arrived in Austin, I got a FaceTime from Billy Porter. I'd never met him but I've always admired him. There was a light that drew me to him. The fashion world shifted on its axis when Billy wore a Christian Siriano gown to the Oscars in 2019—that was a courageous move, and I loved the risks he took with his looks. In a predominately tuxedo/suit world, Billy shook things up, making men's fashion relevant on the red carpet.

People think Billy's success came overnight, but he'd been working at his craft forever. Though he had been on Broadway for years, he wasn't rewarded for living his truth and being himself until he was fifty-one. I love it when people succeed later in life, when their dreams come true despite long odds and public assumption that they won't. I was inspired in the same way when Susan Boyle became an overnight sensation after appearing on *Britain's Got Talent*. Although I've accomplished a lot, there are still so many things I want to do. Stories like Billy's and Susan's help me let go of the feeling that I'm too old to try new things. Miracles can happen at any age.

When Billy called me that day, when I was at one of my lowest points, he said, "Child, I know you're on a retirement, but I need you to come out of retirement and style me. I want to work with you." I spent more than an hour and a half on the phone with Billy getting to know him. He's a beautiful person. What really made me take the job was the fact that he's been with the same management and the same assistant for twenty-nine years. That touched me because that kind of loyalty is rare. It reminded me of working

with Beyoncé and the Destiny's Child family, and of our deep dedication to one another. I told him I would take the job because I knew that he was a loyal person.

Working with Billy has been so refreshing. I can be creative in a stress-free environment. Billy is in his own lane. It's rare that you can shop both the men's and women's sections for the same person. That flexibility has opened the door to let me be creative and experiment. He is also easy to work with, and it's been fun making magic together.

Billy Porter has the same work ethic as Beyoncé. He's a busy man who is constantly working, and that pushes and motivates me. He is a special being who has made me see that I can do more than I ever thought. I wrote a script and I'm doing more designing. I'm working on a line of handbags with my friend Manuel. I want to do more books and more TV and film. Most importantly, I'm at a place now where I can be as busy as I need to be, but I've learned to balance that busyness with time for family and friends. At the end of the day, that is what I care about most.

It takes time to figure out your priorities, and they will shift as you move through different stages of your career, of your love relationships, of raising your children or caring for your parents. Life is filled with transitions; the key to thriving is learning through each transition how to become your true self.

You have to celebrate even the hard stuff because it brings you to a place where you can love yourself. I'm proud of who I've become—not what everyone else sees but my whole self, spiritually and internally. I've been through—and am still going through—a lot. I've learned to live in the dark times, to deal with them and face them head-on. Working through the dark times helps me grow and move forward.

I sometimes wonder what would have happened if I hadn't been outed, if Joseph Kahn hadn't told me I was wasting my potential, if Barack Obama hadn't said, "Where do you go from here?" Where would I be today? Who would I be? But I'm excited about who I am today and what the future holds. I've put out a lot of positive energy and encouraged people in so many ways. In the past, I sometimes questioned the good things that happened to me. Now I'm in a place of acceptance because I know I deserve every good thing that comes my way. I went from "God, why me?" to "God, why not me?" The more blessed I am, the more I can bless others in a meaningful way. I want to do valuable things in the world and impact people in a positive way. I'm looking forward not just to my next chapter in life, but to my next book full of colorful chapters!

Ty's Takeaways

> Don't be afraid to be yourself. Other people's opinions of you are not your business—they don't know your struggles. What you think about yourself is what's important. To build confidence and self-esteem, practice being your own biggest fan.

> You may feel like you've been working toward your goals for so long and like other people got to theirs so much faster and easier. But you haven't reached your goals yet because it's not your time. Focus on your passion. Pour your energy into doing what you love; that makes you more complete, which helps you achieve your goals. Looking at the versions people present of their lives— on social media and elsewhere—can create a lot of self-doubt, but don't let it get to you. The best thing you can do is clap for the other person. Your time will come when you're ready. We block our own blessings when we're jealous of or judge other people.

> Take time out to recharge and connect with the world around you. We're so into our phones and gadgets that we sometimes forget to appreciate what we have. Put your phone away for a while. Feel the sun's warmth on your skin. Take your shoes off at the park and feel the grass under your feet. When you're with your grandparents, your sister, your best friend, really spend that time together. These are the people who know the real you and love you for who you are. Let them know you love them back. Take a break from technology and just be present. These are the moments you'll look back on and appreciate.

> Let people know they are not alone. It costs nothing to help others, and there's real value in lifting someone else up. Be true to your story, whether you are posting to the world on social media or sharing with loved ones and friends. Your words might offer someone a blueprint for finding their way out of a dark time. As bad as things may seem, there's always hope that tomorrow will be better, and showing that possibility to people allows them to benefit from your experiences. I'm living proof that confronting what you think is the worst possible situation can turn into the biggest gift. As bad as your situation may be, somebody else has come through worse and is still able to shine. Never be ashamed of who you are or where you came from. Just keep pushing forward. Every day is a new chance to make yourself over from within.

Ty Came into My World...

by

Billy Porter

Ty serves us quiet-strength-realness through a very purposeful and arresting stillness. One would assume that, having been part of the iconic rise of Destiny's Child and then the subsequent world domination of Beyoncé a.k.a. Miss Queen B herself, taking over the entire cultural planet, Ty would have some sort of extreme ego for us mere mortals to navigate on eggshells. However, after our first meeting over FaceTime during Miss Quarantina, I had to check myself. Because, you see, I have actually been on the other side of such assumptions. I too have been labeled ego-ic, difficult, and hard to work with by people who only see the persona and have never worked with me, met me, or even been in my presence. I too have been unrightfully judged by folk who don't know the actual human being behind the work—at all! What's the old adage? To assume makes an ass out of you and me. That shit is real, y'all, and I had to check myself.

In my late forties, as my star began to rise, I knew that fashion needed to be a part of my "brand." I had no idea what I was doing, but the door to success had finally been swung wide open to me in a huge, life-altering way. The proverbial train had left the station and I found myself sometimes barely hanging on. I was trying to cement my place in a cultural movement, a queer revolution, an activist-based, de-gendering of fashion, if you will. My vision was to be a walking piece of art and activism every time I show up! I had a stylist. We made a monumental mark in a very short period of time. Case in point: the Christian Siriano, antebellum, tuxedo Oscar gown that broke the internet and changed the world of fashion forever. Yup—that is I!

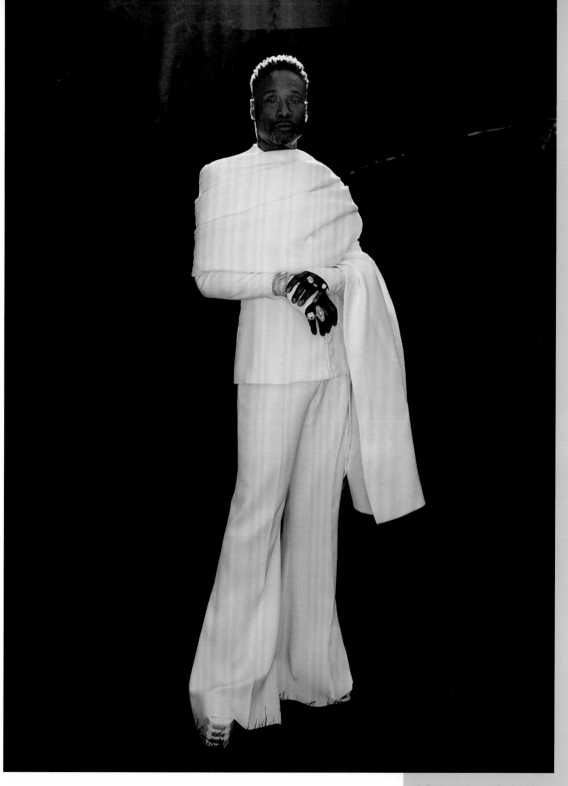

Billy wearing Ashi Studio

Downtime with Billy

And . . . what next? How does one build upon such an iconic moment? Everything was happening so fast and I was swirling out of control. I found myself struggling with the idea that I had to somehow keep up with the constant demand to "outdo" or "top" myself. For what? For whom? I didn't like this concept. I rejected it. I didn't like the pressure and I needed to shift the focus. Get control of my own narrative. That meant I needed an artistic partner who could help take me to the next level—whatever that meant. I needed a visionary artisan who understood my purpose, my calling, my ministry, and my intentional desire to make a difference in the world through my art.

"You can have anybody you want!" my husband yelled at me one day during a conflict. "You could have Beyoncé's stylist!" I scoffed. I thought to myself, How on earth does this man think that my name could be uttered in the same breath with an artist on that level? "I thought, 'Chile, B's stylist don't even know my name.'" Now don't get it twisted: I've never not believed in myself. Quite the contrary, I've always known I'd "make it" someday. And here I was . . . "making it!" And . . . I was just making my splash, and the volume of the work I had to keep up with kept me in a bubble. I didn't know. I truly didn't understand that in the span of one year's time, I had become a whole-ass celebrity!

Enter Ty-silent-assassin-Hunter, a visionary artist of the highest order! Just what I had been searching for. Ty came into my world and effortlessly turnt me out! When we spoke on the phone, he claimed that he had recently retired and was looking for something new to creatively engage with. And then in the next sentence he said, "I believe you are that something new. I believe we can make magic together. I'm comin' out of retirement for you!" And there you have it! Just like my husband said.

Ty's emotions are hard to read. He doesn't give anything away—ever! He's been in rooms with the kind of royalty who can sometimes be incomprehensible.

Ty is a protector. And as a Black, queer man navigating how to move with grace in the public eye, one who has never felt protected or cared for, I feel safe with Ty. We'll be at an event together and I'll forget, once again, that I may be a little famous now, and decide I'm going to take myself to the bathroom without backup. I'll just take off—and in about five seconds flat, Ty is right beside me. Calm, cool, and collected. Covering me. Protecting me.

I can now tell when he's happy about a lewk because he'll scan me up and down and say, "You so disrespectful!" Or, "You ain't gonna have no friends!" You know you doing good when you get that stamp. Since Ty has joined my team, I finally feel taken care of. Looked after. Seen. Protected. So in this moment, I wanna say, thank you, Ty. Thank you for seeing me. Thank you for sharing your brilliance with me and thereby changing the whole-ass world in the process. The earth is a better place having you in it. Love you, boo.

Acknowledgments

I want to thank the creative and knowledgeable staff at **Chronicle Books**, especially editor **Becca Hunt** for her dedication and tremendous encouragement.

Eila Mell, thank you for this long journey—it's been over five years now. I couldn't have done it without you. You gave me the push I needed during all those long days and nights. You're super talented and I'm so happy to create this awesome project with you. I love you much.

Christopher Navratil, thank you for allowing me to tell my story. You recognized and shared my vision and helped bring it to life to share with the world.

Tim Palin and **Susan Lauzau**, thank you for your hard work and dedication. You are both so talented, and working with you was an honor and a pleasure.

To the talented **Ricky Day**, thank you for the pictures.

Beyoncé and **Billy Porter**, your fine words mean so much. I love you guys.

Miss Tina Knowles, I wouldn't be who I am today it if weren't for you. Thank you for giving this country boy from Austin, Texas, a chance. You believed and saw something in me before I saw it in myself, and that allowed me to use all my God-given talents at once. I am forever grateful to you.

Thank you to my family and friends—too many to mention (you know who you are).

To my godmother, **Ethel**, thank you for always being there and being the backbone and ear I needed. I love you.

To my little brother, **Cedric**, thank you for all you do and allowing me to win the fights growing up. We both know you really could have kicked my butt! LOL!

Thank you to my angels—my dad, **Mama Bea**, and **Grandma Georgia**, as well as all my loved ones who have passed.

To **my daughter** and **my mom**—my girls—thank you for motivating me and pushing me in everything I do. I do it for you.

Image Credits

Growing Wildflowers

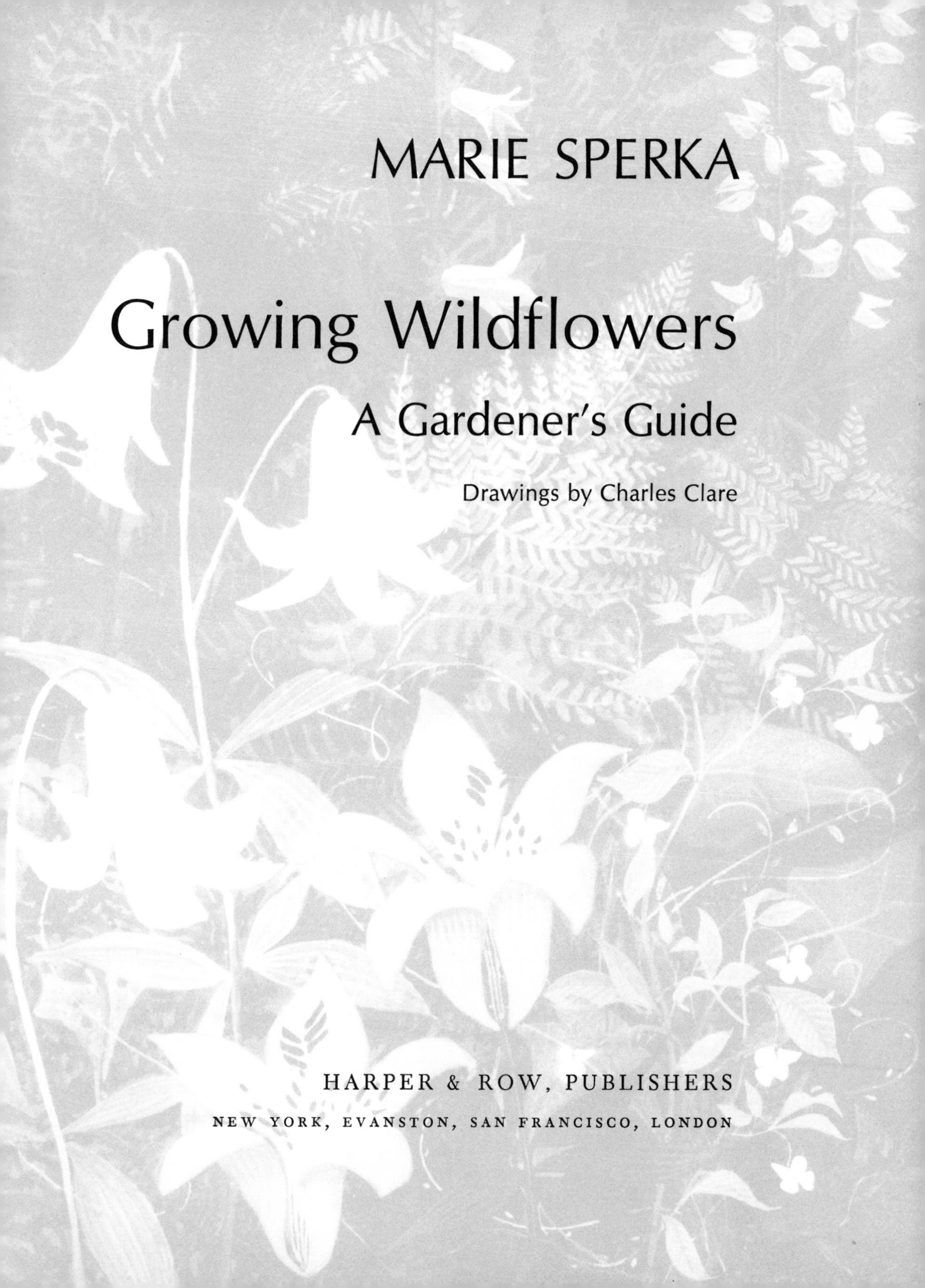

MARIE SPERKA

Growing Wildflowers
A Gardener's Guide

Drawings by Charles Clare

HARPER & ROW, PUBLISHERS

NEW YORK, EVANSTON, SAN FRANCISCO, LONDON

GROWING WILDFLOWERS: A GARDENER'S GUIDE. Copyright © 1973 by Marie Sperka. All rights reserved. Printed in the United States of America. No part of this book may be used or reproduced in any manner whatsoever without written permission except in the case of brief quotations embodied in critical articles and reviews. For information address Harper & Row, Publishers, Inc., 10 East 53rd Street, New York, N.Y. 10022. Published simultaneously in Canada by Fitzhenry & Whiteside Limited, Toronto.

FIRST EDITION

Designed by Lydia Link

Library of Congress Cataloging in Publication Data

Sperka, Marie.
  Growing wildflowers.
  1. Wild flower gardening. I. Title.
SB439.S63   635.9'676   76–156553
ISBN 0–06–013959–5

Contents

Perennial Wildflowers for Permanence

Foreword

The native flora of our prairies, mountains, and woodlands are a living part of the American heritage, as valuable and irreplaceable as any we have. But daily our wilderness and woodlands are vanishing, and with it the plants they nurture. Unless we act quickly, our wildlings will disappear.

Wildflowers, ferns, and other native flora have been my lifelong interest, and in this book I would like to share with my readers my experience in growing and propagating them. Although the cultivation of wildlings is in no way a substitute for their preservation in their natural habitats, it does give to the care of the amateur gardener, the expert, and the nurseryman a small piece of the American wilderness and keeps before us living treasures of our natural heritage.

Please note that many of the flowers I list here are already becoming rare; some are on protected lists. Before you acquire a rare plant, make sure that you have the proper conditions for its growth—and never pick the blooms before they have scattered their seeds if the plant is on the protected list in your state.

The cultivation and propagation practices discussed in this book are those that I have developed and used over years of successful wildflower and fern cultivation, first for my own pleasure and then later as a business. My nursery, Woodland Acres Nursery, is located in the Nicolet Forest area of northeastern Wisconsin. Most of the land there is uncultivated: forest crop or wilderness, a network of lakes and streams, stretches of reforested areas, prairie land, and rolling hills. The climate is severe. Summers are hot and often dry, and in winter the temperatures can drop to thirty degrees below zero and even lower.

Yet I have found that, with care, even in such conditions, it is often possible to grow wild plants in an environment entirely different from their native habitat. In the text of this book I have given detailed instructions on how to cultivate various species. Should any readers know of better methods or have different results to report, I would be very interested in hearing from them.

I would like to thank everyone who encouraged me to put my experience into book form so that I might share the knowledge and satisfaction I have gained from my years of working with wildflowers and ferns.

Marie Sperka

Crivitz, Wisconsin
Winter, 1973

Growing Wildflowers

Some forty years of watching wildflowers grow in the woods and on the prairie, along streams and lakes, among rocks and boulders, and in my nursery, have taught me what I know about their requirements. Their needs in most instances are few, but they are extremely specific and must be followed exactly if the plants are to be grown successfully. Although it appears that wildflowers and ferns thrive under conditions that would kill most cultivated perennials, most of them have, in fact, very particular requirements for soil, sunlight, moisture, and nutrients, and are at least as demanding as domestic plants in these respects.

In this section of the book, general techniques and principles are given for preparing the soil and surroundings so that you may cultivate a lovely wild-flower area under varying conditions.

There are two main types of wildflowers. Those that have a root or bulb system that enable the plant to live for many years and faithfully reappear each spring are called the *perennials*. Those that bloom, set seed, and die in the same year or in two years are called the *annuals* and *biennials*. Most of them are grown directly from seed. Mature perennials, planted while dormant, are the mainstay of an established natural garden. The annuals and biennials provide a ready means of naturalizing a large open area, and they are also used to fill in the bare perennial beds until the perennial plants can take over.

The annuals and biennials are treated individually in the section starting on page 27. Perennial plants are discussed in the section starting on page 41.

Both the botanical name and common name are given for each wildflower. Common names, of course, vary from area to area, and sometimes a plant is known by several names at once. The botanical names are given by family, genus, and species according to *Gray's Manual of Botany* (Merritt Lyndon Fernald, 8th edition, 1950, corrected printing, 1970). Certain wildflowers, which have been imported from foreign lands, will not be found in *Gray's*.

3

PREPARING THE SOIL AND SURROUNDINGS

Reclaiming Barren Earth

Rebuilding infertile soils to make them productive can often pose a real problem, but with a little patience, energy, and planning, wonders can be accomplished. Sandy hillsides, gravelly or gritty soils, barren earth, and even blow sands—any land of low fertility—can be greatly improved and conditioned.

More than fifteen years ago I reclaimed two small plots of land, one of a desert type near where we now have our garden pool and the other a barren excavation next to our house. They could not have seemed more hopeless.

The first plot was a deep hole that I filled with the earth dug out to make the pool. The fill consisted of sand with a mixture of grit and a small amount of clay; humus was nonexistent. For a whole year the area lay bare but was kept free of weeds by frequent hoeing.

Finally the long process began of making the soil suitable for growing something. A layer several inches deep of compost and small leaves was strewn over the entire area. (This was before I had come upon the method listed below for reclaiming soil.) Here and there I made pockets in the earth and filled them with fertile soil, mixing some of the barren earth with it, and planted a few hardy wildflowers. I also planted a seedling birch and a small balsam fir, about twenty-five feet apart. At first the tiny trees seemed too far apart, but as they grew the span closed and today I see that this was the right spacing. The birch is now about twenty-five feet tall, and the balsam fir about twenty feet.

Over the years I have continued to add small leaves, old marsh hay, and weathered straw to the sandy soil. Now hepaticas, bloodroot, and *Trillium grandiflorum* flourish beneath the white birch. They have multiplied, indicating that organic matter has built up sufficiently to grow the woodland wildflowers.

Some half-ton boulders were brought in to create a realistic woodland setting. The untrimmed branches of the balsam fir now sweep the ground.

4

In sunny open spots, prairie-type wildflowers have taken a firm hold. The entire problem area has been transformed from an arid waste into a spot of natural beauty.

The other barren plot was a hollow filled with earth excavated from the basement of my house. A ten-foot strip along a walk was marked off for a perennial flower bed, and the remaining filled area was readied for a lawn.

The key to working up a fertile soil is the humus: the type, the amount, and the way it is scattered on the soil or combined with it. I call this method of reclaiming barren areas "A Dozen Steps to Success."

1. Start with an area of about 1,000 square feet (for example, a plot 20 by 50 feet). Remove any unwanted growth and all debris.

2. Spread six bushels of peatmoss—it must be damp or wet—over the entire area, and over this spread six bushels of good compost or well-decayed, weed-free manure. (The more life-giving humus material you add, the better will be the finished soil, so add more if it is available.)

3. Ten to twelve bales of combined, weed-free oat straw are needed. Combined straw is preferred as it has usually been exposed to the weather for several weeks before baling and is easier to handle. Old clean straw or weathered hay may be substituted. Spread five bales of the straw evenly (about a half bale for every 100 square feet). Loosen the pads as you spread the straw. This is important. As you walk over the straw while spreading it, some will settle.

4. When the entire area is covered with the five bales of straw, sprinkle on twenty pounds of 10-10-10 commercial fertilizer.

5. Over this, sow one-fourth bushel of clean, weed-free oats.

6. Now spread the remaining five bales of straw as you did in step 3.

7. Thoroughly wet down the entire area and roll with a lawn roller or tamp down to settle the straw and flatten the surface. Wetting the straw is not absolutely necessary, but it hastens the germination of the oat seed and dissolves some of the nutrients in the fertilizer.

8. To keep the straw from blowing away, it is desirable to peg the plot down until the oat plants are several inches tall. Place one-inch-square stakes or strong sticks one foot apart along all four sides of the plot. Tie one end of a ball of strong twine to the bottom of one corner-stake and walk back and

forth with it the entire length of the plot, looping the twine around each stake. Now do the same along the width of the plot. This will form a pattern of one-foot squares outlined in twine. In a windy area it is especially important to keep the straw down until the oats have grown tall enough to anchor the straw.

9. As soon as the oat crop is a few inches tall, remove the twine. (It may be saved and used again.)

10. If the project was started in the spring, the oats will be ripe by mid-summer. Now it is time to repeat the enriching process. As soon as the oats have ripened and before the birds can steal the seeds, roll the entire area to flatten the stalks to the earth. The ripened seeds will resow the plot.

11. Sprinkle the plot with ten pounds of 10-10-10 commercial fertilizer again, plus ten pounds of bonemeal. Bloodmeal may also be added, but I find that where dogs run loose this is a poor practice—dogs like to dig wherever bloodmeal is spread.

12. Cover the area with another five to six bales of combined straw, as in step 3. Repeat steps 7, 8, and 9.

The second crop of oats will not ripen, but it will make a good mulch that will be winter-killed and then laid down by the weight of the snow.

The next spring repeat the process beginning with step 4, using more commercial fertilizer if you wish. The addition of fertilizer depends on what you wish to plant when the soil is brought back to good fertility level. Follow through with the remaining steps. This process may be repeated another year in cases of extremely barren soil. Woodland flowers, most perennials, and good lawns need fertile soil. Very few soils will be ready for planting at the end of the first year. Usually it is best to treat a plot for two years or longer.

The poorer sun-exposed soils are best suited for planting the prairie type of wildflower or the sun-lovers of lean meadows, such as butterfly flower, hoary puccoon, bergamot, and ox-eye daisy. When the wildflowers are planted, the coarse mulch should be pushed aside and the rich humus worked into the earth in a circle three to four inches deep. A little extra compost may be added. After planting, return the coarse mulch around the plants. When planning a prairie garden, grasses of the prairie type may be left to grow in tufts here and there for a more natural effect.

Beware of quack grass (also called couch grass) and wild oats. Should they or any other creeping grasses appear, uproot them at once and add more mulch to that spot. The remaining roots will eventually come to the surface as they cannot tolerate deep mulching. Quack grass will literally work its roots right out of the soil if enough mulch is applied.

Where you plant the woodland wildflowers, rather than the prairie type, you must provide shade and continue to build up the soil with humus, as these plants require a rich, fertile soil and protection from intense sunlight. Consider your newly acquired earth a step in good conservation.

When the soil has been enriched to a good depth by decaying mulch and by the addition of humus in planting pockets, you are ready to grow a variety of woodland wildflowers—hepaticas, bloodroot, trilliums in variety, Dutchman's-breeches, mertensia and wild blue phlox, as well as many of the wildflowers of drier woodlands. Continue to mulch your plot until the trees grow their own mulch, and then let the falling leaves take over. It is important to water in periods of drought, but do not water trees after the first of August.

Time and effort go into reclaiming barren earth, but the beautiful and natural results are well worth it.

Reclaiming Overgrown Lands

Woodland wildflowers require uncultivated soil that contains a lot of decaying humus and abundance of fungi. Large areas of wild land can be reclaimed, and your woodland garden expanded, with the simple method given below.

In your selected site, mark desirable wildflowers with a stake so that they will not be accidentally destroyed or smothered. Now dig out all the undesirable wild shrubs, leaving only the fine hair-roots interlaced with the mycorhizal fungus that are beneficial to the growth of lady's-slippers. Remove young trees and saplings where there is crowding; be sure to cut the stumps even with the ground, and remove the bark down to at least three inches below the soil level to prevent new shoots.

The soil in the entire area should not be disturbed any more than necessary. Since fertility is not a problem, all that remains is to smother undesirable grasses and plants. It is best to do this in spring, especially after a heavy rain. Here is my method.

First, spread newspapers, three to five sheets thick, over the entire site. Cardboard can also be used, but it does not deteriorate as quickly. On paths and trails, magazines can be used. Then, spread a generous layer of old straw and marsh hay over all the paper. Finally, scatter a generous amount of 10-10-10 commercial fertilizer over the entire area to hasten the decay of the mulch and newspaper.

If you are laying the newspaper on a hillside, always start from the highest point and work downward (the reverse of shingling a roof). You want to absorb the rain as it falls rather than have it run downhill.

Next spring, if plant life beneath the newspaper has not died, repeat the mulch and fertilizer process. The fertilizer will have leached before planting time in the fall.

Pull back the mulch when you are ready to set plants in the new plot. If any newspaper remains, remove it to the compost heap. Do not spade! Disturb the soil only enough to remove any coarse lifeless roots that remain— and perhaps a few unwanted living ones. Now carefully insert wildflowers into the new soil, spreading the roots and then pulling the mulch up around the stems. Add more mulch where needed, as you would in a garden plot. This type of reclaimed area is an excellent home for all woodland wildflowers and ferns.

Even quack grass will give up under a heavy layer of newspaper and mulch. Quack grass roots need air to grow and cannot stand smothering with a heavy mulch. The roots will grow toward the top, and you will be able to lift them out.

By this method I reclaimed an old chicken yard that had grown up in quack grass; it took several years, but it was worth the effort. The reclaimed area is a very fertile piece of land in the shade of some large oak trees. In open spots I planted a few birch trees. I had always envisioned the yard as ideal for growing lady's-slippers and woodland ferns, and it has indeed proved to be wonderful. The ferns grow luxuriantly. The lady's-slippers thrive, continually growing new roots and multiplying—many two-crowned plants now send up five to seven flower stalks.

Steep Banks, Hillsides, and Rugged Slopes

There are many ways to plant steep and rugged areas that have a tendency to erode. The quickest method is to plant a groundcover suitable to the terrain. The groundcover should have strong spreading roots, which will hold the soil in place. This method is satisfactory if the soil has not eroded and is fertile enough to support the plants you have selected.

Rather than planting steep areas with groundcover, I prefer the method outlined below, even when the soil is fertile. To me it seems wiser to lay down a cover of natural mulch before planting.

1. Lightly rake the selected area and sprinkle with ten pounds of 10-10-10 commercial fertilizer for every 100 square feet (for example, 10 feet by 10 feet). The fertilizer is used only to grow more luxuriant oat plants and will have leached considerably before it is time to plant the wildflowers.

2. Sow broadcast some clean oat seed over the area.

3. Mulch moderately to lightly with clean straw or old marsh hay. The latter is preferred.

4. Sprinkle the area thoroughly with water, being careful to avoid letting the surplus run down hill and cut tiny rivulets that can later contribute to the soil's washing away.

5. Roll the entire area with a lawn roller or tamp down with a board. Unless the area is windy, it is not necessary to peg down the straw until the oat seed germinates.

In a short time this area will be covered with a good stand of oat plants, the roots of which will hold the soil on the slope. The plot should not be disturbed any further, except to push aside the mulch to insert the desired plants.

The oats are best planted in mid-August. The plants will grow only six to ten inches and not set seed. In late fall, the oats will winter-kill and then be packed down by the snow. Plant only oats and not rye, as rye will live over winter and continue to grow the following spring when you will want to insert the plants.

9

Let us assume that the plot is fertile and in the shade. Woodland wild-flowers with strong roots will furnish support to the soil and flourish here. Among these are mayapple, wild ginger, Greek valerian, foamflower in patches, hepaticas in clumps, wild geraniums in drifts, and large colonies of wild violets (except birdfoot, which is for sun only). At the bottom of the slope some of the taller woodland ferns will adapt themselves readily.

In such a shady area it is desirable to continue to add some mulch, unless there are enough leaves each fall to take over naturally. As added fertility builds up the soil, you can add many of the wildflowers that need humus. Trilliums planted in colonies among bloodroot make an appealing picture.

Suppose that the plot is in full sun. It will then need no further mulching, unless weeds are a problem. The addition of tufts of nonspreading grasses will add interest. Suitable wildflowers are butterfly flower, hoary puccoon, gray goldenrod, black-eyed Susans, *Phlox pilosa*, *Liatris scariosa*, and *Monarda fistulosa*. Ox-eye daisies for an early splash of white can take over a whole area. In open sandy spots an addition of drifts of birdfoot violet will spread a wave of blue across the slope in late May and early June.

Clay Soils

The addition of organic matter to clay soils will help to make them porous and easier to work. The method outlined below should give good results. Let us start with a plot about 1,000 feet square.

1. Remove any unwanted growth or debris from the area before starting your project. If large rocks are present and can be moved to one side, it will make for easier tilling or spading later.

2. Over the entire area spread an inch or two of coarse sand or gravelly earth with sand.

3. Over this, spread six bushels of rich organic compost, preferably coarse, or spread some strawy manure. Also spread a bushel or two of damp peatmoss. The more organic matter you add, combined with a balance of sand, the better the condition of the new soil will be. Leafmold from an old leaf pile is also desirable.

4. Sprinkle on ten pounds of 10-10-10 commercial fertilizer.

5. Sow broadcast one-fourth bushel of clean, weed-free oat seed. Cover the oat seed by raking or add some more compost.

6. Wet down entire area thoroughly to hasten germination of the oat seed.

As soon as the oats crop is about seven inches tall, it should be turned under. In a large area, it may be necessary to till several times for best results. Small plots can be spaded by hand. When the vegetation is turned under, it decays and adds the much-needed humus to give texture to the clay soil. With liberal amounts of humus added to clay, the soil will not be as gummy nor bake as readily during periods of drought.

The process may have to be repeated until the desired soil texture is obtained.

Mucklands

Most heavy mucklands require tilling or ditching to drain off the excess moisture that would otherwise stand. In this type of soil, organic matter is usually very abundant and no more need be added. But the addition of coarse grit or sand is advisable in some cases to make the soil less pasty and sticky.

Plants that flourish in mucklands, provided there is no stagnant water, are turtlehead, Joe-pye, boneset, red and blue lobelias, and other plants native to moist areas. The wild calla is one wildflower that will grow in stagnant water.

If I had such an area to work with, I would try making a pool not more than two feet deep at the lowest end. In it I would plant cattails in a container (or they will claim the whole area); at poolside *Iris versicolor* in clumps. I have noticed that these plants can survive undamaged even when the water around them freezes. Around the edges of the pool I would place some large rocks at intervals and in groups. Between the areas where the pool and land meet, fern would make good groundcover and would prevent any silt from washing into the pool during heavy rains. Royal and cinnamon ferns do very well in partial shade.

Highly Acid Soils

Under conifers there are usually bare spots with exposed gnarled roots. Also, the soil is very acid but lacking in the type of humus found under trees in the deciduous woodland.

The soil under spruce trees is usually toxic, and most of the needles should be removed before spading in organic matter. It is a good practice to reserve other evergreen needles for mulching only; that is, for acid-loving plants. Leafmold, damp peatmoss, and organic matter worked only a few inches into the soil among the tree roots will greatly improve the overall condition for planting shallow-rooted, acid-loving wildflowers such as wintergreen berry, goldthread and bunchberry. These make an excellent groundcover requiring a minimum of moisture.

For very acid soils rich in humus, with sufficient shade and ample moisture, select galax, pyrola, pink lady's-slipper, potted bunchberry, clintonia, and painted trillium. Bunchberry, goldthread, and wintergreen will also thrive here. The oakfern quickly forms colonies in this type of soil and adds a note of interest to the wildflowers.

Rocks, Trees, and Fungi

A woodland garden is at its most distinctive when you incorporate into the surroundings the natural elements they grow among in the wild. It will also ensure the success of some of your flowers.

ROCKS. Rocks in a garden recall hills, outcroppings, and ledges as well as fieldstones. When you are landscaping or planning a garden, rocks also mean materials with which to build terraces, stone walls, tree wells, paths, or pools with fountains. Besides lending interest to the landscape, rocks also conserve moisture for the plants growing near their base. Many plants take on an air of elegance when planted beside a large rock or among a group of medium-sized rocks, and some plants, especially the showy lady's-slippers, like to run their roots under the rocks, where they are assured of extra moisture.

A drive down a winding country road often provides lessons in rock positions. At first glance the rocks along the fencerow seem to lie haphazardly, but a closer look reveals that many of them lie at interesting angles and in groupings. A camera or a pad and pencil will aid in making notes about a spot you may want to duplicate later.

Formerly, road builders and farmers had a knack for placing rocks in the most interesting positions. Lacking power equipment, they pushed rocks along the fence lines, glad to have the bigger ones out of their immediate

12

way. Today roadways are made clean, and farmers hire bulldozers to bury the rocks.

Old rocks that have weathered for a considerable time are more interesting than freshly unearthed ones—but use the fresh rocks if you have them. They will take several years to age. Rocks lying in the shade age faster than those exposed to full sun, possibly because shade promotes humidity, which in turn fosters the growth of small fungi. After some years, the flat limestone around our pool is beginning to show a flush of green, adding a touch of permanence to the area. With age, rocks acquire a distinctive beauty and character.

In the woodland garden it is best to use mostly granite rocks of all sizes, up to those that have to be brought in by heavy machinery. Woodland ferns especially thrive when planted among rocks where humus stays and roots are kept cool. The rocks also help to keep the winds from sweeping through. Granite rocks contribute to the acidity of the soil over a long period of time, but rarely is it enough to be measurable.

In the prairie garden I prefer the odd-shaped limestone with rough, weathered textures. Its light color is better suited to the open sunlight. Limestone will make the soil in the immediate area less acid. But this, too, is negligible, unless the limestone is crumbly.

Another rock, found only occasionally, is to all appearances a piece of brownish-red sponge over which glitter has been sprinkled. It is an excellent rock to use in shade, where an aged look is important. When it is used in a moist shady nook, mosses soon grow over it, covering the entire surface. It is very desirable in the woodland garden among small plants such as starflowers, oakferns, clintonias, Canada mayflower, and bunchberries. Sprinkling a little soil from the woodland where mosses are present will hasten growth.

If you are fortunate enough to find rocks with small ledges and indentations, plant mosses and dainty ferns in them. This creates a very natural formation. Common polypody fern (*Polypodium vulgare*) does well in rocky crevices, even if there is only a small opening in which to tuck a bit of humus on which the fern can anchor its root.

One can learn much by studying the wildflowers and ferns that grow among the rocks in the wilderness. You will find long stretches between rocks, and small outcroppings, yet a continuous growth of vegetation. When you place rocks in your own landscape, you will be able to tell whether they look natural.

TREES. If you would like to plant a tree among wildflowers, consider a white birch, which is easy to grow. Select a young tree that is only two to four feet tall and has not yet peeled its bark. Lay aside the coarse mulch and dig a hole one foot deep and three feet in diameter. Shovel some old compost or humus-rich garden soil into the bottom. Woods soil is the best if it is available. (No manure should ever be put into the hole when planting a tree or any other plant: in the process of decaying, the manure will generate heat and burn the roots.) Put the tree into the hole and spread the roots. Fill the hole with soil and replace the mulch, adding more if needed.

A nursery-grown dormant birch tree has a much heavier root system than one dug from the wild and will adapt more readily to the rugged environment of reclaimed soil. By the time the birch has grown seven to nine feet tall, it will usually peel its dark-colored bark and show the much desired paper-white bark.

FUNGI. Mushrooms and toadstools often spring up in areas of a woodland garden where the humus and leafmold are plentiful and moist conditions encourage their growth. A scattering of fungi in a woodland garden lends a note of realism. Huge fungi found growing on old stumps are often gorgeous. Even the rare poisonous fungi lend a beauty all their own to a little spot where they reign a short while and die.

If fungi become too plentiful, simply remove them. (They should be sealed in a plastic bag so that spores cannot ripen and spread before they are disposed of.)

The threadlike mycorhizal fungus and mycelia of other fungi literally web the humus-rich earth of the woodland as they form a lacework on the fine roots of shrubs and trees. These fungi are beneficial to some acid-loving plants, wildflowers, and ferns that flourish best in woodland soil. This type of environment is especially necessary for the successful growth of pink lady's-slippers (see Appendix II, Successful Lady's-slipper Cultivation).

Mulches

It has already been made obvious that no gardener, especially the wildflower gardener, can do without mulches. They are used to kill unwanted

14

growth, to hold moisture in the soil, to protect plants from severe winter cold, and to provide nourishment to the soil. Below is an assortment of mulches for various purposes.

MARSH HAY MULCH. The finer marsh hay is preferable, but I have used hay that contained a considerable amount of cattails and found it satisfactory for mulching larger plants. Marsh hay does not decay as quickly as straw and it lies flatter. It has a neater appearance and does not blow away as easily.

STRAW MULCH. Because it is easier to handle, I prefer oat straw that has weathered for a week or more and then has been baled. During weathering the straw loses its high gloss; I have found that the gloss is detrimental to plants when used as a mulch during the summer, when the sun is stronger.

LEAF MULCH. White birch, soft maple, willow, mountain ash, and other small leaves are preferable to the coarser oak leaves. The small leaves turn to humus more quickly and do not smother the smaller plants as readily. All oak leaves except those of the white and bur oaks make a good mulch for the coarser and more robust wildflowers and ferns. For a coarse mulch that will not blow, run the lawnmower over oak leaves that the wind has swept into rows. The bur and white oak leaves, when shredded, are excellent for mulching in paths and rows of larger plants. Decay is slow. When run through a one-inch screen in a compost grinder, oak leaves and other wood-land litter, even dead branches, make an excellent all-round mulch. It is best put down in fall: the snows and spring rains will settle and moisten it thoroughly.

GRASS MULCH. You are fortunate, indeed, if your lawnmower is equipped with a bag to catch grass clippings. The clippings make an excellent mulch for lady's-slippers, especially the showy lady's-slippers. Each time you mow your lawn, add a light dressing of fresh grass clippings to your lady's-slipper bed. Over the years the grass clippings will build up a rich humus.

EVERGREEN NEEDLE MULCH. The needles of the white pine and Norway pine are excellent for mulching acid-loving plants—for example, pink lady's-slipper, clintonia, bunchberry, Canada mayflower, goldthread, and winter-green. I have never used needles of the balsam tree, but I noticed that in the wild the goldthread and wintergreen berry flourish beneath the balsams. The needles of the spruce tree are supposedly toxic; in yards and woodlands where the large spruces grow, you rarely see plant life beneath their branches.

15

STALKS AND BRANCHES AS MULCH. Disease-free flower stalks of New England aster, blue false indigo, goldenrods, and other tall flowers make a good coarse, airy mulch if you remove their seed heads first. Lobelias usually come through the winter retaining their fall foliage if protected with such mulches. Balsam branches also offer an airy mulch, especially for bearberry vines.

COARSE-SCREENED GRAVEL MULCH. Gravel is a good mulch for the wildflowers of the dry prairies. Gravel mulch helps retain moisture and holds down weeds. Screen gravel through a half-inch mesh, then use a smaller screen to remove the fine sand. Very coarse gravel is also used for mulch. Butterfly flower and blazing star especially flourish when these mulches are used. Hoary puccoon does well with a mulch of fine screened sand.

PEATMOSS MULCH. Damp peatmoss is very beneficial. It is best used next to the earth and then covered with a mulch of hay, straw, or small leaves. As a top mulch, peatmoss dries out and prevents rain from penetrating to the soil. Beneath other mulches, the damp peatmoss retains its moisture and lets other moisture through readily.

SPHAGNUM MOSS MULCH. Like peatmoss, this is best used as an undercover mulch. Both peatmoss and sphagnum moss are long lasting.

COMPOST MULCH. When vegetable matter has decayed to an unrecognizable point, it, too, can be used as mulch. Unless it is very coarse, it should be used as an undercover mulch.

ROCK MULCH. Flat rocks make good mulches when they are laid among plants to cover most of the area. Some cracks should be left, however, so rain can get through. Screened gravel may be used in the cracks. Rocks will offer no enrichment to the soil other than a small amount of minerals. For this reason, I prefer to lay down a compost or other humus-rich mulch before putting down a permanent rock mulch. With a rock mulch you may let falling leaves remain to hide some of the surface. In a prairie garden, rocks will settle somewhat and spreading grasses will eventually hide them.

WOODCHIP AND ROTTED SAWDUST MULCH. I have used sawdust only sparingly. Very old sawdust is excellent. Woodchips are also excellent for woodland paths among coarser plants.

OTHER MULCHES. The list is endless, but I have named those that are easiest to obtain. Any organic matter that decays over a period of years makes good humus. I sometimes use old newspapers and magazines in pathways among large plants where the soil is rich in humus (magazines are slow to decay and should be covered with other mulch to keep the area neat). And several layers of paper of any kind makes a good mulch to kill unwanted growth.

MAKING THE WILDFLOWERS GROW

PERENNIALS. Perennials are almost always planted from dormant stock—that is, from roots, rhizomes, stolons (nodes), or bulbs. Left in the ground, the root system will spread and the plants will reappear each spring. Some perennials may be grown from rootstock bare of sod (bareroot stock) and some must have fresh sod clinging to the roots. Some may be transplanted in their entirety provided they are past their period of bloom. It is usually best to start with stock from mature plants.

Perennial stock can be ordered from nurseries or gathered from the wild. The nurseries either grow the stock from plants they have cultivated (nursery-grown stock) or they collect stock from plants that have good qualities of size, bloom, and hardiness (quality collected stock). When you plan to collect your own stock from the wild, find plants with good quality, mark them with a stake, and dig them up later when they are dormant. Specific instructions for each plant are given in the section devoted to perennials.

Some very attractive perennials have vigorous spreading root systems that have discouraged gardeners from growing them for fear that they might crowd out other plants. For years I have been burying bottomless containers of various sizes to restrict some otherwise aggressive plants. A bottomless gallon container buried at soil level will enable you to grow interesting plants that would otherwise choke out their neighbors. When plants become crowded in the container, remove them and fill the can with new soil. Then replant some of the new shoots of the original stock. Blossoms of such plants should be cut back as they fade to keep them from setting seed.

17

The fine and small perennial seeds often germinate readily, but the larger seeds are usually slow to germinate and many years are required to bring them into bloom. This is especially true of the fleshy rooted and bulbous types. Cuttings or divisions are more desirable than seeds if you already have stock with which to work. I certainly recommend for the beginner plants large enough to bloom.

Fall planting is best for all early-blooming perennials, especially those with heavy roots. For the woodland flowers, a shady border in the garden or a place under high open shade is best. The sun-loving wildflowers will do well on a leaner, drier soil. Whatever your selection, be sure that the plants are suited to your environment.

ANNUALS. Annual wildflowers are grown from seeds, usually sown in early spring or left to self-sow. These flowers bloom, set seed, and die in the same year.

Biennial wildflowers require two years of growth to bloom. Then they, too, set seed and die.

Often the annual and biennial wildflowers can be used to fill in bare spots until perennial wildflowers mature. As well as being interesting and useful, they are an inexpensive way to naturalize a large open area.

With a little special attention and care, most of the annual or biennial wildflowers listed in this book can be grown easily from seeds. Seeds scattered after the plant has bloomed will usually germinate at the proper time. An open area where grasses are sparse is an ideal spot, as most of these wildflowers need sun to complete their short life-spans.

Divisions and Root Cuttings

Dividing large clumps of plants is one of the easiest methods of propagating wildflowers, although it is not always advisable (for example, it is not wise to divide plants that have been recently shipped through the mails). A better method is to grow the plants for at least a year before making the divisions. The best propagating times are early spring, late summer, or fall, depending on the species.

To make a division, carefully break up the clump either by pulling it apart or by cutting it. Each rooted portion may be planted separately, and in one to three years you will have several adult plants.

The division of forking rhizomes is another method that often gives good results. Solomon's plume and bluebeard lily are examples of plants that propagate successfully with rhizome division.

Many plants with very fleshy roots will grow new roots and buds when cut into pieces. Among these are butterfly flower, spikenard, and ginseng. Each root portion is planted separately and is regularly watered to encourage it to form a new plant. When planting pieces of root, remember that the side facing up will grow shoots and the side facing the soil below will grow roots. To prevent accidentally planting the root upside down, cut the top of the piece straight across and cut the bottom at an angle. Special instructions for propagation are discussed under the species name.

Most lily bulbs can be reproduced from scales as well as from seeds and bulbils.

The liatris family, among others, propagates well by the division of corms. All liatris tubers may be cut into pieces as one would cut potatoes, leaving one to two eyes or buds on each piece. Let the pieces dry a little before replanting. Spring is the best time to plant by corm division.

Seeds and Seedlings

Growing perennial wildflowers from seed can be a great challenge, but it is definitely not for the person who expects quick returns. Many wildflower seeds are slow to germinate, and once sprouted, are slow to mature.

Most wildflower seeds are best planted in the fall so nature can do the job of stratification. The hard-shelled seeds, such as baneberry and blue cohosh, require two or more years to germinate. You can file a nick into large seeds to hasten germination, but this is a tiresome task. I have had bearberry and horse gentian remain dormant for four years; germination was then very uneven. Do not be too quick to discard a flat because the seeds failed to germinate in the expected time. Trilliums, for instance, can be very slow at times.

The seeds of trillium and bloodroot must be planted as harvested or they will not germinate the next spring. If the bit of white matter (caruncle) that is attached to a fresh trillium or bloodroot seed is left to dry out, the seed usually takes two years to germinate. The caruncle helps the freshly planted seed to absorb moisture and therefore plays an important part in germination.

For potting soil, one third should be composed of damp peatmoss and sharp sand (or vermiculite), and two parts each of rich compost and woods soil (or garden soil). Thoroughly mix these ingredients before putting them into flats or pots. Make certain that all containers have good drainage. Some seeds may also be sown in a protected woodland area; those for sunny areas may be sown in the garden.

Mix dust-fine seeds with a teaspoonful of fine sand and scatter them on top of the soil without covering. If seed-flat soil is a little uneven, the seeds will settle. It is best to water these fine seeds from the bottom. After planting, the fine seeds should be dusted lightly with a bit of sharp sand.

The medium-sized seeds should be covered with one-quarter inch of sharp sand. The sharp sand prevents damping off as seedlings emerge.

A general rule for seed flats and seed beds: All plants that grow naturally in damp soil will need more moisture than those that require only constant moisture when growing in a permanent location. Therefore, the containers with seeds for damp areas should be watered a little more often. But under no condition should any of the seed flats or seed beds be allowed to dry out, even for only an hour. Seeds in the germination stage are very tender and quickly killed.

When seedlings have developed their second or third set of true leaves, they may be successfully moved to small pots or flats if handled with care. Early August is a good time to transplant seedlings, when they still have time to make considerable growth while the weather is favorable. Unless seedlings have made exceptionally good growth, it is best to winter them in a cold frame. Protect them from mice. After the plants have filled their pots with roots, they are usually ready to be moved to their permanent location.

Water all transplants regularly and mulch very lightly. A little Rapid-Gro in a weak solution helps to prevent transplant shock in both the seedling stage and the well-developed stage when the plants are moved to their permanent sites.

Most seedlings that have fibrous roots usually bloom the first year after transplanting. The seedlings with fleshy roots often do not bloom until the third or fourth year, and some require many years to bloom. Dog-tooth violets take about the longest.

Stem Cuttings

In most of the colder northeastern areas, the period from late June to late July is the most suitable time to make stem cuttings from propagating wild-flowers. This is usually before the plants have set any buds.

The soil mixture used for stem cuttings is made up of one part of sharp sand or (preferably) vermiculite, one part of fine compost, one part of damp peatmoss, and two parts of good garden soil or fine woods soil. Add a half cup of bonemeal for every ten quarts of the mixture. Mix all thoroughly and moisten a little if necessary. Use a 2¼-inch plastic pot for each cutting.

For propagation, select a mature healthy plant with good qualities, remembering that the plants grown from stem cuttings will inherit all the characteristics of the parent plant.

Each stem cutting should have four joints, two above the soil and two below.

Clip the leaves carefully from the two lower joints. Avoid destroying the axillary buds hidden in the axils of the leaves. These buds are responsible for sending new growth above the soil when the cutting shows signs of life.

Nip out the terminal leaf bud to prevent continued upward growth and to promote root growth and new growth from axillary buds.

Dip the lower two joints from which the leaves have been removed into the rooting compound and insert the cutting in a little hole made in the rooting mixture in the pot. Fill the hole with sharp sand.

Firm the soil and continue to treat all the cuttings in the same manner.

Set the pots containing the treated cuttings in a pan of water until moisture shows on the surface of the pot soil.

Remove the pots to flats for easier handling, and then put the flats in a propagation frame or in a cold frame with windows.

Cover the frame closely and keep the inside moist by spraying occasionally with a fine sprayer. Humidity must be maintained within the frame at all times.

A spot with filtered sunlight is ideal for a frame for propagating purposes.

Most cuttings will root in about four weeks. Bottom heat hastens rooting. When roots begin to come out of the bottom of the pot, the flat can be removed from the frame and placed in a sheltered, partially sunny area to harden. Gradually bring the flat into stronger sunlight until the new plants can tolerate full sun. Water carefully at all times.

The hardening process usually requires two weeks or gradually moving the rooted cuttings to stronger light every few days. When cuttings are fully hardened, they may be planted in their permanent location and treated as you would young seedlings.

Immediately after transplanting, give the new little plants a weak liquid fertilizer. I prefer Rapid-Gro. It will not burn foliage or roots if used according to directions. Later in the fall, when the ground is slightly frozen, it is wise to mulch the young plants for winter protection.

Most cuttings are better left in the pots in the cold frame if they have not made good growth at the end of four weeks. Remove the windows, but mulch lightly. Gradually remove the mulch in spring. Some hardening in the frame without the windows is advisable.

In spring, the young plants are ready to transfer to the open ground. Water faithfully to establish them, and mulch those that require it. Diligent care will bring excellent results.

SHADE TERMS

The special names given to the degrees of light and shade required by plants are known as "shade terms." They are used throughout this book according to the following definitions.

Full Sun. Totally unshaded. At no time during the day should the plant be in shadow, although shade after 4 p.m. is permissible.

Sun. At least eight hours of sunshine a day, preferably beginning early in the morning; do not count the time after 4 p.m.

Filtered Sunlight or Light Shade. A dappled light, such as spring-blossoming woodland plants receive through the young leaves of deciduous trees.

Open Shade. The plants may be shaded by buildings or nearby trees, but there should be no canopy of trees or extended eaves overhead.

Moderate to Partial Shade. As the sun moves, the plant receives both shade and light during the day, with brief exposure to direct sun.

High Open Shade. Trees with high branches let some light through, and some light comes from the slanting rays of the morning and late afternoon sun.

Deep Shade. Where evergreen trees grow or where deciduous trees stand close together, the shade is denser. Here temperatures will be several degrees lower and the moisture content of the air higher. Winds do not sweep through so readily.

Annual and Biennial Wildflowers
for Quick Color and Cover

CHENOPODIACEAE [Goosefoot Family]

Chenopodium capitatum • strawberry blite

ANNUAL

HEIGHT: 6 to 12 inches

Strawberry blite is suitable for either a moist sunny area or slight shade where the soil is humus-rich. The flowers are greenish and not pretty, but the plant is grown for its showy clusters of pulpy red fruits that are suggestive of lush ripe strawberries.

The seeds within the cluster are shiny black. Sow them in the fall. The strawberry blite self-sows.

PERIOD OF BLOOM: June–August.

PAPAVERACEAE [Poppy Family]

Eschscholtzia californica • California poppy

ANNUAL

HEIGHT: 6 to 10 inches

The California poppy has light blue-green, finely cut foliage and an abundance of four-petaled yellow or orange flowers. It blooms best on sunny days; the flowers close at night.

The seeds are offered in most garden seed catalogs; they are best sown in spring in full sun. California poppy is easy to grow. Seeds self-sow in the West.

PERIOD OF BLOOM: All summer.

27

Argemone intermedia • prickly poppy

ANNUAL

HEIGHT: 2 feet

The stocky stem has prickly alternate foliage shaped much like that of a slender oak leaf. The blossoms are single 3-inch flowers in shades of yellow or white. The plant will grow in any soil in full sun. Sow seeds in fall or early spring. The prickly poppy rarely self-sows in my area.

In the West, where this poppy is native, it is considered poisonous to cattle, and ranchers battle to destroy it.

PERIOD OF BLOOM: All summer.

Corydalis sempervirens • pale corydalis

BIENNIAL

HEIGHT: 12 to 24 inches

The shiny black seeds of pale corydalis are planted in August and grow to dainty rosettes of blue-green fernlike foliage during the first season. The following season, in May, a single, many-branched stalk appears, bearing countless half-hearts of clear pink with a touch of bright yellow. The plant is quite ornamental in the fruiting stage, when each blossom is replaced by a long slender seed capsule.

When cultivated and given room, pale corydalis will attain the size of a bushel basket. In the wilderness the plants are straggly and not nearly so large.

Pale corydalis is often found growing in full sun among boulders and in the crevices of rocks.

PERIOD OF BLOOM: May into September.

Adlumia fungosa • Allegheny vine

BIENNIAL

LENGTH: 6 to 12 foot vine

The Allegheny vine has airy, bleeding-heart foliage and many pinkish hearts over a long season. It is native to the Allegheny Mountains but will grow in any spot where there is high open shade.

The plant readily self-sows, but I prefer to plant seeds each year as they ripen to ensure spring germination.

PERIOD OF BLOOM: June until frost.

GERANIACEAE [Geranium Family]

Geranium Robertianum • herb-Robert

ANNUAL

HEIGHT: 3 to 5 inches

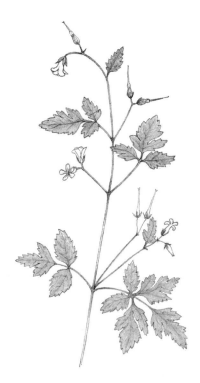

Herb-Robert has delicate, fernlike green foliage, often with a hint of red later in the season. The dainty trumpet-shaped, rose-colored flowers persist all summer in shade in reasonably moist woodland. It is best grown where it can naturalize.

Herb-Robert sets seeds and disperses them in the same way as its larger cousin, the cranesbill: the pods open with a surprising abruptness and the seeds scatter far and wide, making them difficult to collect. Sow seeds as they ripen or in early fall.

PERIOD OF BLOOM: All summer.

BALSAMINACEAE [Touch-me-not Family]

Impatiens capensis • jewelweed

ANNUAL

HEIGHT: 2 to 4 feet

The orange-spotted flowers of the jewelweed are as worthy of praise as an orchid. The many branches and large succulent stems are characteristic of the species. The entire plant is fragile and should be cultivated in close groupings or in protected areas. When a single plant can be grown to display its full development, the jewelweed is at its loveliest.

Jewelweed is found growing in moist, partially shaded areas, but in my gardens it volunteers almost anywhere. The roots are shallow and the plant is easily uprooted. A seed capsule will explode at the touch of a finger and send the seeds flying, hence the popular name touch-me-not. Sow seeds when ripe.

The juice of the jewelweed is often recommended as a treatment for poison ivy, but I have not found it effective.

PERIOD OF BLOOM: July until frost.

UMBELLIFERAE [Parsley Family]

Heracleum maximum • cow parsnip

BIENNIAL

HEIGHT: 3 to 6 feet

Seeds planted in fall send up several large leaves during the first spring. The leaves resemble those of the maple and are about the size of an outstretched hand.

30

The second spring, a stout but hollow leafy stalk appears, bearing two or three large flat-topped umbels, similar to but larger than those of the cultivated parsnip.

The plant, which has a strong odor of parsnip, is found in moist, shady thickets along creek bottoms. It is a fine plant for the bog garden but will grow equally well anywhere there is constant moisture.

PERIOD OF BLOOM: July.

Daucus Carota • Queen Anne's lace

BIENNIAL

HEIGHT: 1 to 3 feet

The leafy stem with its lacy foliage resembles that of its edible cousin, the garden carrot. The seeds are also similar to those of the carrot, but the Queen Anne's lace seeds have barbs which aid in spreading. When the lacy white flowers fade, the outer parts of the umbel curl inward to take on a shape like a bird's nest, and it is often referred to as the bird's-nest flower.

In some areas, Queen Anne's lace is found growing abundantly along fencerows and roadsides. Sow the seeds in fall. It self-sows readily.

The flower stalks are charming in dry floral arrangements. Pick them before the seeds fully ripen.

PERIOD OF BLOOM: June into August.

COMPOSITAE [Composite Family]

Anaphalis margaritacea • pearly everlasting

ANNUAL

HEIGHT: 8 to 12 inches

The willowlike leaves of pearly everlasting are sage green with a white blush. The crushed foliage has a lemon-lime fragrance, which can be used in sachets. The flowers are terminal clusters, and each flower head is round with a yellow eye encircled in pearly white. It is found in wastelands and along roadsides.

Pearly everlasting is an excellent flower for dry floral arrangements. Pick the flowers just as the yellow eye begins to appear. Hang it upside down in a dry place to cure.

The seeds must be sown in fall; in wastelands it self-sows.

PERIOD OF BLOOM: August to September.

Rudbeckia hirta • black-eyed Susan

BIENNIAL

HEIGHT: 1 to 2 feet

The foliage of the black-eyed Susan is mostly basal and hairy. The flowers have deep yellow petals and a prominent raised center of dark glossy brown.

The plant is often abundant in wastelands, old hayfields, and along roadsides where grasses are sparse.

If the blossoms are cut immediately after blooming, the plant often acts as a perennial and persists for several years. When cultivated, the black-eyed Susan is much prettier than when growing in the wild. Large expanses make a colorful display, and they are excellent for naturalizing in large areas.

Sow seeds as soon as they ripen. The plant self-sows freely.

PERIOD OF BLOOM: June to September.

Tragopogon pratensis · yellow goatsbeard

BIENNIAL

HEIGHT: 1 to 2 feet

The yellow goatsbeard, found along roadsides and in wastelands, has slender ribbonlike foliage and a partially leafy stem. Pale yellow-rayed flowers crown the stiff stalk.

The ripening seed forms a globe larger than that of the dandelion. The globes are excellent for dry floral arrangements and are much sought for this purpose. Pick the flower just as it is about to open, and place each stalk in a wire holder, spacing them well apart. When a full globe emerges, spray it with clear hair spray or spray paint (gold is usually chosen). Hold the spray can about 18 to 24 inches away from the globes so that the pressure will not destroy their fragile structure. Dust them immediately with glitter to add a touch of sparkle and color. The globes make interesting displays in bowls of harmonizing colors.

Sow the seeds as soon as they ripen.

In some areas this plant is on the noxious weed list.

PERIOD OF BLOOM: June to September.

CUCURBITACEAE [Gourd Family]

Echinocystis lobata · wild cucumber

ANNUAL

LENGTH: 6 to 12 foot vine

The leaves of the wild cucumber are shaped much like that of the ivy house plants, but they are thinner and lighter green. The vine anchors itself with tendrils as it climbs over fences and through thickets, where it is usually found.

The four-seeded burr resembles a tiny cucumber with spines. The seeds must be planted in fall or they will not germinate the following spring. The plant self-sows readily.

PERIOD OF BLOOM: All summer.

MALVACEAE [Mallow Family]

Abutilon Theophrasti • Indian mallow

ANNUAL

HEIGHT: 3 to 5 feet

A robust plant with large, heart-shaped leaves and single yellow flowers, the Indian mallow is usually found in legume crops, wastelands, and along fencerows.

Sow seeds in fall, preferably in fertile soil. The plant does not self-sow readily.

Because of its cup-shaped seed pod with a disklike pattern, Indian mallow is also called butter print.

PERIOD OF BLOOM: July to September.

GENTIANACEAE [Gentian Family]

Gentiana crinita • fringed gentian

BIENNIAL

HEIGHT: 1 to 3 feet

Fringed gentian is the most coveted and elusive biennial wildflower, and it has proved a trial to many who have tried to grow it from seed. Potted stock is easiest to transplant.

This wildflower needs no further identification than its distinctive fringed blossoms. It grows along still lakes where the damp shores are partly taken over by grasses. It also grows in wet roadside ditches, and I have even found it growing in a little patch of dwarf moss on the north side of a hill where scrub oak grew. As a rule it is quite scarce.

The small tan seeds are very light and are easily blown by the wind. Fresh seeds should be sown immediately, in peatpots or flats or directly where you are able to naturalize the plant. Place the seeds on top of the soil and cover them with evergreen branches. Remove the branches in spring as seedlings appear. Grow the seedlings in partial shade, never letting the soil become dry. The plants grow very little during the first year. The following spring, transplant potted stock in a damp meadow or any other suitable place. With care and regular watering the seedlings will grow to maturity, bloom, set seed, and die, completing their life cycle in the second year.

You will need to set out seedlings for two consecutive years if you want to establish a colony. If the plants are growing in an ideal location, they will self-propagate.

Make every effort to preserve this wildflower in its natural state, and try to establish new colonies where conditions are suitable.

PERIOD OF BLOOM: August to October.

Never pick this rare wildflower.

SCROPHULARIACEAE [Figwort Family]

Verbascum Thapsus • common mullein

BIENNIAL

HEIGHT: 3 to 6 feet

Mullein, also called "velvet plant," is often found growing in dry sunny wastelands. It forms a rosette of gray woolly leaves in the first year. In the second, it sends up a heavy spike with a raceme of small yellow flowers.

For dry floral arrangements, cut the spikes right after they bloom. The seeds are very fine and should be sown in fall.

PERIOD OF BLOOM: June into August.

Gerardia virginica • smooth false foxglove

BIENNIAL

HEIGHT: 2 to 4 feet

The leafy stem of the smooth false foxglove appears in the second year. At the top of the stem, the leaves are gradually replaced by yellow or occasionally white flowers growing like flared tubes in the axils of the smaller upper leaves. The plant is found in dry woodlands and thickets, but will grow in gardens in full sunlight.

Sow seeds in June or late fall. When the smooth false foxglove is in close proximity with other plants in protected areas of open shade, especially where leaves fall to provide additional protection, it often forms clumps and lasts for years.

PERIOD OF BLOOM: July into August.

Castilleja coccinea • Indian paintbrush

BIENNIAL

HEIGHT: 12 to 18 inches

The true flowers are yellow, but the red bracts give the Indian paintbrush its color. Flowers grow on the upper third of the stem. The plants tend to be parasitic and grow best in a soil containing some decaying humus.

Whole colonies often disappear for several years, only to reappear for long stretches again. I have known it to grow year after year on an old logging trail where shade is high and open.

The plant will grow in wet ditches among sparse grasses where the soil is lean but where decaying humus is present on the surface. The plant is not easy to establish. If you wish to naturalize it, select a spot where grass is sparse; or you can choose an open spot and scatter some oat seed, then cut the oats back, leaving about a six-inch stubble to shelter the seedlings. Scatter the fine seed as soon as it ripens and do not disturb the soil. Once established, the plant will reappear from time to time. Try growing this wildflower in a damp woodland trail in high open shade where the soil is damp most of the year.

PERIOD OF BLOOM: May into July.

Never pick this rare wildflower.

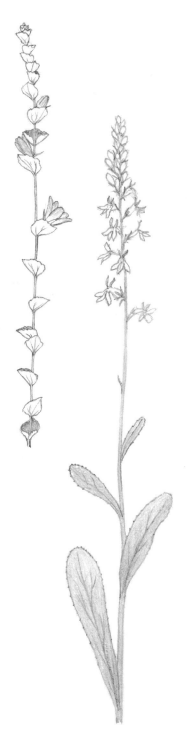

CAMPANULACEAE [Bluebell Family]

Specularia perfoliata • Venus's looking-glass

ANNUAL

HEIGHT: 10 to 20 inches

Each tiny rosette of Venus's looking-glass sends up a single spike bearing dainty starlike flowers of intense purple in the axils of the clasping leaves.

The seeds must be sown in fall for spring germination. Cultivated plants are huskier than wildlings, and small seedlings transplant easily. The plant also readily self-sows.

PERIOD OF BLOOM: June into August.

Lobelia spicata • spiked lobelia

BIENNIAL

HEIGHT: 2 feet

A single stem rises from a small rosette of basal foliage, bearing a slender spike of pale blue-lipped flowers. When growing in masses it is unusually pretty.

Spiked lobelia can be found along roadsides and in wastelands. It often volunteers in land that has not been cultivated for a few years.

Sow the seeds as soon as they are ripe. Where the soil is open, the spiked lobelia self-sows readily.

PERIOD OF BLOOM: June.

Perennial Wildflowers
for Permanence

TYPHACEAE [Cattail Family]

Typha latifolia • common cattail

DESCRIPTION: 4 to 6 feet tall. The common cattail has 6 to 8 inch yellow or brown flower spikes, each supported by a solitary heavy stem. Ribbonlike leaves, as long as the stem, extend from the base. As the upper male portion of the flower withers, the lower female portion grows fatter, becoming the cylindrical spike we know as the cattail.

Cattails are found in wet open swamplands, along low lake shores, and often in roadside ditches where water collects in early spring.

PERIOD OF BLOOM: June into July.

SOIL: Neutral to acid soils that are always moist, or at least quite damp.

LOCATION AND EXPOSURE: Cattails are not suited to every wild-flower garden because they demand constant moisture and because of their vigorous growth. Do not underestimate their power to reproduce; where conditions are favorable, they can take over large areas. However, they are ideal for naturalizing along a stream or lake shore or for planting singly in a container in a small pond.

PLANTING TIME: Spring or fall.

ROOT SYSTEM: A stout creeping rhizome with feeder roots that have a strong tendency to multiply in wet areas, especially once the plant has become established in sunny marshes. The rhizomes are edible. The Indians cooked the fleshy portions, which are rich in starch.

PLANTING DEPTH AND SPACING: Space about 1 to 2 feet apart. Set plants at the same level at which they previously grew, making certain to tuck in all the rhizomes and any stray roots.

PLANTING STOCK AND PROPAGATION: Few, if any, nurseries grow cattails for sale. Take your own quality collected stock by di-

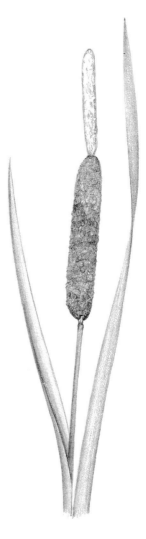

viding the creeping rhizomes, preferably in spring in the colder climates.

COMMENTS: The leaves of cattails laid lengthwise among tall wildflowers furnish a long-lasting mulch.

For dried floral arrangements, the cattail spikes should be picked when only half grown or else the cylinders will break open into a mass of fuzz. When completely ripe, the cylinders may be loosened and used to stuff pillows. Be certain to use a fine quality of ticking.

ARACEAE [Arum Family]

Arisaema triphyllum • Jack-in-the-pulpit

DESCRIPTION: 15 to 30 inches tall. Brown-and-green hooded flowers rest above thrice-parted leaves. In August the plant produces bright red berries. Jack-in-the-pulpit is found in rich moist woods, wet swamps, or drier areas in high open shade where soil is rich in humus though of only moderate moisture content.

PERIOD OF BLOOM: Late May into June.

SOIL: Any humus-rich soil of moderate acidity, preferably a little moist, especially in spring.

LOCATION AND EXPOSURE: Deep to light shade. "Jacks" can be planted in small colonies among other woodland flowers, or they can be used effectively as bold accents when placed as lone "sentinels" in a well-chosen rocky spot. They are also outstanding when interspersed with maidenhair fern.

PLANTING TIME: Preferably fall, but it is also possible to plant in early spring when the plants are still dormant or have only slightly sprouted.

ROOT SYSTEM: A corm, increasing in size with age, has feeder roots on its upper side just below the new shoot. These roots seek nutrients from the soil and humus. The feeder roots are not present on dormant stock held in storage, but new roots develop in spring. Cormlets often appear at the upper and outer edges of larger corms.

PLANTING DEPTH AND SPACING: Planting depth is best determined by the size of the corms. Small corms up to the size of a nickel should be planted 2 to 4 inches deep, larger corms 5 to 8 inches deep. Depth also depends on whether or not the soil is heavy or humus-rich.

If you live in a colder region and have trouble with your "Jacks" coming up too soon and being cut down by frost, add some extra mulch as soon as the ground freezes in late fall. This will help to hold the frost in the ground and retard spring growth. Remove the extra mulch a few weeks later than usual.

PLANTING STOCK AND PROPAGATION: Plant nursery-grown corms or quality collected stock.

Pulp-free seeds may be planted in flats or in the woodland as soon as they ripen. Sometimes seeds do not germinate until the second spring. Seedlings usually do not bloom until the third year. Chipmunks are very fond of the seeds and cormlets and will often plant and replant them.

COMMENTS: The Jack-in-the-pulpit is a stately flower which has many uses in the woodland garden. Years ago the Indians cooked the corms for food, hence the common name Indian turnip. Uncooked, the corm is supposedly poisonous, at least for humans. I doubt that it is harmful to other animals, especially bears: One fall a mother bear and her cub uprooted our "Jack" bed, leaving behind a mess of half-eaten stalks and corms.

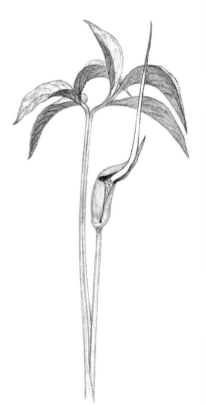

Arisaema Dracontium • green dragon

DESCRIPTION: 1 to 3 feet tall. A long, slender, green spadix extends from a greenish half-opened spathe above the fan-shaped compound leaves. The white flower is tinged or streaked with green. Orange fruits appear in early fall.

The green dragon is usually found in wet, rich woods and along woodland brooks, often interspersed with its cousin, the Jack-in-the-pulpit.

PERIOD OF BLOOM: May into June.

SOIL: Humus-rich, acid to slightly acid woodland soil.

LOCATION AND EXPOSURE: Green dragon grows best in cool open shade where constant moisture is available. It provides a bold accent in the moist wild garden. In damp shady areas I have seen it reach a height of 4 feet.

PLANTING TIME: Spring or fall, while dormant or only slightly sprouted.

ROOT SYSTEM: The corm has a prominent new shoot from which many white feeder roots penetrate the soil. This corm is very similar to that of Jack-in-the-pulpit. Sometimes the parent corm produces cormlets.

PLANTING DEPTH AND SPACING: Set small corms 2 to 4 inches deep, and larger corms 5 to 7 inches deep. Plant in small colonies or at random for best effect.

PLANTING STOCK AND PROPAGATION: Use nursery-grown stock. Quality collected stock is very scarce.

The offsets of large corms give quicker results than propagating by seed. Seeds sown when they ripen in fall take several years to become big blooming-sized corms.

COMMENTS: Green dragon is a novelty in the wild garden when planted beside a rock, along a path, or in a shady spot beside a pool where it can reflect in the water.

Calla palustris • wild calla

DESCRIPTION: 5 to 10 inches tall. Wild calla has fleshy, jointed prostrate stalks and medium heart-shaped leaves on upright stems. The flower is white with a hint of green, on a round spadix. It is held on 4 to 5 inch stems above the forking and creeping root-stock. The clusters of fruit are shaped much like pineapples, but are only about 1½ inches long.

Wild calla is usually found in lake indentations, bogs, and swales, in cool open shade where the water is still and shallow and apparently stagnant. Much of its rootstock shows.

One August I found a large colony of wild calla growing in a wet peat bog, with water several inches deep in places. The plants crept along amid fallen branches and wood litter; it was apparently an ideal location. Some plants had already set fruit that was turning reddish, while other plants were just coming into bloom.

PERIOD OF BLOOM: June into late fall.

SOIL: Slightly acid soil with constant moisture or where water is still and shallow. Wild calla cannot survive a dry spell.

LOCATION AND EXPOSURE: An excellent plant for naturalizing at the edge of a still body of shallow water in a cool shady spot. For years I grew a few plants in an old five-gallon container that was buried in the ground to the top edge. I punctured several holes in the container to allow for slow seepage. The container was filled within two inches from the top with mucky soil from a nearby lake where swamp and water met. A generous handful of bonemeal should be mixed into the top few inches of earth. It grew in this container for many years, until one extremely cold, snowless December the plant winter-killed because of lack of cover. A light mulch might have saved it.

PLANTING TIME: Early spring or fall. Moves easily.

ROOT SYSTEM: A jointed, creeping rootstock with some feeder roots at nodes on the underside. The plant moves about as it grows, the old portion dying as new joints are formed to produce next year's growth and bloom. The cycle is continually repeated, and as the stalks fork the colony becomes denser and larger.

PLANTING DEPTH AND SPACING: Plant close together if you wish rootstocks to overlap. The roots that grow along the bottom of the rootstock should be anchored into the earth, but leave the creeping rootstock at soil level or barely covered. A winter mulch is suggested for very cold climates.

PLANTING STOCK AND PROPAGATION: Nursery-grown potted stock is much preferred, but you can use quality collected stock.

Cuttings taken in July and set into peat-muck rooting medium give fair results. Fill a container with a few inches of water, and place the peat pots in it. Then moisture will be constantly available.

Pulp-free seeds may be planted in muck or very wet swampy soil as soon as they are ripe. Seedlings will bloom in a few years.

COMMENTS: If you can meet the needs of the wild calla, by all means grow it. In general the plant is rather scarce, but I have been fortunate in finding some large colonies.

Symplocarpus foetidus • skunk cabbage

DESCRIPTION: 1 to 3 feet tall. Very early in spring, the greenish yellow spadix of the skunk cabbage appears, enclosed by a reddish brown spathe that is open at one side and looks very much like a dwarf's hut with the door ajar. As the flower in the spadix wilts, the green leaves unfold.

45

Skunk cabbage is usually found in swales and amid hummocks in grassy swamplands. At the Keshena Indian Reservation (now Menominee County) I have seen large colonies of skunk cabbage growing in full sun in grassy lowlands and along small brooks.

PERIOD OF BLOOM: April into May, often before the snow has completely thawed.

SOIL: Damp, humus-rich soil, neutral to slightly acid.

LOCATION AND EXPOSURE: Preferably a shady spot, unless the soil is very moist. Plant the skunk cabbage where you want it to stay, since a full-grown plant will have a bushel of soil adhering to its roots, and is next to impossible to move.

PLANTING TIME: Fall planting is best.

ROOT SYSTEM: A stout rhizome with long, stringy, white roots.

PLANTING DEPTH AND SPACING: Space plants several feet apart to allow for development. Set young dormant plants with the shoot just at soil level. Mulch heavily with forest litter or old marsh hay.

PLANTING STOCK AND PROPAGATION: Nursery-grown seedlings are best. Quality collected young stock with good roots will also do well.

To propagate from seed, sow the seeds when ripe in a peaty soil that is kept constantly moist. Seedlings require considerable time to mature.

COMMENTS: The bruised leaves have a foul odor which gives the skunk cabbage its name. The plant has no odor otherwise. Do not hesitate to grow skunk cabbage near the house if you have a suitable location. Its large quilted green leaves are handsome.

LILIACEAE [Lily Family]

Uvularia grandiflora · merrybells

DESCRIPTION: 10 to 15 inches tall. Merrybells have clear, lemon-yellow flowers and three-cornered green seed capsules. From forked stalks and leafy stems, sparse clusters of long, loosely bell-shaped flowers hang on arching stems.

In woodlands, on shaded slopes, large colonies of merrybells bloom each spring beneath the high branches of white birches and oaks. Here leafmold is deep and there is very little competition from other large wildflowers. Fringed polygalas and, when there has been a wet August, ghostly Indian pipes (*Monotropa uniflora*) are often found as companion plants.

PERIOD OF BLOOM: May into June, depending on location.

SOIL: Any humus-rich woodland soil that is slightly acid.

LOCATION AND EXPOSURE: Light, open shade where leafless trees allow the sun to filter through in spring but shut out its burning rays in the summer. Merrybell's bountiful foliage matures after bloom and makes a good groundcover for the bare spots left by mertensias, which bloom at the same time. The two combine well.

PLANTING TIME: While dormant in spring or fall.

ROOT SYSTEM: A pure white rhizome with stringy white roots, very similar to that of pink lady's-slipper but not as coarse.

PLANTING DEPTH AND SPACING: Space plants 1 to 2 feet apart. Give ample room, as each plant becomes a clump. Plant the short rhizomes about 1½ inches deep with the tip of the new shoot slightly below soil level. Spread roots carefully.

PLANTING STOCK AND PROPAGATION: Nursery-grown stock is huskier, but freshly dug collected stock may also be used.

Clumps may be divided for propagation by pulling them apart very carefully and planting each separately. To propagate from seeds, sow as soon as they are ripe. The plant often self-sows. Seedlings mature enough to bloom about the third or fourth year.

COMMENTS: Merrybells benefit greatly from transplanting. The plants will form clumps a few seasons after being moved, whereas plants growing in the wild stay much the same. A generous mulching of old straw, weathered marsh hay, or old leaves is helpful.

Another common name for the merrybell is bellwort.

Uvularia sessilifolia • wild oats

DESCRIPTION: 6 to 10 inches tall. Dainty 1 inch yellow bells are held jauntily above light-green, oval, tapering foliage. Later they are replaced by three-cornered green seed capsules.

47

This small type of merrybell is at home in moist woodlands where the soil is rich in humus. It has a habit of colonizing in groups to carpet the forest floor.

PERIOD OF BLOOM: May into June. The little flowers are long lasting.

SOIL: Neutral to slightly acid soil that is rich in leafmold and retains some moisture.

LOCATION AND EXPOSURE: High open shade where some sun can filter through to the forest floor. Because this merrybell is both dainty and small, it should be planted in colonies to give the best color effect. Wild oats are lovely when planted in patches alternating with small airy ferns.

PLANTING TIME: While dormant in spring or fall.

ROOT SYSTEM: A small white rhizome with stringy white roots.

PLANTING DEPTH AND SPACING: Space 4 to 6 inches apart, or plant at random in colonies of a dozen or more. Set the rhizome about 1 inch deep with the tip of the new shoot just barely below soil level. Mulch lightly.

PLANTING STOCK AND PROPAGATION: Use nursery-grown stock or freshly dug collected stock of good quality. When colonies become crowded, separate the rhizomes and replant at once.

Sow seeds as soon as they ripen; they are sometimes slow to germinate. Seedlings are slow to bloom.

COMMENTS: The wild oat is a dainty wildflower for a choice spot in your woodland garden. Its little bells are precisely shaped and droop gracefully above the neat foliage.

Allium cernuum • nodding wild onion

DESCRIPTION: 18 to 20 inches tall. A nodding umbel of loose florets and flat ribbonlike foliage. The florets are pale rose-lavender with a faint pinkish cast.

The wild onion is usually found in shaded woodland and rocky areas where the soil is humus-rich; it is also found in prairies.

PERIOD OF BLOOM: July into August.

SOIL: Neutral to slightly acid soil. (I use a sandy loam.)

LOCATION AND EXPOSURE: Although its native habitats are shady woodlands, the wild onion blooms more profusely in full sun.

Plant it in colonies or scatter bulbs among other wildflowers. It is very easy to grow.

PLANTING TIME: While dormant in early spring or fall.

ROOT SYSTEM: A white bulb with white basal roots, looking very much like the edible green garden onions.

PLANTING DEPTH AND SPACING: Set the bulbs 1 inch deep and space 3 to 5 inches apart. Or plant at random in a rock garden.

PLANTING STOCK AND PROPAGATION: Use nursery-grown stock or quality collected stock.

Divide clumps in very early spring. To propagate by seed, sow them in shallow soil in fall or very early spring. The plant rarely self-sows.

COMMENTS: I grew the nodding wild onion for several years before it established itself sufficiently for me to enjoy its beauty.

Lilium philadelphicum • wood lily

DESCRIPTION: 1 to 3 feet tall. Upright stems with willowlike foliage grow in whorls at intervals along the entire stem. Vase-shaped flowers grow one or two to a stalk, rarely three. They are reddish orange, with brown-purple dots from the center of the blossom to the throat.

The wood lily inhabits dry prairielike areas and open cut-over woodlands. Sometimes it is found growing in colonies, transforming a common grassland into a glistening sea of orange.

PERIOD OF BLOOM: June into July.

SOIL: Acid to moderately acid sandy loam. Good drainage is important.

LOCATION AND EXPOSURE: Full sun or very light open shade where the flower can benefit from the morning sun. Intersperse the wood lily with other prairie wildflowers. It does best where there is a groundcover of grasses and is, therefore, a fine plant for naturalizing in a meadow.

PLANTING TIME: While dormant in very early spring or fall. It resists transplanting.

ROOT SYSTEM: A scaly white bulb with lower fibrous feeder roots.

PLANTING DEPTH AND SPACING: Set bulbs 4 to 5 inches deep and space 8 to 12 inches apart; or plant them at random for a more natural effect.

PLANTING STOCK AND PROPAGATION: Nursery-grown stock is best. Quality collected stock may be dug up in fall—place a marker in summer because the plants go dormant in August.

This lily can be successfully increased by removing scales from the parent plant and planting them in flats or in large, squat pots. Use a humus-rich soil. Winter over in the cold frame. The following summer tiny new shoots will emerge and new bulblets will form. As soon as the bulblets are the size of small acorns, plant them in a permanent location to mature. You can expect excellent results.

Sow seeds as soon as they ripen. Seeds sown in flats produce only a single leaf the first year. Seedlings bloom in four to five years.

COMMENTS: The wood lily is on the protected list and is quite scarce. Flowers last only one day in a bouquet, and the blossoms are better left alone to set seed.

Lilium canadense • Canada lily

DESCRIPTION: 3 to 5 feet tall. The Canada lily has graceful, partially nodding flowers with large, slightly curved petals. The flowers grow in groups on arching stems. They are yellow on the outside, orange-colored with dark spots on the inside. Smooth, lanceolate green leaves grow in whorls along the sturdy, upright stalk.

The Canada lily haunts wet meadows and lowlands.

PERIOD OF BLOOM: June into July.

SOIL: Fertile, moist, slightly acid soil is best.

LOCATION AND EXPOSURE: The Canada lily can be grown in full sun in wetlands and in moist shade in open woodland. In areas where the soil is unshaded, a generous mulching will protect the plant and keep its roots cool.

PLANTING TIME: Early fall is best, but spring is satisfactory if bulbs are still dormant.

ROOT SYSTEM: A white scaly bulb with basal white feeder roots.

PLANTING DEPTH AND SPACING: Set bulbs 5 to 8 inches deep, depending on size. Space 1 foot apart in scattered colonies in meadows.

PLANTING STOCK AND PROPAGATION: Use nursery-grown stock or quality collected stock.

For propagation, scales removed from the parent plant right after bloom give the quickest results. Grow the scales in a humus-rich soil to which a considerable amount of sharp sand has been added. Grow them in flats or in a protected area for two years before moving the medium-sized new bulbs to their permanent location.

Sow seeds as soon as they ripen. It takes as many as five years to produce a bulb large enough to bloom.

COMMENTS: The Canada lily is truly a showy plant. It is best suited for a partially shaded woodland area or a damp-to-wet open meadow.

Lilium michiganense • Michigan lily

DESCRIPTION: 2 to 3 feet tall. The flowers of the Michigan lily are deep orange with brown spots and distinctly curved petals. The foliage is alternate on sturdy stems.

This lily inhabits wet prairies and meadows as well as moist woodlands and the thickets at river bottoms.

PERIOD OF BLOOM: July into August.

SOIL: Fertile, slightly acid to neutral soil with constant moisture.

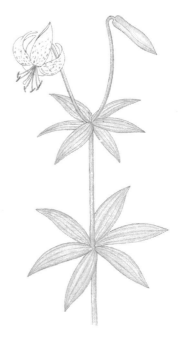

LOCATION AND EXPOSURE: Grow Michigan lilies in full sun or in high open shade in moist woodland. Planted in a wet meadow with other wildflowers, they will provide a lovely contrast.

PLANTING TIME: Early fall is best.

ROOT SYSTEM: A scaly, pale yellow bulb with horizontal rhizomes which produce new plants to form colonies.

PLANTING DEPTH AND SPACING: Set the bulbs 4 to 6 inches deep, depending on size. Space 1 foot or more apart. Often this flower does not bloom until the second year after it has been moved.

PLANTING STOCK AND PROPAGATION: Nursery-grown stock mature enough to bloom is best. Quality collected stock may also be used.

To propagate, divide the clumps that are formed by new rhizomes (if large enough, these often bloom in the second year), or sow seeds in fall as soon as they ripen. Seeds do not always germinate the following spring or summer. Several years may elapse before seedlings will bloom.

COMMENTS: In my garden I have a colony of Michigan lilies in a spot which was once used as a burning pile and then as a compost heap. Here they grow in high open shade on a slope, mulched with marsh hay. Some of the older plants have flowers in clusters of eight to ten blossoms. These lilies have grown so well that I now believe compost and wood ash are helpful in promoting luxuriant growth. Although the Michigan lily is usually no more than 3 feet tall, mine grow to 5 feet in moist, partly shaded spots.

Lilium superbum • Turk's-cap lily

DESCRIPTION: 3 to 6 feet tall. The several orange flowers with their deeply curved petals and the stately stems make this a distinctive lily. The upper foliage is alternating, and the lower foliage often grows in tiers.

The Turk's-cap graces wet meadows and marshy lowlands with its elegance. Sometimes it is found in damp roadside ditches, accompanied by the fringed gentian.

PERIOD OF BLOOM: July into August.

SOIL: Fertile, loose, somewhat acid soil with reasonably good drainage.

LOCATION AND EXPOSURE: The Turk's-cap is a good plant for high open shade in moist woodland or for a sunny meadow. For best results, plant this flower in colonies in the meadow in full sun, and shade the roots by using a good mulch or companion planting.

PLANTING TIME: Early fall is best.

ROOT SYSTEM: A scaly white bulb with basal feeder roots.

PLANTING DEPTH AND SPACING: Set the bulbs 4 to 6 inches deep, depending on size. Space 1 foot or more apart. For naturalizing, plant in colonies. As with other wild lilies, Turk's-cap may not always bloom in the first year after transplanting.

PLANTING STOCK AND PROPAGATION: Two-year-old, nursery-grown stock is best. But also use quality collected stock.

Scales removed from the parent bulbs will produce new bulbs the following year and will be ready to be moved to a permanent location. Large bulbs usually give good results, but I find the scale method quickest.

To propagate from seed, sow the seeds in flats or in the open as soon as they ripen. Be sure to keep the seed bed area moist all through the year. There should be good germination the following spring and early summer. Seedlings are usually large enough to move the third fall.

COMMENTS: The Turk's-cap is very similar to the Michigan lily and may be confused with it. Turk's-cap is smaller and darker.

Lilium tigrinum • tiger lily

DESCRIPTION: 2 to 4 feet tall. Clusters of orange-red flowers grow at the top of a single stem; the curved petals are covered with dark spots. Leaves alternate along the length of the stem, with black bulbils forming in the leaf axil.

The tiger lily is an Asian garden lily that took kindly to our fields and thickets. It is often found in very old gardens and around deserted homesteads. Rodents carry the seeds away and help to spread it.

PERIOD OF BLOOM: July into late August.

SOIL: Ordinary fertile garden soil or humus-rich woodland soil. It is not demanding.

LOCATION AND EXPOSURE: Full sun or light open shade. It is excellent in a border planted among blue flowers for deep contrast.

PLANTING TIME: Fall planting is best.

ROOT SYSTEM: A large white bulb with white basal roots.

PLANTING DEPTH AND SPACING: Set the bulbs 3 to 5 inches deep. Space 10 to 15 inches apart or plant in small colonies.

PLANTING STOCK AND PROPAGATION: Nursery-grown stock or bulbs collected from old gardens or fencerows should grow well.

To propagate, plant bulbils ½ inch deep as they fall from the parent plant. These bulbils will produce only one true leaf the following spring. Young plants can be moved at almost any time of the year.

The tiger lilies in my garden never set seed.

COMMENTS: Originally grown only in cultivation, this is an excellent lily for naturalizing along a rail fence.

Erythronium americanum • trout lily

DESCRIPTION: 5 to 8 inches tall. The flared, bell-shaped yellow flowers are flushed with brown on the outside. They droop over the slender, leafless stems. There is also a rare white species with

an orchid-lavender flush on the outside, but it is rarely found in the same woodland.

The trout lily grows in rich, deciduous woods, in thickets, and in areas where the soil is heavy.

PERIOD OF BLOOM: May.

SOIL: A slightly acid soil that is humus-rich or fertile to a good depth.

LOCATION AND EXPOSURE: Light open shade in the woodland where the sun filters through or in partial shade among other wildflowers. Since it goes dormant after bloom, plant the trout lily among other small wildflowers that retain their foliage. Blue phlox or hepaticas are excellent for interplanting.

PLANTING TIME: While dormant in late summer or fall.

ROOT SYSTEM: Small, light tan, teardrop-shaped bulbs with white basal roots.

PLANTING DEPTH AND SPACING: Set the bulbs 3 to 5 inches deep; they will work down to their correct level. Plant at random for a natural effect. Often years pass before transplanted bulbs will bloom again. Trout lilies planted where early spring sun is at its fullest will bloom sooner than those planted in shadier areas.

PLANTING STOCK AND PROPAGATION: Nursery-grown stock planted in peat pots will give the best results. Set the peat pots 2 to 3 inches deep and cover with earth and mulch. Quality collected stock of good size may also be used. Because trout lilies grow deeper into the ground each year, old bulbs are hard to find.

Seed production is poor and germination is even poorer. It often takes eight years for seedlings to mature enough to bloom.

COMMENTS: I wonder if the speckled foliage accounts for the name of trout lily.

Camassia scilloides • eastern camass

DESCRIPTION: 10 to 15 inches tall. Pale blue (or, more rarely, white) starlike flowers grow in spikes above foliage resembling those of the leek.

The eastern camass inhabits damp meadows and very open woodlands.

PERIOD OF BLOOM: May into June.

SOIL: Neutral to slightly acid soil of good fertility.

LOCATION AND EXPOSURE: Naturalize in damp sunny meadows or plant in open woodland in patches among birches or other deciduous trees. Interplant with ragwort for color.

PLANTING TIME: While dormant in late summer or early fall.

ROOT SYSTEM: A white onionlike bulb with white basal roots.

PLANTING DEPTH AND SPACING: Set the bulbs 3 to 5 inches deep. Space about 6 inches apart. In an ideal location each bulb will soon become a clump. Mulch. Insert an identifying tag into the ground of planted areas since the eastern camass often goes dormant right after the seeds ripen.

PLANTING STOCK AND PROPAGATION: Nursery-grown stock of good size is best. Or use quality collected stock of good size.

As soon as seeds ripen, sow them in flats. They will produce one slender spear of green the following spring. Several years elapse before seedlings are mature enough to bloom.

COMMENTS: Many years ago some species of camass were used by the Indians as food, but other species are very poisonous.

Camassia esculenta • western camass

DESCRIPTION: 1 to 2 feet tall. Starlike flowers grow in spikes above grasslike foliage. The flowers are an intense copen blue, or (rarely) white.

Western camass forms a sea of blue in moist meadows and open woods along streams.

PERIOD OF BLOOM: June.

SOIL: Fertile garden soil or humus-rich woods soil. Mix in some sand for drainage, which is important during dormancy.

LOCATION AND EXPOSURE: Best planted in clumps among other wildflowers with good foliage that will provide color when the camass goes dormant. Excellent in colonies in damp meadows.

PLANTING TIME: When bulbs become dormant, or early fall.

ROOT SYSTEM: A white onionlike bulb with basal white fibrous roots and a tan paperlike covering.

PLANTING DEPTH AND SPACING: Set the bulbs 4 to 5 inches deep. Space 8 inches or more apart since each bulb forms a clump.

PLANTING STOCK AND PROPAGATION: Use nursery-grown stock or quality collected stock of good size.

Camass can be multiplied by removing offsets from larger bulbs and planting them separately. Do not plant small bulbs more than 2 inches deep. They often bloom in the second year.

Seeds sown when ripe or in early fall germinate the following spring and produce one spearlike leaf, which then becomes dormant about midsummer. Several years elapse before the seedlings mature enough to bloom.

COMMENTS: The intense blue of this camass is spectacular, rivaling other wildflowers that bloom at the same time.

Ornithogalum umbellatum • star-of-Bethlehem

DESCRIPTION: 5 to 8 inches tall. The waxy-white starlike flowers have a greenish tint on the outside. The leaves resemble those of the crocus; they are linear, with a white midrib.

Originally grown only in cultivation, the star-of-Bethlehem is now found in old fields and meadows among grasses.

PERIOD OF BLOOM: Late May into June.

SOIL: Ordinary garden or woodland soil. Not fussy.

LOCATION AND EXPOSURE: Very light open shade or a place where the morning sun shines briefly. A fine plant for the semishaded rock garden or along a woodland path. Excellent to naturalize in patches. Star-of-Bethlehem quickly becomes dormant after bloom.

PLANTING TIME: While dormant in spring or fall. Fall is preferable.

ROOT SYSTEM: A small white bulb with white fibrous roots.

PLANTING DEPTH AND SPACING: Set the bulbs 1 inch deep. Space 4 to 6 inches apart, since each bulb forms a clump.

PLANTING STOCK AND PROPAGATION: Use nursery-grown stock or quality collected stock.

Propagation by division of bulb colonies in early spring or fall offers a fast method of increasing stock. I have never noticed seeds.

COMMENTS: Star-of-Bethlehem is interesting planted among low groundcovers that retain their foliage.

Muscari botryoides • grape hyacinth

DESCRIPTION: 6 to 10 inches tall. An elongated cluster of neat little porcelain-blue bells clings closely to an upright spike. A rare white variety also exists. The foliage is ribbonlike.

At one time grown only in cultivation, grape hyacinth is now found in deserted gardens and along fencerows.

PERIOD OF BLOOM: Early May.

SOIL: Ordinary garden soil or rich woods soil that is neutral to only slightly acid.

LOCATION AND EXPOSURE: There are many uses for this blue early-spring flower. I planted it along a sunny path to our pool and under a nearby birch among hepaticas, bloodroot, and white trilliums.

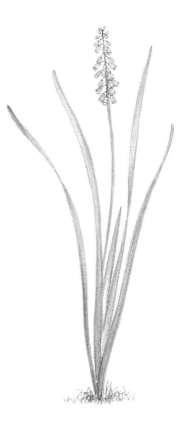

PLANTING TIME: Transplant after blooming when the foliage fades or anytime thereafter into the fall.

ROOT SYSTEM: A white onionlike bulb with white basal roots. It multiplies readily.

PLANTING DEPTH AND SPACING: Set the bulbs 2 to 3 inches deep. Space 3 to 6 inches apart. Each bulb will form a neat little clump. For naturalizing, plant at random, or tuck the plants in niches of a rock garden.

PLANTING STOCK AND PROPAGATION: Use nursery-grown stock or divide clumps if the grape hyacinth is already in your garden. Or use quality collected stock.

This plant rarely sets seed. Division of clumps is the best method of propagation.

COMMENTS: Wherever you choose to grow grape hyacinths they will be welcome bursts of heavenly blue in the early spring sunshine, but grow them where other plants will provide interest when the hyacinth goes dormant shortly after blooming.

Smilacina stellata • star-flowered false Solomon's seal

DESCRIPTION: 10 to 18 inches tall. This variety of false Solomon's seal is referred to as the star-flowered; a sparse plume of starry white flowers grows at the top of a leafy stem. The stem is arching and grows in a slightly zigzag fashion. Dark red berries appear in the fall.

The plant is often found in moist woods with good drainage and along sandy roadsides where there is some shade during the heat of the day.

PERIOD OF BLOOM: Late May into June.

SOIL: Fertile or sandy soil that is slightly acid. Good drainage is important.

LOCATION AND EXPOSURE: Partial shade where tree branches are high overhead. It is excellent for naturalizing or as groundcover in the woodland. If you wish to keep a few plants within bounds in a small garden, plant them in bottomless gallon cans.

PLANTING TIME: Early spring or anytime after dormancy until late fall.

ROOT SYSTEM: A pale, slender, creeping rhizome that frequently sends up new plants, forming large colonies that take over wide areas.

PLANTING DEPTH AND SPACING: Plant the rhizomes horizontally, 1 inch deep with the eye almost at soil level. Point each rhizome in a different direction since each will creep and fork to form a colony. Space at least 1 foot apart.

PLANTING STOCK AND PROPAGATION: Use nursery-grown stock or quality collected stock.

Fall is the best time to propagate from divisions. Divide rhizomes at the forks, leaving one newly formed shoot in each division.

Seeds sown in fall often do not germinate until the second year, and seedlings bloom several years later.

COMMENTS: In our area of the Nicolet National Forest this plant claims countless miles, growing in older Jack pine plantations.

Smilacina racemosa • false spikenard

DESCRIPTION: 1 to 3 feet tall. A leafy stem arching at the top bears a solitary white to creamy-white plume. Speckled berries appear in August and provide excellent food for grouse.

False spikenard is found in dry open woodlands where the soil is rich in humus. In our woodland the chipmunks have been carrying and burying seeds for some time now, and several colonies of the plant have been established as a result of their activities.

PERIOD OF BLOOM: May into June.

SOIL: Rich soil of moderate acidity.

LOCATION AND EXPOSURE: A fine plant for open woodlands or in the shade as a groundcover among shrubs. False spikenard is best grown where humus is deep. Planted in colonies under deciduous trees, it will spread after once becoming established. Mulch generously.

PLANTING TIME: While dormant in spring or fall.

ROOT SYSTEM: A coarse tannish rhizome with many rings and coarse white feeder roots. Newly formed eyes remain below the ground for a year before emerging.

PLANTING DEPTH AND SPACING: Plant the rhizomes horizontally, 2 inches deep, with the tip just below soil level. Space at least 1 foot apart since the rhizome forks as it creeps along.

PLANTING STOCK AND PROPAGATION: Nursery-grown stock has a heavier root system and thicker rhizomes, but quality collected stock from plants mature enough to bloom may be used.

Divide the rhizomes for propagation, preferably in fall. Seeds planted as soon as they ripen usually require two years to germinate and another five years to bloom.

COMMENTS: The false spikenard should be planted in its permanent home since it resists moving and often will not bloom the first year after transplanting. It is also known as Solomon's plume.

Clintonia borealis • bluebead lily

DESCRIPTION: 6 to 8 inches tall. Clusters of small, greenish yellow bells rise on upright stems above broad, glossy leaves. Steel-blue berries appear in August.

In cool, damp, deciduous woodlands and among evergreens, where the soil is humus-rich and mulch is plentiful, the bluebead lily grows in huge colonies among cinnamon fern, starflower, and bunchberry. In drier, shaded areas it grows among bracken fern, blooming before the ferns unfurl their fronds.

PERIOD OF BLOOM: Late May into early June.

SOIL: Humus-rich acid to slightly acid soil. Add a generous amount of damp peatmoss to the soil.

LOCATION AND EXPOSURE: The bluebead lily cannot tolerate the hot summer sun on its leaves. It is an ideal plant for deep shade, where many other wildflowers would fail.

59

PLANTING TIME: Fall planting is preferable, but plants can be moved in the spring while still dormant.

ROOT SYSTEM: A slender creeping rhizome that divides at the nodes to form additional plants. Collected stock has only a few feeder roots at each node, while nursery-grown stock has a vigorous root system.

PLANTING DEPTH AND SPACING: Place the rhizome horizontally about ½ to 1 inch deep with the new shoot-tip just about at soil level. Mulch with partly decayed oak leaves, weathered straw, or old marsh hay.

The clintonias are ramblers. When planting a colony, point the tips of the rhizomes in different directions so that they can spread outward. New rhizomes form, and these will fork also.

PLANTING STOCK AND PROPAGATION: Nursery-grown stock is far superior to collected stock in root system and vitality, but quality collected stock with ample roots may be used.

Division of rhizomes in fall is the quickest method of propagation.

Sow pulp-free seeds as soon as they are ripe or in early fall. Next spring, each seed that germinates sends up one tiny green spear. Each succeeding year the spear lengthens and broadens until a single leaf on each plant has almost reached maturity. Over the next few years some of the plants will produce two mature leaves. Blooms appear only when the plant has matured sufficiently to produce three or four leaves. A bluebead lily bed that I started from seeds about twelve years ago is finally displaying some plants with three leaves that should grow to full size this year. Next year I hope to be rewarded with some bloom.

COMMENTS: I know of no other wildflower that takes as long as *Clintonia borealis* to grow from seed to the flowering stage. But the glossy foliage is like a carpet of green velvet in shaded forest nooks, and it is one of the few plants that retains its quality of foliage throughout the growing season.

Disporum maculatum • nodding mandarin

DESCRIPTION: 1 to 2 feet tall. Nodding bells grow on a forked stalk with alternate, ovate, quilted leaves tapering to a point. Flowers are cream-colored to yellow with brownish-purple speckles.

This mandarin is a native to shaded woodlands where there is a carpet of deep humus.

PERIOD OF BLOOM: May into June.

SOIL: Neutral to slightly acid, rich woods soil. It must have constant moisture if it is to set seed.

LOCATION AND EXPOSURE: A fine, showy plant for naturalizing in a colony in open shade.

PLANTING TIME: While dormant in spring or fall.

ROOT SYSTEM: A white rootstock that forms a clump to develop new plants. Very much like that of merrybells.

PLANTING DEPTH AND SPACING: Space the rootstock 1 to 2 feet apart, to leave room for clumps to spread. Set 1 inch deep and mulch.

PLANTING STOCK AND PROPAGATION: Use nursery-grown stock, or quality collected stock where available.

Divide rootstocks while dormant in spring or fall. Seeds should be sown when ripe. They are slow to germinate.

COMMENTS: The nodding mandarin is an excellent plant to grow in colonies because of its showy flared bells and its distinctively textured, deeply veined foliage. Other disporum flowers are not as showy as those of the nodding mandarin.

Maianthemum canadense • Canada mayflower

DESCRIPTION: 3 to 6 inches tall. The Canada mayflower looks very much like a miniature lily of the valley and is sometimes called false lily of the valley. It has fragrant, tiny white flowers in an oval spike and bright red berries from August into September.

Canada mayflower covers woodland floors, where it grows among clintonia and bunchberry. On drier wooded hillsides it is found among wintergreen and pyrola. It also tends to form colonies around fallen logs of evergreen trees and stumps of the white pine, sending its rhizomes through the decaying wood.

PERIOD OF BLOOM: Late May into June.

SOIL: Humus-rich to slightly acid soil. But I have also found it growing in fire furrows in pure sand where it was mulched by falling leaves. Plenty of mulch will help this plant to spread more quickly.

LOCATION AND EXPOSURE: A good groundcover for partial or deep shade. Grow it among pink lady's-slippers or clintonias. Canada mayflower is very neat and easy to cultivate.

PLANTING TIME: While dormant in spring or fall. Potted stock may be planted anytime.

ROOT SYSTEM: A very extensive and forking rootstock consisting of slender, jointed, white rhizomes that creep at about 1 inch below soil level.

PLANTING DEPTH AND SPACING: Plant bareroot stock horizontally, cover with 1 inch of earth, and mulch. If you are planting stock grown in peat pots, sink to soil level and mulch lightly. Space either stock 6 to 12 inches apart. If planting sods, sink to soil level, space 1 foot or more apart, and mulch lightly.

PLANTING STOCK AND PROPAGATION: Nursery-grown stock in peat pots is best and gives the quickest results. Freshly dug bareroot stock may be used; unless sods are large, many of the eyes will be severed from the parent rootstock.

Sow seeds in the fall in individual pots. Later, set the pots in their permanent location. Propagating from seed is slow, and it takes several years for the plants to bloom.

COMMENTS: The Canada mayflower is one of the best ground-covers to grow among lady's-slippers and other acid-loving wild-flowers. It spreads surprisingly fast when mulched with leaves of soft maple and white birch. Old weathered straw and partly decayed marsh hay also make an excellent mulch; they must be put down in fall so that snow can settle the mulch.

Streptopus roseus • rose mandarin

DESCRIPTION: 1 to 2 feet tall. The dainty, drooping bells in the axils of the upper leaves are dull rose to pink. The leafy, twisted stalk has ovate leaves which taper to a point. Red berries appear in the fall. The plant grows in colonies in deciduous woods that have plentiful leafmold.

PERIOD OF BLOOM: Late May into June.

SOIL: Humus-rich, neutral to slightly acid soil. Moist but not wet.

LOCATION AND EXPOSURE: Plant rose mandarin in deep to open

shade or among rocks and stumps in a woodland garden. Or grow it in colonies to serve as groundcover.

PLANTING TIME: While dormant in spring or fall.

ROOT SYSTEM: A matted rhizome that divides at frequent intervals to send up new plants.

PLANTING DEPTH AND SPACING: Set the rhizomes horizontally, 1 inch deep, and spread the fibrous feeder roots carefully. Mulch.

PLANTING STOCK AND PROPAGATION: Use nursery-grown stock or quality collected stock.

Divide rhizomes while the plant is dormant. Sow seeds as soon as they ripen or in the fall. Germination is slow, and the plant will take several years to bloom.

COMMENTS: The rose mandarin, also known as rosy twisted stalk, is a showy plant, especially suited for groundcover in forest areas with high open shade. It can be planted in small groups or in large colonies.

Polygonatum biflorum • Solomon's seal

DESCRIPTION: 1 to 3 feet tall. Tiny, elongated pale yellow or greenish bells hang in pairs in the axils of the leaves on arching stems. Dark blue berries, flushed with white, appear in the fall. Solomon's seal grows in moist woodlands, in deep shade where the soil is humus-rich. I found it growing among rocks along a shaded river bank where the mulch had accumulated in pockets.

PERIOD OF BLOOM: June into July.

SOIL: Slightly acid, humus-rich soil retaining some moisture.

LOCATION AND EXPOSURE: Plant in light shade or even in high, open, deep shade among rocks, on hillsides, or in colonies along with *Trillium grandiflorum* and *Trillium cernuum*. It contrasts nicely with medium-sized ferns.

PLANTING TIME: While dormant in spring or fall.

ROOT SYSTEM: A twisted, heavy white rhizome that forms a shoot at each node. The shoot branches off to start a new plant.

PLANTING DEPTH AND SPACING: Plant the rhizome horizontally, 1 to 2 inches deep, with the tip just below the surface of the soil. Space 1 foot apart or intersperse with other wildflowers.

PLANTING STOCK AND PROPAGATION: Nursery-grown stock is more heavily rooted, but you can also use quality collected stock of good size.

Divide rhizomes in spring or while dormant. Sow seeds as soon as they are ripe. Germination is uneven and seedlings are slow to mature, but I found that when freshly gathered seed was planted next to a shady stone foundation germination was much better, possibly due to even moisture.

COMMENTS: This excellent groundcover is especially handsome under large trees or among shrubs. When the berries turn blue they have a blush like Concord grapes.

A coarser version of Solomon's seal is the great Solomon's seal (*Polygonatum commutatum*). It requires more moisture. A lone specimen turned up in my garden and grew to a height of 6 feet. But because there was a dry spell that summer it did not set seed.

Medeola virginiana • Indian cucumber

DESCRIPTION: 1 to 2 feet tall. Above a whorl of light green leaves, the Indian cucumber displays an umbel of small, greenish yellow drooping flowers with curved petals. The flowers are replaced by green berries that turn black in the fall.

Indian cucumber grows naturally in moist woods where the soil is humus-rich and the earth is reasonably moist throughout the growing season. It can also grow in shade on rocky hillsides.

PERIOD OF BLOOM: May into June.

SOIL: Moist, slightly acid, rich woods soil.

LOCATION AND EXPOSURE: Ideal for naturalizing in deep to moderate shade in deciduous woodlands. Plant in colonies, or among smaller ferns or low-growing wildflowers for contrast.

PLANTING TIME: While dormant in spring or fall.

ROOT SYSTEM: An odd-shaped oblong and fleshy white tuber that tastes like cucumber.

PLANTING DEPTH AND SPACING: Plant the tubers horizontally 1 to 2 inches deep. Space 6 to 8 inches apart.

PLANTING STOCK AND PROPAGATION: Use nursery-grown stock or quality collected stock.

Divide tubers, preferably in spring. Seeds sown when ripe may germinate the following spring, but it takes several years for seedlings to mature.

COMMENTS: Indian cucumber is an unusual and worthwhile addition to the wild garden if you can meet its requirements. I find it demanding at times, but not always. In fall, as the berries ripen, the leaves take on a maroon flush which makes an interesting contrast with evergreen ferns.

Trillium luteum • yellow trillium

DESCRIPTION: 10 to 15 inches tall. A whorl of three brown-mottled green leaves grow on a sturdy stalk. At the top, just above the leaves, is a solitary, pale-yellow to clear-lemon-yellow flower with three petals. The straight, narrow petals come to a point and are partly opened. Sometimes there is a wave or slight twist in each. A close sniff suggests a hint of lemon.

This trillium is found in deciduous woods where leafmold is deep. Though it commonly grows far south of Wisconsin, it has thrived here despite our severe winters.

PERIOD OF BLOOM: May into June. This variety blooms longer than any other trillium, usually for a full month.

SOIL: Neutral to slightly acid, humus-rich soil. I find that when replanted, all trillium rhizomes do best when a bit of sand is placed at their base.

LOCATION AND EXPOSURE: While blooming, this wildflower requires filtered sunlight; at all other times it needs shade. For the best display, plant yellow trillium in groups alongside other wildflowers.

PLANTING TIME: Fall planting is highly recommended to ensure stronger bloom and good foliage development.

ROOT SYSTEM: A large rhizome with many stringy white feeder roots. A strong grower, occasionally sending up two stalks from one node.

PLANTING DEPTH AND SPACING: Plant the tuberlike rhizome 2 to 4 inches deep, depending on the size of the rhizome and the texture of the soil. In heavy soils, plant shallow. All trilliums require a year-round mulch.

PLANTING STOCK AND PROPAGATION: Use nursery-grown stock or freshly dug quality collected stock.

65

I have never known the seeds to mature, possibly because of the severe climate in my area.

COMMENTS: A most unusual addition to the woodland garden. The fragrant, long-lasting blossoms have a beauty all their own.

Trillium recurvatum • prairie trillium

DESCRIPTION: 10 to 15 inches tall. A solitary maroon flower with three upright petals rests above a whorl of three mottled ovate leaves. The upper part of the petal is often flushed with green.

This trillium is found in moist woods and thickets south of Wisconsin. It has also thrived well in my area, much farther north.

PERIOD OF BLOOM: May.

SOIL: Neutral to slightly acid soil, rich in humus.

LOCATION AND EXPOSURE: Grow in open woods where the plants will be protected from the summer sun. Plant them in colonies or intersperse with other trilliums for contrast.

PLANTING TIME: Fall is best.

ROOT SYSTEM: A medium-sized rhizome with white stringy roots.

PLANTING DEPTH AND SPACING: Set the rhizomes 2 to 4 inches deep. Space several inches apart or in groups.

PLANTING STOCK AND PROPAGATION: Use nursery-grown stock or freshly dug collected stock of good quality.

Seeds must be sown as soon as they are picked or germination will be delayed a year.

COMMENTS: This trillium is grown for its mottled foliage rather than for its flower.

Trillium sessile • toadshade

DESCRIPTION: 6 to 10 inches tall. Mottled green leaves, 1½ to 4 inches long, grow in groups of three or occasionally more; they are almost twice as long as they are wide. The upright flower petals are narrower than those of the yellow trillium; they are fragrant and long-lasting, and come in a distinctive shade of wine maroon.

This trillium is native to the Central States but has proved hardy in northern Wisconsin.

PERIOD OF BLOOM: May into June.

SOIL: Humus-rich soil that is only slightly acid.

LOCATION AND EXPOSURE: Moist woods where the soil is humus-rich. An excellent trillium to grow for contrast among yellow trillium and rose trillium, which finish blooming a little later. Plant toadshade in the foreground of ferns, preferably in high open shade.

PLANTING TIME: Fall is preferable.

ROOT SYSTEM: A stout rhizome with many stringy roots.

PLANTING DEPTH AND SPACING: Plant the rhizomes 2 to 4 inches deep, depending on whether the soil is heavy or sandy. In heavy soil, plant about 3 inches deep.

PLANTING STOCK AND PROPAGATION: Use nursery-grown stock or freshly dug collected stock of good quality.

The toadshade has not set seed in our garden, but new plants will occasionally sprout from the small rhizomes that grow around the parent plant.

COMMENTS: The wine-maroon petals of the toadshade make a handsome display against the background of the mottled green leaves.

Trillium cernuum • nodding trillium

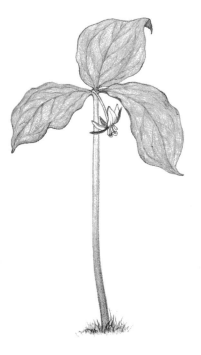

DESCRIPTION: 12 to 18 inches tall. A nodding flower with three wavy petals hides beneath a whorl of three large leaves. The flower is white with deep rose to maroon anthers. Occasionally the blossoms are yellow, pink, or even rose colored, and then the anthers are usually pale yellow or white. A handsome, three-cornered berry forms after the flower blooms, and turns red in July.

The nodding trillium is found in woods where the soil is humus-rich and moist. It also grows along the edge of evergreen swamps.

PERIOD OF BLOOM: May into June.

SOIL: Moderately acid woods soil, moist to wet, but good drainage is important. If the moisture is constant, it will also grow in drier woodlands. The soil in our trillium beds has a pH of 6.

LOCATION AND EXPOSURE: Grow in high open shade with moderately moist, humus-rich soil and plentiful mulch. Planted in groups of three, this tall trillium provides a bold contrast with smaller varieties. For a natural effect, try growing it in colonies— or in small groups with leatherwood fern or florist fern—among rocks where leafmold is deep.

PLANTING TIME: Fall is preferable for all trilliums because the rhizomes continue to grow throughout late fall and early winter as well as in very early spring, and the new shoots are easily broken in moving.

ROOT SYSTEM: A large rhizome with many stringy feeder roots. Occasionally a single rhizome will send up two stalks during one season and only a single stalk the next season. In my wildflower garden, next to a foundation, a nodding trillium planted ten years ago now sends up six flower stalks.

PLANTING DEPTH AND SPACING: Plant the rhizomes 2 to 4 inches deep in groups of three. Space 6 or more inches apart or plant at random (groups of three together make a better display.)

PLANTING STOCK AND PROPAGATION: Use nursery-grown stock or freshly dug collected stock.

When the seeds are ripe they should be removed from the pulpy hull and immediately planted in flats or in a permanent location. The seedlings may take as many as ten years to bloom.

COMMENTS: This trillium is unusual and outstanding. I especially like its showy red berry, which lasts a long time.

The flowers are sweet-scented.

Trillium erectum • purple trillium

DESCRIPTION: 10 to 15 inches tall. This trillium has a short sturdy stem with a whorl of three ovate leaves at the top. The medium-sized maroon flower in the center of the leaves has an offensive odor (occasionally pale-yellow blossoms come up that have no odor).

Purple trillium grows in moist, rich woods in deep to open shade.

PERIOD OF BLOOM: May.

SOIL: Neutral to slightly acid, humus-rich soil.

LOCATION AND EXPOSURE: Open to deep shade in woodland where leafmold is plentiful. A striking companion for *Trillium grandiflorum*.

PLANTING TIME: Fall is best for all trilliums.

ROOT SYSTEM: Large rhizomes with many stringy roots. Older rhizomes often develop tiny rhizomes which may be detached and planted separately. Plant them only 2 inches deep and they will seek their own level.

PLANTING DEPTH AND SPACING: Plant the rhizomes 2 to 4 inches deep. Space 8 inches or more apart, or plant in groups of three or interspersed with other wildflowers.

PLANTING STOCK AND PROPAGATION: Use nursery-grown stock or freshly dug quality collected stock.

Propagate by removing small rhizomes from the parent plant. Seeds sown as soon as they ripen are slow to germinate and require years to bring to the blooming stage.

COMMENTS: The maroon-red flowers make an excellent contrast for other spring flowers such as the wild blue phlox and other trilliums.

Wake robin is another name for this trillium. It is also called stinking Benjamin because of the foul odor of the blossom. I find that the odor is not noticeable unless one sniffs closely.

Trillium grandiflorum • large white trillium

DESCRIPTION: 12 to 18 inches tall. Three broad, ovate leaves in a whorl top a sturdy stem. (I have found a few plants with four leaves and four petals, but one of the petals was partially curled.) The single pure white flower with yellow anthers is long lasting. The slightly curved, often wavy, petals deepen to a blush pink as they wither. There is also an extremely rare double white form, a gardenialike flower, which is highly prized.

This trillium is found throughout much of the eastern half of the United States and is abundant in Wisconsin. It carpets large areas with green and white, usually growing in colonies in open to deep shade. From year to year it reappears in dry upland woods as well as in wooded gullies. It is rarely found among evergreens.

PERIOD OF BLOOM: May into June.

SOIL: Neutral to slightly acid soil with plenty of humus. In the wild state, the rhizome is often found in sandy soil under the top layer of earth containing the humus.

LOCATION AND EXPOSURE: A woodland spot or a sloping hillside where the sun can filter through leafless trees in spring makes an ideal home for this lovely flower. It can also grow in deep shade. In the wild, *Trillium grandiflorum* always grows in large colonies, but some occasionally stray.

PLANTING TIME: Fall is best.

ROOT SYSTEM: A husky rhizome with many stringy roots.

PLANTING DEPTH AND SPACING: Plant the rhizome 2 to 4 inches deep. Space 8 inches or more apart, or plant in colonies or in groups of three. The plant looks interesting in groups among hepaticas and bloodroots.

PLANTING STOCK AND PROPAGATION: Use nursery-grown stock or freshly dug quality collected stock.

I find that rhizomes planted 2 inches deep and given a good mulch produce a number of rhizomes over a period of years. Be wary of shallow planting in light soil; it invites rodent damage.

Sow seeds as soon as they are ripe, before the caruncle dries. Seedlings require several years to bloom. The double white *Trillium grandiflorum* does not set seed and can only be propagated by detaching the tiny rhizomes from parent stock. This is a slow but rewarding method.

COMMENTS: The *Trillium grandiflorum* is the showiest of the trillium group, often covering hillsides and woodlands with patches of "snow." It is also easily cultivated.

This flower is really two in one, first a splendor of purest white and then a splash of pink turning to rose as it withers.

Trillium undulatum · painted trillium

DESCRIPTION: 8 to 12 inches tall. A white flower with three crimson-streaked petals sits just above a whorl of three leaves. The leaves are medium green and thin textured. In fall, the plant produces a red berry.

This wildflower inhabits cool woods and rarely grows in colonies.

PERIOD OF BLOOM: May into June.

SOIL: Requires a fertile, wet, acid soil, which can be pasty.

LOCATION AND EXPOSURE: A cool, damp, shady nook is ideal. It is also lovely scattered among occasional clintonias in a moist area carpeted with goldthread.

PLANTING TIME: Fall.

ROOT SYSTEM: A medium-sized rhizome that is slow to multiply.

PLANTING DEPTH AND SPACING: Plant rhizomes 3 to 5 inches deep, 1 to 2 feet apart in a random fashion for a natural effect.

PLANTING STOCK AND PROPAGATION: Nursery-grown stock is best. Also use quality collected stock, freshly dug.

I have never grown this trillium from seed, but I presume sowing the seeds as soon as they are ripe will give the same results as it does with other trilliums.

COMMENTS: The flower is of unusual beauty. Recently a seedling appeared in my garden in the shade of a black cherry tree. When I removed some of the earth carefully to bare the rhizome without disturbing the roots, I found the rhizome top was 3½ inches down in rich humus. The seedling reappeared the following spring.

This trillium will become dormant shortly after blooming unless continued moisture is available.

Trillium ozarkanum · Ozark trillium

DESCRIPTION: 4 to 6 inches tall. This trillium, of the *virginianum* variety, has a dainty white flower which turns rose as the blossom fades, prominent anthers, and an extremely prominent calyx the same size as the blossom. After the flower withers, the calyx almost doubles in size and hides the seed pod. The stem is a striking wine-red color.

The Ozark trillium is found in woodlands south of Wisconsin wherever the soil is moist and somewhat acid.

PERIOD OF BLOOM: In its native home the Ozark trillium blooms in April, but farther north it blooms in May.

SOIL: Neutral to acid soil rich in humus. Constant moisture helps all trilliums retain their foliage throughout the growing season.

LOCATION AND EXPOSURE: A good trillium to plant in front of the taller *Trillium cernuum* in an open woodland spot.

PLANTING TIME: Fall is preferable for all trilliums.

ROOT SYSTEM: A small white rhizome, rarely more than an inch long. Tiny rhizomes form around the adult rhizome to form a clump.

PLANTING DEPTH AND SPACING: Plant 2 to 4 inches deep. Space 8 to 12 inches apart. Avoid planting in clumps since each rhizome forms a clump with age.

PLANTING STOCK AND PROPAGATION: Use nursery-grown stock or quality collected stock where available.

The Ozark trillium is best propagated by removing small rhizomes from the parent plant in fall only. Do not divide the clumps until 4 or 5 mature stalks appear.

Seeds must be sown as soon as harvested. The following spring only one leaf will appear, and the seedlings usually require three to six years to bloom.

COMMENTS: The Ozark trillium is particularly handsome because of its wine-red stalk.

Trillium stylosum • rose trillium

DESCRIPTION: 10 to 12 inches tall. Slightly nodding flowers, with narrow curved petals, are pink to rose colored with a little white on the undersides. The rather long stems grow out of a whorl of three medium-sized leaves.

The rose trillium naturally inhabits rocky regions of the Appalachian Mountains; it has also proved hardy in northern Wisconsin.

PERIOD OF BLOOM: Early June. It is the last trillium to bloom.

SOIL: Fertile woodland soil that is neutral to slightly acid. Constant moisture is important to all trilliums.

LOCATION AND EXPOSURE: Plant in woodlands among medium-sized feathery ferns.

PLANTING TIME: In fall, only while dormant.

ROOT SYSTEM: A medium-sized rhizome with stringy fibrous feeder roots.

PLANTING DEPTH AND SPACING: Plant 2 to 4 inches deep. Space 6 to 12 inches apart or plant at random.

PLANTING STOCK AND PROPAGATION: Use nursery-grown stock, or quality collected stock where available.

Sow seeds as soon as they are ripe. Several years elapse before the seedlings bloom.

COMMENTS: The rose trillium is the last of the trilliums to bloom in my garden; it just begins to blossom when *Trillium grandiflorum* is fading to pink. It is good company for *Trillium luteum*, which blooms throughout the trillium season.

Trillium nivale • snow trillium

DESCRIPTION: 3 to 4 inches tall. The dainty white blossoms are occasionally streaked with pink. Three bluish green, petiolate leaves grow in a whorl. It is found in rich woodlands and glens.

PERIOD OF BLOOM: In northern Wisconsin it blooms in early April. A tiny node of green appears through the leafmold as soon as the snow melts. Sometimes this trillium blooms during spring snowstorms.

SOIL: Humus-rich soil with a pH of 6 gives fine results.

LOCATION AND EXPOSURE: A dainty little trillium to grow beneath taller shrubs or in colonies in open woodlands.

PLANTING TIME: Fall only.

ROOT SYSTEM: A small rhizome that is slow to multiply.

PLANTING DEPTH AND SPACING: Set the small rhizomes 2 inches deep. They will adjust to their own depth. Plant in groups or colonies.

PLANTING STOCK AND PROPAGATION: Use nursery-grown stock or quality collected stock.

My *Trillium nivale* has never set seed, possibly because there are no bees around to pollinate it when it blooms.

COMMENTS: Drifts of this little trillium are a welcome sight in early spring; they are sometimes covered for a day or so by slushy snows.

AMARYLLIDACEAE [Amaryllis Family]

Hypoxis hirsuta • yellow stargrass

DESCRIPTION: 4 to 6 inches tall. The hairy, upright foliage appears to be folded lengthwise. Bright-yellow starlike flowers,

greenish on the outside, grow midway up the foliage on a single stem.

Usually found in grassy meadows, along roadsides, and often in very open woodlands, this wildflower also grows in prairie regions.

PERIOD OF BLOOM: Late May into July, with scattered blossoms throughout the summer.

SOIL: Many types of fertile, slightly acid to acid soil as well as sandy loam. Constant moisture promotes superior growth and bloom.

LOCATION AND EXPOSURE: Yellow stargrass is native to prairies and open woodland; I find it grows best in full sun where the soil never bakes dry. Excellent for a rock garden amidst blue-eyed grass.

PLANTING TIME: While dormant in spring or fall, but I have moved it in midsummer, cutting back the foliage considerably and letting it grow anew.

ROOT SYSTEM: An almost round, onionlike corm covered with a fibrous papery brown hull.

PLANTING DEPTH AND SPACING: Set the corms a few inches apart in small groups and plant 1½ inches deep. In northern areas, mulch unless grown among grasses.

PLANTING STOCK AND PROPAGATION: Use nursery-grown stock or quality collected stock.

Separate the tiny corms that form around the parent plant. You must inspect the plants every day if you want to collect the elusive black seeds. Sow them in fall and barely cover them with earth.

COMMENTS: The foliage and flowers of yellow stargrass contrast beautifully with those of blue-eyed grass. They are of two different families.

IRIDACEAE [Iris Family]

Iris cristata • crested dwarf iris

DESCRIPTION: 3 to 8 inches tall. Sword-shaped leaves grow in groups up the short flower stem. Often tucked in among the foliage, the dainty flowers are light blue to lavender-blue, with bright yellow crests on each lower petal. The white form is rare.

Crested dwarf iris grows naturally in rich, rocky woods and along streams and lakes. It also grows abundantly in some eastern parts of Wisconsin.

PERIOD OF BLOOM: May.

SOIL: Neutral to slightly acid soil of good fertility.

LOCATION AND EXPOSURE: This iris makes a fine groundcover in high open shade or in sun with constant moisture. Plant it among limestone rocks or in fertile garden soil. It spreads to form mats.

PLANTING TIME: Spring or fall.

ROOT SYSTEM: A small slender rhizome with fibrous roots. Each rhizome sends out new rhizomes in a fan shape to form a clump.

PLANTING DEPTH AND SPACING: Set the rhizomes almost at soil level, leaving the tips partly exposed. Space 6 or more inches apart, depending on the effect wanted. Carefully tuck the fine feeder roots into the soil, and water often. If you are placing the newly transplanted stock in a sunny spot it is wise to provide shade for a week to ten days.

PLANTING STOCK AND PROPAGATION: Use nursery-grown stock or quality collected stock.

Divide plants in very early spring or right after blooming. My crested iris have never set seed.

COMMENTS: The blossoms of this little iris are strikingly different from those of other wild irises. The rhizome has a tendency to creep in a beadlike fashion as it grows, while the feeder roots penetrate deep into the soil.

I find the white form, *Iris cristata alba*, equally easy to grow. It is a prize addition to the wild garden.

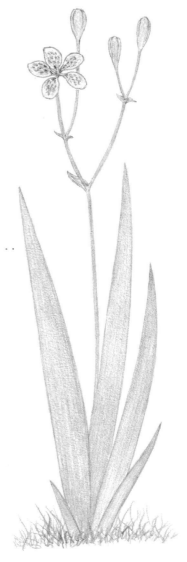

Belamcanda chinensis • blackberry lily

DESCRIPTION: 2 to 3 feet tall. Orange flowers with dark spots grow on a single slender stem. The foliage resembles that of the iris. In fall this lily produces a shiny blackberrylike seed cluster.

The blackberry lily is found in wastelands, along roadsides, and around old homesteads. It was originally a cultivated flower, but now grows wild.

PERIOD OF BLOOM: July into September.

75

SOIL: Ordinary fertile garden soil. It requires no special care.

LOCATION AND EXPOSURE: Plant the blackberry lily in an airy, sunny spot. If crowded, it sometimes develops leaf spot.

PLANTING TIME: While dormant in spring or fall.

ROOT SYSTEM: An orange-yellow rootstock with a few fibrous roots.

PLANTING DEPTH AND SPACING: Plant the rhizome 1½ inches deep and space 1 foot apart. It forms clumps.

PLANTING STOCK AND PROPAGATION: Use nursery-grown stock or plants collected from old gardens or waysides.

Divide the clumps in early spring or fall. Sow the seeds as soon as they are ripe. Often two years elapse before the seeds germinate, and another two years before the seedlings bloom.

COMMENTS: This flower is often referred to as the leopard lily because of the spots on the flower petals. The dried seed clusters are interesting in floral arrangements.

Sisyrinchium angustifolium • blue-eyed grass

DESCRIPTION: 6 to 10 inches tall. Flat flower stems are studded with clusters of dainty starlike flowers. The flowers are light blue to deep violet-blue, and the slender irislike foliage is blue-green.

Blue-eyed grass is usually found in dry, sunny meadows among grasses. In my area it graces roadsides, growing in gravelly earth.

PERIOD OF BLOOM: May into June.

SOIL: Slightly acid sandy loam to poor sandy soils. Good drainage is important. When cultivated, blue-eyed grass quickly forms large clumps.

LOCATION AND EXPOSURE: Blue-eyed grass blooms profusely in full sun and fertile soil. It is an interesting plant for a sunny rock garden or as edging along a stony walk in full sun.

PLANTING TIME: Spring or fall. Moves easily.

ROOT SYSTEM: Coarse fibrous roots, pale tan-yellow in color.

PLANTING DEPTH AND SPACING: Set the crown about ¼ to ½ inch deep. Space 6 inches apart, or farther apart in fertile soils. It forms clumps.

PLANTING STOCK AND PROPAGATION: Nursery-grown stock has a heavier root system, but you may also use quality collected stock.

Divide clumps in spring or fall. Seeds sown when ripe will

germinate the following spring, and the seedlings will reach a good size the next summer. When grown in barren areas, it readily self-sows.

COMMENTS: Each six-petaled, starlike flower opens for one day and shortly after sets seed. On cloudy days the flower rarely opens. Blue-eyed grass is very interesting in the seed stage. I marvel to see such tiny flowers produce fruit the size of small peas.

Iris versicolor • blue flag

DESCRIPTION: 2 feet tall. The orchidlike flowers are medium-blue with splashes of gold. They resemble cultivated irises although they are smaller. The sword-shaped foliage is long and graceful.

Blue flag grows in wet meadows and marshes, along lakes and brooks, and even in ditches where there is standing water in spring.

PERIOD OF BLOOM: June.

SOIL: Blue flag grows readily in any fertile soil.

LOCATION AND EXPOSURE: For the best bloom, plant blue flag in full sun. If you prefer to emphasize the foliage, plant in a shaded spot next to a rock or at the edge of a pool.

PLANTING TIME: Early spring, or late August into fall.

ROOT SYSTEM: A stout, cream-colored rhizome that creeps in a fanlike manner.

PLANTING DEPTH AND SPACING: Plant the rhizome horizontally, barely below the surface of the soil and with the crown at soil level. Space 1 foot apart. For best bloom, divide and transplant every third year.

PLANTING STOCK AND PROPAGATION: Nursery-grown stock is superior to collected stock.

Division of the rhizomes in August gives good results. Seeds sown as soon as they ripen and kept reasonably moist will produce blooming plants in three years.

COMMENTS: Blue flag deserves a prominent place in a wild garden. Although naturally found in very wet places, seedlings and nursery-grown stock can be grown successfully in ordinary garden soil of good fertility and average moisture.

ORCHIDACEAE [Orchis Family]

Cypripedium Calceolus • large yellow lady's-slipper

DESCRIPTION: 10 to 20 inches tall. Leafy stems bear one or two flowers which resemble pouches or slippers with two twisted frills for ties. The flowers are clear yellow with brown frills.

This large lady's-slipper (the *pubescens* variety) is found in moist deciduous woods that are often somewhat drier in summer. It also grows on hummocks in swamps.

PERIOD OF BLOOM: May into June.

SOIL: Neutral to slightly acid soil, rich in humus and with ample moisture gives best results. Mix some damp peatmoss into the soil. Woods soil is best, as it contains fungi that are beneficial to these plants.

LOCATION AND EXPOSURE: Partial shade in open woods is preferable. Yellow lady's-slippers are especially handsome interspersed with leatherwood and florist ferns. One of the easiest lady's-slippers to establish, it can be grown extensively in wild gardens.

PLANTING TIME: While dormant in spring or fall.

ROOT SYSTEM: A cream-colored, extremely stringy, creeping rootstock that is rather flexible in comparison to that of the pink lady's-slipper. The rhizome of the yellow lady's-slipper works itself down, and in fully established plants the crown may reach 1½ to 2 inches deep.

PLANTING DEPTH AND SPACING: Set the rhizome about 1 to 1½ inches deep with the base of the dormant bud ¾ to 1¼ inches below the soil level. Slant the roots slightly downward so that the tips will be slightly deeper than the base of the bud. Mulch with decaying leaves, weathered straw, or old marsh hay. Mulching helps retain the moisture and also keeps the roots cool in summer. Plants should be spaced 12 to 18 inches apart or planted at random. Multiple-crowned plants should be given ample room. A few rocks in the area lend an air of spaciousness and help protect the roots.

PLANTING STOCK AND PROPAGATION: Nursery-grown collected sods are easiest to move, but you can also use quality collected stock with good roots.

The division of lady's-slipper rhizomes is not always successful, as rot can set in at the crown and destroy both divisions. When the buds are far enough apart, division is less complicated.

As to seeds, there seem to be thousands in each capsule. Although I have never tried growing these plants from seed, I do know people who claim that yellow lady's-slippers appeared in their woods several years after seeds were scattered. It is well worth a trial.

COMMENTS: Give the lady's-slippers a little additional mulch each year unless falling leaves have taken over. The leaves of white birch and soft maple are especially good. The decaying humus will feed the plant and make for better specimens. All lady's-slippers benefit when the soil is kept moist, especially by mulching.

There is a smaller, less common version of the yellow lady's-slipper, the dainty *Cypripedium Calceolus parviflorum*. When established, it too spreads to form a clump. Do not plant it quite as deep as the large yellow lady's-slipper.

Cypripedium reginae • showy lady's-slipper

DESCRIPTION: 1 to 2 feet and taller. The flowers are shaped like large pouches or moccasins; they grow along the stem singly, in pairs, or even in groups of three. Flowers are white, flushed with magenta—pure white flowers are rare. Stems are stout with many broad-pleated leaves. Both stems and leaves are hairy.

The showy lady's-slipper is found in evergreen swamps and moist woods. Throughout our area it is found only off the beaten path.

PERIOD OF BLOOM: June, when other lady's-slippers are fading.

SOIL: Rich soil, neutral to slightly acid, with a generous addition of damp peatmoss mixed in to help retain moisture. Woods soil is essential; the showy lady's-slipper will not grow in cultivated garden soil.

LOCATION AND EXPOSURE: High open woods with shade where the soil does not dry out excessively. Constant moisture is best.

79

Some fifteen years ago I planted a few showy lady's-slippers in the shade of a large oak tree where the soil was virgin. Here a portion of their roots could creep under a large granite boulder. With a carpet of oak fern and some other small wildflowers planted nearby, the showy lady's-slippers seem to thrive. Each June they put on a regal display, with two to three pouches on each sturdy stem. It takes time to establish showy lady's-slippers, but once established their beauty increases yearly.

PLANTING TIME: While dormant in spring or fall. I prefer fall planting for all lady's-slippers unless they are moved in sods.

ROOT SYSTEM: Fibrous stringy roots extend from the rootstock. The roots are not as coarse as those of the pink lady's-slipper.

This species is a shallow grower. As plants become established, the crowns work up and some new roots will be barely below soil level. Some may even creep at soil level if the humus is well decayed. This is why a rock mulch over a good layer of humus is so beneficial.

PLANTING DEPTH AND SPACING: Set the rhizomes ½ to 1 inch deep, spreading the roots evenly. Cover with woods soil so that the top of the dormant bud is barely at soil level. Taper the tips of the roots slightly downward, a little deeper than the base of the shoot. Showy lady's-slipper plants should be spaced 2 to 3 feet apart. Allow room for future growth and space for the roots to run.

Mulch lightly with old decaying leaves, weathered marsh hay, or old straw. A combination of partly decayed straw, soft maple leaves, and birch leaves is ideal. A little extra mulch may be given the first fall but should be removed in spring.

Large rocks laid around the lady's-slipper plants encourage the roots to run beneath and help to keep the roots cool, which will promote more luxuriant growth. When planting the lady's-slipper, a twig should be put next to each crown so that rocks will not be laid over the buds later on. Winter snow will firm the mulch, and if too much is added, the shoots will not emerge. In this case, the twigs will mark where the plants should come up and some of the mulch can be removed. Once the plants have sprouted, a few inches of mulch can be put back around the stem. The addition of grass clippings as a mulch each time the grass is cut does wonders for this particular plant.

PLANTING STOCK AND PROPAGATION: Stock that has been growing in the nursery for two or more years is by far the best but you can also use sods or quality collected bareroot stock.

I have never tried divisions, as the plants grow much better when left in clumps where each plant helps the other.

Mature, established plants set a quantity of seed, but they do not germinate when sown in a flat. Try scattering seeds in a moist woodland instead.

COMMENTS: Showy lady's-slipper plants develop and improve with age. Established plants should never be moved. At best, it takes several years for a plant to multiply. With time the quality of the bloom improves and the plant becomes more stately. Always keep your showy lady's-slippers reasonably moist, but never soaking wet.

A friend of mine moved her showy lady's-slipper five or six times in as many years. When she built a new home, the "showy" was moved again. With each moving the plant became less vigorous. Now my friend has a permanent home for her clump of showy lady's-slippers on the north side of the house where a large shallow planter is filled with woods soil and damp peatmoss. The planter is bottomless. Following my instructions, she faithfully mulched the clump with fresh grass clippings each time the lawn was mowed. Now, some six years later, the showy lady's-slipper has 23 slippers and has formed a large clump.

Cypripedium acaule • pink lady's-slipper

DESCRIPTION: 6 to 8 inches tall. Each stem bears a single, moccasin-shaped flower and two single, oblong basal leaves. The flowers are rose-pink with reddish veins and wine-colored frills. Pure white ones are rare, indeed, and they have yellow frills.

The pink lady's-slipper grows in dry, open shade in oak woods where moisture and leafmold are ample. Established plants do not seem affected by dryness in the summer in these woodland regions. They are also found under the shade of cedars and balsams, on ridges and hummocks in swampy areas, and at the base of white pine stumps in the shade.

PERIOD OF BLOOM: May into June.

SOIL: Use fertile, acid to slightly acid, humus-rich woods soil and well decayed leafmold, preferably oak. A generous amount of damp peatmoss should also be mixed in, and the soil should be capable of retaining moisture. It is especially important to keep the roots moist the first few years after transplanting. Mycorhizal fungus must be present in the soil if the plant is to grow successfully.

LOCATION AND EXPOSURE: Partial to deep shade in an open woodland. For a natural effect, plant randomly and intersperse with low groundcovers such as bunchberry, goldthread, and oak fern, or all of these running into each other. Plant a few *Clintonia borealis* and a vine of moneywort for an unusual and beautiful effect. If the soil and location are right, the pink lady's-slipper will grow for years; some will even have multiple crowns.

In one small nook I have some pink lady's-slippers growing under Norway pine with clintonia, bunchberry, and some moneywort. I add a little oak-leaf mulch when it is needed, and nature adds pine needles each fall. This little colony has thrived for over ten years.

PLANTING TIME: Spring or fall, but I prefer fall. One mid-June I rescued a quantity of pink lady's-slippers from an area where a bulldozer was cutting through a road. I removed all the seed pods and flowers from the plants to conserve their strength and vitality. Whenever possible I lifted each plant with some soil adhering, or in a sod, and I planted at the same level under tall evergreens in our yard. A few plants had bare roots. But with care and faithful watering almost every plant survived the move, and most of them bloomed the following year.

ROOT SYSTEM: The rhizomes have coarse, stringy white roots which are very brittle. At no time should the roots of any lady's-slippers be exposed to wind or sun.

The rhizome of this species tends to work upward, and established plants may be only a fraction of an inch under the soil. When the plant is in this condition the buds will be plump in the fall, and most plants will bloom the following spring.

PLANTING DEPTH AND SPACING: Set the rhizome about 1 inch deep with the base of the dormant bud ½ to 1 inch below soil level and the tip of the roots slightly downward, a little deeper than the base of the shoot. Spread the roots carefully when planting and make certain that a liberal amount of damp peatmoss is mixed into the woods soil that covers the roots. A mulch of old straw or decaying oak leaves and some old marsh hay is excellent. When planting, place a twig upright near each plant just in case the mulch was spread too generously and the shoot fails to emerge the following spring. Water all the plants liberally immediately after planting, and never let the soil dry out. (This applies to all lady's-slippers as well as to all transplanted stock.)

In fall my lady's-slipper beds are left to themselves, as leaves scatter across the plot. Never place mulch over freshly fallen leaves; the leaves might heat and smother the plants. If the beds need mulching, do it before the leaves fall in autumn.

PLANTING STOCK AND PROPAGATION: Rhizomes in sods are most desirable, but not easy to obtain. Use stock that has grown in the nursery for a year or more or collected stock with plenty of good roots.

Division of rhizomes is most trying, and I find that it is better to keep them growing in clumps rather than attempting to divide them.

It is extremely difficult to get lady's-slipper seeds to germinate, especially in flats. Ten years ago I scattered seeds in an oak-pine woods and pink lady's-slippers are now blooming there. A nurseryman wrote to me that he had succeeded in getting the seeds to germinate but lost the tender seedlings when he tried to transplant them.

COMMENTS: Growing pink-lady's-slippers can be a challenge. But it is also a great satisfaction. Although these plants are supposedly difficult to grow, I have found that it is quite possible to supply all the necessary conditions.

Cypripedium montanum • mountain lady's-slipper

DESCRIPTION: 12 to 18 inches tall. One or two white moccasin-shaped flowers flushed with purplish-blue and with brown frills grow on leafy stems. The mountain lady's-slipper is a western species, haunting brushlands and meadows where the soil is well drained and slightly acid. It is very rare and becoming more so.

PERIOD OF BLOOM: May and June.

SOIL: We grew a few plants in slightly acid and humus-rich soil, but one spring they failed to appear.

LOCATION AND EXPOSURE: We grew the mountain lady's-slipper in

83

high open shade with yellow lady's slippers and trilliums.

PLANTING TIME: While dormant in spring or fall.

ROOT SYSTEM: Fibrous stringy roots and medium rootstock.

PLANTING DEPTH AND SPACING: Set the rhizome about 1 inch deep with the base of the dormant bud ½ to 1 inch below soil level and the root tips tapering slightly downward somewhat lower than the base of the shoot.

PLANTING STOCK AND PROPAGATION: Use wild stock transplanted to the nursery and grown one or more years, or collected stock if it is available.

I have never tried scattering the seeds.

COMMENTS: The pouches of the mountain lady's-slipper are very similar in shape to those of the yellow lady's slipper and are slightly larger than those of the small white lady's-slipper. In fact, I can see little difference between this species and the small white lady's-slipper except that the mountain lady's-slipper tends to become dormant in August.

Cypripedium candidum • small white lady's-slipper

DESCRIPTION: 6 to 10 inches tall. The flowers are small white pouches (or slippers) with a faint bluish tint. The stems are leafy.

The small white lady's-slipper is very rare. It is supposedly found near lake shores, but I have not been fortunate enough to find a single specimen in the wild. A few years ago a man from southern Wisconsin brought me two plants which he had found in an abandoned pasture where there was ample moisture.

PERIOD OF BLOOM: Early June.

SOIL: My small white lady's-slippers grow in neutral to slightly acid soil (pH around 6), rich in humus. They thrive where yellow and showy lady's-slippers grow.

LOCATION AND EXPOSURE: We grow our few specimens with dainty oak fern in open woodland with high intermittent shade. Each plant has formed a clump, which indicates that this location is satisfactory.

PLANTING TIME: While dormant in spring or fall, preferably fall.

ROOT SYSTEM: Small rhizomes with medium-sized, stringy roots.

This species, like the yellow lady's-slipper, has a tendency to work its way downward. The roots of our plants are 1½ inches deep.

PLANTING DEPTH AND SPACING: Set the rhizomes about 1 inch deep with the base of the dormant bud ¾ to 1 inch below soil level and the root tips slightly downward, a little deeper than the base of the shoot. We use very old decaying oat straw for mulch.

PLANTING STOCK AND PROPAGATION: Nursery-grown stock obtained from divisions is the only kind I have ever seen offered, and even that is seldom available. Collected stock is not available since the plant is very rare.

Our plants have not set seed; the blossoms usually blast right after blooming.

COMMENTS: This lady's-slipper is similar to the yellow in its growth habits but is not as rugged. The small white lady's-slipper should only be planted if you can give it a perfect home.

In the yellow lady's-slipper bed, near but not in the planted row, I found a white lady's-slipper flushed with blue. I have no idea where it came from but I like to think a seed germinated and brought this prize to my wild garden.

ARISTOLOCHIACEAE [Birthwort Family]

Asarum canadense • wild ginger

DESCRIPTION: 4 to 6 inches tall. The handsome leaves are light green and heart-shaped. They hide tiny flowers that resemble little brown stone crocks. The flowers are maroon flushed with soft gray-green on the outside.

Wild ginger inhabits dense, rich woods and partly shaded areas where grass is sparse. It grows in large colonies among rocks in deciduous woods.

PERIOD OF BLOOM: May into June. Blossoms are long-lasting.

SOIL: Woods soil rich in humus is preferable, but I have grown wild ginger with success in fertile garden soil that is neutral to slightly acid.

LOCATION AND EXPOSURE: Wild ginger is an excellent groundcover

85

to plant between taller wildflowers in a woodland region. I have several patches that have formed dense mats on the north side of a stone wall. Under an oak tree another colony is rapidly covering a large area. The plants are near a water pump and often get extra water; the soil is quite dry otherwise.

PLANTING TIME: While dormant in spring or fall.

ROOT SYSTEM: A creeping rootstock forms roots at the nodes and forks as it creeps along. The rhizomes have a spicy, ginger-like fragrance and are pleasant to dig up.

PLANTING DEPTH AND SPACING: Plant the rhizomes horizontally about ½ inch deep, easing the tip to soil level. Make certain to tuck in all the roots along the stolon. Mulch in fall.

PLANTING STOCK AND PROPAGATION: Use nursery-grown or quality collected stock.

Divide the creeping rootstocks, especially where patches have become crowded. Cuttings taken after bloom form roots easily. Seeds are hard to collect, but wild ginger self-sows readily where the earth is constantly moist.

COMMENTS: An old gardener once told me that this plant depends entirely on slugs for pollination. In my garden the chipmunks carry the coarse seeds away and plant them at odd intervals. Wild ginger volunteers in the nursery in the most precarious places. The Indians used the spicy rhizomes for seasoning.

Aristolochia macrophylla • Dutchman's-pipe

DESCRIPTION: A 10 foot vine that entwines itself around nearby plants. The heart-shaped leaves usually grow in pairs along the stem. The brownish purple flower is a 1 inch tube shaped much like an old-time pipe with a flare at the top.

Although it grows naturally in rich, moist woods in regions much farther south, Dutchman's-pipe will grow hardily as far north as Wisconsin, though it may have scant bloom.

PERIOD OF BLOOM: May into June.

SOIL: Woods soil rich in humus, neutral to only slightly acid.

LOCATION AND EXPOSURE: Grow Dutchman's-pipe in open shade. Choose a spot where it can climb on taller flowers or on a support. It will attach itself to anything within reach.

PLANTING TIME: While dormant in fall.

ROOT SYSTEM: Fibrous orange roots and a sturdy rootstock.

PLANTING DEPTH AND SPACING: Space 3 feet or more apart. Set the next year's basal shoot just below soil level.

PLANTING STOCK AND PROPAGATION: Use nursery-grown or quality collected stock.

With age, the Dutchman's-pipe develops a woody stem. It might be possible to grow new plants from soft-wood cuttings, as one can with honeysuckles and bittersweet.

Seeds may be sown as soon as they ripen.

COMMENTS: I grew Dutchman's-pipe only as a novelty and was surprised to find that it had clambered onto a nearby wild cherry.

PORTULACACEAE [Purslane Family]

Claytonia virginica · spring beauty

DESCRIPTION: 4 to 6 inches tall. This plant often grows in a reclining position. A small cluster of dainty, starlike flowers rests at the end of a fragile stem. The flowers are white or delicate pink, with darker pink to rose-colored veining. The entire plant is succulent.

Spring beauty is found in moist open woods, usually with deep leafmold. As a child I remember picking the flowers along a woodland stream where they literally carpeted the earth with their fragile beauty.

PERIOD OF BLOOM: May.

SOIL: Humus-rich, moist woods soil is best, but I also grow them in drier woodland soil where there is plentiful moisture during their bloom period. The soil may be neutral to only slightly acid, but humus content is more important than pH.

LOCATION AND EXPOSURE: Grow spring beauty in the high open shade of soft maples, aspens, birches, or elms, where the sun filters through leafless trees in spring. Interplant with oak fern, as spring beauty soon disappears after blooming.

PLANTING TIME: As soon as dormant into fall.

ROOT SYSTEM: A tiny, dark-colored tuber shaped much like a potato, with many tiny eyes protruding.

PLANTING DEPTH AND SPACING: Set the tubers 2 to 3 inches deep. Space 4 to 6 inches apart or plant in small colonies.

PLANTING STOCK AND PROPAGATION: Use nursery-grown stock or quality collected stock of good size.

Seeds are difficult to collect. Sow them as soon as they ripen. Spring beauty self-sows readily in the wild.

COMMENTS: This little charmer is excellent in a rock garden among small ferns that will stay green when it becomes dormant.

RANUNCULACEAE [Crowfoot Family]

Thalictrum dioicum • early meadowrue

DESCRIPTION: 1 to 2 feet tall. Greenish yellow to mauve airy panicles are held above compound leaves with many divisions.

In rich dry woodlands early meadowrue grows in colonies, making a lovely display.

PERIOD OF BLOOM: June.

SOIL: Humus-rich woods soil or fertile, slightly acid garden soil.

LOCATION AND EXPOSURE: Plant early meadowrue in open shade or along the edge of a woodland area where it is exposed to the early morning sun. It is an excellent substitute for ferns in regions where the soil is dry or there is a great deal of sun or wind. The foliage is sturdy and makes a fine groundcover when it is scattered in colonies either in semishaded areas or in full sun if moisture is unfluctuating.

PLANTING TIME: While dormant in spring or fall.

ROOT SYSTEM: Fibrous. The parent plant dies and forms two or more new offsets which will become parent plants the following year.

PLANTING DEPTH AND SPACING: Plant with the crown at soil level and mulch if you wish. Space 1 to 2 feet apart. The new shoots are purple when first emerging in springtime.

PLANTING STOCK AND PROPAGATION: Use nursery-grown stock or divisions of offsets collected in fall or early spring, or freshly dug collected stock. Remove all old roots before replanting.

Seeds should be sown as soon as they ripen. Early meadowrue

self-sows readily, especially if there is crumbly humus on the forest floor. Seedlings bloom the third year.

COMMENTS: A good plant to grow for the texture of its foliage and for its airy flowers. I stress the use of early meadowrue as a substitute for ferns where soil is not moist enough for ferns.

The seeds are held in the airy panicles. Male and female flowers grow on separate plants, so that not all plants will set seed. The male meadowrue has greenish yellow blossoms, while the female has an additional tinge of mauve.

Thalictrum polygamum • tall meadowrue

DESCRIPTION: 3 to 4 feet tall. Large plumes of airy white are held above divided, compound foliage on stout, hollow stems. Occasionally a bold lavender plume appears.

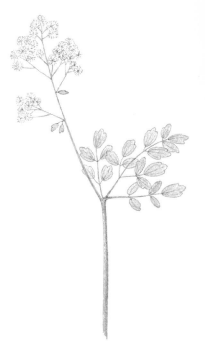

Tall meadowrue is found along brooks, in wet meadows, and along roadside ditches where it displays its beauty in full sun. It grows taller in very wet places.

PERIOD OF BLOOM: Late June into August.

SOIL: Use fertile, slightly acid soil, wet or of average moisture. When grown in ordinary garden soil that is not wet, the plant may not be as tall as it is in the wild but the flowers will be just as beautiful.

LOCATION AND EXPOSURE: Tall meadowrue grows best in full sun, but it will grow in partial shade and still flower. In the wild, it is found among Joe-pye and swamp milkweed.

PLANTING TIME: While dormant in spring or fall.

ROOT SYSTEM: Fibrous. Each year after blooming, new offsets form at the base of the parent plant which then dies, leaving the new shoots to produce the next year's flowers.

PLANTING DEPTH AND SPACING: Set plants with the crown at soil level and mulch. Space plants at least 12 to 18 inches apart. Tall meadowrue does not make as dense a clump of foliage as does early meadowrue, but if the flowers and stalks are cut to the ground new growth soon appears.

PLANTING STOCK AND PROPAGATION: Use nursery-grown stock or freshly dug collected stock.

Divide offsets while dormant in spring or fall. Plant seeds as soon as they ripen. Seed germination is much slower than that of the early meadowrue. Often many of the seeds will not germinate until the second year.

COMMENTS: Tall meadowrue is a bold wildflower that commands attention wherever it grows. Plant it next to water where its beauty can be reflected. I grow it beside our pool with *Gentiana Saponaria* and *Lobelia Cardinalis*.

Anemonella thalictroides • rue anemone

DESCRIPTION: 4 to 6 inches tall. In late April, little red stems with folded rose-colored foliage appear through the leafmold. Shortly after some warm spring morning rain, clusters of flowers resembling the hepatica appear. They are held above a lacy spread of foliage resembling meadowrue. The flowers are fragile and come in shades of pink and white; their petals have a quality like fine china.

Rue anemone grows in protected woodlands in high open shade, often among other wildflowers.

PERIOD OF BLOOM: Early May into June. The flowers are long-lasting.

SOIL: Neutral to slightly acid soil, rich in humus.

LOCATION AND EXPOSURE: Open shade with filtered sunlight in a spot protected from strong winds. Plant rue anemone along a partly shaded path, in little colonies among small rocks, or with late wildflowers such as the showy lady's-slipper.

PLANTING TIME: Summer into late fall after the plants go dormant. Rue anemone can be transplanted in spring, even when in flower, but I prefer fall planting.

ROOT SYSTEM: A cluster of tubers resembling those of the dahlia in miniature.

PLANTING DEPTH AND SPACING: Plant tubers about 1 inch deep. Space 4 inches apart or plant closer together in small patches. Mulch with old marsh hay or with small leaves such as birch or willow. Oak leaves are too coarse and tend to smother the plants.

PLANTING STOCK AND PROPAGATION: Use nursery-grown stock.

Propagation may be by division of clusters after bloom, but this is a touchy job, as each tuber must have an eye.

Sow seeds as soon as they ripen; this requires close watching. Seedlings usually do not bloom until the third year.

COMMENTS: The flowering period of this dainty flower is four to six weeks. The plants then set seed and quickly become dormant. I marvel at the capacity of such small tubers to bloom so profusely over such a long period of time.

There is a double pink rue anemone known as Schaaf's double pink. It is lovely, and blossoms last a month.

Hepatica americana • hepatica

DESCRIPTION: 3 to 4 inches tall. In early spring, bouquets of single flowers with individual stems appear from the center of a clump of last year's foliage. The foliage is round-lobed and leathery, wine colored on the underside. The flowers are white or pastel shades of blue and purple. A pink color is the rarest. (I once found a pale yellow hepatica which never grew larger or set seed.) Colors vary with the pH of the soil. As the flowers fade, new furry leaves appear and soon grow to maturity.

In aspen and soft maple woodlands rich in leafmold, colonies of hepaticas suddenly appear in the spring morning sunlight. On cloudy days the flowers do not open. In my area hepaticas are also found on shady slopes, along streams, and in rocky terrain.

PERIOD OF BLOOM: Late April into May.

SOIL: Slightly acid, humus-rich soil is preferable, but I have found it growing nicely in sandy loam and in the black heavy soil of river bottoms.

LOCATION AND EXPOSURE: An excellent flower for open woodlands, or anywhere it is exposed to the morning sun. Hepaticas make a superior groundcover when grown in large colonies or among other wildflowers of equal height.

PLANTING TIME: Early spring or fall.

ROOT SYSTEM: Fibrous. Clumps enlarge with age.

PLANTING DEPTH AND SPACING: Space 8 to 12 inches apart. Plant the crowns at about soil level with the shoots just barely above the earth. Mulch with old straw or small leaves, tucking the mulch around and beneath the foliage. Later in the season (about October), scatter leaves or a little marsh hay to protect the foliage from freezing rain, especially if the bed is in a place where winter sunscald might occur. In spring, pull the mulch away from where the plants have sprouted, but leave some mulch between

91

the plants. The mulch can be used again later for the self-sowing process which follows.

PLANTING STOCK AND PROPAGATION: Use nursery-grown stock or quality collected stock.

Divide the clumps in fall, but you will find they are slow to increase. When dividing a clump, it is best to leave two or three buds in each division. Clumps can be moved with soil adhering right after blooming and before new leaves have completely developed. This method is the quickest way to establish a showy colony.

Sow the seeds in flats or in the open as soon as they ripen. Cover with a thin layer of old mulch. To promote self-sowing, wait until the plants have stopped blooming and the fruit has reached the stage where they start to bend the stems; new leaves will be little bundles of fuzz. Then cover the entire bed with a light dressing of marsh hay to discourage chipmunks from raiding the seed supply. A good sprinkling of water will settle the hay, and soon new leaves will sprout through the mulch. The seeds will fall into the old mulch, and in a few years the colony of hepaticas will be heavily populated with flowering plants. If thinning is necessary, some plants can be moved in the fall of the second or third year.

COMMENTS: Most hepaticas have eight petals, but occasionally you may find some with twelve to eighteen. I call these semi-doubles. There is a true double form, which is rare.

Hepatica acutiloba is identical with *Hepatica americana* except that the foliage lobes are acute instead of round. I have found the two growing in the same environment, which indicates that their growth requirements are the same.

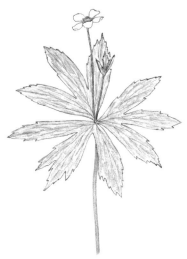

Anemone canadensis • Canada anemone

DESCRIPTION: 1 to 2 feet tall. Pure white, single flowers with prominent golden centers are held above lanced foliage. The foliage is quite similar to that of the cranesbill geranium.

The Canada anemone is found in moist sunny meadows, along lakes and streams, and beside roadside ditches, often blanketing the whole area in glistening white.

PERIOD OF BLOOM: Late May into July if there is ample moisture.

SOIL: Reasonably fertile soil that is damp or has constant moisture. Otherwise it is adaptable and will spread readily to form colonies.

LOCATION AND EXPOSURE: The Canada anemone is best grown in moist sunny areas where it can spread without restriction. Full sun is preferable, but it will tolerate partial shade.

PLANTING TIME: While dormant in spring or fall. It can also be moved in spring when only a leaf or two has developed.

ROOT SYSTEM: Very slender, almost threadlike, dark rhizomes which often pause to send up several new crowns and then travel on to repeat the process. Rhizomes spread quickly under ideal conditions.

PLANTING DEPTH AND SPACING: Space the rhizomes 6 to 12 inches apart. Plant them not more than ½ inch deep with the eye at soil level. Mulch the area with weathered marsh hay, old straw, or leave bare to weed. Mulch helps to retain moisture in soil.

PLANTING STOCK AND PROPAGATION: Use nursery-grown stock or quality collected stock.

Divide matted clumps in spring or fall.

Each blossom produces a burrlike fruit. As soon as the seeds ripen, sow them in a flat or in a moist open area. Seedlings usually bloom the third year.

COMMENTS: Canada anemone is a vigorous grower and must be restricted in a small garden. Set a few plants in a bottomless gallon can and cut the fruit before the seeds ripen. The pure white blossoms complement the colors of other flowers in the wild garden.

Anemone quinquefolia • wood anemone

DESCRIPTION: 3 to 6 inches tall. The leaves of the wood anemone are thrice-divided and compound. A short stem bears a single flower, white inside, with outside color varying from rose to purple.

Wood anemone congregates in colonies in sheltered, open woods, often making a carpet of color.

PERIOD OF BLOOM: May into June.

SOIL: Slightly acid, rich woods soil. I have also grown it under a grape arbor where the garden soil was moderately fertile.

93

LOCATION AND EXPOSURE: The wood anemone is an ideal ground-cover mixed with taller flowers in an open shaded woods. This small flower should be grown in masses for best effect.

PLANTING TIME: Potted stock can be planted anytime during the growing season. Sods and bare rootstock should be planted very early in spring or in fall.

ROOT SYSTEM: A very brittle, cinnamon colored rhizome which forks and sends up new shoots.

PLANTING DEPTH AND SPACING: Space potted stock 6 inches apart, setting the pot at soil level. Sods should be planted at the same level and spaced 1 foot apart. Bareroot stock should be planted 1 inch deep and 4 to 6 inches apart. All should be mulched with an airy mulch to a depth of an inch or so.

PLANTING STOCK AND PROPAGATION: Nursery-grown potted stock is best.

Seeds ripen quickly and when sown immediately after ripening will produce flowering plants in three or sometimes four years. The blossoms produce burrlike fruit similar to but smaller than those of the Canada anemone.

COMMENTS: This delicate little plant is very persistent. Where we cleared an area of woodland to add to our lawn, the wood anemone continued to appear despite frequent mowing.

Anemone patens • pasque flower

DESCRIPTION: 4 to 6 inches tall. This variety of the pasque flower (*Wolfgangiana*) has a large, single, lavender-blue flower at the top of the foliage. The color may vary; creamy white ones are rare. The foliage is divided, heavily cut, and mostly basal—often there is one small leaf on each stalk. The flowers are soon replaced by a silky plume which bears the seed and quickly disappears.

The pasque flower inhabits dry prairies and sunny slopes where it carpets the earth with color.

PERIOD OF BLOOM: April into May.

SOIL: A neutral or sandy, slightly fertile loam is ideal. Moisture is important at time of bloom, but the plant can stand considerable drought thereafter.

LOCATION AND EXPOSURE: Grow the pasque flower in open areas

where a splash of early spring color is desired. Good drainage is important.

PLANTING TIME: While dormant in very early spring or fall.

ROOT SYSTEM: A vigorous diffused root system in which many of the fibrous roots become fleshy and send out secondary roots in search of food. All pieces of root more than ⅛ inch in diameter left in the ground will produce new plants.

PLANTING DEPTH AND SPACING: Space 1 to 2 feet apart or plant at random among scattered old rocks in a prairie area. Set the plants with the crown 1 inch deep in very cold climates to protect them from alternate thawing and freezing in spring. It is best to mulch for winter.

PLANTING STOCK AND PROPAGATION: Use nursery-grown stock. Quality collected stock also does well, but pasque flower is on the protected list in most areas.

Two-inch root cuttings give quick results for propagation. Insert the cuttings in a rooting medium and keep them slightly moist. Divide large plants in very early spring.

Seeds sown in spring germinate readily. Transplant the seedlings to their permanent location the following spring. The seedlings will bloom the spring after they have been moved and will quickly grow to maturity.

COMMENTS: Prairie smoke is a good companion for the pasque flower, as it will grow under the same conditions. The two contrast well in foliage and flower, and make an interesting display. Goldfinches steal the seeds of both species before they ripen. Cover the silky plumes with wire cages to protect the seed crop.

Anemone pulsatilla • pasque flower

DESCRIPTION: 8 to 10 inches tall. The flower stalks are raised above a carpet of much-divided basal foliage. *Anemone patens* and *Anemone pulsatilla* are often spoken of as the same plant, but there is a considerable difference when they are seen growing side by side. The foliage of the latter is silkier when emerging in spring, the flowers are deeper in color, the bloom period is longer, and the silky plumes are showier and last longer. The flowers of the *Anemone pulsatilla* range from purple-blue to wine-

95

purple and from lavender to creamy white. Flowers and silky plumes appear on the plant at the same time. The white flowers have greenish plumes; the colored flowers have plumes with a hint of purple.

The *Anemone pulsatilla,* like *Anemone patens,* grows in dry prairies and sunny exposed slopes, carpeting the earth with color.

PERIOD OF BLOOM: April into June. When cultivated, the plant occasionally sends up a blossom at any time during the summer.

SOIL: Use either a gritty or a sandy loam soil that is fertile. Good drainage is important. Established plants can stand drought.

LOCATION AND EXPOSURE: This pasque flower is an excellent plant to use for edging along a sunny border. The foliage is good throughout the summer and into fall. Each spring the flowers burst into glorious bloom, and the silky plumes last long into summer.

PLANTING TIME: While dormant in very early spring or fall.

ROOT SYSTEM: A vigorous diffused root system. Many of the fibrous roots become fleshy and send out secondary roots in search of nutrients. All root pieces more than ⅛ inch in diameter left in the ground produce new plants.

PLANTING DEPTH AND SPACING: Space 1 to 2 feet apart, depending on the desired effect. Set the plants with the crowns 1 to 2 inches deep, depending on the size of the plant. This protects the plants from alternate thawing and freezing in spring. I find that no mulch is needed when they are planted in spring.

PLANTING STOCK AND PROPAGATION: Nursery-grown stock of medium size is best and easiest to transplant. Also use quality collected stock when it is available, but this pasque flower is on the protected list.

To propagate, 2 inch root cuttings give quick results. You can divide large plants in spring, but I get better results by planting seedlings.

Seeds sown in spring germinate readily. Transplant the seedlings after one year. They will bloom the second year and rapidly become showy specimens.

COMMENTS: The pasque flower is one of the earliest spring flowers. Every gardener will want this choice plant with its vibrant colors and silky plumes. Goldfinches and other birds are attracted by the ripening plumes.

Caltha palustris • marsh marigold

DESCRIPTION: 12 to 18 inches tall. The marsh marigold has lightly toothed round basal foliage, hollow stems, and single, glistening yellow flowers with showy centers.

Marsh marigold is found growing along brooks, in roadside ditches with standing water, in swamps, and in sunny meadows. In spring it transforms large areas into patches of gold, but by midsummer the plant has almost disappeared.

PERIOD OF BLOOM: May.

SOIL: Use very fertile slightly acid or neutral soil that is wet or has constant moisture. The marsh marigold will grow in drier areas if enough water is supplied during the growing period.

LOCATION AND EXPOSURE: Full sun or high open shade. The marsh marigold is a fine plant for naturalizing along a brook or near a pool. Always grow it with other plants that retain their foliage. Use a mulch if you are growing the plant in an exposed area.

PLANTING TIME: After spring blooms; the plant will remain dormant into fall.

ROOT SYSTEM: An extensive, very coarse and fibrous, stringy root.

PLANTING DEPTH AND SPACING: Space 1 to 2 feet apart. Spread the roots evenly with the crown set at soil level.

PLANTING STOCK AND PROPAGATION: Use nursery-grown or quality collected stock.

Divide clumps after the plants bloom. As soon as seeds ripen, sow them in a wet place or in a container where the soil can be kept moist. Seedlings sometimes bloom the second year.

COMMENTS: Surprisingly, one rarely sees the pretty marsh marigold growing in the wildflower garden. Its color makes an interesting contrast with other spring wildflowers. It is also known as the cowslip, and is often gathered as a pot herb.

Coptis groenlandica • goldthread

DESCRIPTION: 3 to 4 inches tall. The evergreen foliage of the goldthread is toothed, thrice-parted and glossy. It resembles the barren strawberry. The plant has wiry stems holding dainty single white flowers just above the foliage.

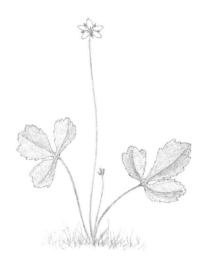

I have seen goldthread literally carpet the floor of evergreen forests. In late autumn the evergreen needles form a light blanket to protect the plants against inclement winter weather. It grows among bunchberry, pink lady's-slipper, wintergreen, and clintonia.

PERIOD OF BLOOM: May into June.

SOIL: Acid to slightly acid humus-rich soil that is wet to slightly damp.

LOCATION AND EXPOSURE: Open or deep shade. Goldthread is an excellent groundcover; it forms a carpet of glossy green.

PLANTING TIME: Spring or fall. Plant potted stock anytime.

ROOT SYSTEM: A dainty, threadlike, creeping rhizome with fine, sparse hair roots. It is bright yellow and forks at frequent intervals. It is easily identified.

PLANTING DEPTH AND SPACING: Set potted stock or collected stock at soil level and mulch lightly, preferably with pine needles. Space in small colonies a few inches apart or plant at random.

PLANTING STOCK AND PROPAGATION: Nursery-grown potted stock is much the best, but you can also use quality collected sods. Bareroot stock dries out too quickly.

Seeds are hard to collect. Sow them in acid to slightly acid soil that can be kept moist.

COMMENTS: Goldthread is a most unusual and admirable groundcover to use with larger plants that grow in acid to slightly acid soils. It can be used as an extensive carpeting under evergreens, where grass cannot grow. Goldthread is an outstanding plant, one of my favorites.

Aquilegia canadensis • wild columbine

DESCRIPTION: 2 to 3 feet tall. Drooping flowers have yellow and scarlet corollas. The coarsely divided compound foliage is mostly basal.

In rough, rocky terrain you will find wild columbine growing at odd angles, sometimes precariously perched among rocks where soil is scarce, but its roots reach deep into the earth. It is also found along the borders of open woods or along roadsides.

PERIOD OF BLOOM: May into June.

SOIL: Any slightly acid to neutral soil with good drainage. Sandy loam is preferable.

LOCATION AND EXPOSURE: Columbine grows readily at the edge of a woodland or a partly shaded hillside. It is equally at home in the rock garden, or in a sunny border with other flowers. Plant the columbine where you want it to stay, as old roots do not move readily.

PLANTING TIME: Early spring (before the new growth is 1 inch high), or in fall while dormant.

ROOT SYSTEM: A fleshy, brittle root, gray to black. Large crowns do not divide readily and have a tendency to be short-lived when divided.

PLANTING DEPTH AND SPACING: Space 1 to 2 feet apart and set crowns at soil level. In the rock garden, place some rocks over the root area after planting.

PLANTING STOCK AND PROPAGATION: Young nursery-grown stock is far superior to collected stock. If you use collected stock, it must be young, as old roots are too gnarled to be moved successfully.

Seeds sown in the garden or in flats produce seedlings that bloom in the second year. Sow the seeds as soon as they are ripe or in fall. Columbine self-sows readily when growing where the earth is bare.

COMMENTS: Our native columbine is an easy wildflower to grow, and one of outstanding beauty. When the blossoms sway in a breeze they call to mind a group of skirted elves dancing to the music of rustling leaves. For a charming effect, try growing columbine in a rocky outcropping near a pool where it can be reflected in the water.

Cimicifuga americana • American bugbane

DESCRIPTION: 2 to 4 feet tall. American bugbane is similar to its sister plant, black cohosh, but it blooms later. It is a bold perennial with a few compound leaves on a long stalk. Its slender wand of creamy white flowers has a feathery elegance.

Bugbane is found in moist rock woods. Although its natural range is farther south and east, it has proved hardy in Wisconsin despite our bitter cold winters.

PERIOD OF BLOOM: Late August into September and often into October if not injured by frosts.

SOIL: Neutral to slightly acid soil rich in humus and with constant moisture.

LOCATION AND EXPOSURE: Grow bugbane in high shade or along a woods border where it can get only a small amount of morning sunlight. This species can be grown in full sunlight if the soil is rather moist. In areas where frost comes early, it is best planted in a sheltered spot near a foundation.

PLANTING TIME: While dormant in spring or fall.

ROOT SYSTEM: A knotted rootstock with wiry fibrous roots which develop new shoots with age.

PLANTING DEPTH AND SPACING: Space 2 feet or more apart. Spread the roots carefully so that new shoots will be about 1 inch below soil level. Mulch continuously. Bugbane is a good plant for specimen display when planted among rocks where leafmold is deep.

PLANTING STOCK AND PROPAGATION: Nursery-grown stock is much the best, but you can also use quality collected stock where available.

Divide clumps in spring or fall while the plant is dormant. Sow seeds as soon as they ripen. Seeds do not ripen as far north as Wisconsin.

COMMENTS: The white spires are lovely in autumn when few white flowers are blooming. This species blooms about the same time as the cultivated bugbanes offered as perennials under the names of *Cimicifuga simplex* and white pearl. There is a slight difference in foliage.

Cimicifuga racemosa • black cohosh

DESCRIPTION: 3 to 5 feet tall. The black cohosh has ample green foliage with much-divided leaves. Feathery racemes of tiny white flowers grow on tall wands.

Black cohosh is found in deep woodlands and along the borders or woods where the shade is open and the soil is humus-rich. I have also found it growing in river bottoms with *Trillium grandiflorum,* wild ginger, and patches of maidenhair fern. It grows very tall in shaded moist areas where the soil is deep.

PERIOD OF BLOOM: July into August.

SOIL: Fertile, acid to slightly acid humus-rich with an average-to-high moisture content. Good drainage is necessary.

LOCATION AND EXPOSURE: Black cohosh is best suited to a woodland garden in deep shade where branches are high overhead, or to a lightly shaded border. If exposed to sunlight for several hours a day, the white spires will be crooked and grow haphazardly instead of in a stately fashion. Black cohosh is striking when grown with a background of tall ferns among large rocks where humus is plentiful and mulch gathers each fall.

PLANTING TIME: While dormant in spring or fall. Plant black cohosh where you want it to remain, as it resists transplanting and usually does not bloom until the second or third year after being moved.

ROOT SYSTEM: A very knotted rhizome developing many eyes with age. Some of the rhizomes elongate and establish new plants.

PLANTING DEPTH AND SPACING: Space 2 to 4 feet apart. Set the plants with eyes 1 to 1½ inches below soil level. Mulch with leaves or other partly decayed humus. It requires a rich soil.

PLANTING STOCK AND PROPAGATION: Nursery stock is best because the plants have a heavier root system, but you can also use quality collected stock.

Divide the clumps, leaving two or more eyes in each division. Sow seeds in rich woodland soil as they ripen. Germination is slow and uneven. Seedlings usually do not bloom until the fourth year.

COMMENTS: Block cohosh is a bold wildflower, wonderful for the woodland garden or border. Its long-lasting spires are a welcome sight on hot summer days. But do not plant black cohosh where its oversweet odor will be offensive.

The beadlike wands which develop in the seed stage are excellent for dry floral arrangements. In my area black cohosh is known as fairy candles, which I think is a more appropriate name.

Actaea rubra • red baneberry

DESCRIPTION: 1½ to 2 feet tall. The red baneberry has compound toothed foliage and white flower clusters made up of many tiny flowers. A cluster of brilliant red, shiny berries appears in August and September.

101

The baneberry is found in rich woods where leafmold is deep and often where other wildflowers carpet the forest floor.

PERIOD OF BLOOM: Late May into June.

SOIL: Slightly acid, rich woods soil that is humus-rich and does not dry out.

LOCATION AND EXPOSURE: Plant under high branches where shade is open to deep. Baneberry contrasts well with royal, cinnamon, and maidenhair ferns or with white baneberries.

PLANTING TIME: While dormant in spring or fall.

ROOT SYSTEM: Coarse fibrous roots on a rootstock that develops many eyes with age.

PLANTING DEPTH AND SPACING: Plant the rootstock with eyes or new shoots about 1 inch below soil level. Mulch with leaves, old straw, or weathered marsh hay. Space 1½ to 2 feet apart or plant at odd intervals.

PLANTING STOCK AND PROPAGATION: Nursery-grown stock has a superior root system. Quality collected stock should have strong eyes.

If you divide clumps, leave two or more eyes in each division. Sow the seeds as soon as they ripen, as old seeds often remain dormant for over a year before germinating. Fresh seeds planted in fall should germinate the following spring. The seed bed must never dry out. Seedlings often bloom in the third year.

COMMENTS: All baneberry fruits are poisonous. The chipmunks steal the seeds and plant them, but I do not know if they eat any.

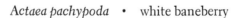

Actaea pachypoda • white baneberry

DESCRIPTION: About 2 feet tall. Each stalk bears a single white oblong flower cluster above toothed compound foliage. This flower head is replaced by a cluster of china white berries, each with a conspicuous black eye on a showy red stem, hence the common name "doll's eyes."

Red and white baneberries are often found growing together in rich woods in deep to moderate shade. But when growing alone, the white baneberry is usually found in a drier woodland.

PERIOD OF BLOOM: Flowers, late May into June. Berries, August into September.

SOIL: Slightly acid humus-rich soil. It must not dry out completely or the plant will become dormant that year.

LOCATION AND EXPOSURE: Baneberries must have some shade or their foliage will burn. Light to deep shade under high branches is ideal. Grow baneberries in groups of three or interplant them with ferns. Bloodroot will make nice carpeting in such an area if there is constant moisture.

PLANTING TIME: While dormant in spring or fall.

ROOT SYSTEM: Coarse fibrous roots on a rootstock that develops many new eyes with age. Old rootstocks show scars of previous growth.

PLANTING DEPTH AND SPACING: Space about 2 feet apart. Plant the roots with new shoots or eyes about 1 inch below soil level and mulch. For an outstanding effect, place several plants or a single large one in a shaded opening.

PLANTING STOCK AND PROPAGATION: Nursery-grown stock is best. Choose quality collected stock with prominent eyes.

Divide large clumps, leaving several eyes to each division.

Sow pulp-free seeds as soon as they ripen. The white baneberry seems to be slower to germinate than the red. Seedlings usually bloom the third year.

COMMENTS: The berries of the white baneberry are very attractive and provide a focal point in the wild garden. Occasionally the baneberries form hybrids. I have had several unusual white ones. A white baneberry seedling has pink berries, but the black eyes are missing. Another seedling has the doll's-eyes berries but is set apart from the others by its foliage, which is coarser, not quilted, and has a definite cast of blue-green.

Hydrastis canadensis • golden seal

DESCRIPTION: 6 to 12 inches tall. Golden seal looks something like a maple seedling, but is distinguished by a greenish white globelike flower head, a red-berried seed cluster in fall, and heavily veined leaves which have deeper lobes than those of the maple.

Golden seal is occasionally found in rich maple hardwoods and often in the company of ginseng. The plant is becoming very scarce in the wild.

PERIOD OF BLOOM: May.

SOIL: Humus-rich woods soil that is neutral to only slightly acid.

LOCATION AND EXPOSURE: Light to deep open shade. Golden seal is a good plant for the cool woodland garden where it can be planted in little colonies for a unique display.

PLANTING TIME: Early spring or fall, but with care golden seal can be moved earlier or later.

ROOT SYSTEM: A knotty yellow rhizome with many fibrous roots.

PLANTING DEPTH AND SPACING: Space 6 to 10 inches apart, preferably in little groups. Plant the rhizome ½ to 1 inch deep, depending on the size of the plant.

PLANTING STOCK AND PROPAGATION: Use nursery-grown stock. Quality collected stock is rare because golden seal has been ruthlessly dug up by collectors for its medicinal value.

To propagate by division, divide the rhizomes when the plant is dormant. To grow from seed, pick the berry as soon as it turns scarlet and separate the seeds from the pulp. Sow the seeds in a selected spot where the loose leafmold has been raked to one side. Cover lightly. The seeds will stratify by themselves. Keep the bed moist at all times. Germination can be slow unless conditions are ideal.

To grow by layering, cut the roots into ¼ to ½ inch pieces, leaving the fine hair-roots intact. Put the cuttings in a box in layers with a mixture of sandy loam and sharp sand separating them. Keep them moist but not wet. Put the box in a frost-free place or in the basement over winter. Most pieces will have new plants in about six months. Cuttings put down in November are ready to plant in the open in early spring. Set the new plants barely ½ inch deep and mulch lightly, preferably with leafmold or with old decaying mulch.

My own method is to cut the roots up into pieces of ¼ to ½ inch and layer them in damp sphagnum moss in a plastic bag. I tie the bag and put it in the well pit, which is frost-free. In spring, most of the cuttings are ready to plant. New plants are formed on the cuttings. I get very good results.

COMMENTS: Golden seal derives its name from the golden color of its roots. At one time it was grown commercially in some areas of Wisconsin for its medicinal value as an alterative and tonic.

BERBERIDACEAE [Barberry Family]

Jeffersonia diphylla • twinleaf

DESCRIPTION: 8 to 10 inches tall. A single white hepaticalike flower which is short-lived and produces yellow-green seed capsules with green "lids." The flower rests on a stalk with two leaves rising from the base. Each leaf is like a pair of outstretched bird's wings. After the flower withers both the foliage and the stalk continue to grow, hiding the seed capsule.

Twinleaf is found in open deciduous woods where the soil is humus-rich. It is not found in my immediate area of Wisconsin.

PERIOD OF BLOOM: May into June.

SOIL: Neutral to moderately acid soil with an abundance of humus.

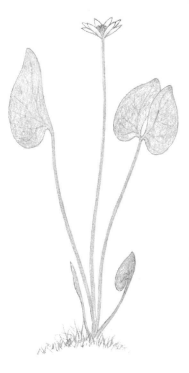

LOCATION AND EXPOSURE: Grow twinleaf in partial to open shade, or plant in colonies like hepaticas. The foliage makes an excellent contrast with other plants.

PLANTING TIME: While dormant in spring or fall.

ROOT SYSTEM: A heavy rootstock with many coarse, fibrous, slightly wavy roots that are light tan.

PLANTING DEPTH AND SPACING: Space 6 to 8 inches apart when planted among groundcover or in colonies. Or plant at random to accent the foliage.

PLANTING STOCK AND PROPAGATION: Nursery-grown stock is huskier, but also use quality collected stock.

Divide clumps in fall. Sow seeds as soon as they ripen. Seedlings are slow to reach the flowering stage.

COMMENTS: Twinleaf is grown for its interesting foliage. The leaves resemble a pair of bird's wings poised for flight.

The seeds form in rows in a capsule shaped like a miniature inverted pear. The top of the capsule has a flap like a coin purse horizontally zipped. It is a unique plant.

Caulophyllum thalictroides • blue cohosh

DESCRIPTION: 1 to 3 feet tall. Tiny flowers in drooping clusters grow above coarsely cut blue-green foliage with blunt lobes. The flowers are green to greenish yellow, often with a red tinge. In August, striking, bright blue berries and white blooms vie for attention.

Blue cohosh is found growing in rich, rocky woods and well-drained river bottoms, usually with red baneberry, black cohosh, and *Trillium grandiflorum* under a canopy of soft maples, basswoods or elms.

PERIOD OF BLOOM: May.

SOIL: Neutral to slightly acid fertile soil with a moderate supply of constant moisture. Blue cohosh will also grow in drier woods with a good mulching to retain moisture.

LOCATION AND EXPOSURE: Light to deep high shade. You can alternate blue cohosh with mertensia to fill in the bare spots when mertensia becomes dormant. The foliage contrasts well with tall ferns. When grown with red baneberry, the colors of the berries contrast strikingly.

PLANTING TIME: While dormant in spring or fall; fall is preferable.

ROOT SYSTEM: A sturdy, angled rootstock with coarse, slightly wavy, fibrous roots. It develops many eyes with age.

PLANTING DEPTH AND SPACING: Space 1½ or more feet apart. The plant forms a clump with age, becoming very showy. Spread the roots carefully when planting and have the new shoots about 1 inch below soil level. Keep covered with a mulch of leaves or decaying straw.

PLANTING STOCK AND PROPAGATION: Nursery-grown stock has a better developed root system than collected stock, but also use freshly dug collected stock.

Divide clumps, leaving two to three eyes in each division. Plant the seeds as soon as they ripen in humus-rich woods soil kept constantly moist. Often two to four years pass before the seeds germinate, but the process can be hastened by filing a nick in each seed. Seedlings often commence blooming the third year.

COMMENTS: The blue berries and the handsome foliage of the blue cohosh provide a fine contrast with other plants, and will enhance the beauty and charm of any shaded area in a wildflower garden.

Podophyllum peltatum • mayapple

DESCRIPTION: 12 to 18 inches tall. Two umbrella-shaped, round-lobed leaves hide a single creamy-white waxy flower on a solitary stalk. The flower has a lovely fragrance and produces yellow fruit in August, which is edible.

Mayapples carpet large areas under deciduous trees in moist open woods. They also grow in thickets and in dense shade, though not as abundantly.

PERIOD OF BLOOM: Late May into June.

SOIL: Neutral to slightly acid soil very rich in humus or leafmold.

LOCATION AND EXPOSURE: Mayapple blooms more often when planted in open shade, but it will also grow in denser shade where the woods are cool. I find that it is best grown in colonies where it carpets forest floors under a canopy of deciduous trees. Or try planting it randomly in a rocky woodland for a most unusual effect. It grows vigorously and makes an excellent ground-cover for large shady areas.

To enjoy mayapple in a small garden it is best to restrict it to a limited area. Plant one or two rhizomes in a bottomless gallon can sunk at soil level; when the plants begin to crowd the container, remove all the rhizomes and start anew.

PLANTING TIME: Fall is preferred.

PLANTING DEPTH AND SPACING: Set the stocky horizontal rhizome about 1 to 1½ inches deep with the tip leading to soil level. Space 1 foot or more apart.

ROOT SYSTEM: The rhizome is coarse, about as thick as a lead pencil, and pale tan in color. It pauses often to fork and send up new growth.

PLANTING STOCK AND PROPAGATION: Nursery-grown stock is best. If you buy collected stock make certain that the rhizome has an eye and is not just a piece.

Sow seeds in autumn. I have had little luck growing it from seed and find that root division in fall is easiest.

COMMENTS: Mayapples are best grown in spacious, shaded woodlands. The fruit was once popular in traditional American cooking; the rootstock is poisonous.

107

PAPAVERACEAE [Poppy Family]

Sanguinaria canadensis • bloodroot

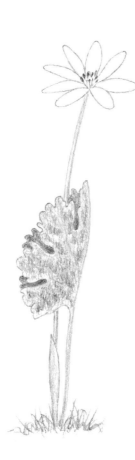

DESCRIPTION: 6 to 9 inches tall. A starlike, fragile blossom with 8 petals rests on a solitary stem. This short-lived flower is white with a yellow center. There is a rare double form and also a semidouble. The large, deeply lobed leaves are pale green with lighter green underneath.

Bloodroot is found in rich woods or in thickets on river bottoms where the leafmold is deep. It frequently grows in the vicinity of *Trillium grandiflorum*.

PERIOD OF BLOOM: Late April into May, depending on when spring arrives and whether there is enough filtered sunlight to warm the ground.

SOIL: The pH is not important, but good humus content and moisture are necessary.

LOCATION AND EXPOSURE: Bloodroot grows best in a sheltered woodland where spring sunshine filters through leafless trees, and where it will later be protected from the strong summer sun. After blooming, the leaves continue to develop and make good groundcover for large areas that do not dry out. In dry woodlands bloodroot becomes dormant in August. Interplant in colonies with clumps of maidenhair fern for continuous groundcover.

PLANTING TIME: Fall planting is preferable, but bloodroot can be moved in spring if growth is not too far advanced.

ROOT SYSTEM: A forking salmon-colored rhizome that oozes red juice when broken, hence the name bloodroot.

PLANTING DEPTH AND SPACING: Space 6 inches or more apart. Plant the rhizome horizontally ½ to 1 inch deep with the budded tip leading to soil level. Mulch continually with decaying leaves or old straw.

PLANTING STOCK AND PROPAGATION: Multiple-crown nursery stock gives the best results, even blooming the first year after transplanting. Also use quality collected stock.

Divide crowded rhizomes. Seeds must be sown as soon as they are harvested, before the caruncle (the little white attached portion) has a chance to dry out. If the caruncle dries out, the seed will stay dormant for a year. This is true of all seeds having caruncles.

Seedlings often bloom the third year.

COMMENTS: The very rare double white form, which does not set seed, was first found in the wilds of lower Michigan and was taken to the Netherlands where it is now grown for export to the United States. Like its single-petaled kin, the double blood-root flower closes each sundown, its petals resembling hands folded in prayer. The white peonylike flowers last about a week and then quickly disappear.

Stylophorum diphyllum · celandine poppy

DESCRIPTION: 10 to 15 inches tall. A showy, deep yellow flower with four petals is supported by a slender, leafy stem. The gray-green oblong foliage is mostly basal and unevenly lobed. The seed pod is oblong, with a rough outer cover and droops on the stem.

Celandine poppy inhabits rich woods where the soil is fertile and damp in spring.

PERIOD OF BLOOM: May into June. The plants produce an occasional flower at any time during the summer if they are grown in a reasonably damp area and do not dry out.

SOIL: Fertile soil, preferably rich in humus, that does not dry out completely. The plant can also be grown in fertile garden soil with constant moisture.

LOCATION AND EXPOSURE: Plant celandine poppy in a woodland garden in very high open shade, or where the sun filters through leaves in early spring. I find that it grows equally well in an open garden with full sun and fertile soil. When grown in the open, the plants should be mulched where winters are severe.

For an outstanding effect, grow celandine poppy in groups of three or more, or intersperse with other woodland plants such as mertensia, trilliums, and medium-sized ferns—especially maidenhair fern for foliage contrast.

PLANTING TIME: While dormant in spring or fall.

ROOT SYSTEM: A pinkish to salmon-colored, brittle rhizome which, like bloodroot, oozes an orange juice.

PLANTING DEPTH AND SPACING: Space the fleshy rhizomes 8 to 12 inches apart or farther if you wish them to develop into showy clumps. Set with the eye 1 inch below soil level and mulch.

PLANTING STOCK AND PROPAGATION: Nursery-grown stock is huskier than collected stock and develops into a showy specimen sooner. Quality collected stock must have strong eyes.

Divide large rhizomes with many eyes, leaving two eyes in each division. Growth may be quite slow. Seeds must be sown as soon as they ripen; they bear a caruncle which must not dry out. Seeds germinate readily the following spring, and seedlings usually bloom the second year. Guard the seeds closely, as chipmunks are very fond of them.

COMMENTS: The gray-green lobed foliage of the celandine poppy makes a unique contrast with other wildflowers.

Dicentra Cucullaria • Dutchman's-breeches

DESCRIPTION: 6 to 10 inches tall. Snow-white to pinkish flowers (occasionally a delicate pink one is found in a colony) hang like pantaloons on arched stems. The foliage is a delicate green and fernlike.

Dutchman's-breeches grows in large colonies, literally carpeting the floor of rich deciduous woods where the leafmold is deep. Usually other vegetation is sparse while these flowers are in full bloom.

PERIOD OF BLOOM: Late April into May.

SOIL: Neutral to slightly acid soil rich in humus. Like all members of the fumitory family, they require rich soil. In fertile woodland soil the plants will bloom profusely.

LOCATION AND EXPOSURE: Grow Dutchman's-breeches in open shade where filtered sunshine can warm the earth in early spring. For a good display, always plant them in groups or in small colonies among other wildflowers like tall white snakeroot or citronella that will bloom much later and grow only slightly in early spring. Maidenhair fern can also be scattered among the colonies to give a lovely effect later in the season when the Dutchman's-breeches become dormant.

PLANTING TIME: Plant anytime after dormancy into late fall.

Spring transplanting is not advisable; the plants begin to sprout as soon as the frost leaves the ground.

ROOT SYSTEM: A small scaly bulb with white fibrous roots. Each bulb is made up of many tiny white or pink kernels. Usually only one or two of the larger bulblets in a cluster contain the internal flower bud which produces the next year's display.

PLANTING DEPTH AND SPACING: Space 4 to 6 inches apart in colonies. Set the bulbs about 1 to 1½ inches deep and mulch with small leaves, old straw, or marsh hay. The bulbs multiply to form clumps.

PLANTING STOCK AND PROPAGATION: Use nursery-grown or quality collected stock with all the kernels intact and forming a compact bulblet (or bulb).

To divide the bulbs, break the tiny kernels from the main bulblet and plant them only about ½ inch deep. Mulch with a light layer of old straw or small leaves. Several years will elapse before these bulblets bloom.

Use the seeds if you catch them in time. Sow them in flats as soon as they ripen, and keep them moderately moist. Mulch the flats lightly. Seedlings may appear slowly, often continuing to emerge throughout the second year. Planting seeds is a slower process than dividing mature bulbs. You can expect some self-sowing.

COMMENTS: Often sizable colonies of Dutchman's-breeches carpet large areas under tall hardwoods where filtered sunlight makes a dappled pattern on their foliage. Here they look like countless pantaloons hung very carefully upside down.

In my woodland garden, where the plants are mulched, I find that I can grow vigorous and beautiful Dutchman's-breeches. Plants do not usually reach their peak until the third year after transplanting.

Dicentra canadensis • squirrel corn

DESCRIPTION: 6 to 10 inches tall. The foliage of the squirrel corn is smooth, blue-gray, and fernlike. The flowers are dainty broad hearts; they are fragrant and pinkish white, sometimes with a pale lavender tint.

Squirrel corn is often found with Dutchman's-breeches in open deciduous woods where leafmold is deep.

111

PERIOD OF BLOOM: May.

SOIL: Slightly acid humus-rich soil or a neutral soil rich in leaf-mold.

LOCATION AND EXPOSURE: Grow squirrel corn in open woodland where the spring sun filters through leafless trees. Plants become dormant soon after they bloom and should be planted in colonies with later-blooming small plants to keep the woodland floor from looking bare later in the season. Moneywort is an excellent groundcover to use with squirrel corn.

PLANTING TIME: The tiny tubers are best planted after dormancy and into late fall.

ROOT SYSTEM: The tiny tubers look very much like several small yellow peas linked together with a white string. In fall, each tuber sends out tiny white fibrous roots.

PLANTING DEPTH AND SPACING: Plant the tubers 2 inches deep in groups of 3 or more, or in small colonies. Mulch. If you have trouble with rodents stealing the tubers, cover the planted area with ½ inch mesh galvanized wire before mulching; the plants will grow through the wire the next season. Chipmunks love to transplant squirrel corn.

PLANTING STOCK AND PROPAGATION: Use nursery-grown stock or quality collected stock.

The seeds should be sown as soon as they ripen, but it is difficult to catch them before they disperse. They self-sow very readily.

COMMENTS: Mice and chipmunks are adept at carrying away the tubers and planting them elsewhere. Covering the beds with wire mesh before mulching has discouraged further raiding of our beds, and our squirrel corn now grows in lovely colonies each season.

Dicentra eximia • pink bleeding heart

DESCRIPTION: 12 to 20 inches tall. The pink bleeding heart has the familiar cluster of heart-shaped flowers drooping on arched stems. The foliage is green and fernlike. Usually rose-pink, the flowers occasionally have a hint of lavender. The color depends mostly on the amount of sunlight available and soil fertility. Catalogs frequently call this the fern-leafed bleeding heart.

The bleeding heart is usually found in rocky woods with humus-rich soil. Although not a native of Wisconsin, it withstands our severe climate very well.

PERIOD OF BLOOM: Flower buds appear with the first spring foliage, and the plant continues to bloom until the first killing frost. It is one of our longest-blooming wildflowers. If there is heavy rainfall in June and July, this flower often blooms sparsely in August but perks up again in September.

SOIL: Garden or woods soil is suitable.

LOCATION AND EXPOSURE: Pink bleeding heart blooms profusely in high open shade or preferably in full sun. It is also an excellent groundcover under tall, sparsely planted trees where the soil is fertile.

PLANTING TIME: Early spring, late summer, or very early fall.

ROOT SYSTEM: A coarse fibrous rootstock that forms a clump as it grows new eyes for the next year's growth.

PLANTING DEPTH AND SPACING: Space 2 feet apart in fertile soil. Dig a fairly good-sized hole, and plant so that the top pink eyes will be about 1 inch below soil level. Mulch if grown in open shade.

PLANTING STOCK AND PROPAGATION: Use nursery-grown or quality collected stock.

When dividing old rootstocks and old crowns make certain that each plant has at least three strong pink eyes in each division. The old crowns die as they finish blooming and new ones take over each year. To keep the plants growing vigorously, divide them every second or third year, otherwise the dead growth will choke the new eyes as they form. This is very important if you want your bleeding hearts to bloom continuously.

Seeds should be sown as soon as they have been picked, otherwise the caruncle will dry out and the seeds will not germinate until the second spring. Seedlings are very delicate at first and should not be transferred to their permanent home until late July or the following spring.

COMMENTS: Bonemeal and a complete fertilizer (10-10-10) worked into the soil a few inches from the plant in spring and again in midsummer will assure continuous bloom throughout the growing season.

Dicentra formosa • western bleeding heart

DESCRIPTION: 6 to 10 inches tall. Pink heart-shaped flowers flushed with lavender are attached to leafless stems in drooping clusters. The foliage is fernlike. There is a pure white variety known as white sweetheart. Its foliage is fernlike, but paler green in color.

Western bleeding heart is native to western states and southwest Canada. In high cool shade it carpets the ground, displaying its lovely hearts.

PERIOD OF BLOOM: Late May until killing frosts.

SOIL: Slightly acid, humus-rich woods soil that is fertile to a good depth and has constant moisture. Both the pink and the white form need a plentiful supply of organic matter and must be kept mulched with decaying humus.

LOCATION AND EXPOSURE: A cool shady nook protected from the heat of the sun is ideal for bleeding heart. This delightful plant is an excellent groundcover for rich woodlands, where decaying humus and vegetation have made a deep bed of humus-rich soil. In cold climates the western bleeding heart should be heavily mulched with old marsh hay or small leaves during the winter. Remove some of this mulch in spring at about the time when the frost leaves the ground.

PLANTING TIME: Late May when the plants have just begun to grow or when potted stock has shown its first buds.

ROOT SYSTEM: Extensive, very brittle rhizomes that fork and spread to establish colonies. The rootstock spreads at soil level beneath the damp old mulch, sending its feeder roots into the earth. Bleeding heart must have a heavy mulch of decaying old straw, marsh hay, or fine leaves if it is to prosper. The decaying organic matter also helps retain the needed moisture.

PLANTING DEPTH AND SPACING: Bareroot stock should be planted ½ to 1 inch deep with the new shoot leading to soil level. Insert pot-grown nursery stock at soil level. Mulch.

PLANTING STOCK AND PROPAGATION: Pot-grown nursery stock is much the best; collected stock should have a considerable quantity of roots at the rhizome joints.

Rhizomes planted vertically in 2 inch wet peat pots with the eye at soil level will produce small plants that bloom quite well the following year. Potted stock should be kept in an uncovered cold frame over the winter and mulched heavily.

COMMENTS: In cold climates like my own, where the temperature occasionally dips to −35 degrees in winter, it is important to mulch the plants carefully. The pink species seems a little hardier than the white.

Corydalis bulbosa · purple corydalis

DESCRIPTION: 4 to 6 inches tall. Rosy-purple flower clusters are held on a single stem above fernlike, blue-green foliage.

Purple corydalis is a particularly hardy wildflower native to Switzerland; it is not easily damaged by early spring frosts. Many times I have seen my corydalis lying flat on its face after a hard frost only to perk up again when the sun came out.

PERIOD OF BLOOM: Late April into May. Dormant by June.

SOIL: Humus-rich soil that is neutral to only slightly acid.

LOCATION AND EXPOSURE: I find this plant very adaptable. It blooms best when exposed to morning sunlight or to sunlight filtered through leafless branches. Tuck the bulbs among rocks in the garden or plant along the edge of a tulip bed. Corydalis may also be interplanted with very small ferns or later-flowering dwarf groundcovers.

PLANTING TIME: Bulbs are best planted after dormancy in early summer and into late fall. Corydalis blooms too early to be transplanted in spring.

ROOT SYSTEM: A small yellow bulb that looks like an oversized shelled acorn half. White feeder roots develop in late summer. Bulbs usually divide every year or two when conditions are favorable.

PLANTING DEPTH AND SPACING: Space about 6 inches apart. Set the bulbs 2 to 3 inches deep. If the area is ideal, the corydalis will multiply readily.

PLANTING STOCK AND PROPAGATION: Use nursery-grown stock.

You can divide bulbs every two or three years. Seeds are hard to collect, but corydalis occasionally self-sows.

COMMENTS: This little flower is so lovely that all who see it will admire it. *Corydalis solida*, which is very similar to *Corydalis bulbosa*, has not proved hardy in our cold climate.

CRUCIFERAE [Mustard Family]

Dentaria diphylla • two-leaved toothwort

DESCRIPTION: 8 to 10 inches tall. Two toothed leaves grow opposite each other halfway up the stalk. The stalk is topped by a loose cluster of four-petaled white flowers which turn pinkish with age. Basal foliage is similar to that on the stalk.

Two-leaved toothwort inhabits moist rich woods. It is also found in deep woods, growing along streams with hepaticas and fringed orchis.

PERIOD OF BLOOM: May.

SOIL: Neutral to slightly acid humus-rich soil with constant moisture. I have found that toothwort does well in soil that is damp in spring and not too dry in summer.

LOCATION AND EXPOSURE: Grow this toothwort in colonies as a very low groundcover. The foliage stays neat and green all summer. Select an open spot where the shade is high.

PLANTING TIME: While dormant in spring or fall.

ROOT SYSTEM: A slender white rhizome that is brittle, crinkled, and easily broken. It often sends up new growth as it creeps along. The feeder roots are white.

PLANTING DEPTH AND SPACING: Space about 10 inches apart since the rhizomes will spread. Plant the slender rhizomes 1 inch deep. Mulch lightly.

PLANTING STOCK AND PROPAGATION: Use nursery-grown or quality collected stock.

Divide the rhizomes into segments while the plant is dormant. Pot them in a flat for one year before setting them out in a permanent location. Each broken portion will produce a new plant. Seeds sown when ripe will germinate though I have had little luck collecting them before the chipmunks make off with the harvest. The plant self-sows.

COMMENTS: This easily grown plant is rarely found in woodland gardens. Because of its crinkled root it is sometimes called crinkleroot.

Dentaria laciniata • cut-leaved toothwort

DESCRIPTION: 8 to 12 inches tall. Usually two palmate leaves grow midway up the stem. A loose cluster of four-petaled white flowers, occasionally flushed with pink or lavender, grows on top. The foliage is narrower, deeper cut, and more tapered than that of two-leaved toothwort.

This toothwort is found in moist rich woods and along river bottoms in deep shade. I have found it along trout streams that slightly overflow their banks in spring.

PERIOD OF BLOOM: May into June.

SOIL: Humus-rich soil a little on the damp side is best.

LOCATION AND EXPOSURE: Plant in colonies in open-shaded woodland. It can be interspersed with smaller ferns.

PLANTING TIME: Spring or fall when dormant.

ROOT SYSTEM: The tan, jointed rootstock with fibrous roots divides easily. Each portion eventually forms a new plant.

PLANTING DEPTH AND SPACING: Space 10 to 15 inches apart. It will spread. Set the slender rhizomes horizontally 2 to 3 inches deep and mulch.

PLANTING STOCK AND PROPAGATION: Use nursery-grown stock or quality collected stock of good size.

Be careful not to divide dormant rhizomes into sections that are too small.

Sow ripe seeds immediately in rich woods soil.

COMMENTS: This toothwort has a showier blossom than the two-leaved toothwort. Toothworts are also called pepper roots because the rootstock has a piquant taste.

SAXIFRAGACEAE [Saxifrage Family]

Tiarella cordifolia • foamflower

DESCRIPTION: 6 to 8 inches tall. The foamflower has feathery white flower spikes and graceful, maplelike, hairy basal foliage. There is also a rare variety with delicate pink flowers.

In rich cool woods, it carpets large areas. When grown in a protected area, the leaves stay green all winter.

PERIOD OF BLOOM: Late May into June.

SOIL: Humus-rich soil that does not dry out readily. Neutral to slightly acid, rich in leafmold.

LOCATION AND EXPOSURE: Foamflower is a choice plant for a shaded garden. It also makes an excellent groundcover under deciduous trees; it does not fare well under evergreens.

PLANTING TIME: Spring when plants begin to grow or fall while dormant.

ROOT SYSTEM: The parent plant has fibrous roots. In the spring the crown sends out many pinkish runners which develop fine hairy roots at the joints. Each section forms a new plant, which can be severed from the parent plant as soon as the foliage crown develops.

PLANTING DEPTH AND SPACING: Space 6 to 12 inches apart, depending on the desired effect. Set crowns at soil level, spreading the roots carefully. Cover the tiny roots on the runners lightly with damp humus. Mulch with birch, soft maple, or other small leaves. Old straw or weathered marsh hay make good mulches too.

PLANTING STOCK AND PROPAGATION: Use nursery-grown or quality collected stock with good roots.

Divide the rhizomes (rooted runners) of mature plants. Sow seeds on top of rich soil in a flat. Keep them protected the first year, preferably in a cold frame. In Wisconsin our plants rarely set seed.

COMMENTS: The star-shaped flower spikes and the lovely patterned foliage of foamflower lend an airy beauty to the woodland garden. As new leaves appear in spring, old foliage bronzes and disappears, adding a bit of humus to the soil.

Heuchera villosa • hairy alumroot

DESCRIPTION: 6 to 10 inches tall. The white feathery plumes and the foliage are similar to those of the foamflower. Alumroot, however, does not send out rhizomes like the foamflower. Its natural habitat is farther south and east, although it has proved hardy in Wisconsin.

PERIOD OF BLOOM: August into September.

118

SOIL: Neutral to slightly acid soil that retains some moisture in summer. A moist woodland where leafmold is plentiful is ideal.

LOCATION AND EXPOSURE: Plant hairy alumroot in woodland among rocks in pockets of humus-rich soil. The flower is delightful in late summer when most woodland wildflowers have faded. Alumroot can also grow in fertile garden soil when shade is provided during midday heat.

PLANTING TIME: Spring or fall.

ROOT SYSTEM: A coarse rhizome with many fibrous roots that multiply at the crown.

PLANTING DEPTH AND SPACING: Space 10 to 15 inches apart. The plants will form clumps. Set the crown at soil level, which is usually ½ to 1½ inches deeper than the level at which it previously grew; the plants tend to raise their crowns above the soil as they mature. In rich soil with constant moisture they will form larger clumps if they are set slightly deeper.

PLANTING STOCK AND PROPAGATION: Use nursery-grown stock. Use only the young crowns of quality collected stock.

Divide clumps in spring, and water faithfully. Our plants have never set seed.

COMMENTS: To prolong the beauty of your foamflower bed, interplant it with hairy alumroot. The foliage and flower of the two plants are so similar that only a very close look will reveal the difference. Interplanting gives your foamflower bed a second chance to display its springtime beauty.

Heuchera americana • rock geranium

DESCRIPTION: 1 to 3 feet tall. Several spikes bearing many dainty cream-colored or greenish bells rise up from a rosette of large round scalloped leaves.

Rock geranium is found in moist to dry rocky woods and uplands. I have also found it in rocky crevices where no soil was visible.

PERIOD OF BLOOM: June.

SOIL: Neutral to slightly acid soil. The texture of the soil is not important.

LOCATION AND EXPOSURE: Rock geranium grows in open shade or filtered sunlight. It will also grow in the open if it is protected from strong afternoon sunlight.

119

PLANTING TIME: Spring or fall, preferably spring.

ROOT SYSTEM: Coarse black rootstock with some fibrous roots. It forms clumps.

PLANTING DEPTH AND SPACING: Space 18 to 24 inches apart. The flowers are most striking when planted singly.

PLANTING STOCK AND PROPAGATION: Young nursery-grown stock transplants more readily than young quality collected stock.

Divide large clumps in spring, discarding the old knotty ones, but this is not always successful. Scatter seeds on a flat as soon as they ripen. Transplant the seedlings when they are half grown.

COMMENTS: The leaves are almost evergreen, especially when there has been ample snow cover. When grown among rocks or when there is some sun, the leaves tend to bronze on the outer edges, the older leaves gradually becoming completely bronze with autumn frosts.

The foliage is similar to that of our house geranium, which explains the common name rock geranium. In my area it is also called crevice alumroot.

Mitella diphylla • bishop's-cap

DESCRIPTION: 8 to 10 inches tall. Two leaves grow opposite each other midway up each flowering stem. The delicate, airy, white flowers are contained in a narrow raceme. The foliage somewhat resembles that of the foamflower but is smaller. Bishop's-cap remains in a neat clump and does not send out runners like the foamflower. After the flowers fade, the plant produces exposed, shiny jet-black seeds which give it new beauty.

Bishop's-cap is found growing with hepaticas, *Trillium grandiflorum*, and bloodroot in moist rich woods and well-shaded woodlands where humus is plentiful.

PERIOD OF BLOOM: May into June.

SOIL: Slightly acid, fertile soil that is damp or only slightly moist. Bishop's-cap is easy to grow.

LOCATION AND EXPOSURE: Bishop's-cap makes excellent groundcover in deep shady woods. It also provides points of interest when grown among rocks where there is deep humus and adequate moisture. Or it can be interspersed with other woodland wildflowers. Its leaves are almost evergreen.

PLANTING TIME: Spring or fall.

120

ROOT SYSTEM: The rootstock is a rather twisted, pinkish, scaly rhizome that forks but stays close to the parent plant, creating a clumplike effect.

PLANTING DEPTH AND SPACING: When planting in colonies, space 6 inches or more apart. Among rocks, plant at random. Set the crowns of young plants, older plants, and divisions at soil level.

PLANTING STOCK AND PROPAGATION: Use nursery-grown or quality collected stock.

Divide rooted rhizomes. If there are insufficient roots, the plants should be potted and transplanted in the autumn.

Ripe seeds sown at soil level germinate fairly well. A balsam or spruce branch placed over the flat will help retain moisture. Seedlings usually start to bloom in the third year.

COMMENTS: A charming, dainty plant with many uses in a woodland garden. It makes a fine substitute for foamflower in an area that is too small for a plant that spreads so quickly.

Parnassia glauca • grass of Parnassus

DESCRIPTION: 6 to 10 inches tall. There is a single leaf midway up each flower stalk, and one solitary anemonelike flower at the top. Flowers are waxy white with green veins. The heart-shaped, light-green basal foliage forms a clump.

Grass of Parnassus is found growing in colonies along brooks, grassy lake shores, and in wet marshes. I know a dry hillside where it grows abundantly and blooms in great profusion. I marvel at how this flower manages to survive there. Stock from this dry area has not transplanted successfully.

PERIOD OF BLOOM: August into September.

SOIL: Moist, neutral to slightly acid, fertile soil. Add a sprinkling of lime.

LOCATION AND EXPOSURE: Grow grass of Parnassus among sparse grasses in wet meadows where it might possibly self-sow. I started a colony in an old kitchen sink buried at soil level. I filled the sink with fertile loam and worked in a handful of garden lime. I tucked a mulch of decaying straw around each plant to keep them reasonably moist. The hole in the bottom of the sink provided ample drainage. The first summer I was rewarded with lovely bloom and abundant seeds.

PLANTING TIME: Fall is best.

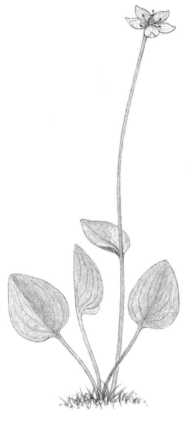

ROOT SYSTEM: Fibrous roots. The plants form clumps.

PLANTING DEPTH AND SPACING: Space 6 to 12 inches apart. Leave a clump of earth adhering to the roots, and set the plants at the level at which they previously grew. Tuck mulch around the plants and keep moist.

PLANTING STOCK AND PROPAGATION: Nursery-grown stock in a sizable ball of earth is best. Quality collected stock with soil adhering is scarce.

Wild seeds are hard to collect since the slightest breeze will send them scattering as soon as the oval capsule opens. Collect the seeds daily in your garden and plant them immediately. Seeds scattered over a flat containing natural, fertile loam with a sprinkling of lime produce some seedlings that bloom the second year. I cover the flat with ½ inch mesh wire before mulching for the winter; this keeps the rodents from eating the crowns and destroying the young plants. Remove the mulch in spring but keep the wire a bit longer if possible. Germination may be slow and uneven. Seedlings should not be transferred to peat pots until the summer of the second year. When transplanting, remember to leave some of the earth from the flat adhering to the tiny roots. The plants can be moved to their permanent bed in the summer of the third year.

COMMENTS: Grass of Parnassus is not easy to grow, but it is well worth the extra effort.

ROSACEAE [Rose Family]

Gillenia trifoliata • bowman's root

DESCRIPTION: 2 to 3 feet tall. Thrice divided, compound leaves alternate on branching stems. The white to pale pink terminal flowers grow in open clusters.

Bowman's root is found in rich, open woodlands in high shade.

PERIOD OF BLOOM: June into July.

SOIL: Moderately acid soil with good fertility. It should be damp or moderately moist.

LOCATION AND EXPOSURE: Bowman's root is easily grown in wild gardens with high open shade or along borders of deciduous woodland.

PLANTING TIME: Spring is preferable.

ROOT SYSTEM: A coarse root once thought to have medicinal value.

PLANTING DEPTH AND SPACING: Space 1 to 2 feet apart with crowns at soil level. Mulch.

PLANTING STOCK AND PROPAGATION: Use nursery-grown stock or quality collected stock.

Divide crowns in early spring. I have not tried stem cuttings. Seeds sown in fall usually grow to blooming-sized seedlings the second year.

COMMENTS: Bowman's root is best planted in a showy colony or among ferns.

Waldsteinia fragarioides • barren strawberry

DESCRIPTION: 3 to 6 inches tall. Single ½ inch bright yellow flowers grow on bare stems. The shiny green leaves are thrice-parted like those of the strawberry, but lobed like those of the goldthread, which it resembles more closely.

Barren strawberry is found in moist to dry woodlands and cutover lands, especially where aspen and oaks provide shade. It often grows among wintergreen.

PERIOD OF BLOOM: May into June. Long-lasting flowers.

SOIL: Slightly acid, humus-rich woods soil with some moisture and good drainage. In damp areas the barren strawberry sends out many stolons which carpet the forest floor.

LOCATION AND EXPOSURE: Use this plant as a groundcover in the high open shade of woodland, or grow it in small colonies among other wildflowers. It also provides a good groundcover for sunny areas if it has constant moisture. A few single-crown plants set out in full sun in my garden formed neat clumps in one year and proved more vigorous than plants grown in shade.

PLANTING TIME: Early spring or fall.

ROOT SYSTEM: Each plant sends out stolons from the crown, and these form new plants which stay close to the parent. Roots are fibrous and sparse.

PLANTING DEPTH AND SPACING: Space 6 or more inches apart. The

main crown should be at soil level with new leafless shoots and side stolons about ½ inch deep. Mulch the first winter. Keep moist.

PLANTING STOCK AND PROPAGATION: Nursery-grown stock has more fibrous roots, but you can also use quality collected stock.

Divide clumps in early spring or fall. The seeds are always harvested by rodents before I can collect them. They do germinate easily, however.

COMMENTS: I rarely see this plant offered in wildflower catalogs. It makes a neat, conservative groundcover and has a unique beauty.

Fragaria vesca • woodland strawberry

DESCRIPTION: 6 inches tall. Single white ½ inch flowers appear in step fashion above lush, green, upright foliage. The 1 inch long conical fruit bears seeds on the outside, unlike the fruit of *Fragaria virginiana*, which is round with sunken seeds. The fruit of the woodland strawberry is red, occasionally yellow or white.

I have always found the woodland strawberry growing in rather moist cutover lands where the soil is fertile. Its lush green foliage carpets large areas.

PERIOD OF BLOOM: May. Fruit in June and July.

SOIL: Woodland strawberry grows well in fertile garden soil.

LOCATION AND EXPOSURE: Grow the woodland strawberry in full sun in the garden or in high open woodland where there is ample room for it to spread. It is an excellent groundcover and also useful for bordering walks and paths. Some sunshine is essential if the plants are to blossom and bear fruit.

PLANTING TIME: Spring or fall.

ROOT SYSTEM: Each plant has many fibrous roots and forms several crowns.

PLANTING DEPTH AND SPACING: Space 1 foot apart. Set the crowns at soil level.

PLANTING STOCK AND PROPAGATION: Use nursery-grown potted seedlings or quality collected young runners with good fibrous roots.

Seeds sown very early in the greenhouse will produce flowering plants by August and fruit a few weeks later. Seeds are sometimes offered in catalogs under the name "alpine strawberry."

COMMENTS: I recall happy childhood days when I used to gather pailfuls of these luscious strawberries for jams and canning and for eating fresh. The berries are easy to pick, as the calyx remains on the stalk.

Potentilla canadensis · common cinquefoil

DESCRIPTION: 8 to 20 inch prostrate vines develop from a rhizome. The ½ inch five-petaled flowers are bright yellow with yellow centers. The foliage is divided and often referred to as "five-fingers." The stems are reddish.

Common cinquefoil is usually found growing in colonies along the edge of woodlands and in old fields.

PERIOD OF BLOOM: Late May into July.

SOIL: Any dry to average garden or woods soil.

LOCATION AND EXPOSURE: High open shade or full sun is best. Use cinquefoil for groundcover between taller plants that are spaced far apart.

PLANTING TIME: While dormant in spring or fall.

ROOT SYSTEM: A pink-flushed bulblike rhizome with many fibrous roots. Cinquefoil, like strawberries, spreads by runners; the nodes root where they touch damp soil.

PLANTING DEPTH AND SPACING: Space 1 or more feet apart. Set rhizomes about ½ to ¾ inch deep.

PLANTING STOCK AND PROPAGATION: Use quality collected stock.

Cinquefoil self-sows a little, but spreads mostly by rooting runners.

COMMENTS: Some people consider common cinquefoil a weed, but I cannot find it listed in any weed books. A few plants grew up along the path to our pool and have neatly covered an otherwise barren area.

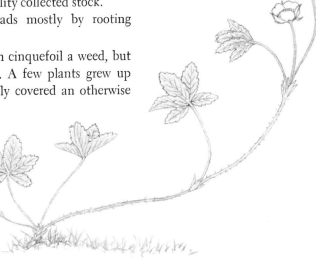

125

Potentilla anserina • silverweed

DESCRIPTION: 6 to 9 inches tall. Solitary ¾ to 1 inch golden yellow flowers are held on slender stems above pinnate silvery foliage, which shimmers when covered with dew.

In colder climates silverweed is found in damp meadows or around old homesteads, usually carpeting a large area. It is originally from Eurasia.

PERIOD OF BLOOM: June into summer.

SOIL: Silverweed will grow in any but extremely acid soil, but neutral to slightly acid soil is best. Constant moisture is important.

LOCATION AND EXPOSURE: Silverweed thrives in full sun or high open shade. It spreads rapidly and is used where extensive ground-cover is wanted quickly. It does not do well in hot climates, but is extremely hardy in cold ones.

PLANTING TIME: Spring or fall.

ROOT SYSTEM: Silverweed spreads by sending runners from the parent plant in several directions. The stolons root quickly to form new plants.

PLANTING DEPTH AND SPACING: Set the plants as they previously grew with crowns at soil level.

PLANTING STOCK AND PROPAGATION: Use nursery-grown or collected stock where available. Its range is limited to colder climates.

The plant is so easily reproduced by stolons that it is not worth the trouble to grow it from seed.

COMMENTS: Because of the golden yellow flowers and silvery gray foliage, this showy plant is also called silver-and-gold.

Geum triflorum • prairie smoke

DESCRIPTION: 8 to 15 inches tall. Crimson to rose-pink nodding flowers support an upright puff of mauve-pink which is the fruit. The plant is very showy in its budding stage. The basal foliage is oblong, irregularly lobed, and almost evergreen.

Prairie smoke is found in deserted hayfields and prairies where the soil is rocky and often sandy. Each plant forms a horseshoe-shaped clump as it multiplies. Its basal foliage chokes out the grasses as it spreads.

PERIOD OF BLOOM: June into July. In my garden where the soil is a rich sandy loam, it often blooms again later in the summer if there has been enough rain.

126

SOIL: Good drainage is very important. Slightly acid to neutral, sandy soils are best. Garden soil is good too.

LOCATION AND EXPOSURE: An excellent plant to grow along a sunny path or among low rocks in a sunny rock garden. It rarely blooms or multiplies in shade.

PLANTING TIME: Spring or fall. A light temporary mulch is advisable if you plant prairie smoke in fall.

ROOT SYSTEM: A heavy creeping rootstock with many coarse fibrous roots. The newer roots, which are white and lighter than the old ones, are most important for the growth of the plant. Eventually old roots and rootstock die and decay. Be careful not to break off too much of the old rhizome when transplanting, otherwise the plants may not bloom for a year.

PLANTING DEPTH AND SPACING: Space 1 to 2 feet apart, as each plant will multiply in a horseshoe fashion. Set the plants with the crowns at soil level.

PLANTING STOCK AND PROPAGATION: Nursery-grown stock is usually best, especially when it has been divided regularly. Quality collected stock is rare.

Division of rhizomes is the best and easiest method of propagation. As to seeds, I find germination poor.

COMMENTS: I rarely find prairie smoke in wild gardens. It is a striking and unusual plant that is worth growing. Plant it in a sunny garden or in a meadow where patches of grass have been cleared. Prairie smoke is the prettiest of the wild geums. Goldfinches are very fond of the seeds.

Alchemilla pratensis • lady's mantle

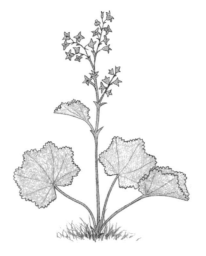

DESCRIPTION: 6 to 10 inches tall. Clusters of airy yellow flowers grow above mounds of fluted round leaves with serrated edges.

Originally from Europe, lady's mantle is now native to some eastern states; its range is limited. It is found in dry, gravelly soil.

PERIOD OF BLOOM: Early July to late August.

SOIL: Lady's mantle thrives in a variety of soils as long as there is good drainage. This plant cannot tolerate wet roots. I grow it in sandy loam.

LOCATION AND EXPOSURE: Grow in full sun or very light open shade. Lady's mantle can be used effectively to make a bright, attractive border.

PLANTING TIME: Spring or fall, but I prefer spring.

ROOT SYSTEM: A heavy rootstock with coarse fibrous roots. The rootstock forms a clump which can be divided.

PLANTING DEPTH AND SPACING: Space the plants about 1 foot apart, giving them room to form showy clumps. Set the crown ½ to 1 inch deeper than it previously grew.

PLANTING STOCK AND PROPAGATION: Use nursery-grown stock or quality collected stock if available.

For propagation, divisions of clumps will give the best results. Seeds are slow to germinate.

COMMENTS: Lady's mantle is a particularly beautiful plant. The foliage is silvery gray when beaded with rain or dew and is easily preserved in glycerine for use in dry floral arrangements.

Filipendula rubra · queen of the prairie

DESCRIPTION: 3 to 5 feet tall. Sprays of pink flowers bloom outward from the center of the cluster. The leaves are textured, compound, and very pinnate.

Queen of the prairie is found in moist meadows as well as in soils with average moisture. It grows in full sun.

PERIOD OF BLOOM: Late June into August.

SOIL: Neutral to slightly acid soils or very fertile soils. The moisture content should be high to average.

LOCATION AND EXPOSURE: To bloom well this flower should be planted in full sun. It can be used effectively as a showy border, or naturalized in a meadow. Continuous mulching will promote spreading.

PLANTING TIME: While dormant in spring or fall.

ROOT SYSTEM: A creeping pinkish rhizome, dividing at the nodes to send up new shoots.

PLANTING DEPTH AND SPACING: Set the rhizomes about 1 inch deep with the tip of the plant at soil level. Mulch. Space 1 to 2 feet apart.

PLANTING STOCK AND PROPAGATION: Use nursery-grown stock.

COMMENTS: The airy pink blossoms are elegant, but last only a short while after being cut. The fruit is excellent for use in dried floral arrangements.

LEGUMINOSAE [Pulse Family]

Cassia marilandica • wild senna

DESCRIPTION: 3 to 4 feet tall. The loose racemes of golden yellow flowers with prominent dark-brown anthers remind one of the delphinium "bee." The leafy stalks have pinnate leaves similar to those of the honey locust, and the whole plant becomes quite bushy.

Wild senna naturally inhabits moist open woods and thickets in a region much farther south than Wisconsin. But with a generous mulch of oak leaves, it has proved hardy here.

PERIOD OF BLOOM: July into August.

SOIL: Slightly acid, fertile, sandy loam or any good garden soil with adequate drainage.

LOCATION AND EXPOSURE: I find this plant grows best in full sun. Given enough room, it develops into a handsome deciduous bush. Wild senna is also a good choice for a sunny woodland border.

PLANTING TIME: While dormant in fall or spring. Mulch in winter in cold climates.

ROOT SYSTEM: A coarse and fibrous, fleshy black rootstock that enlarges with age and produces many new eyes.

PLANTING DEPTH AND SPACING: Space 3 feet or more apart. Set the eyes about 1 inch below level with the roots at least an inch deeper. Cultivate or mulch. Mulching is preferable since new shoots come up near the parent stems.

PLANTING STOCK AND PROPAGATION: Use nursery-grown stock or young collected stock where available.

Dividing the clumps in spring gives good results for propagation. New growth is slow to appear. The seeds are hard-shelled and often slow to germinate. Sow them in fall. Seedlings bloom the third year.

COMMENTS: Wild senna is a bold vigorous plant of unusual beauty. This large perennial can be used in place of a shrub. In clusters, the seed pods make good material for dry floral arrangements.

129

Baptisia australis • false blue indigo

DESCRIPTION: 3 to 4 feet tall. The bushy plants have pealike flowers and foliage of the legume type. The flowers are usually indigo-blue, although there is a white species and a related species (*Baptisia tinctoria*) with smaller, yellow flowers. The latter grows naturally farther south, but a few have survived in my garden. False blue indigo was originally cultivated in the southern states, and now grows wild there in open sandy fields or old gardens.

PERIOD OF BLOOM: Late May into July.

SOIL: False blue indigo prefers a sandy loam, but also grows well in a heavier, more fertile soil if drainage is good.

LOCATION AND EXPOSURE: A showy plant for a border or along the edge of a woodland where there is ample sunshine. I prefer to grow it in full sun.

PLANTING TIME: While dormant in spring or fall, but spring-planted stock grows sooner.

ROOT SYSTEM: A fleshy rootstock that sends out long, stringy, white roots and produces many eyes in a close cluster. Digging up a large plant can be difficult because of its extensive root system, but many roots can be cut without injuring the plant.

PLANTING DEPTH AND SPACING: Set the plants 2 feet apart to allow room for growth. Plant so that the upper eyes are 2 inches below soil level. This encourages the rootstock to send up more new shoots to form a large plant. When transplanting, trim the old roots to 3 inches.

PLANTING STOCK AND PROPAGATION: Nursery-grown stock is best. Quality collected stock may be used if available.

To propagate, divide large plants in spring while they are dormant. Cut each rootstock into pieces, leaving about three eyes in each division and trimming the stringy roots back to 3 or 4 inches. Each of the new eyes will develop a whole new root system.

Sow seeds when they are ripe. Some seedlings will appear the first spring and others may keep appearing throughout the summer and the following spring. Some will bloom in the third year. Often plants do not fully mature until the fifth year.

COMMENTS: Seeds are formed in the black, "bloated" enclosures shaped like pea-pods. They rattle when ripe. For dry floral arrangements, cut the stalks with pods when they first show a little black and are not yet fully ripe. Hang them upside down to dry.

Lupinus perennis • wild lupine

DESCRIPTION: 1 to 2 feet tall. Wild lupine usually grows in a semiprostrate position but holds its pealike blossoms erect in terminal racemes. The flowers are clear blue with a hint of purple inside. There are also rare white and pink forms which I have not yet been fortunate enough to find. The blue-green palmate leaves have many divisions.

Wild lupine is found along roadsides, in wastelands and in old hayfields. It blooms profusely in June sunshine, forming a sea of blue. Plants that grow in the shade have few blossoms. The soil in such areas is not fertile but usually sandy, and grasses grow sparsely. In such dry areas the plants quickly go dormant and often do not set seed in drought years.

PERIOD OF BLOOM: June.

SOIL: This lupine prefers a slightly acid, sandy loam soil with good drainage. But it can be grown successfully in a garden where the soil is heavier and drainage is good.

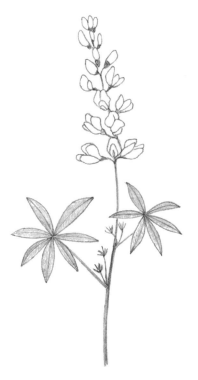

LOCATION AND EXPOSURES: The wild lupine grows best in a well-drained spot with full sun. It goes dormant after setting seed, but after a wet August new foliage appears in early fall. Interplant this lupine with other wildflowers, such as butterfly flower, that will cover bare spots and bloom when the lupines fade. The foliage may mildew if air circulation is poor.

PLANTING TIME: While dormant in spring or fall.

ROOT SYSTEM: A young plant has one tapering rhizome with a few feeder roots. As the rhizome develops, eyes form along its length and send up new growth which forms a clump. You will often find small clumps of nitrogen nodules attached here and there to the distorted branching rhizomes. The roots go deep into the earth in search of minerals.

PLANTING DEPTH AND SPACING: Space the plants 10 to 12 inches apart, setting the eyes of the white shoot about 1 inch below soil

131

level. If green foliage has formed, then plant with the crown at soil level.

PLANTING STOCK AND PROPAGATION: Use young nursery-grown stock or quality collected young stock. It is a waste of time and effort to try transplanting old plants.

The easiest method of propagation is to sow the seeds in tiny pots and transfer them to a permanent location when the second true leaf appears. To hasten germination, soak the seeds in tepid water 15 minutes before sowing. Seedlings bloom the following summer.

COMMENTS: Wild lupine is a very hardy, long-lived wildflower that grows nicely in a sunny, well-drained garden. It is not difficult to cultivate if young plants are used. Old plants usually die when moved. The foliage is supposedly poisonous to cattle.

GERANIACEAE [Geranium Family]

Geranium maculatum • spotted cranesbill

DESCRIPTION: 1 to 2 feet tall. A loose cluster of single magenta-pink flowers are borne on a rigid stem above deeply toothed basal foliage. Two leaves grow midway up the flower stalk. At first glance the foliage is very similar to that of the Canada anemone.

Spotted cranesbill grows in places that are protected from strong winds. It is found in open shade on hillsides and shaded roadsides, where it often grows in the company of false Solomon's seal.

PERIOD OF BLOOM: Late May into June.

SOIL: Average to fertile woodland soils that are neutral to slightly acid. I grow it in garden soil with mulch.

LOCATION AND EXPOSURE: Plant in open shade. If you plant on a hillside, choose a spot protected from strong winds. I also grow spotted cranesbill in the garden in full sun. When planted in a colony, it makes a charming display.

PLANTING TIME: While dormant in fall, or spring when only slightly sprouted.

ROOT SYSTEM: A stout many-branched rhizome that spreads horizontally. When plants become crowded the roots rise above soil level and freeze. The blunt white tips of the rhizomes hold the next year's bud. The smaller white tips will not send shoots above the earth until a year later.

PLANTING DEPTH AND SPACING: Space 10 or more inches apart. Set the rhizome 1 inch deep with the eyes leading to the surface. Mulch. If the nodes on the rhizome are not well developed the plant may stay dormant for a year. If the area is kept moist the plant usually blooms the following year.

PLANTING STOCK AND PROPAGATION: Use nursery-grown stock or quality collected stock.

To propagate, divide clumps in early spring or fall, leaving several plump eyes on each division.

Seeds sown when ripe usually mature enough to bloom in the second or third year. Cranesbill self-sows readily where leafmold is bare.

COMMENTS: The beaklike seed capsule is most unusual and interesting when the seed has been dispersed. The seeds themselves are difficult to collect because the pods open suddenly—changing from green to almost black overnight, they almost burst open and scatter the seeds far and wide.

POLYGALACEAE [Milkwort Family]

Polygala paucifolia • fringed polygala

DESCRIPTION: 3 to 5 inches tall. Dainty, orchidlike flowers, ranging in color from rose-purple to magenta, grow in the axils of oval-shaped leaves. Rarely, the flowers are white. The leaves form on the upper part of the purple stems; they take on a bronze cast in autumn.

Fringed polygala usually grows in rich dry woods and on hillsides under deciduous trees where the forest floor is quite free of grasses. Shinleaf and merrybells are often found nearby.

PERIOD OF BLOOM: May into July.

SOIL: Acid to slightly acid woods soil rich in humus and not too dry in summer.

133

LOCATION AND EXPOSURE: Fringed polygala is a choice plant for a woodland garden where sunlight filters through the trees in spring. It is a very neat groundcover to grow between taller wildflowers that bloom later. Or grow it in small neat colonies. Its foliage lasts late into fall and often remains through the winter.

PLANTING TIME: Sods are best moved in fall. Potted stock can be planted either in spring or fall.

ROOT SYSTEM: The extensive white stringlike rhizomes wander far from the parent plant to form new plants. Like some violets, it bears, in addition to its larger blossoms, cleistogamous (closed, self-pollinated) flowers, and subterranean fruit. This double system of propagation ensures rapid spreading.

PLANTING DEPTH AND SPACING: Space sods 1 foot apart and potted stock 6 inches apart. Plant both at soil level. Mulch with birch or other small thin leaves.

PLANTING STOCK AND PROPAGATION: Nursery-grown potted stock is superior, but is not always available.

Large sods with soil adhering give good results. Sods are best selected from an area where the plants grow close together.

Stem cuttings taken in early summer and put in a propagating frame give fair results.

COMMENTS: The plant is also called gay wings. It is not easy to establish, but once established it spreads readily.

Polygala Senega • Seneca snakeroot

DESCRIPTION: 8 to 15 inches tall. Upright stems with narrow, willowlike leaves bear spikes of white to greenish white flowers in dense racemes. The racemes are also interesting in the seed stage.

Seneca snakeroot grows in dry meadows where the grass is short, along gravelly roadsides, and at sunny edges of woodland.

PERIOD OF BLOOM: May into June.

SOIL: Sandy loam or garden soil that is only slightly acid and has good drainage.

LOCATION AND EXPOSURE: Naturalize Seneca snakeroot among other wildflowers or sparse grasses. It needs full sun or very light open shade. It is not easy to establish.

PLANTING TIME: While dormant in spring or fall.

ROOT SYSTEM: A stout, wiry, cream-tan rhizome with few feeder roots.

PLANTING DEPTH AND SPACING: Space 10 to 15 inches apart to allow room for it to form a clump. Set the plants with eyes about ½ inch below soil level, making certain that the taproot is planted straight down since it seeks deep levels.

PLANTING STOCK AND PROPAGATION: Use young nursery-grown stock or quality collected young stock.

Take cuttings in July or as soon as the stalk seems firm and mature. Cuttings should have at least three or four nodes in the soil and 2 inches of leafy stalk above the soil. Remove the flowering portion of the stalk or tip if the flowers have not yet developed. Pot individually and put in a propagating frame.

Sow seeds when ripe and keep moist. Seedlings usually send up one flowering stalk the second or third year.

COMMENTS: Seneca snakeroot is not a strikingly beautiful plant, but its tiny flowers and beadlike seeds lend it an air of loftiness. Plant it where you want it to remain as it resists transplanting.

There is a dainty pink species, *Polygala polygama*, which occasionally appears in my garden. It tends to die out, however, and does not transplant readily although it has a compact root system and produces subterranean seeds like the fringed polygala. None of the polygalas are easy to establish.

EUPHORBIACEAE [Spurge Family]

Euphorbia Cyparissias • Cypress spurge

DESCRIPTION: 4 to 6 inches tall. The showy, leaflike yellow flowers of the Cypress spurge turn reddish as they fade. The foliage is very fine and feathery on very upright stems; it, too, turns yellow and often reddish in fall.

Cypress spurge is found along roadsides, in dry sandy fields, and around old homesteads. Originally from the Old World, this plant has found its way to North America and has readily established itself here.

PERIOD OF BLOOM: June into July.

SOIL: Any sandy, gritty, or poor soil with good drainage. The pH is not important.

LOCATION AND EXPOSURE: Plant the Cypress spurge in full sun and very poor soil for the best display and compact beauty. In shade it grows rampantly, sometimes becoming a nuisance, and for this reason is not suited for a garden. But it is perfect for hot, sunny, sandy, gravelly areas where little else grows and groundcover is needed to keep the earth from blowing or washing away. Cypress spurge can be easily cultivated in such areas and serves its purpose well. If you do want to grow Cypress spurge in your wild garden, plant it in the sun in a bottomless gallon can to restrict its growth.

PLANTING TIME: While dormant in spring or fall.

ROOT SYSTEM: A creeping rhizome that often sends up new shoots and forms dense clumps. The rootstock is scaly and white with pink eyes which will produce next year's growth.

PLANTING DEPTH AND SPACING: Set the plants ½ to 1 inch deep. Space only 6 inches apart for quick groundcover. Clumps may be spaced even farther apart.

PLANTING STOCK AND PROPAGATION: Pot-grown stock is easiest to plant. To propagate, divide rhizomes.

COMMENTS: Cypress spurge is a good, neat groundcover for those dry, sandy areas where little else survives. I also find it very ornamental; the foliage remains long into fall and is strikingly colorful. But it can become a pest if not planted with care.

MALVACEAE [Mallow Family]

Malva moschata • musk mallow

DESCRIPTION: 1 to 2 feet tall. The single flowers with notched petals ranging from rose-pink to purest white resemble those of the wild rose. The deeply cut, leafy foliage grows on rigid stems.

Musk mallow is found along roadside fences, in old fields, and around abandoned homesteads. Originally grown only in cultivation, it has taken readily to the wild.

PERIOD OF BLOOM: June into late August and often into September.

SOIL: Any neutral to slightly acid garden soil with average moisture content.

LOCATION AND EXPOSURE: Musk mallow blooms best in full sun but will tolerate light open shade. It is a good plant for a border. When musk mallow is naturalized in meadows it should be planted in patches where the grass is sparse or the grass will choke out the plants. A little mulch helps keep the grass down.

PLANTING TIME: While dormant in spring or fall.

ROOT SYSTEM: A wiry, coarse, fibrous, white rootstock that does not transplant well when mature.

PLANTING DEPTH AND SPACING: Space 1 foot apart. When given enough room the plants develop into nice bushes. Set the crowns at soil level and spread the roots evenly. Mulch if you wish.

PLANTING STOCK AND PROPAGATION: Use young nursery-grown stock or quality collected young stock.

I have not been successful in propagating by division of clumps. Cuttings may be taken in July, but they, too, give poor results. Seeds sown in fall or spring will produce blooming-sized plants the second year.

COMMENTS: The outstanding leafy foliage of the musk mallow provides an excellent contrast to plants with linear foliage. Musk mallow derives its name from its musky odor.

Callirhoe involucrata • wine cups

DESCRIPTION: 1· to 2 foot trailer with forking vines. Wine cups have beautiful rose-shaped flowers and blunt-tipped, deeply lanced foliage. The color of the flowers ranges from a luscious wine-red to the color of an American beauty rose. The seed pods are little circles, resembling those of hollyhocks.

Wine cups are native to the southern and southwestern prairies of the Dakotas.

PERIOD OF BLOOM: June until hard-killing frosts.

SOIL: Neutral to slightly acid soil, either sandy or fertile. Good drainage is very important.

LOCATION AND EXPOSURE: The wine cups requires full sun throughout the day for best bloom. It is an excellent plant for a dry sunny spot where it can spread or for a rock garden on a sunny bank. If grown in the open, mulch in winter.

ROOT SYSTEM: The rootstock is white and resembles a small slender parsnip.

PLANTING TIME: Early spring or fall. Spring is preferred.

PLANTING DEPTH AND SPACING: Set root at crown level and space two feet apart, as they will run.

PLANTING STOCK AND PROPAGATION: Use young nursery-grown stock or, where available, young collected stock.

Seeds sown when ripe or in very early spring will produce blooming sized seedlings the second year. Transplant the seedlings to a permanent location before they mature.

COMMENTS: For continuous bloom it is best not to let the plant set seed and to water it during periods of extreme drought.

Wine cups are charming as they spread their vivid colorful flowers over bare areas. The plant is also known as buffalo rose and poppy mallow.

VIOLACEAE [Violet Family]

Viola pedata • birdfoot violet

DESCRIPTION: 3 to 5 inches tall. The pansylike flowers with outstanding yellow eyes are usually shades of lavender-blue. The color varies from plant to plant depending on soil fertility, acidity, and location. There is also a bicolored variety with two upper petals of rich royal purple. On rare occasions a white flower with dark veins appears among the blues. The foliage is deeply toothed and resembles an outstretched bird's foot.

As early woodland flowers fade, birdfoot violets blanket sunny fields and roadsides with sandy banks. When the prairie grasses grow tall this showy violet becomes partly dormant until August rains revive it.

PERIOD OF BLOOM: May into June. I find that when the birdfoot violet is cultivated it blooms again in August and does not go dormant after blooming in early summer. Blossoms continue to appear until the plant is killed by frost.

SOIL: Acid to slightly acid sandy soil with good drainage. Birdfoot violets will also flourish in average garden soils. In its native habitat, it tends to grow in poor sandy soils or in areas with little humus. When cultivated, it thrives in good but not too fertile soil with good drainage. Cultivated plants are showier and do not go dormant in midsummer. They need mulch over the winter or they may winter-kill. The wild birdfoot violets are protected by grasses.

LOCATION AND EXPOSURE: The birdfoot violet must have full sun to grow and bloom vigorously, otherwise it gradually weakens and dies. In a sunny spot each plant will form a showy clump. This is an excellent wildflower for planting in a rock garden, on a slope, or along a walk where the sun shines all day.

PLANTING TIME: Early spring or fall for nursery-grown stock. Collect wild plants just after they finish blooming and before they go dormant. Or move plants in late August when the rains encourage new growth.

ROOT SYSTEM: The rootstock is very different from that of other violets. It is bulblike and looks much like a miniature celeriac root with coarse feeder roots.

PLANTING DEPTH AND SPACING: Space 6 to 12 inches apart, depending on the fertility of the soil. Set the rhizome about ½ to 1 inch deep and spread the roots evenly.

PLANTING STOCK AND PROPAGATION: Nursery-grown stock is superior to quality collected stock.

Divide the clumps in late summer, fall, or early spring. Plant "bulbs" about 1 inch deep in sandy loam soil that retains moisture. Remove some of the upper feeder roots from the rootstock. Many small bulblike rootstocks will form; these can be transplanted and usually bloom in the second year.

The seeds are difficult to find, especially when they are dispersed among grasses. In sandy areas the birdfoot violet self-sows readily. The bi-colored and white forms rarely retain their distinctive coloring when planted from seed.

Birdfoot violets seem to fare better and make a much prettier display when they are permitted to take over an entire area. Find a sunny nook where they can grow among sparse prairie grasses, and they will propagate themselves.

COMMENTS: The birdfoot violet is our choicest native violet, growing profusely in dry, sunny areas. Reforestation has killed huge patches of these violets; it is painful indeed to see young trees grow taller while the birdfoot beneath them grows scarcer and more precious each year. Do not pick the birdfoot violet since it does not have self-fertile hidden seed pods, as do most of the other violets without leafy stems, and requires the flower to produce seed.

Viola papilionacea • common blue violet

DESCRIPTION: 4 to 5 inches tall. The common blue violet blooms profusely. The flowers are rich purple-blue with a white throat and dark veining on the inside of the lower petal toward the base. The *albiflora* form is white with dark veining and a touch of blue or chartreuse on the inside of the lower petal towards the base. The white flowers make a pretty contrast with the purple-blue ones. The deep green foliage is long-lasting in either sun or shade if the soil is not too dry.

Blue violets are often found around old homesteads, in sunny open meadows, and along roadsides.

PERIOD OF BLOOM: May into June.

SOIL: This violet grows vigorously in any ordinary garden soil with average moisture.

LOCATION AND EXPOSURE: The common blue violet grows equally well in sunlight or open shade. It makes a quick groundcover for a slope, spreading rapidly by self-sowing. It spreads too profusely for the small garden and is best when naturalized among tall plants of equal vigor.

PLANTING TIME: Spring or fall. Moves easily with care at other times as well.

ROOT SYSTEM: A knotty rootstock with many fibrous feeder roots.

PLANTING DEPTH AND SPACING: Space 10 inches or more apart, depending on the effect wanted. Set the crown ½ to 1 inch deep. I have tilled the rootstock of this plant into the earth to a depth of several inches—they not only persisted but grew even more vigorously, forming large clumps.

PLANTING STOCK AND PROPAGATION: Use nursery-grown stock or quality collected stock.

Divide the clumps in spring, fall, or right after blooming. Keep the plants well watered until they are established. This violet self-sows freely. It has many hidden seed pods which disperse the seeds widely and establish new colonies.

COMMENTS: The lovely purple-blue flowers are intriguing despite the plant's tendency to overrun small gardens. For slopes and large areas it is unexcelled as a quick low groundcover. I find that the white variety is not quite so aggressive.

Viola Priceana • Confederate violet

DESCRIPTION: 4 to 6 inches tall. The white flowers are flushed with gray-blue or lavender. Although the Confederate violet is considered a variation of *Viola papilionacea*, its foliage is a little lighter green and possibly a little broader. It is not as aggressive unless grown in very fertile soil.

The Confederate violet is usually found in old gardens and around deserted homesteads where it was probably once cultivated.

PERIOD OF BLOOM: May into June.

SOIL: Slightly acid to neutral soils. This violet grows readily in most soils.

LOCATION AND EXPOSURE: Grow the Confederate violet in woodlands, along a border of deciduous woods, or in a shaded area at the base of a stone wall. In cold areas it should be mulched, as it does not seem to be as hardy as *Viola papilionacea*, nor does it do as well when cultivated in the hot sun.

PLANTING TIME: Spring or fall.

ROOT SYSTEM: A coarse knotty rhizome with many fibrous feeder roots.

PLANTING DEPTH AND SPACING: Space rhizomes 6 to 10 inches apart. The crown should be ½ to 1 inch below the surface of the soil. Mulch lightly. The Confederate violet has a tendency to grow itself out of the soil. In cold climates this will winter-kill it unless some extra mulch is added in late fall.

PLANTING STOCK AND PROPAGATION: Use nursery-grown or quality collected stock.

Divide the rootstocks in spring or fall. Also grow from seed. This violet self-sows to some extent.

COMMENTS: The Confederate violet is one of the showy spring violets that is especially lovely when planted in a colony. It produces self-fertile hidden seed pods near the surface of the soil. When these pods ripen they burst open and scatter seeds far and wide.

Viola (a sport) • Jessie's red violet

DESCRIPTION: 3 to 4 inches tall. The dainty, orchid-red flowers have wine-colored veins extending into their pale chartreuse throats.

141

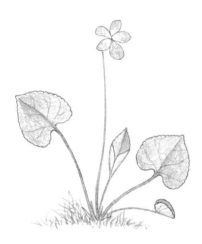

The leaves are medium green and heart-shaped. The white form is known as Jessie's white violet and has a clear chartreuse throat veined with purple. It is not as robust as *Viola papilionacea albiflora*. Examination leads me to believe Jessie's red violet is a smaller offspring of *Viola papilionacea albiflora*, the major difference being that Jessie's red violet is smaller.

My plants came from a grower in New York who had had them so long he could not recall their source.

PERIOD OF BLOOM: May into June. If there is sufficient rainfall in August, Jessie's red violet will often bloom again in September.

SOIL: Neutral to slightly acid garden soil. I grow it in sandy garden loam.

LOCATION AND EXPOSURE: Jessie's red violet is very adaptable. In our nursery it grows in colonies in open shade, full sun, and in one spot with an eastern exposure, where it has morning sunlight.

PLANTING TIME: Spring, fall, or after blooming.

ROOT SYSTEM: The medium-sized rootstock is knotty and has many fibrous feeder roots.

PLANTING DEPTH AND SPACING: Space 4 to 8 inches apart, as the violets form small clumps. Set the rootstock ½ to 1 inch deep.

PLANTING STOCK AND PROPAGATION: Use nursery-grown stock.

Clumps can be divided in spring or fall.

Jessie's red violet self-sows. Do not transplant until the seedlings are large enough to bloom.

COMMENTS: A most unusual violet. The orchid-red flower provides a welcome color contrast with other wild violets or small spring wildflowers.

Viola latiuscula • broad-leaved wood violet

DESCRIPTION: 4 to 6 inches tall. The medium-blue flowers of this violet are dark-veined and have a white throat. The leaves are broad and continue to develop after the plant has ceased to bloom.

The broad-leaved wood violet is found in meadows where it grows in the shade of other plants and in open woodlands where leafmold is plentiful.

PERIOD OF BLOOM: May into June.

SOIL: Ordinary garden soil or slightly acid woods soil. This violet is very easy to grow.

LOCATION AND EXPOSURE: Select an open woodland or a partly shaded area.

PLANTING TIME: Spring or fall.

ROOT SYSTEM: A knotty rhizome with fibrous feeder roots.

PLANTING DEPTH AND SPACING: Space 6 to 12 inches apart. Set the crowns ½ to 1 inch deep and mulch. Each crown will form a showy clump. This wood violet does not grow as aggressively as the common blue violet.

PLANTING STOCK AND PROPAGATION: Use nursery-grown stock or quality collected stock.

Divide the clumps in spring or fall. This violet is easily grown from seeds. It self-sows readily—many hidden self-fertile seed pods just below the soil surface rise and disperse the seeds as they ripen.

COMMENTS: You will know this species by its seed pods which are flushed with purple or frequently completely purple flushed with green. This is a neat violet that will not crowd out other woodland plants.

Viola palmata • early blue violet

DESCRIPTION: 5 to 8 inches tall. The dark blue flowers have light cream-colored throats. The lower petals are veined with purple. There is little variation in color within this species. The coarsely cut foliage is deeply toothed, somewhat resembling that of the birdfoot but not as airy.

Early blue violets are found in rich deciduous woods in light to partial shade, growing in large colonies.

PERIOD OF BLOOM: May into June.

SOIL: Average to dry fertile soils that are neutral to slightly acid.

LOCATION AND EXPOSURE: Early blue violets grow vigorously in high open shade. They are suitable for colonizing in shaded woodlands under the branches of tall trees. Or use them as groundcover between taller wildflowers that bloom later.

PLANTING TIME: Spring or fall.

ROOT SYSTEM: The coarse rhizome has many fibrous feeder roots. It becomes knotty with age.

PLANTING DEPTH AND SPACING: Space 6 to 12 inches apart, as each plant forms a neat clump. Set the rootstocks ½ to 1 inch

deep and mulch. When crowded, these violets have a tendency to grow out of the soil. They must be mulched in winter in cold climates.

PLANTING STOCK AND PROPAGATION: Use nursery-grown stock or quality collected stock where available.

Divide the clumps in spring or fall. This violet self-sows readily in open woodland soil.

COMMENTS: When seedlings first emerge, the first leaves are plain and not palmate. Usually the third to fifth leaf produced by a seedling starts to show the toothing of the parent plant.

Early blue violets look lovely when planted in large groups.

Viola blanda · sweet white violet

DESCRIPTION: 2 to 3 inches tall. This violet has light green, heart-shaped foliage and tiny flowers. The fragrant blossoms are white with purple veins extending toward the throat. The stems are flushed with a red that is especially bright on plants that grow in dry sunny areas.

Sweet white violet is very adaptable. It can be found in damp cool swamps, moist meadows, and partly shaded areas in deciduous woods where it makes a neat groundcover. It even grows in woodland soil that becomes very dry during the summer.

PERIOD OF BLOOM: May, sometimes into June.

SOIL: Neutral to slightly acid fertile soil with average to very high moisture content. Sweet white violet will also grow in drier woodlands where leafmold is plentiful.

LOCATION AND EXPOSURE: The sweet white violet is equally at home in a partly shaded dry woodland and in a sunny, moist spot. Plant it among taller wildflowers in shady woods or use it as groundcover under mulched shrubs. It is a very neat groundcover and spreads quickly when given a light fall mulching of partly decayed leaves or old marsh hay.

PLANTING TIME: While dormant in spring or fall. Potted stock may be planted anytime.

ROOT SYSTEM: A dainty fibrous rhizome that forks and sends out white filiform stolons which grow tiny feeder roots and eventually become mature plants. The sweet white violet spreads prolifically when planted where leafmold is plentiful. When planted in the open in ordinary garden soil without mulch, it stays in a neat clump and does not set new rhizomes as freely.

PLANTING DEPTH AND SPACING: Space 6 to 10 inches apart. This violet spreads to make neat mats. Set the crown of the main plant at soil level, making certain to cover all the smaller rhizomes and tiny rootlets. Mulch lightly with old humus or preferably with partially decayed small leaves.

PLANTING STOCK AND PROPAGATION: Nursery-grown potted stock is the easiest to transplant. You can also use wild quality collected stock.

The rhizomes can be divided when an area becomes too crowded. The tiny, plump, red-flushed seed pods burst and scatter the seeds widely, thus populating more distant areas.

COMMENTS: The sweet white violet is an excellent small low groundcover to use between taller wildflowers such as baneberries, black cohosh, and even lady's-slippers.

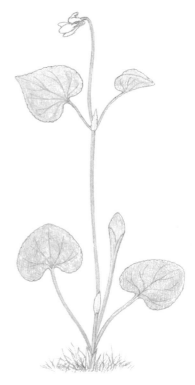

Viola pubescens • downy yellow violet

DESCRIPTION: 9 to 12 inches tall. Bright yellow flowers, veined with purple toward the throat, grow on leafy stems above sturdy green foliage.

The downy yellow violet is found in rich, dry, deciduous woods where the sunlight filters through leafless branches in spring. It is rarely found growing in large patches.

PERIOD OF BLOOM: May into June.

SOIL: Average to dry fertile soils that are neutral to only slightly acid. I have grown this violet in full sun in sandy garden loam; the foliage remained green and the plant set an abundance of seed.

LOCATION AND EXPOSURE: The downy yellow violet is an excellent flower to grow in a deciduous woods or along a border exposed to brief morning sunlight. Plant at least three or more together or they will not be very noticeable. This plant, unlike so many violets without leafy stalks, does not form clumps.

PLANTING TIME: While dormant in spring or fall.

ROOT SYSTEM: A medium-sized rhizome with fibrous feeder roots.

PLANTING DEPTH AND SPACING: Space about 6 inches apart. Set the plants so that the crown is barely ½ inch below soil level. Mulch.

PLANTING STOCK AND PROPAGATION: Use nursery-grown stock or, when available, quality collected stock.

If you propagate by planting seeds in flats, do not transplant the seedlings until the second year. The plant self-sows under ideal conditions where there is an abundance of leafmold.

COMMENTS: This violet never becomes weedy. In my garden the chipmunks steal the downy seed pods just before they ripen, thus cheating me of my seed supply. To outfox them, I set wire cages over several plants.

Watch the seed pods closely. Pick them when they are ready to pop open, just as they are about to turn tan, and drop them into a glass jar with a piece of tissue to keep them from molding. Do not use a shallow container; the seeds may disperse when the pods pop open.

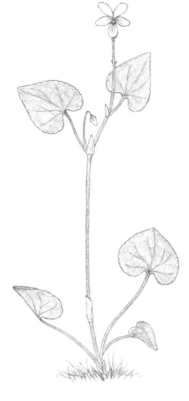

Viola pensylvanica • smooth yellow violet

DESCRIPTION: This small violet (Var. *eriocarpa*) has small flowers that are clear yellow with black veins deep in their throats. The stems are leafy, and there is some basal foliage. The smooth yellow violet resembles the downy yellow but is smaller, has lighter green foliage, and lacks the downiness on the leaves and seed pods.

It is found in moist woodlands, often with *Trillium grandiflorum* and bloodroot.

PERIOD OF BLOOM: May into June.

SOIL: Humus-rich soil that is neutral to only slightly acid. The soil can be moist or have the average moisture content of garden soils.

LOCATION AND EXPOSURE: The smooth yellow violet is an excellent plant to grow in small colonies in the woodland among rocks or tall spring wildflowers. When planted in dry woodland it will become dormant in periods of drought. It can be grown in full sunlight.

PLANTING TIME: Spring or fall, while at least partially dormant.

ROOT SYSTEM: A compact rootstock with stringy fibrous roots which form a large clump. A vigorous grower, it forms large colonies quickly.

This violet self-sows readily wherever the ground is open. Collecting seeds is a problem, as the seed capsules burst open un-expectedly.

PLANTING DEPTH AND SPACING: Space 4 to 6 inches or more apart. Spread the roots evenly and barely cover the crowns. Mulch lightly.

PLANTING STOCK AND PROPAGATION: Use nursery-grown stock or, when available, quality collected stock.

If you propagate by planting seeds in flats, do not transplant the seedlings until the second year. The plant self-sows under ideal conditions where there is an abundance of leafmold.

COMMENTS: Smooth yellow violet is best suited for planting among taller, more robust woodland wildflowers. It provides a neat groundcover for moist areas.

Viola canadensis • Canada violet

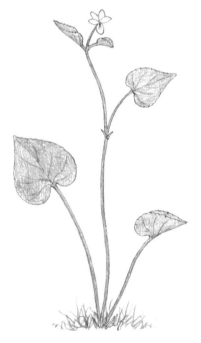

DESCRIPTION: 10 to 15 inches tall. The pointed heart-shaped leaves of the Canada violet grow on leafy stems. The flowers are pre-dominantly white; the plant may simultaneously bear white, magenta-flushed, and lavender-flushed flowers. They have dark purple veins inside, from the lower part of the petals to the base, and yellow centers.

The Canada violet grows in cool shady woods, usually in rocky terrain and often with Dutchman's breeches and wild blue phlox. It favors cold climates.

PERIOD OF BLOOM: May through June, often into midsummer.

SOIL: Neutral to slightly acid soil that is rich in humus and reason-ably moist. Once established, the plants can withstand drought as well as severe cold without mulch.

LOCATION AND EXPOSURE: Cool shaded woodland where the soil is rich in humus and rather rocky; such a spot is often found near a brook. Grow the Canada violet in colonies to promote longer periods of bloom.

PLANTING TIME: While dormant in spring or fall. This violet should not be moved bareroot once it has begun to grow.

ROOT SYSTEM: A knotty rhizome with many fibrous roots. It forms a compact clump that is difficult to divide.

PLANTING DEPTH AND SPACING: Space 1 inch apart or more. Set the rootstock with the crown just barely below soil level.

147

PLANTING STOCK AND PROPAGATION: Use nursery-grown stock or quality collected stock.

Seeds are scarce, but sowing is the best method of propagation. This violet self-sows to some extent, but spreads very slowly and never becomes weedy.

COMMENTS: The peculiarity of having white and partly colored flowers on the same plant at the same time makes the Canada violet an interesting specimen. The blossoms are long-lasting.

Viola conspersa • American dog violet

DESCRIPTION: 2 to 6 inches tall. The dainty flowers are light to medium blue, with dark veining extending into the white throat. The stems are slender, with a number of rounded leaves. Each plant usually has two to four flowering stalks.

The American dog violet grows in dry, open woodland with sparse grasses or in damp, rocky woods. When we cleared land to make our lawn, the dog violet volunteered abundantly and still persists in some shady spots.

PERIOD OF BLOOM: May into June.

SOIL: Neutral to slightly acid soil of average fertility.

LOCATION AND EXPOSURE: Partial to high open shade or places exposed to the morning sun. Plant this violet in colonies among other small wildflowers, or tuck it into shady, humus-filled niches of a rock garden.

PLANTING TIME: While dormant in early spring or fall. This variety does not transplant easily once it has begun to grow.

ROOT SYSTEM: A small rootstock with fibrous roots.

PLANTING DEPTH AND SPACING: Set the plants about 4 inches apart and as deep as the level at which they previously grew. Always move the plants with a little dirt adhering to the roots.

PLANTING STOCK AND PROPAGATION: Use nursery-grown stock or collected stock with soil adhering.

Seeds are hard to collect. This violet self-sows to some extent.

COMMENTS: Along with the sweet white, the American dog violet is our daintiest violet. Unlike the former, it does not spread by rhizomes; it multiplies slowly and never gets weedy. To make the dog violet more noticeable, plant in groups of three to six.

Viola (a sport?) • an unidentified violet

A short while ago I found in my wild garden a strange new violet growing where *Viola papilionacea*, the common blue violet, had previously grown. The flower is a delicate sky-blue and the lower petal is flushed with a deeper blue and veined with dark purple. The two lateral petals are downy toward the throat, which is a delicate chartreuse. The foliage is light green and similar in shape to that of Jessie's red violet. It does well in either full sun or light shade.

The intruder has been separated from the other plants and I am now waiting to see what the seedlings will be like. Will their flowers be purple-blue like the common blue violet's, or remain, like their parents', a lovely sky blue?

LYTHRACEAE [Loosestrife Family]

Lythrum Salicaria • purple loosestrife

DESCRIPTION: 2 to 4 feet tall. The showy flower spikes have tiny flowers ranging from rose-purple to magenta. The leafy square stems have lanced foliage on either side.

Purple loosestrife is found in damp ditches, sunny wet meadows, and marshes. It grows very tall and stately in wet places. I first came upon it growing in a wet ditch, where it has continued to grow for years.

PERIOD OF BLOOM: June through September, reaching its peak in July and August.

SOIL: Slightly acid to neutral, fertile soils with constant moisture, though not necessarily wet. Purple loosestrife does reasonably well in ordinary garden soil that does not bake dry.

LOCATION AND EXPOSURE: To best display their beauty, set the plants singly or in groups of three. Plant all members of the loosestrife family where you want them to remain, since they develop heavy roots with age. A single plant sends up many spikes as it matures. Purple loosestrife is excellent for naturalizing in a wet meadow or as a specimen plant at the back of a border.

PLANTING TIME: While dormant in spring or fall.

ROOT SYSTEM: A very unyielding, woody rootstock with fine fibrous roots. When moving old plants, prune the roots considerably to encourage new growth.

PLANTING DEPTH AND SPACING: Space 1 to 3 feet apart. Set young or medium-sized plants with the pink eye about 1 inch below soil level. Trim off ragged old roots, leaving only the fine fibrous ones.

PLANTING STOCK AND PROPAGATION: Use young to medium-sized nursery-grown stock or quality collected young stock. Use old plants only as a last resort.

Cuttings taken from the center length of the stem in July give very good results and is the best method of propagation. Purple loosestrife self-sows in some areas.

COMMENTS: Purple loosestrife is a bold plant that lends color and beauty to the landscape. Originally found only in cultivation, it has taken to the wild and prospered remarkably well.

ARALIACEAE [Ginseng Family]

Aralia racemosa • spikenard

DESCRIPTION: 2 to 5 feet tall. The large, tapered flower clusters, made up of many tiny flowers, are white with a tint of yellow or green. They grow upright above large compound foliage on heavy, leafy stems. The stems are a wine-flushed green. Purple-red to wine-colored berries ripen in the fall and are very showy. Spikenard is a robust grower, and seems almost tropical. You will know this bold plant whenever you meet it, which will usually be quite unexpectedly.

Spikenard is rarely found in large patches. It seeks high open shade in deciduous woods where leafmold is deep but where the terrain is rocky and bare of other vegetation.

PERIOD OF BLOOM: Late June into July.

SOIL: Slightly acid to neutral rich woods soil with constant moisture is best. But I have also grown spikenard in partial shade and in full sun in a fertile sandy loam with no more than average moisture.

LOCATION AND EXPOSURE: For a bold effect, plant spikenard alone in full display, with a shady border as background, or along the border of open woodlands. It is equally effective when planted in high open shade where only leafmold or small wildflowers and ferns carpet the forest floor. A few plants here and there are sure to draw favorable comments.

PLANTING TIME: While dormant in spring or fall.

ROOT SYSTEM: A large knotty and scarred rhizome grayish in color and forked several times. Each year's growth leaves a scar on the rootstock. The roots have a very pleasing aroma. It is next to impossible to dig up large rootstocks without breaking them, but this does not hinder future growth. The top growth is deciduous.

PLANTING DEPTH AND SPACING: Cut the heavy portion of rootstocks into 4 to 5 inch lengths and plant horizontally 1 to 2 inches deep in sandy loam in partial shade. Keep the soil reasonably moist.

PLANTING STOCK AND PROPAGATION: Nursery-grown transplants between one and two years old are best. Or use quality collected stock that is not too large. Young plants that have not yet bloomed are easiest to move.

Divide old rootstocks. During the fall the plants go dormant. A good number of the divisions will grow into plants worth transplanting. Some may bloom the following year.

I have had considerable success with cuttings by packing them in plastic bags with damp sphagnum moss and keeping them in the well pit over the winter. I set the cuttings out in mid-June, mulch them, and keep them moist. Over 85 percent grew.

COMMENTS: The large compound leaves and colorful fall fruit of the spikenard make it an unusual plant of great beauty. Planted alone in full display, it is a bold specimen. The plants are slow to bloom after being disturbed, but they are not demanding; once established they last for many years.

Aralia nudicaulis • wild sarsaparilla

DESCRIPTION: 8 to 12 inches tall. A solitary stem bears three compound leaves, which usually grow horizontally. Each flowering plant has only one bare stalk topped with one to three round flower heads. The flower heads are made up of many tiny greenish florets. Green berries turn black in fall.

Wild sarsaparilla is found growing in conservative little colonies in dry deciduous woods and thickets.

PERIOD OF BLOOM: May into June.

SOIL: Acid to slightly acid woods soil or garden soil. The plant is easily cultivated.

LOCATION AND EXPOSURE: Wild sarsaparilla makes a good open groundcover in high shade where the forest floor is covered with leafmold and other vegetation is sparse. If you grow it along the edge of the woodland it will usually work its way inward.

PLANTING TIME: While dormant in spring or fall.

ROOT SYSTEM: The knotty rootstock, bearing scars of each previous year's growth, forms rhizomes that send up new plants at frequent intervals.

PLANTING DEPTH AND SPACING: Space 12 to 18 inches apart. Set plants with dormant shoots at soil level and mulch. Any attached rhizomes should be planted horizontally.

PLANTING STOCK AND PROPAGATION: Use nursery-grown stock or quality collected stock.

Divide rootstocks when they are dormant. Sarsaparilla can be grown from seeds sown when ripe, but it propagates so easily from rootstock divisions that I hardly ever bother with seeds. Seedlings mature slowly.

COMMENTS: The foliage of the wild sarsaparilla makes a striking contrast interspersed with other woodland plants. Do not plant it among very small woodland plants or it may block out too much light. My plants send up new shoots at intervals of 6 to 10 inches, but this might vary according to soil fertility.

The wild sarsaparilla is not of the sarsaparilla family but derives its name from the similar flavor of its roots, which are often used as a substitute for making syrup and medicinal extracts.

Panax quinquefolium • ginseng

DESCRIPTION: 8 to 15 inches tall. Each plant sends up a solitary stalk with three compound leaves and one round, white to yellowish flower cluster. In early autumn the crimson berries appear. The rootstock is yellowish brown.

Ginseng is found in northeastern and north central hardwood forests, in cool shade where leafmold is plentiful. It is rare.

PERIOD OF BLOOM: July.

SOIL: Ginseng will grow only in a humus-rich woodland soil. The soil should be preferably from hardwood areas—never from the high-acid evergreen areas.

LOCATION AND EXPOSURE: This plant must have shade. Cool shade in an open woods is ideal. In the wild garden, ginseng is grown mainly for the contrast of its foliage and the bright color of its berry rather than for its flower. Because of its history, ginseng is certain to be a conversation piece in any wild garden.

PLANTING TIME: While dormant in spring or fall.

ROOT SYSTEM: A cylindrical, fleshy rootstock of a yellowish brown color that forks as it matures. It is aromatic.

PLANTING DEPTH AND SPACING: Space 8 or more inches apart. Or plant a few at random. Set the eyes of the rootstock 2 to 3 inches deep, making certain that the tapering rootstock is not bent over. Mulch lightly, preferably with old leafmold.

PLANTING STOCK AND PROPAGATION: Nursery-grown stock, one to two years old, is best. Or use quality collected stock if you are fortunate enough to find it. Ginseng is becoming increasingly rare in the wild.

Ginseng seeds take eighteen months to germinate; they should never be allowed to dry out. Fresh seeds should be layered immediately in damp earth and kept until the following August or September, then planted in beds in the open. Space them several inches apart. Or try sowing the seeds in the open and letting them fend for themselves. This method has given me the best results. Seedlings may appear the second spring. They require about two years to bloom, and five years to mature.

COMMENTS: Ginseng once grew abundantly in our hardwood forests. Unfortunately, so many plants were dug up for export to China, where they were prized for the medicinal value of their roots, that it is now rarely found growing wild.

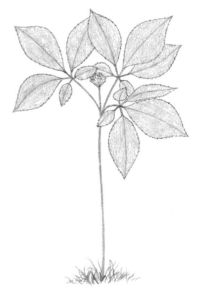

Panax trifolium • dwarf ginseng

DESCRIPTION: 3 to 5 inches tall. This neat little plant has a small ball of tiny white florets above a whorl of three small, compound palmate leaves. Yellow berries appear in the fall.

Dwarf ginseng is found in moist rich woods, usually where there is a mixture of evergreen and deciduous trees. It may be found on moist hummocks in high open shade. It is quite rare.

PERIOD OF BLOOM: May into June.

SOIL: Acid to slightly acid humus-rich woods soil that retains moisture. Add some damp peatmoss to the soil.

LOCATION AND EXPOSURE: Plant dwarf ginseng in damp, moist woodland or at the edge of a shady bog that is free from grass and covered with low sphagnum moss.

PLANTING TIME: Fall is best. The plant must be dormant.

ROOT SYSTEM: A tiny, globe-shaped, blackish tuber.

PLANTING DEPTH AND SPACING: Space only about 4 inches apart in a small colony. Set the tubers 2 inches deep; in the wild they are even deeper.

PLANTING STOCK AND PROPAGATION: Nursery-grown stock is rarely offered. Use quality collected stock dug in fall. Never transplant dwarf ginseng until it goes dormant. Mark the area where you find it growing and return to collect it in fall.

Sow the seeds when they are ripe. The seeds are scarce.

COMMENTS: Dwarf ginseng is a dainty, much prized plant for the wildflower garden. Always set out three or more tubers in a colony —otherwise they will be obscured by the surrounding plants. A small colony perched on a hummock makes a delightful picture.

CORNACEAE [Dogwood Family]

Cornus canadensis • bunchberry

DESCRIPTION: 3 to 5 inches tall. Four white dogwood-like bracts with yellow centers give the effect of a full-bodied flower. The flower grows on a single short, rigid stem above a whorl of four to six almost ovate leaves. Heavy clusters of bright orange-red berries appear in fall.

154

Bunchberry is found in deep, cool woodlands. It creeps over old decaying logs and sends rhizomes through rotted pine logs. I have even found it growing at the top and along the sides of decaying white pine stumps where chipmunks evidently hid some seeds.

Bunchberry has a way of taking over old logging roads that had the soil scraped bare. When the road is in the shade, bunchberry grows luxuriantly, blooms abundantly, and sets out a heavy seed crop. In sunnier, moister areas the plant is smaller.

PERIOD OF BLOOM: Late May into July.

SOIL: Very acid to slightly acid humus-rich soil with high to average moisture content. However, I once found bunchberry growing along an old logging road in a bank of pure red sand with barely a sprinkling of humus. Since it was on a shady hillside the moisture was constant, and a nice colony of blooming plants was firmly established despite the poor soil.

One little colony which has persisted and bloomed freely along a concrete walk grows in soil with a pH of only 6. I am therefore inclined to believe that shade, constant moisture with good drainage, humus-rich soil or damp sand, are much more important than an acid soil.

LOCATION AND EXPOSURE: Bunchberry is an excellent groundcover under evergreens or deciduous trees where there is ample humus and where falling needles and leaves furnish a continuous mulch and make the soil sufficiently acidic and fertile. Bunchberry is a good companion plant for the pink lady's-slipper or bluebeard lily. All three need shade but tolerate filtered spring sunlight or shifting shade in summer.

PLANTING TIME: Plant bareroot stock while dormant in spring or fall. Potted stock can be planted almost anytime.

ROOT SYSTEM: A slender rhizome, forking and spreading in many directions to send up new plants. New rhizomes are white or pinkish with rose-colored buds. They become woody as they mature and therefore more troublesome to establish. When several plants are confined to a small container (2¼ inch rose pot) of woods soil and kept moist, they develop a great many roots in one growing season under ideal conditions. When the plants are removed from the container intact and planted in a permanent home, they soon form a neat colony.

PLANTING DEPTH AND SPACING: Space bareroot stock 6 inches apart

and potted stock 1 foot apart. Set the eye of bareroot stock about ¼ inch deep and mulch lightly. Keep moist. Potted stock should be planted at soil level and also mulched and kept moist. A light mulch of evergreen needles or partly decayed leaves is excellent.

PLANTING STOCK AND PROPAGATION: Nursery-grown potted stock is far superior. You can also use quality collected sods taken from an area where the plants grow close together. Replant the sods at the same soil level. Bareroot stock can be difficult to establish. It must be freshly dug for fair results. I do not recommend it.

Pulp-free seeds planted in peat pots and kept moist sometimes give excellent results. Plant 6 to 8 seeds in each pot. They may not germinate until the second or third year.

COMMENTS: Bunchberry is one of our choicest groundcovers but often difficult to grow successfully. Once established, however, it will continue to spread, densely carpeting the forest floor. Bunchberries do not seem to thrive in isolation; it is best to plant them in groups of three or more.

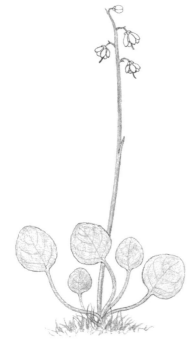

PYROLACEAE [Wintergreen Family]

Pyrola virens • shinleaf

DESCRIPTION: 6 to 8 inches tall. A solitary stem bears a raceme of waxy-white fragrant flowers above roundish basal foliage. The flowers are reminiscent of widely opened lily of the valley.

Shinleaf is found in dry to moist deciduous woods. It grows among fringed polygala and large merrybells on slopes where tall birches, soft maples, aspens, and a few oaks furnish shade. It blooms best where the shade is not too deep.

PERIOD OF BLOOM: June into July.

SOIL: Slightly acid to acid, humus-rich woods soil with some moisture available while the plants are blooming.

LOCATION AND EXPOSURE: High open woodlands where the sun filters through leafless trees in spring. Grow shinleaf in colonies or among other small woodland plants that also thrive in humus-rich soil.

PLANTING TIME: While dormant in spring or fall.

ROOT SYSTEM: The running, threadlike white rhizome is very extensive, making it difficult to collect sods with enough rhizomes in each clump.

PLANTING DEPTH AND SPACING: Space about 1 foot apart. Set potted stock or sods at soil level and mulch lightly wth small leaves, preferably birch or willow.

PLANTING STOCK AND PROPAGATION: Nursery-grown potted stock is best, but not often available. Plant quality collected sods, at least 8 inches square, in fall.

You can plant the seeds if they are available, though germination is poor.

COMMENTS: Pyrolas are choice plants with lovely delicate flowers. They make excellent groundcovers but are very difficult plants to establish unless all their requirements are met.

ERICACEAE [Heath Family]

Epigaea repens • trailing arbutus

DESCRIPTION: A 6 to 10 inch creeper. The stems of this vinelike plant are woody and have oval, hairy but somewhat leathery leaves. The clusters of delicate, tubular flowers are white to pale pink and fragrant.

By scuffling the fallen leaves in an oak-pine wood, you may discover trailing arbutus growing in lovely mats. It usually grows in the vicinity of bunchberry, wintergreen, starflower, clintonia, and goldthread.

PERIOD OF BLOOM: May.

SOIL: An acid to moderately acid sandy loam soil, rich in humus to a shallow depth, and with a sandy soil below providing good drainage. I use a soil with a pH of 6.

LOCATION AND EXPOSURE: Trailing arbutus grows well in a cool open woods where it is protected from the hot summer sun but where early spring sunshine filters through leafless branches. Choose a spot where the forest floor is covered with decaying leaves or evergreen needles. Also, woodland soil contains the mycorhizal fungi that are beneficial to the plant.

157

PLANTING TIME: Plant sods in spring or fall. Potted stock can be planted almost anytime.

ROOT SYSTEM: Except for the taproot, the plant feeds on the first few inches of soil. Feeder roots develop where the vines are covered with damp humus.

PLANTING DEPTH AND SPACING: Set sods or potted stock at soil level and mulch by scattering a mixture of evergreen needles, birch leaves, and soft maple leaves. Keep the plants moist until they are well established.

PLANTING STOCK AND PROPAGATION: Nursery-grown potted stock is superior to quality collected sods.

Cuttings taken in early fall should be put in a sand–peat mixture and placed in a cold frame over the winter. A hormone rooting compound is beneficial. Mulch the cuttings lightly for the winter. There will usually be good stock at the end of the second year (though not always). Diligent care and patience is important.

Seeds sown in a humus-rich acid soil produce a sparse scattering of seedlings. Germination is poor.

COMMENTS: Trailing arbutus is on the protected list in Wisconsin and should never be dug or picked without the permission of the landowner. It is best not to pick arbutus at any time, but rather to enjoy its beauty in the wild. Some of these plants must be preserved for future generations to see.

Gaultheria procumbens • wintergreen

DESCRIPTION: 2 to 4 inches tall. The tiny white bell-shaped flowers, often tinged with pink, are hidden by three thick aromatic leaves. The red berries that appear in fall last a long while, sometimes until spring. These edible berries are known for their flavor.

Wintergreen is often found carpeting large areas of woodland, whether damp or dry, deciduous or evergreen.

PERIOD OF BLOOM: Late June into August.

SOIL: Acid to only slightly acid humus-rich soil with some sandy base beneath to ensure good drainage. Sometimes wintergreen is found growing in peaty soil, usually on hummocks.

LOCATION AND EXPOSURE: Wintergreen grows well under the open shade of oaks and pines. It makes a sturdy groundcover for large woodland areas free from underbrush. It can also be grown in the shade of sparsely planted tall wildflowers or ferns.

PLANTING TIME: Spring or fall. Plant potted stock anytime.

ROOT SYSTEM: A creeping rootstock 1 to 2 inches beneath the soil forks to send out new rhizomes which form new plants. These rhizomes are white to deep pink, and pinkest at the end where the new bud is to form.

PLANTING DEPTH AND SPACING: Space about 1 inch apart exactly at soil level. Mulch lightly with small decaying leaves, pine needles, or preferably a mixture of both.

PLANTING STOCK AND PROPAGATION: Potted nursery-grown stock is best but is rarely offered. Use quality collected sods from areas where the plants grow close together.

You can take cuttings of new plants or rhizomes in July, but I do not get very good results. Seeds are very slow to germinate and give very poor results.

COMMENTS: The mealy red berries have a mild and pleasant minty flavor; they stay on the plants unless plucked by birds or rodents. The leaves also have the wintergreen flavor and can be dried and used as a tea.

Gaultheria hispidula • creeping snowberry

DESCRIPTION: 3 to 6 inch dainty trailing vine. Tiny round evergreen leaves, which taste like wintergreen, are opposite each other on a brown woody stem. The tiny white flowers are bell-shaped. The small aromatic berry that appears later is also white.

I searched for a bed of creeping snowberry for a long time until my husband showed me a patch he had found in a white-spruce swamp while hunting. This patch made a showy carpet. It grew protected from hot sun on hummocklike spots overgrown by dense hugging mosses, on old logs decayed almost to humus, and it reached out into sphagnum-moss beds where an occasional pitcher plant stood out boldly.

PERIOD OF BLOOM: May into June.

SOIL: I found the snowberry growing in a medium that could hardly be called soil; it was composed of moss-covered decaying wood covered with layers of old needles, tiny mosses, and decaying

vegetation. I constructed a similar medium by the following process, which proved successful. Select a cool dampy site and dig a hole. Make a rim around the top of the hole with a ring of metal at least 6 inches wide. Fill the hole to the top with equal portions of sharp sand, coarsely sifted rotted pine wood, shredded damp sphagnum moss, and damp peatmoss, all mixed together thoroughly. Moisten and firm the mixture as you fill the hole.

If you can find a well rotted white pine log in your woodland just let the snowberry ramble over it, and skip the above procedure.

LOCATION AND EXPOSURE: Creeping snowberry requires deep cool shade and a constant supply of moisture. Moisture is *very* important. Plant the creeping snowberry in a carefully prepared bed or near a rotted log where it can ramble to form a dense colony.

PLANTING TIME: Plant sods in spring or fall. Potted stock can be planted anytime.

ROOT SYSTEM: Fine hairy roots form on the underside of the woody stems wherever the plant lies on damp moss or decaying humus. These tiny roots do not continue growing when planted directly into ordinary woods soil.

PLANTING DEPTH AND SPACING: Space 1 foot apart. Set potted stock or sod at soil level, tucking in any tiny rootlets that may have formed along the stems. When you grow snowberry in a prepared bed try to find a piece of rotted, moss-covered wood to put nearby to create a natural effect. If the wood is kept moist, some of the stems will root and gradually spread over the entire surface.

PLANTING STOCK AND PROPAGATION: Nursery-grown potted stock is by far the best, but rarely offered. With proper care, quality collected stock will give good results in an ideal location.

Seeds are very scarce and very slow to germinate.

Six-inch cuttings taken in early May give good results. My method of propagation: Place a plastic sheet about 6 by 24 inches on a table. Cover half of it lengthwise with damp shredded sphagnum moss. Over this, lay the 6 inch cuttings on their sides so that the lower 2 inches (trimmed of tiny leaves) rest on the moss and the upper 4 inches extend 1 inch beyond the other side of the 6 inch plastic width. Sprinkle another ½ inch layer of damp sphagnum moss over the stems on the mossy side of the plastic. Now fold the clear side of the plastic over the mossy side; roll up the entire length of the sheet carefully and tie it. This should give you a roll with the 1 inch of leafy stems covering one end. Place the roll with the leafy side up in a tin can punched with holes, and loosely invert a plastic bag over both. Put the whole thing in the propagating frame or cold frame. In the propagating frame the cuttings may be ready for potting in late August; in the cold frame they will take another year. Always keep the moss moist.

Pot the cuttings in the mixture described above in the soil section. Hold the potted cuttings in a cold frame for a year or two before moving them to their permanent bed.

When transplanting to pots, let any moss adhering to the fragile roots remain. Particular care must be taken at this time not to injure the fine roots. This method will produce stock that should grow into showy specimens.

COMMENTS: Cultivating creeping snowberry is a challenging pursuit needing special care and patience; you may well be proud once you have succeeded in establishing it.

Arctostaphylos Uva-ursi • bearberry

DESCRIPTION: 8 to 20 inch trailing vines. The small, white to pinkish flowers resemble those of blueberry and wintergreen. The small, ovate, alternate leaves on a woody vine form a dense carpet of glossy green. The stems of vines over two years old are often tinted with red. Long-lasting red berries appear in August.

Bearberry grows along sandy roadsides, in open oak and pine woods, and in places where there is barely an inch of top soil and plenty of red sand. On sunny sandy banks in reforested areas, where fire lanes interlace the countryside, bearberry is often found crawling along and rooting as it travels. Bearberry is beautiful in such areas, always lush and green.

PERIOD OF BLOOM: Late May.

SOIL: Acid to moderately acid, gritty soil. It should be moist enough to allow for good growth, but must always have good drainage. A generous amount of sharp sand and damp peatmoss should be added to average soils.

LOCATION AND EXPOSURE: Bearberry is an unexcelled groundcover for sandy soil on a gently sloped bank or in wide patches of open sand. It blooms best in sunny areas. It is also a good groundcover

161

to plant in intermittent sunlight under high-branched evergreens.

PLANTING TIME: Plant potted stock or sods in early spring or fall.

ROOT SYSTEM: Fine hairy roots develop wherever the tender young vines rest on the damp earth as they creep along. When the vines become woody the hairy roots break away, and the plant dies from lack of nourishment.

PLANTING DEPTH AND SPACING: Set potted stock at soil level or slightly deeper. Cover any bare branches with soil. New roots will develop on two-year-old stems. Space potted stock or sods about 1 foot apart. Time and patience are required to establish this plant successfully, but once established it grows luxuriantly.

PLANTING STOCK AND PROPAGATION: Nursery-grown potted stock is best though expensive. Sods are difficult to dig up and not always reliable. Planting bareroot stock is a waste of time and money.

Cuttings taken in July give poor results, but cuttings taken in early September when the wood has hardened a little give better results. You may use the same procedure that I described for propagating from creeping snowberry cuttings. Or dip the cuttings in a hormone rooting compound, pot them in a sand-peat mixture, and put them in a propagating frame. It may take one or two years before the plants can be placed in their permanent home.

Seeds sown as soon as they ripen may take two years to germinate and another two or three years for the seedlings to mature enough to bloom.

COMMENTS: Bearberry is not an easy plant to grow, but once established it quickly carpets large areas with glossy green.

In autumn, when the foliage takes on a bronze tinge, the partridges come searching for bearberries to eat.

DIAPENSIACEAE [Diapensia Family]

Galax aphylla • galax

DESCRIPTION: 8 to 15 inches tall. Racemes of dainty white flowers grow on leafless stalks. The round basal foliage is a lustrous shiny green, often with a reddish tint. The leaves are slightly toothed and have a leathery texture.

Galax grows naturally in rocky mountainous woods with heavy soils in the southern part of the country.

PERIOD OF BLOOM: May into June.

SOIL: In the wild, galax grows in heavy clay soil. In my wild garden I grow it in an acid to slightly acid woods soil with a generous layer of decaying oak leafmold. It needs constant moisture.

LOCATION AND EXPOSURE: Galax is an excellent groundcover to grow in the deep shade of high open oak and evergreen woods where there is humus to hold in the moisture. It is best displayed when grown in its own exclusive colony.

PLANTING TIME: Spring or fall.

ROOT SYSTEM: A knotty, twisted, pinkish-red rhizome that forks to send up new shoots. It has fibrous feeder roots.

PLANTING DEPTH AND SPACING: Space 6 to 12 inches apart. Set bare roots horizontally about 1 inch deep with the red tip leading to soil level. Set potted stock or sods at the same level at which they previously grew. Give extra mulch in winter in very cold climates.

PLANTING STOCK AND PROPAGATION: Nursery-grown potted stock is best, but you can also use quality collected sods.

When dividing large clumps, leave soil adhering. I have never grown galax from seeds, as the plant does not set seed this far north.

COMMENTS: Galax, which is also known as beetleweed or wand-flower, is a plant of high quality, but difficult to grow. It is much sought after by florists for its long-lasting, leathery leaves.

I had almost given up hope of growing galax this far north; despite frequent waterings, my plants did not flourish. Then, after a good soaking, I decided to smother them with decaying oak leaves (no white oak). I set the galax in an out-of-the-way place and completely neglected them. Late in August I went back to the site and was surprised to find that all the plants had sent up healthy new leaves. They had taken hold despite neglect and severe drought, and I can only attribute this growth to the 6 to 8 inch layer of oak leaves I had spread over the area.

I will take some root cuttings from this acclimated stock in early spring before new growth appears.

PRIMULACEAE [Primrose Family]

Dodecatheon Meadia • shooting star

DESCRIPTION: 10 to 15 inches tall. Clusters of starlike flowers with curved petals are borne on sturdy hollow stems above a rosette of round-lobed oblong foliage. The stars vary in color from white to pink or lavender. (The white variety is supposedly rare, but most of my plants are white.) The centers of the flowers are yellow with blackish circles. The interesting cuplike seed pods have little toothed edges.

Shooting star is found in open woods, fertile prairies, meadows, and old cemeteries.

PERIOD OF BLOOM: May into June.

SOIL: Fertile sandy loam, heavier soils, or humus-rich woodland soil that is neutral to slightly acid. The plants must have moisture when they are blooming.

LOCATION AND EXPOSURE: Plant shooting stars along a path, among rocks in shade, or in the open woodland where they will have sun during the spring. Shooting stars can also be planted in full sun among other plants that will take over when it goes dormant. Established plants can endure extreme drought if they are well mulched. I keep the nursery beds under continuous mulch, adding some each year after the plants go dormant.

PLANTING TIME: Fall is preferable.

ROOT SYSTEM: A coarse rootstock with white fibrous roots and many feeder rootlets. As the plant grows older, it sends up several crowns. Mature plants form little eyes near the crown, and these develop into new plants. The rootstock is very fragrant.

PLANTING DEPTH AND SPACING: Space 10 to 15 inches apart. Set the eye of the dormant stock about ½ inch deep, making sure to spread the roots evenly. Mulch.

PLANTING STOCK AND PROPAGATION: Use nursery-grown or quality collected stock, the latter will not usually bloom the first year.

The easiest method of propagation is to divide the crowns in late summer or fall. To divide the rootstock, break away from the mother plant each segment that bears an eye. Remove part of the lower portion so that the new segment is about 3 inches long. Set in a flat or in a pot. Usually two years elapse before new plants will bloom.

Seeds are plentiful but very slow to germinate. Seedlings are very fragile for the first two years and may die in transplanting.

COMMENTS: There is a much showier species, *Dodecatheon amethystinum*, with blossoms in shades of glowing amethyst and magenta. They require more moisture, however, and are not as easily grown as the more common *Dodecatheon Meadia*. Shooting star is sometimes known as American cowslip.

Lysimachia terrestris • swamp candles

DESCRIPTION: 10 to 15 inches tall. The upright stalks have willow-like leaves and are topped with a wand of clear yellow, starlike flowers with reddish purple markings. The flowers bloom over a long period if there is ample moisture. Bulbils form in the axils of the leaves.

Swamp candles are found in lowlands and roadside ditches. Once plentiful in my area, they are now found only along lesser country roads because of weed spraying along the highways.

PERIOD OF BLOOM: June through August, and sometimes into September.

SOIL: Moist to wet soils of moderate acidity and fertility. When swamp candles are grown in average garden soil that is constantly moist, the blossoms will be smaller and will not last as long.

LOCATION AND EXPOSURE: Swamp candles are best planted in colonies in a dampish place where they can spread to form a large mass. Mulch or plant among sparse grasses. Full sun is necessary for good bloom.

PLANTING TIME: Spring or fall, but I have moved swamp candles with soil adhering while they were blooming. I watered them carefully and they continued to bloom.

ROOT SYSTEM: Creeping rhizomes with a pinkish tint often send up new shoots which eventually develop into plants large enough to bloom.

PLANTING DEPTH AND SPACING: Space the plants at least 1 or more feet apart since they spread. Plant the rhizomes horizontally 1 inch deep and mulch. It is best to weed the beds by hand when

the plants are growing in cultivated soil, as young plants continuously appear beside parent plants.

PLANTING STOCK AND PROPAGATION: Use nursery-grown stock or quality collected stock.

Divide crowded clumps. Bulbils planted as soon as they ripen produce plants which are often mature enough to bloom in the second year.

COMMENTS: I had searched long and hard to find this plant when I came upon it quite by accident in a swamp not far from home.

Lysimachia Nummularia • moneywort

DESCRIPTION: 6 to 15 inch vines. Moneywort forks as it creeps along and has round leaves opposite each other on the vine. Single, bright yellow flowers are found in the axils of the leaves.

Moneywort is found in damp areas, dry open fields, and in old gardens. It was orginally grown only in cultivation.

PERIOD OF BLOOM: Late June into August.

SOIL: Poor sandy soil to soil of good fertility that is slightly acid. Damp soil and soil which never becomes extremely dry is satisfactory.

LOCATION AND EXPOSURE: Moneywort will grow in sun or light shade, but it blooms more profusely when grown in full sun and fertile damp soils. This neat groundcover hugs the earth closely and is excellent used with wildflowers such as lady's-slippers, trilliums, or baneberries. It is also useful as a hanging vine in window boxes.

PLANTING TIME: Spring or fall.

ROOT SYSTEM: Tiny white roots form along the vines wherever the nodes touch the damp earth or where a little mulch falls over the vines. At these intervals, where the new roots form, clusters of pink eyes soon appear, giving rise to a new plant.

PLANTING DEPTH AND SPACING: Space 1 foot or more apart to allow for spreading. Set the crowns at soil level, but any pink eyes at

the base of the crown should be planted ¼ inch below soil level.

PLANTING STOCK AND PROPAGATION: Use nursery-grown or quality collected stock. Potted or bareroot stock should have several leaders. To propagate, divide well-rooted vines that have formed a colony of new plants, or take stem cuttings in June or July. I have not tried growing moneywort from seed, since it is too easily propagated by other means.

COMMENTS: Moneywort is a good plant to use where there is too much shade or the soil is not fertile enough for grass to grow. Moneywort makes dense mats and stays green all summer. It is not damaged by mowing, and its spreading is easily restricted since its roots are very shallow.

Trientalis borealis • starflower

DESCRIPTION: 4 to 8 inches tall. A single wiry stem supports a whorl of six or more leaves. Above this on a short stem appear one or two showy white stars. These are replaced later by a tiny white seed-ball containing several seeds.

Starflower is found in the damp, deep shade of hardwoods as well as in somewhat drier woods of oak, aspens, soft maple, and occasional balsams. Leafmold is always deep and humus abundant.

PERIOD OF BLOOM: May into June.

SOIL: Acid to moderately acid soil, rich in leafmold and humus, with constant moisture.

LOCATION AND EXPOSURE: Starflower must have some shade. If the soil is too dry the plant goes dormant shortly after blooming. Starflower is an excellent groundcover. I have planted a few in the shade of a birch tree among rocks and mulched them with an inch-deep layer of sphagnum moss. Over this I placed a thin sod of dainty growing mosses. Each spring the starflowers emerge through the mosses and put on a lovely show of their own, always adding new plants to their growing colony.

PLANTING TIME: Fall planting is best; the plant is too easily broken in spring when growth has started.

ROOT SYSTEM: A tiny, irregular-shaped tuber with many white threadlike roots. The tubers are connected by threadlike stolons, which pause at intervals to produce new tubers.

PLANTING DEPTH AND SPACING: Always plant in colonies, spacing

167

6 to 9 inches apart. Plant bareroot stock 1 inch deep in moist, humus-rich soil and plant potted stock at soil level. Starflowers spread gradually by slender rhizomes.

PLANTING STOCK AND PROPAGATION: Nursery-grown potted stock is best: the root system will not have to be disturbed during transplanting and the tubers have usually multiplied. If you collect stock, gather a bit of the immediately surrounding leafmold to add around the roots when transplanting.

Sow seeds in flats ½ inch deep as soon as they ripen—the soil in the flat should contain a lot of leafmold. Place an evergreen bough over the flat to shelter it in winter. When the seeds germinate, give them light shade. A slow process, but fun to try.

COMMENTS: The delicate starflower will naturalize and spread once it is established. When transplanted, it may stay dormant for a year before showing any growth.

GENTIANACEAE [Gentian Family]

Gentiana Andrewsii • bottle gentian

DESCRIPTION: 1 to 2 feet tall. Clusters of bottle-shaped flowers are a gorgeous copen blue of great intensity. White flowers are rare. These clusters are located in the axils of the upper leaves. Pointed and lanceolate leaves on opposing sides of the stem are often tipped with bronze late in summer.

The bottle gentian grows in damp sunny meadows and among the sparse grasses along shady brooks and lake shores.

PERIOD OF BLOOM: August into September.

SOIL: Neutral to slightly acid fertile but sandy soil as well as heavier black soils. I grow bottle gentian in sandy loam of average fertility with moderate to ample moisture. The soil need not be as wet as in its native habitat.

LOCATION AND EXPOSURE: When grown in open, damp sunny meadows with Cardinal flowers bottle gentians are outstanding. Or grow in light shade beside a brook or next to a pool. The bottle gentians adapt readily when transplanted if you do not disturb the soil around their roots. Mulch for best results or plant at a shallow depth.

168

PLANTING TIME: Fall transplanting is best. Stock transplanted in spring requires watering to establish. Never transplant gentians after they are a few inches tall.

ROOT SYSTEM: A coarse rootstock with many fleshy white roots extending away from the crown. In nursery-grown stock with trimmed roots, many new fibrous roots develop.

PLANTING DEPTH AND SPACING: Space 8 to 12 inches apart. In the wild, I find that the roots are near the surface, but in cultivation I get better results by setting the crown at least 1 inch deep, especially for large plants. Always trim all the roots back to 3 to 4 inches before transplanting. This encourages new fibrous roots to grow, and the plants will be more vigorous.

PLANTING STOCK AND PROPAGATION: Nursery-grown stock is best. You can also use freshly dug collected stock with roots trimmed to 3 to 4 inches so that new fibrous ones may develop from the cut ends.

Scatter seeds on a flat when ripe and cover with a ½ inch mesh to protect them from rodents and wind. Cover with an evergreen bough or light mulch until spring. Seedlings should be left in the flats until the end of the second growing season or early the following spring. Then trim the roots and transplant to their permanent home.

COMMENTS: A colony of blue-flowered bottle gentian makes a memorable sight. Gentians are choice long-lived wildflowers. They need little care other than keeping them free of weeds.

Gentiana Saponaria • soapwort gentian

DESCRIPTION: 18 to 30 inches tall. Bottle-shaped flowers are a slightly lighter blue than bottle gentian and fade to lavender with age. White flowers are rare. The blossoms are long-lived and bloom well. The pointed lanceolate foliage, with opposing leaves, is narrower than that of the bottle gentian.

Soapwort is found in roadside ditches, along wet lake shores and brooks, at the edge of marshes, and in damp meadows. It often grows in large colonies, especially to the west of us along the Wisconsin River.

PERIOD OF BLOOM: Late July into August. It is the first gentian to bloom.

SOIL: Neutral to slightly acid soil of good fertility. In the nursery we grow it in fertile sandy loam, sometimes in very light shade, but mostly in full sun.

LOCATION AND EXPOSURE: Interplant soapwort gentian with other gentians to extend the blooming period of the area. Near our pool, where the soil is sandy and barren and overrun by a groundcover of wine cups, a lone gentian seedling volunteered. In a few years it grew into a large flowering clump despite the poor, dry soil. It is growing next to a stone, which may account for its ability to thrive without watering and endure periods of drought.

PLANTING TIME: While dormant in spring or (preferably) fall.

ROOT SYSTEM: A coarse rootstock with many white stringy roots that are fleshy and tapering. Unpruned roots of seedlings that are left to develop without transplanting may reach up to 2 feet for moisture and nutrients.

PLANTING DEPTH AND SPACING: Space about 10 inches or more apart. Trim the roots to 3 to 4 inches before planting. Set the crowns 1 to 1½ inches deep. Because the roots are trimmed and set deeper than wildlings, with age, the plants develop extra flower stalks and form larger clumps.

PLANTING STOCK AND PROPAGATION: Nursery-grown stock has a better, more compact, heavier root system than collected stock. Quality collected stock should have all roots trimmed back to 3 to 4 inches before transplanting.

Gentians rarely self-sow. For seedlings follow the directions for bottle gentian.

COMMENTS: This gentian is the most robust of those mentioned in this book. I prefer it for its long-lasting flowers.

Along the Wisconsin River at a friend's home, I came upon the white form of soapwort gentian. These plants have been moved to the far end of the nursery, away from the blue kind, so that hopefully the seeds may produce white seedlings.

Gentiana decora • Allegheny Mountain gentian

DESCRIPTION: 1 to 2 feet tall. The flowers of this gentian are smaller than those of the bottle or soapwort gentians, and the color is as intensely blue as the bottle gentian. The foliage is narrower and more refined.

The Allegheny Mountain gentian is native to the Allegheny Mountain country and nearby areas of Tennessee. It has also proved hardy in the very severe winters of Wisconsin.

PERIOD OF BLOOM: Late September into November. This gentian blooms somewhat late; its bottles remain blue for a long while, even after frost has faded the foliage.

SOIL: Neutral to slightly acid soil with damp to average moisture. Constant moisture is important for all gentians.

LOCATION AND EXPOSURE: Plant in sun or very light shade. In the north it should be planted in a sheltered area to keep the frost from harming its blossoms.

PLANTING TIME: While dormant in spring or fall; fall is preferable. I find mulching is easier when a bit of old growth is left on the plant.

ROOT SYSTEM: A small crown with fine white stringy roots.

PLANTING DEPTH AND SPACING: Space 8 to 10 inches apart to form neat clumps. Set the crown 1 to 1½ inches deep and spread the trimmed roots evenly. Mulch for winter and keep reasonably moist, but not necessarily wet.

PLANTING STOCK AND PROPAGATION: Nursery-grown stock is best. Or use quality collected stock if available.

In the north, the plant matures too late to set seeds. If seeds are available, follow the directions for sowing other gentians. It is important to plant fresh seeds as soon as they ripen.

COMMENTS: Often some of the bottles of Allegheny Mountain gentian open slightly. This makes it easier for the bees and insects to pollinate this species.

A lovely plant.

APOCYNACEAE [Dogbane Family]

Amsonia Tabernaemontana • amsonia

DESCRIPTION: 2 to 3 feet tall. The willowlike medium-green leaves alternate along the entire length of the stem. At the top of the stem are panicles of pale blue, starlike flowers with narrow petals. Soon after these fade, white clusters of slender cylindrical seed

pods develop. The leafy stalk continues to grow a few more inches and almost hides the seed pods until they begin to ripen. The pods deepen from pinkish to tan. The seeds are cinnamon brown; they are shaped like ¼ inch long pieces of round toothpicks.

Amsonia is native to southern Illinois and spreads both east and west. It has also proved hardy in northern Wisconsin. Some of my plants, now bushy, have lasted more than ten years.

PERIOD OF BLOOM: May into June.

SOIL: Although amsonia grows in standing water or very damp soil in its native habitat, it adapts to ordinary garden soil with only constant moisture and also to neutral and slightly acid woods soil. In the nursery, soil is a sandy fertile loam that retains moisture reasonably well.

LOCATION AND EXPOSURE: Full sun or partial shade. With age the plant sends up many stalks and becomes large and bushy, capable of taking over a large area left by earlier-blooming spring flowers or bulbs.

PLANTING TIME: While dormant in spring or fall.

ROOT SYSTEM: A fine cream-colored taproot on young plants; as plants mature, the root system becomes coarse and fibrous.

PLANTING DEPTH AND SPACING: Space 2 feet apart to allow for growth. Set the taproot with the eyes about 1 inch below soil level. In very cold areas mulch in winter, or all year if you wish.

PLANTING STOCK AND PROPAGATION: Young to medium-sized nursery-grown stock transplants more easily. You can also use quality collected stock of medium size.

Propagation by division of the roots has proved successful. Seeds are more reliable; as soon as they are ripe sow them in flats or in the open. Transplant seedlings to a permanent location in late summer or the following spring. Plants may bloom the third year.

COMMENTS: Although the amsonia normally grows in wet soils, it will thrive in drier soils; once established the roots seek moisture and nutrients at deeper levels. The foliage remains green until hard-killing frosts.

ASCLEPIADACEAE [Milkweed Family]

Asclepias tuberosa • butterfly flower

DESCRIPTION: 1 to 2 feet tall. Each hairy-velvet stem bears many alternating willowlike leaves. The stems are topped with a cluster of showy flowers that attract many butterflies—as well as hummingbirds and bumblebees. Most flowers are orange, ranging from pale orange to deep red-orange or, occasionally, deep yellow.

Butterfly flower grows in sunny areas along roadsides, deserted fields, and grassy lands. It is also found among shorter grasses along fence lines.

PERIOD OF BLOOM: Late June into August. Transplanted plants often bloom again in September.

After plants have become established for several years, they can be cut back completely after the first blooming to induce a second. Only well-established plants can be selected for cutting back, and it should not be done to the same plant year after year.

SOIL: A sandy loam that is acid to almost neutral is preferable, but butterfly flower also grows in gritty or gravelly soils or even heavier soils. Good drainage is essential—it is much more decisive to the plant's life than pH.

LOCATION AND EXPOSURE: Full sun and good drainage are the first considerations. Set in permanent locations immediately, since established roots grow very deep into the soil for food and moisture.

Butterfly flower is an excellent companion plant for other prairie wildflowers such as harebell, prairie phlox, hoary puccoon, and blazing star.

PLANTING TIME: While dormant in spring or fall. The plants do not move readily when foliage is mature.

ROOT SYSTEM: A cream-colored, fleshy tuberous root that is long, very brittle, and delightfully fragrant.

PLANTING DEPTH AND SPACING: Set the fleshy roots with the eyes 2 inches deep. This depth is important! In nature the eyes grow at soil level, so one assumes that in transplanting the same procedure should be followed—this plant is an exception.

Space 1½ to 3 feet apart. Mature plants growing in full sun and good sandy loam will reach the size of a bushel basket in a few seasons.

When transplanting large seedlings from the nursery, cut off all roots at the lower end, making them a uniform length of about 4 inches. New feeder roots grow from the bottom of the severed roots. The result is a more compact, sturdy rootstock. In very cold climates where snow is scarce, the plant should be well mulched in winter.

PLANTING STOCK AND PROPAGATION: Nursery-grown transplanted stock is superior to collected stock. Do not be dismayed if you do not get the entire root when digging in the wild. Trim all jagged ends. Fall is the best time for collecting.

Root cuttings can be made in spring. Insert 2 inch sections of roots upright into a mixture of sharp sand and some peatmoss or shredded sphagnum moss. To make sure the root remains upright, as you work cut the top of the root straight across and the lower end at an angle. Keep reasonably moist but not wet.

At times I have had poor seed germination, with best results from seeds sown in May. Mulch seedlings the first winter and transplant them the following spring to a permanent location.

COMMENTS: The butterfly flower was once widely used as a tonic and expectorant, and was commonly prescribed for pleurisy, hence it is also called pleurisy root. Most botanical books list this lovely flower by the name butterfly weed, but in nursery catalogs you will find it listed as butterfly flower, a name it rightly deserves.

Asclepias incarnata • swamp milkweed

DESCRIPTION: 3 to 4 feet tall. An unusually showy plant with clusters of flat-topped, wine-rose-colored flowers on top of a well-branched stem. White flowers are rare. The heavy stalk is hollow and flushed with wine color. It bears only a few willowlike, lanceolate leaves. The swamp milkweed inhabits wet meadows, brooksides, lake shores and marshes, growing among boneset and Joe-pye.

PERIOD OF BLOOM: July into August.

SOIL: Neutral to slightly acid soil, wetlands to average garden moisture.

LOCATION AND EXPOSURE: Should be grown in full sun, though it tolerates very light shade for part of the day. An excellent plant for open meadows with tall meadowrue, Joe-pye, and goldenrod.

I have grown swamp milkweed in the perennial border where it did well in slightly dry soil.

PLANTING TIME: While dormant in spring or fall.

ROOT SYSTEM: Numerous white threadlike roots, 6 to 8 inches and longer, extend from a sturdy crown with many buds.

PLANTING DEPTH AND SPACING: Space 2 feet apart. Trim the extensive roots back to 3 inches and spread evenly, setting the new shoot at the crown just barely below soil level. The roots should taper slightly downward.

PLANTING STOCK AND PROPAGATION: Use nursery-grown stock of medium size, or quality collected young stock.

Propagate by division of the crowns of the young plants in spring, or sow seed.

My seeds were slow to germinate and gave poor results at times. The plant did, however, volunteer here and there in my garden among the evergreens where the soil is not cultivated and grasses are sparse.

COMMENTS: Every one of my swamp milkweed plants has its own group of butterflies hovering over it.

Asclepias syriaca • common milkweed

DESCRIPTION: 3 to 5 feet tall. A large stout stalk, with blunt-tipped opposite oval leaves, bears large clusters of almost ball-shaped flowers in the axils of the upper leaves. The flowers are mauve-lavender, globe-shaped, and very fragrant.

Found in wastelands, along fence rows and roadsides. Quite common.

PERIOD OF BLOOM: July into August.

SOIL: Easily grown in most soils.

LOCATION AND EXPOSURE: Open sunny areas are best. A dozen plants in a colony make a handsome display. After the plant has bloomed, pull up the stalks; if enough of the root is left in the ground to produce a new plant, it will grow enough to bloom again the following season. If any plants are unwanted, pull up the stalks as they appear and the plant will eventually die.

PLANTING TIME: While dormant in spring or fall.

ROOT SYSTEM: A heavy white rootstock creeps underground and

sends up new shoots at frequent intervals. Rhizomes from the plants by our doorstep have crawled under a 3 foot width of sidewalk to appear in the nearby rock garden.

PLANTING DEPTH AND SPACING: Space 1 foot apart. Set the eyes 1 to 2 inches below soil level. If only one colony is wanted, grow them in a bottomless gallon can buried at soil level.

PLANTING STOCK AND PROPAGATION: Use quality collected stock. The plant self-sows readily.

COMMENTS: The sweet fragrance of the common milkweed permeates the air for a considerable distance from the plant.

POLEMONIACEAE [Polemonium Family]

Polemonium reptans • Greek valerian

DESCRIPTION: 8 to 12 inches tall. The compound leaves resemble those of the Christmas fern but are shorter and a little broader. Leafy stems display china-blue, bell-shaped flowers.

Greek valerian is found in rich deciduous woodlands. It is much improved by cultivation.

PERIOD OF BLOOM: May into June.

SOIL: Ordinary garden soil or rich woods soil, or any soil that is fertile and neutral to only slightly acid.

LOCATION AND EXPOSURE: Grow plants in full sun or shade. Excellent interplanted with mertensia which goes dormant after blooming while the Greek valerian retains its green foliage until hard-killing frosts. This flower goes well with yellow merrybells when grown in shade.

PLANTING TIME: Spring or fall.

ROOT SYSTEM: A tightly crowded clump of fibrous roots.

PLANTING DEPTH AND SPACING: Space 1 to 1½ feet apart since each plant will form a large clump. It should be divided every third year.

PLANTING STOCK AND PROPAGATION: Nursery-grown stock has a more extensive root system, but quality collected stock does well too.

To propagate by division, cut into several clumps in early

spring or mid-August. Sow seeds as soon as they ripen or in very early spring. On bare, uncultivated soil it will self-sow.

COMMENTS: An excellent plant to grow for foliage contrast with plants that have a coarser leaf. Its bright blue flowers vie with the blue of a sunny June day.

Phlox divaricata • wild blue phlox

DESCRIPTION: 8 to 12 inches tall. Opposite lanceolate leaves on wiry stems that support a loose, terminal cluster of single-petaled flowers. The petals often show variation in notching. The flowers are lavender-blue to purple-blue. Occasionally one finds patches of clear blue. Wild blue phlox is often found on shady roadsides, in open woods, and in moist, deciduous rocky woods. Where shade is high it is often found in colonies (especially in Menominee County, Wisconsin).

PERIOD OF BLOOM: Late May into June.

SOIL: Neutral to slightly acid fertile soils. Humus-rich woodland soil is ideal. In the nursery, we grow it in rich garden loam in partial shade.

LOCATION AND EXPOSURE: Filtered sunlight or open shade is preferable. When wild blue phlox is grown with foamflower it offers a lovely blend of blues to accent with white. Cut back the flowering stalks as soon as seeds have dispersed, or sooner if no seed is wanted. In the mulched woodland it does not self-sow readily.

PLANTING TIME: Spring or fall. Also August.

ROOT SYSTEM: A tough, fibrous, stringy root system. New roots will form at the nodes on stems that come into contact with moist earth or even damp mulch.

PLANTING DEPTH AND SPACING: Space about 1 foot apart or scatter in the woodland garden. When transplanting, set the nodes about 1 inch deeper than the level at which the plant previously grew. This will give you a stronger plant because the nodes covered with soil will root and send up extra flower stalks.

PLANTING STOCK AND PROPAGATION: Nursery-grown stock has a more compact and abundant root system. Select quality collected stock with good roots.

Divide clumps in spring (preferably) or in August. Always set plants an inch deeper.

Take cuttings in June from new shoots that appear after flowering stems have been cut back, or take cuttings from the tops of new growth in spring.

The cutting propagation procedures for all varieties of *Phlox divaricata* are the same: Nip out the terminal leaf growth and set cuttings so that two nodes with leaves are above soil level and two nodes without leaves are below soil level. Dip in rooting compound. Pot individually. Put pots in a propagating frame or cover with plastic bags and apply bottom heat. If bottom heat is not available, sink the plastic-covered pots halfway into a "working" compost heap. Enough heat will be present to encourage root growth.

Seeds are not easily collected, but should you get some, sow as soon as they ripen. Seedlings appear the following spring and bloom the following year. Transplant seedlings a few inches high with one node set deeper.

COMMENTS: This is a versatile wildflower that can have many uses —in the rock garden, along a woodland trail, among tulips, or grown along other flower beds in patches for contrast in spring.

Phlox divaricata • phlox

DESCRIPTION: 8 to 12 inches tall. The phlox (var. *Laphamii*) has medium-green foliage on opposing sides of the stem. It holds its color better than other *Phlox divaricata*, rarely having reddish tints in the sky-blue flower. Close observation will show that it is distinctly different. The erect stems are topped by loose terminal clusters of five-petaled flowers. The petals are broader and do not have notches. The bloom is superior, too, but they all make lovely companions in the woodland garden.

Found in rich woodlands in high open shade with other spring wildflowers.

PERIOD OF BLOOM: May into June.

SOIL: Neutral to slightly acid, fertile soil. In humus-rich moist soil the plants form large clumps.

LOCATION AND EXPOSURE: Filtered sunlight is preferred, but it will grow in sun where moisture is constant. Interplant with spring bulbs or other woodland wildflowers. Cut back foliage after blooming. New growth soon appears and remains green late into fall.

PLANTING TIME: Spring or fall.

ROOT SYSTEM: A vigorous but tough fibrous root system, with each node that touches damp earth sending out new roots and later new shoots. Under ideal conditions this plant spreads steadfastly.

PLANTING DEPTH AND SPACING: Space 1 foot or more apart. When transplanting phlox set it deeper so that one or two nodes previously above ground are now covered with soil. These covered nodes will develop new shoots and roots, which will provide heavier bloom the next season. In the woodlands surround the plants with a generous mulching to conserve moisture.

PLANTING STOCK AND PROPAGATION: Cuttings from one-year-old plants are best. Also use quality collected stock when available.

Divide clumps in spring or August, and set plants one or two nodes deeper than previously grown. Take cuttings from new shoots in June before the plant blooms or from the new growth that appears after bloom. Collecting seeds is difficult. Use the cutting propagation procedures described for the wild blue phlox.

COMMENTS: When *Phlox divaricata* varieties are grown together you will readily notice differences among them that are hard to describe. Yet even within this *Laphamii* variety, a bed of these plants grown from cuttings makes an exciting display.

Phlox divaricata • white phlox

DESCRIPTION: 6 to 10 inches tall. White phlox (var. *albiflora*) has wiry stems with light-green lanced leaves and a terminal cluster of five-petaled white blossoms.

The wild white phlox is found in rocky woods east and south of Wisconsin. My original stock came from Kansas and proved as hardy here as native phloxes.

PERIOD OF BLOOM: May into June.

SOIL: Neutral to slightly acid soil with constant moisture. Fertile garden or woodland soil.

LOCATION AND EXPOSURE: Light open shade is preferable. Grow plants in masses for a show of cool white, or plant with colored phloxes for contrast.

PLANTING TIME: Spring or fall.

ROOT SYSTEM: A compact, tough fibrous root system. New roots form where the nodes touch damp earth.

PLANTING DEPTH AND SPACING: Space 6 to 10 inches apart or plant at random among small woodland wildflowers. Always set the plants one or two nodes deeper than their previous level to encourage bushier plants and greater bloom. This is very important!

PLANTING STOCK AND PROPAGATION: Nursery-grown stock is best. Also use quality collected stock where available.

Divide large plants in spring or in August. Take cuttings before or after blooming when new growth appears. Use the cutting propagation procedures described for the wild blue phlox. The white phlox does not take kindly to propagation by cuttings, but rooting hormones will hasten root development. Do not expect the same results with this form as with the colored varieties.

The white phlox is grown more easily from seeds than the colored ones. When the white phlox parent plants are grown unmixed with other phloxes, seedlings usually come 100 percent pure white. If there are a few strays you can distinguish them by their darker green foliage. If white plants are grown next to colored varieties, some colored seedlings will result.

Seedlings may be transplanted when 2 inches tall to pots or to a sheltered place in the open. Always remember to plant one or two nodes deeper than the previous level. This is the secret of getting wild phloxes to form bushy plants that bloom abundantly.

COMMENTS: You will find that this wild phlox requires a little more care, but with fertile soil, light shade, and ample moisture, it will form lovely masses of cool white.

Phlox pilosa • prairie phlox

DESCRIPTION: 1 foot tall. In cultivation, this plant reclines and each rootstock sends up several flower stalks instead of just one. The stalk is slender with opposite linear leaves and bears a loose cluster of flowers, their color varying from pink to violet-lavender. Completely white ones and white ones with red eyes are rare. Occasionally the petals are flared.

Prairie phlox is found in dry prairies, meadows, and along roadsides. In my area of Wisconsin it grows in large colonies along roadsides where the grasses are not too aggressive, making a splash of color.

PERIOD OF BLOOM: June. Cultivated seedlings often bloom again in August and make very bushy plants. Well-established plants may be cut back after blooming, and they, too, often bloom again.

SOIL: Slightly acid sandy loam is best. In the nursery we use fertile but sandy loam. Good drainage is important.

LOCATION AND EXPOSURE: In cultivation, prairie phlox is best planted among sparse prairie grasses or in full sun. If planted in shade, the plants become straggly and die. An open meadow or a rock garden with sun is ideal. In the wild state, the foliage dies after the plant blooms and sets seed but reappears in August. In cultivation, the leaves usually stay green. This is an interesting plant to grow with hoary puccoon.

PLANTING TIME: Spring or fall when new growth is only an inch or so high.

ROOT SYSTEM: Fibrous roots become wiry with age. Old plants do not transplant as readily as young plants. In cultivation each plant develops several buds at the crown, but it cannot be divided and to do so is certain to kill the plant.

PLANTING DEPTH AND SPACING: Set the crowns at soil level and spread the roots evenly outward and slightly downward. Space about 1 foot apart.

PLANTING STOCK AND PROPAGATION: Use nursery-grown stock or young quality collected stock.

Prairie phlox is easily grown from seeds, but they are difficult to collect because the seed pods open immediately after ripening. It self-sows. Seedlings often bloom the first year, but surely the second year.

COMMENTS: Prairie phlox is an excellent plant for dry, open, sunny areas. It must never be moved while blooming or the plants will perish. Should you find an unusual color variation in the wild it is wise to mark the spot and transplant when new growth appears in August.

Phlox ovata • mountain phlox

DESCRIPTION: 4 to 6 inches tall. Mountain phlox has clear pink to rose-colored single flowers on upright stems. White ones are rare. It is almost an evergreen creeper with reclining branches.

Native much farther south and east, mountain phlox has proved very hardy in northern Wisconsin. It is found in thickets and moist open woods where it makes a lovely green carpet with its contrast of pink flowers in spring.

PERIOD OF BLOOM: May into early June.

SOIL: Slightly acid to moderately acid humus-rich soil, somewhat moist, especially while plant is blooming. I grow it under oak trees where the leafmold nourishes the plants.

LOCATION AND EXPOSURE: A fine groundcover for a moist shady area or one that does not become too dry. Given a good location it will soon carpet the forest floor with green. Mountain phlox is a good groundcover to grow with lady's-slippers. It likes to creep among leaf mulch.

PLANTING TIME: Spring or fall. Potted stock anytime.

ROOT SYSTEM: Fibrous. Roots form whenever nodes of the lower branches touch the damp earth. Thus new plants form and new reclining branches appear after blooming.

PLANTING DEPTH AND SPACING: Space 6 inches or more apart. Set the crowns at soil level and tuck any rooted runners gently into the soil surface and mulch. Plant potted stock at soil level. Mulch lightly with small leaves or shredded larger leaves. Let some of the green peek through.

PLANTING STOCK AND PROPAGATION: Potted stock is preferable, either quality nursery-grown or collected bareroot stock.

Divide plants that have formed mats, after blooming or in very early spring. Seeds are very fine and almost impossible to collect. I have had the most success with stem cuttings when I take them in June.

COMMENTS: Mountain phlox is a permanent groundcover that improves in beauty with the years. Ideal.

There is a blue-flowered variety of *Phlox ovata* with similar growing habits.

BORAGINACEAE [Borage Family]

Lithospermum canescens • hoary puccoon

DESCRIPTION: 8 to 10 inches tall. A cluster of golden yellow flowers, shaped like forget-me-nots but larger, are held above gray-green foliage. The foliage tends to be willowlike, blunt-tipped, and downy.

Hoary puccoon graces dry sunny fields and roadsides among

grasses. It is also found growing in gravelly areas, often with prairie phlox.

PERIOD OF BLOOM: June.

SOIL: Poor sandy soils or slightly acid fertile loam. Good drainage is very important. When grown where soil is heavy with clay, a liberal amount of sand should be incorporated into the existing soil.

LOCATION AND EXPOSURE: Place hoary puccoon in a sunny, well-drained spot and each plant will become a clump with age.

PLANTING TIME: While dormant in early spring or fall, but fall is best.

ROOT SYSTEM: The gray-to-black-coated rootstock is very irregular, with few feeder roots. The color depends on root size and age. New roots are usually a light tan, turning grayer as they age and becoming black in about three years. The inside of the fleshy root is pure white.

PLANTING DEPTH AND SPACING: Space 10 to 15 inches apart, depending on the size of the plants and the effect wanted. Planting depth is important. In the wild you will find that the eyes of the plant are just below soil level—a little deeper where it is very sandy; when transplanting, the eyes should be set 2 inches deep. This will give strong plants that will improve with age.

PLANTING STOCK AND PROPAGATION: Two-year-old nursery-grown stock has the best root system for transplanting. Also use quality collected stock, freshly dug, in fall.

For cuttings, use roots about the size of a wood lead pencil. Cut into 2 inch pieces. Cut the top portion of the root straight across and the bottom portion at an angle. This is a signal to yourself to keep the root pieces right side up. Set cuttings in sand or sandy loam about 1 inch deep and keep slightly moist. These cuttings usually root in one year, and some may even bloom the second year.

If roots break off, while digging, new shoots will develop and another plant will grow from the portion left in the soil. Often several eyes are formed on the stub and a plant with a multiple crown is born.

COMMENTS: Hoary puccoon is very effective when grown among tufts of grass in a prairie type of garden.

Try this: Pour about a gallon of sharp sand over a well-established plant that has at least six stems. Spread the sand about 2 inches deep and leave permanently. The tops of the stems should be upright above the sand. The buried portion of the stems will develop new eyes, which in time will send up new multiple shoots. The sand does wonders for this plant.

Myosotis scorpioides • forget-me-not

DESCRIPTION: 6 to 15 inches tall. Angled prostrate stems with light-green, lanced foliage. Short leafy stems grow mostly from each joint and have small, delicate sky-blue flowers with yellow eyes.

The forget-me-not grows in damp areas in sun or very light shade. I first came upon this plant in Menominee County, Wisconsin, where a large colony of forget-me-nots was growing in the wilderness. The plants grew at the edge of a clear, slow-moving shallow brook, their roots firmly anchored in the fine gravel of the creek bed. It was early spring and only here and there a flower had opened, but there were many budded spikes, promising an expanse of gorgeous blue very soon.

PERIOD OF BLOOM: May into August, and even later if faded flowers are picked or if the location is moderately moist. Where moisture is abundant, bloom period is extended into autumn.

SOIL: Slightly acid to neutral soils with constant moisture. Make sure the soil never gets extremely dry. Wet gravel beds at the edge of a creek are choice spots.

LOCATION AND EXPOSURE: Full sun or partial shade. The forget-me-not is adaptable to a wide range of growing conditions. If soil is too dry the plants may become shaggy and tend to go dormant, but with rains or watering they will grow anew. Plant in a rock garden over a protruding rock in light shade. Or plant potted stock in gravelly beds of slow-moving streams that remain rather quiet and clear. Put the plants near shore.

PLANTING TIME: Potted stock anytime. Bareroot stock in spring or fall, but spring is preferred.

ROOT SYSTEM: Fibrous roots. New roots form where stems or branches recline on damp earth.

PLANTING DEPTH AND SPACING: Space 2 feet apart or farther if you wish to keep the effect of individual clumps. Set plants at same level at which they grew previously or slightly deeper.

PLANTING STOCK AND PROPAGATION: Potted nursery stock is best. Clumps from nurseries are also good, as is quality collected stock.

Divide large plants in spring. Cuttings taken in summer root readily. Seeds are difficult to collect.

COMMENTS: Although forget-me-not is at home in the average garden that does not get too dry, it is also ideal for areas that are too damp for most plants. Use it as a groundcover in wet places.

The forget-me-not is an escapee from early gardens.

Mertensia virginica • Virginia bluebell

DESCRIPTION: 1 to 2 feet tall. Drooping clusters of pink buds become beautiful porcelain blue flowers. When new growth first emerges above the mulch in spring, it is somewhat purplish tinted with green. This disappears as the leafy stems develop. The oval leaves are mostly on the lower half of the stem. There is also a white form.

Mertensia is found in woodland rich in leafmold as well as in moist rocky woods and along streams, where it often grows in colonies.

PERIOD OF BLOOM: May into June.

SOIL: Slightly acid to neutral soil of good fertility. Moisture in spring is very important, even if the earth becomes very dry in summer after dormancy.

LOCATION AND EXPOSURE: This wildflower is equally at home in full sun or in a shaded nook. When it is in full sun, bumblebees are attracted in droves. Grow it with other wildflowers that have good foliage and will take over when the Virginia bluebell becomes dormant in early summer. In open shade grow it with wild ginger or with other groundcovers.

PLANTING TIME: As soon as roots become dormant and into late fall.

ROOT SYSTEM: A fleshy but very brittle black-coated tuberous rootstock that takes on many odd shapes. Old, gnarled rootstocks do not produce well and are best discarded. Young roots grown in very sandy soil are cinnamon-brown in color. All roots are white inside.

PLANTING DEPTH AND SPACING: Space 1½ feet apart or farther

185

when interplanted with other wildflowers. Set tubers with the white eyes 1 inch below soil level and mulch generously.

PLANTING STOCK AND PROPAGATION: Nursery-grown stock of medium size is best. Quality collected stock, preferably young roots, is good.

Seed sown as soon as ripe will produce some seedlings large enough to bloom the third year. The plant self-sows readily, especially where the soil is rich in leafmold and somewhat damp.

COMMENTS: A very popular, charming spring wildflower. Beautiful with large golden merrybells, which bloom at the same time and have good foliage.

I call Virginia bluebell the chameleon of my garden because the purplish thumbs that first emerge above the earth turn to green leaves and the pink buds become beautiful blue flowers.

Mertensia albiflora • white mertensia

DESCRIPTION: 10 to 15 inches tall. This is a smaller version of Virginia bluebell (*Mertensia virginica*). Clusters of greenish white buds open to pure white. The foliage is light green, oval, and smaller.

My stock has been grown from a specimen of the white mertensia found in the wild in Iowa. Because of its smaller overall growth I believe it is a white version of the midwestern bluebell known as *Mertensia lanceolata*.

PERIOD OF BLOOM: May into June.

SOIL: Fertile slightly acid woods soil that is moist during the blooming period.

LOCATION AND EXPOSURE: I planted my seeds in open woodland in a cleared area. The soil is rich in leafmold and quite damp in spring. Plants are removed only as needed, but otherwise have remained in their original bed to self-sow. For color contrast, grow the white and blue mertensias together.

PLANTING TIME: After plants become dormant, in early summer into fall.

ROOT SYSTEM: A fleshy, black-coated tuberous rootstock that grows in many fantastic patterns. One root tends to grow directly downward. Rootstocks are very brittle and easily broken while being dug up.

PLANTING DEPTH AND SPACING: Space about 1 foot apart or plant at random among other wildflowers that retain their foliage throughout the season. Set the rootstock with the white eyes 1 to 2 inches deep. In my original bed I find that some of the seedling rootstocks are 5 inches deep. Evidently the plants have sought their own depths.

PLANTING STOCK AND PROPAGATION: To be certain of color, use nursery-grown stock that has already bloomed. Collected stock is very rare.

Seeds sown as soon as they ripen or left to self-sow where leafmold is moist give good results. If your nursery-grown stock was grown with the Virginia bluebells, you may find some blue seedlings appearing in your new bed. Remove them promptly as soon as foliage fades. Also remove all blue buds as they appear to avoid cross-pollination, and mark the plants.

COMMENTS: The unusual beauty of the pure white mertensia is certain to be an added attraction to your wild garden.

VERBENACEAE [Vervain Family]

Verbena canadensis • rose verbena

DESCRIPTION: 2 to 3 feet long. A trailing-vine type of plant, spreading to make a circle. Clusters of rose-colored flowers are held above deeply toothed, ovate, medium-green leaves that are hairy. Where the soil is moist, the reclining branches root at the nodes as they spread.

This verbena is found in sunny, rocky prairies where the soil is lean and sandy. It is native in more southern and western parts of Wisconsin than mine, but I have found it hardy with a cover of mulch in winter.

PERIOD OF BLOOM: Late May until heavy frosts. Pick the spent flowers to encourage bloom.

SOIL: Poor, sandy soils or a fertile, sandy loam with good drainage. Add sand to very fertile, heavy soil. This plant does best on a lean diet.

187

LOCATION AND EXPOSURE: Verbena must be planted in full sun for abundant bloom. It is best suited for the prairie, a sunny garden, or groundcover on a sunny bank.

PLANTING TIME: In areas where the temperatures dip far below zero it is best to plant in spring. In warmer climates, fall planting is practical.

ROOT SYSTEM: Very coarse, fibrous roots becoming wiry with age. The nodes along the trailing branches aboveground send down new roots wherever they touch the damp soil.

PLANTING DEPTH AND SPACING: Space 3 feet apart. For a dense groundcover, space only 2 feet apart. Set the crowns at soil level. Mulch in cold areas during the winter months.

When plants become too crowded, remove some of the older ones. Merely clip the branch and dig up the unwanted plants.

PLANTING STOCK AND PROPAGATION: Pot-grown nursery stock or stock grown in the field for one season have vigorous young root systems.

Select only the younger plants for division. Stem cuttings in July are the easiest method of propagation. Seeds are often slow to germinate, and seedlings bloom the second year. The plant self-sows.

COMMENTS: *Verbena canadensis* makes a fine groundcover for a rocky, sandy area that seems to grow little except weeds.

LABIATAE [Mint Family]

Ajuga reptans • bugleflower

DESCRIPTION: 5 to 8 inches tall. Dainty, semihooded flowers rest on short spikes above oval, lightly scalloped leaves. The spikes are clear blue and occasionally purple. At times a pure white will volunteer among a long-established bed of blues. It is possibly a seedling.

Bugleflower is found on roadsides and hillsides, and in open sunny fields. It usually grows in large colonies.

PERIOD OF BLOOM: May into July.

SOIL: Bugleflower is not particular about soil texture or pH, but it does need good drainage. In fertile soils it grows lavishly.

LOCATION AND EXPOSURE: An excellent groundcover for a sunny spot, a steep hillside to hold the soil in place, or under high shrubs where sunlight is ample. When grown as groundcover, the neat rosettes of basal foliage make an interesting pattern among widely spaced taller flowers in full sun or very light shade.

PLANTING TIME: It moves easily almost anytime except while blooming. Water faithfully when first transplanted and it will soon spread.

ROOT SYSTEM: Some fibrous roots on well-established plants. White cordlike rhizomes creep along just a little below soil level, pausing at intervals to send up new growth.

PLANTING DEPTH AND SPACING: Space about 6 inches apart. Plant crowns at soil level or slightly deeper in well-drained soil. Where climates are severe, mulch in winter if snowfall is scant.

PLANTING STOCK AND PROPAGATION: Nursery-grown stock has a better root system. When collecting stock, select only the stronger plants with good root systems.

Divide offsets when clumps become crowded. Seeds are hard to collect, but the plant self-sows readily.

COMMENTS: Bugleflower is a charming groundcover, useful for replacing grass on steep banks where mowing is difficult. Although this plant is rugged, it does need some moisture to thrive.

Bugleweed is another common name for bugleflower.

Scutellaria ovata • early blue skullcap

DESCRIPTION: 1½ to 2 feet tall. Hooded flowers, violet to clear blue, are held upright on squarish stems with multiple branches. Leaves are ovate and serrated. Seed pods have interesting shapes, usually oval. They resemble miniature old-fashioned bed-warmers.

This skullcap is found in moist, rocky woods in areas that have very little shade, in full sun along river banks, and in the drier parts of meadows.

PERIOD OF BLOOM: Late June into August.

SOIL: Neutral to slightly acid sandy loam or a fertile, heavier soil with good drainage. Constant moisture, though not soaking. Not demanding otherwise.

LOCATION AND EXPOSURE: Full sun or very light shade; direct sunlight produces plants with sturdier stalks. Excellent grown in colonies.

PLANTING TIME: While dormant in spring or fall. Spring only in extremely cold climates.

ROOT SYSTEM: A fibrous root system, purplish in color, with both the eyes for next year's bloom and the side rhizomes sending up new growth.

PLANTING DEPTH AND SPACING: Space 1 foot apart. Set the eyes of the plant 2 inches deep, spreading any attached rhizomes horizontally. In cold climates, mulch over winter (or permanently) with 6 inches of loose straw or marsh hay. Remove some in spring. The roots and eyes cannot tolerate alternate thawing and freezing.

PLANTING STOCK AND PROPAGATION: Nursery-grown stock is far superior to quality collected stock, but the latter is scarce.

To propagate, divide large clumps, preferably in spring, or sow seeds when they ripen. A few seedlings may bloom the first year, but three years are required to form a clump.

Cuttings taken in July and treated with rooting hormones give poor results. Those cuttings that do root should be left in propagation beds until the following June.

COMMENTS: Skullcaps are very seldom seen in wild gardens although they are easily cultivated and have lovely, long-lasting flowers. They are versatile and make a wonderful addition to a garden nook or an open meadow.

Set markers next to all plants since they are slow to sprout in spring. Easier still, leave a few inches of the old stubble if you are not a meticulous gardener.

Scutellaria serrata • showy skullcap

DESCRIPTION: 1 to 2 feet tall. Ovate leaves are located opposite each other on square stems. Usually two or more blue flowers are found on top. The plants form neat clumps.

Showy skullcap inhabits rich woods and glens farther east of and south of Wisconsin. But they have proved hardy in my severe climate when I mulch them for the winter.

PERIOD OF BLOOM: May into June.

SOIL: Slightly acid, humus-rich soil. Also will grow in fertile garden soil (as will all skullcaps). Constant, moderate moisture; do not let the soil get too wet.

LOCATION AND EXPOSURE: Use showy skullcap for naturalizing in an open area in full sun or very high open shade.

PLANTING TIME: While dormant in spring or fall.

ROOT SYSTEM: Fibrous.

PLANTING DEPTH AND SPACING: Space 1 foot apart. Set the rootstock with the eyes 2 inches below soil level. Mulch in winter and remove some in spring.

PLANTING STOCK AND PROPAGATION: Nursery-grown stock, or quality collected stock where available.

To propagate, divide clumps, preferably in spring, or sow seeds when ripe. Some seedlings will bloom the second year. I have never tried growing this one from cuttings.

COMMENTS: The skullcaps should be better known and enjoyed more. Their blue color adds a touch of beauty to the wild garden.

Scutellaria incana • downy skullcap

DESCRIPTION: 1 to 2 feet tall. Medium-blue hooded flowers with serrated, oval foliage on forking square stems. It forms clumps.

Downy skullcap is found in open lightly shaded areas of moist woods, and along river banks, and in drier woods and thickets.

PERIOD OF BLOOM: July into August.

SOIL: Average garden soil that does not get too dry, or a moist, humus-rich soil that is slightly acid.

LOCATION AND EXPOSURE: Although this skullcap is usually found in shade, it does best in full sun. Plant the blue downy along a woodland border with brilliant red Oswego tea for contrast. The addition of early-blooming white snakeroot will give you a red, white, and blue color scheme. Mulch.

PLANTING TIME: While dormant in spring or fall.

ROOT SYSTEM: Fibrous roots are dark gray-black with a purple tint, and the rhizomes are pink tipped. An extensive root system.

PLANTING DEPTH AND SPACING: Space 1 to 1½ feet apart. Set the crowns, with rhizomes attached, about 2 inches deep. Mulch during the winter. Plants are slow to appear in spring. All plants should be marked clearly.

PLANTING STOCK AND PROPAGATION: Nursery-grown stock is best. Also use quality collected stock where available.

Divide clumps in spring, and keep the area moist; the plants are slow to grow. Seeds sown when ripe give some bloom the first year. Stem cuttings I took in July gave fair results. Plants from cuttings must be kept in propagation frames until the following June.

COMMENTS: Skullcaps are beautiful flowers that have many uses in the perennial garden as well as in the wild garden. They are easily cultivated and bloom abundantly over a long period. I cannot praise them too highly.

Scutellaria integrifolia • pink skullcap

DESCRIPTION: 1½ to 2 feet tall. The hooded flowers of the pink skullcap range from a rose-pink to a pale lavender-pink. This plant is a highly prized form of S. *integrifolia*, which is commonly purplish blue with a white throat, the blue of an even deeper hue than that of downy skullcap (S. *incana*). The stems are rigid and square with many serrated, oval leaves.

Pink skullcap is native to open meadows, thickets, and along woodland borders. My original stock came from southern Indiana, but it has proved hardy here with winter mulching.

PERIOD OF BLOOM: July into September.

SOIL: Regular garden soil of good fertility that does not become extremely dry. Constant moisture is best. Neutral to slightly acid soil produces good flowering plants.

LOCATION AND EXPOSURE: Full sun or very light partial shade. Provides a fine contrast among blue skullcaps. Interplant with other wildflowers or grow in a colony on the sunny side of a woodland border.

PLANTING TIME: Fall or spring, preferably spring.

ROOT SYSTEM: A fibrous, purplish root system with eyes for the next year's growth. Rhizomes stay nearby and bloom the following year.

PLANTING DEPTH AND SPACING: Space 1 foot apart. Set the eyes 2 inches deep and spread roots and attached rhizomes horizontally. Mulch with 6 inches of straw or marsh hay in cold climates. Mark planted areas.

PLANTING STOCK AND PROPAGATION: Use nursery-grown stock; collected stock is rare.

192

Divide larger plants, preferably in spring. Seeds sown when ripe produce plants of blooming size the second year. Some blue seedlings may appear, since the plant does not come 100 percent true from seed.

COMMENTS: The pink skullcap is a rare prize.

Scutellaria lateriflora • mad-dog skullcap

DESCRIPTION: 1 to 2 feet tall. This skullcap has many branches. In the upper axils of the ovate leaves, which are opposite each other, the flower sprays form a grand display. The flowers are blue and sometimes have a hint of purple. White ones are rare. This variety of skullcap is readily identifiable because the flowers favor one side of the stem.

Mad-dog skullcap is found along thickets near stream beds, in open damp shady woods, and also in moist meadows. It is very much at home in regular garden soil with only moderate moisture.

PERIOD OF BLOOM: July into September.

SOIL: Fertile, slightly acid soil with constant moisture, though it need not be wet. The soil in our nursery that does not dry out has proved satisfactory.

LOCATION AND EXPOSURE: Skullcaps grow best in full sun or very light partial shade with constant moisture. Reasonably good flowers can be grown under more trying conditions. Mulch helps to protect plants in winter and to retain moisture in summer.

PLANTING TIME: Spring or fall, spring preferred.

ROOT SYSTEM: A fibrous rootstock with eyes and extensive thread-like roots, plus long, slender, creeping rhizomes that send up new plants around the parent plant.

PLANTING DEPTH AND SPACING: Space 1 foot or more apart to leave room for the plant to form neat clumps. Set the eyes 2 inches deep and mulch for winter protection in cold climates. Mark the area.

PLANTING STOCK AND PROPAGATION: Use nursery-grown stock. Collected stock is rare.

Division of parent plants should be done in spring. Seeds sown when ripe give some bloom the second year, and plants mature in three years.

COMMENTS: The skullcaps awaken slowly in spring so it is important that all plants be staked.

193

Scutellaria baicalensis • skullcap blue heaven

DESCRIPTION: 15 to 18 inches tall. The bushy skullcap has terminal clusters of intense medium-blue flowers, which are about 1 inch, tubelike in shape, and hooded. The plant has numerous stems bearing abundant clusters, which give it a tall, moundlike effect. The leaves are opposite to each other and are willowlike. They are not very noticeable during the blooming period. This rare wildflower is a foreigner from Lake Baikal, Siberia. It does well in our cold climate.

PERIOD OF BLOOM: July into August and often September.

SOIL: This skullcap grows well in fertile, slightly acid, sandy loam soil. It can stand some extreme conditions. Constant moisture with good drainage is best.

LOCATION AND EXPOSURE: Give this plant plenty of elbow room when grown in the border or wildflower garden. Full sun is a must for healthy specimens with abundant flowers.

PLANTING TIME: Spring or fall when dormant.

ROOT SYSTEM: The roots are very different from those of all the other species. Its rootstock is a coarse yellowish rhizome with few feeder roots, often forked. It breaks easily and should be handled carefully. Over a period of years additional eyes form at the crown of the plant, and the rhizome becomes very coarse and almost impossible to transplant, often parts of it rotting away for new rhizomes to form (in the same way as the rhubarb).

PLANTING DEPTH AND SPACING: Space at least 1½ feet apart. Set the plants with eyes 1½ to 2 inches deep and dig deep holes to accommodate the tapelike root, which is often forked.

PLANTING STOCK AND PROPAGATION: Young or medium-sized nursery stock is best.

The propagation of skullcap blue heaven is best limited to seeds (which always come up true to the parent plant). Seeds sown as soon as they ripen or in very early spring give small to medium-sized blooming plants the second year.

Root cuttings and stem cuttings produced no satisfactory results.

COMMENTS: Skullcap blue heaven is the prettiest of all the skullcaps. Catalogs and books list it only by its botanical name. I am responsible for giving it the name listed here. When growing in a drift, they remind me of a patch of deep blue sky.

Glechoma hederacea • gill-over-the-ground

DESCRIPTION: A fast-growing vine. Blue-lipped flowers form in the axils of the round, scalloped, opposite leaves.

This wildflower frequents shady damp areas and old homesteads as well as sunny places. Originally it grew only in cultivation.

PERIOD OF BLOOM: May into June, even earlier in warm climates.

SOIL: Use soil of any kind. This is the most versatile plant I know and will adapt itself to a variety of growing conditions.

LOCATION AND EXPOSURE: Fairly deep shade to full sun. Not the least bit particular. Gill-over-the-ground is an excellent vine for problem areas. Use it with grasses to hold the soil on a slope; it hugs the earth closely.

PLANTING TIME: Almost anytime, but during the growing season it must be carefully watered to establish.

ROOT SYSTEM: The main rootstock is a fibrous clump. Tiny roots form where running vines touch the damp earth at the nodes, and soon new plants are born. Each rooted portion may be separated and planted separately.

PLANTING DEPTH AND SPACING: Space ½ to 1 foot apart, depending on the size of the plant. Set the plants with the tiny crowns at soil level. Tuck in carefully.

PLANTING STOCK AND PROPAGATION: Use nursery-grown stock or quality collected stock.

Root propagation is done by cutting rooted vines into pieces between the joints and planting each portion separately. Cuttings taken in July for potting give good results. Seeds are difficult to collect, and the plant self-sows.

COMMENTS: I highly recommend this little plant. When grown in its proper place, it is unsurpassed. But do not plant it where it can run into the lawn or it will become a pest!

I say, "Give me an ash pile, a clinker heap, or a pile of sand, gravel, or earth—and I will soon turn it into a spot of beauty by covering it with gill-over-the-ground."

Physostegia virginiana • false dragonhead

DESCRIPTION: 1 to 3 feet tall. Terminal clusters of lipped flowers on spikes. Rose-lavender is the most common form. There is also a white form, which is rare in the wild but frequently grown in cultivation. A deep vibrant rose variety, *Physostegia vivid*, is offered as a perennial. The stem of the false dragonhead is square with toothed, willowlike leaves growing opposite each other.

False dragonhead grows in colonies in moist meadows, along streams, and around deserted homestead gardens.

PERIOD OF BLOOM: June into September. The rose-lavender variety grows rampantly, while the white grows more conservatively. The *Physostegia vivid* blooms later and is very showy.

SOIL: Ordinary garden soil with constant moisture is quite satisfactory. In damp to wet soils, it grows tall and abundant; in semidry areas, its growth is more restrained.

LOCATION AND EXPOSURE: The rose-lavender species is best grown in an open meadow or where it can spread. The pure white and vivid rose varieties are ideal as a border or near a pool or stream where their beauty can be reflected in the water.

PLANTING TIME: Spring or fall.

ROOT SYSTEM: New shoots form near the parent plant, which dies after blooming. The fibrous roots are coarse, white, and threadlike.

PLANTING DEPTH AND SPACING: Space 1 foot apart. Plants form clumps which should be divided every three years. Only the strong new outside shoots should be used. Set new plants with green growth at the crown just at soil level. Dormant stock should be planted about ½ inch deep. Fall plantings should be mulched.

PLANTING STOCK AND PROPAGATION: Nursery-grown stock is best, or use quality collected stock.

Divide clumps in spring or fall, and select only the husky outer shoots for transplanting.

Seeds sown in fall give mature plants the second year. All three species grow from seed.

COMMENTS: Both the white and vivid rose dragonheads are excellent for cut flower arrangements since they are long lasting. This plant is also called by the name obedient.

Salvia azurea • blue salvia

DESCRIPTION: 1½ to 2 feet tall. The broad lanceolated basal leaves are heavily quilted and prominently veined in pale green against dark green bodies. Numerous erect flower stalks have lateral branches, which form dense spikes in racemes. The large, lipped flowers are intense blue, suggestive of delphinium and monkshood.

Originally grown only in cultivation, blue salvia is now found in dry plains, prairies, and around old homesteads.

PERIOD OF BLOOM: June into July.

SOIL: Easily grown in ordinary garden soil with moderate fertility.

LOCATION AND EXPOSURE: Ideal in a sunny garden where its interesting green foliage will persist until killing frosts. Also, an excellent, showy plant along the border.

PLANTING TIME: Spring or fall.

ROOT SYSTEM: A robust rootstock with coarse fibrous roots.

PLANTING DEPTH AND SPACING: Space the plants 1 foot apart and set the crowns slightly deeper than the level at which they grew previously.

PLANTING STOCK AND PROPAGATION: Use nursery-grown stock, or quality collected stock where available.

Division of clumps is the easiest method of propagation.

Blue salvia is easily grown from cuttings taken after the plant has hardened, usually in mid-July. If cuttings are potted and kept in a propagating frame until rooted, they can be planted in the open in August.

Sow seeds as soon as they ripen or in early spring. Seedlings often bloom the second year.

COMMENTS: Blue salvia is a charming plant grown with earlier wildflowers that go dormant after blooming. Its basal rosette of foliage covers bare spots.

Monarda fistulosa • wild bergamot

DESCRIPTION: 2 to 3 feet tall. Clear lavender flowers are most common; occasionally, a few have hints of lavender-pink. White is very rare (I found a white-flowered plant that propagated well). The flowers end in terminal whorls, with each floret lipped. Stems are square with light gray-green foliage; the leaves are opposite one another and slightly toothed.

The wild bergamot grows along roadsides, in wastelands, and in dry meadows, often in the vicinity of black-eyed Susan, blazing star, frostflower aster, and gray goldenrod.

PERIOD OF BLOOM: Late July into September.

SOIL: Wild bergamot will grow in slightly acid, sandy, barren soils; fertile sandy loam; and soils that are very fertile. It is not demanding, but in lean soil it forms better and the stems do not become weak and twisted.

LOCATION AND EXPOSURE: Full sun to very light shade. A fine plant for naturalizing in meadows with goldenrods, blazing star, and black-eyed Susans.

PLANTING TIME: Spring, preferably.

ROOT SYSTEM: A mat of fibrous roots and many rhizomes from a large clump.

PLANTING DEPTH AND SPACING: Space 1 to 1½ feet apart. Plant the rhizomes horizontally 1 inch deep with the tip leading to the surface.

PLANTING STOCK AND PROPAGATION: Young nursery-grown plants are best, especially seedlings.

Division of old plants is not always successful. Stem cuttings taken in July give some results, but propagation by seed is the easiest.

Sow seeds as soon as they ripen or in fall. Seedlings often bloom in one year.

COMMENTS: Wild bergamot should always be grown where air circulation is good or it may mildew. When used as a border, cut it back right after blooming.

Three or four dried leaves steeped in a cup of boiling water, with sugar or honey added, makes a pleasing tea. Gather leaves in July.

Monarda didyma • Oswego tea

DESCRIPTION: 2 to 3 feet tall. Brilliant, scarlet-red flowers with lipped florets are found in terminal whorls. Leaves are opposite, toothed, and deep green with occasional red flushes. They are aromatic and have a minty fragrance when crushed.

Oswego tea grows naturally in areas south of Wisconsin, inhabiting moist spots along streams and in rich, open woodland.

PERIOD OF BLOOM: July–August; blooms later in cooler climates.

SOIL: Neutral to slightly acid soil with constant moisture. Water during periods of drought.

LOCATION AND EXPOSURE: Full sun or partial shade in a woodland border. An excellent contrast for bottle gentians and white snakeroots.

PLANTING TIME: Spring preferred.

ROOT SYSTEM: A fibrous rootstock with many branches that form a large mat. To keep this species vigorous, divide and replant every spring.

PLANTING DEPTH AND SPACING: Space 1 to 1½ feet apart. Set the rhizomes about 1 inch deep with the tip leading to the soil surface.

PLANTING STOCK AND PROPAGATION: Nursery-grown field stock or potted cuttings are preferable; also use quality collected stock if available.

Stem cuttings taken in July give fairly good results and must be kept in a cold frame for the first winter in very cold climates.

Sow seeds as soon as they ripen. A few seedlings may bloom in one year.

COMMENTS: In cultivation the monardas are short-lived unless replanted every year or two.

Collinsonia canadensis • stoneroot

DESCRIPTION: 2 to 4 feet tall. This plant has many branches with large ovate light-green leaves. The leaves are quilted and toothed. Panicles of airy, lemon-scented yellow flowers have wine-colored tinges in each blossom. They are somewhat orchidlike.

Stoneroot is usually found in rich soil in moist woodlands where it is protected from early spring frosts. Its foliage especially is sensitive to frost.

PERIOD OF BLOOM: August into September.

SOIL: Fertile garden soil with ample moisture—neutral to only slightly acid woods soil is preferable. The plant will not survive severe drought.

LOCATION AND EXPOSURE: Full sun or very light shade, in protected areas where frost cannot injure its foliage. Should frost damage occur, the plant will send up new shoots and bloom a little later. A deep mulch helps keep it dormant longer in spring.

199

PLANTING TIME: While dormant in spring or fall.

ROOT SYSTEM: A black, stonelike knotty rhizome like that of blazing star but much harder.

PLANTING DEPTH AND SPACING: Space 1 to 3 feet apart. Set the rhizomes 2 inches deep and mulch, preferably the year round. In cold climates mulch in winter to avoid winter-kill.

PLANTING STOCK AND PROPAGATION: Use nursery-grown stock or quality collected stock.

Divide rhizomes in spring while dormant. Lay the stonelike rootstock on a firm surface and use a clean, sharp chisel and hammer to cut it into pieces. Leave an eye or two on each piece, and plant with the eye upward. Some natural division also occurs.

Seeds rarely ripen and self-sow.

COMMENTS: Stoneroot, often called citronella or horse balm, is rarely grown in the wild garden, but nearly everyone who sees it in one will comment on its beauty and delightful fragrance.

SCROPHULARIACEAE [Figwort Family]

Chelone glabra • white turtlehead

DESCRIPTION: 1 to 3 feet tall. A dense terminal spike of lipped flowers on a leafy stem. The leaves are opposite, lanceolated, and slightly serrated. Plants with very slender leaves have pure white flowers; the flowers of larger plants are often tinted with pink to mauve. Each flower resembles a turtle's head with open mouth.

White turtlehead is found in wet meadows, along streams and lakes, in wet ditches, and in lowlands.

PERIOD OF BLOOM: July into September. Flowers are long-lasting if moisture is ample.

SOIL: Moderately acid to slightly acid soils, from moderate moisture retention to wet. I grow it in a fertile sandy loam with average moisture.

LOCATION AND EXPOSURE: Select a spot in full sun or very light shade. A lovely plant for the open, damp sunny meadow. More interesting when grown in colonies.

PLANTING TIME: While dormant in spring or fall.

ROOT SYSTEM: A coarse fibrous white rootstock with many white branches that will form new plants. The branches can be separated.

PLANTING DEPTH AND SPACING: Space 1½ to 2 feet apart. Set rootstocks upright and spread any branches attached to them horizontally about 1 inch below soil level. Eyes of the rhizomes and the crown should be almost at soil level. Mulch.

PLANTING STOCK AND PROPAGATION: Nursery-grown stock is far superior to collected stock.

To propagate, divide rhizomes, or take stem cuttings taken in July (moderately good results).

Sow seeds when ripe. White turtlehead self-sows in moist areas. Seedlings bloom the second year.

COMMENTS: An excellent companion for the stately red Cardinal flower.

Try cutting a few turtlehead plants back late in June. You will find that they bloom later and are bushier.

Chelone obliqua · red turtlehead

DESCRIPTION: 3 to 4 feet tall. A more robust grower than the white turtlehead. The foliage is a darker green, and the rose-colored flowers with yellow beards are the same shape but larger. They appear later in the year.

Native below the Mason-Dixon Line, it has proved hardy in cold climates.

PERIOD OF BLOOM: Late August into October.

SOIL: Acid to slightly acid soil of good fertility with moderate constant moisture.

LOCATION AND EXPOSURE: A good border plant for its foliage contrast as well as for the color and shape of its flower. Also valuable for naturalizing along a brook or lake or in a damp sunny meadow.

PLANTING TIME: While dormant in spring or fall.

ROOT SYSTEM: The root system is white. A stout rootstock, with fibrous roots, sends out many rhizomes to form a clump.

PLANTING DEPTH AND SPACING: Space 1 to 2 feet apart. Set the rootstock horizontally, carefully covering with about 1 inch of soil. Let the tips of the rhizomes taper upward, almost to soil surface.

Mulch in winter. A continuous mulch helps to retain much-needed moisture.

PLANTING STOCK AND PROPAGATION: Nursery-grown stock is superior, but you may also use quality collected stock.

Propagate by divisions of clumps, preferably in spring, and stem cuttings taken in early July. In my local area seeds do not ripen. If they are available, sow as soon as they ripen and transplant the seedlings in the spring of the second year.

COMMENTS: Red turtlehead is a charming plant with many good qualities and is an excellent addition to the wild garden.

White snakeroot and red turtlehead make an interesting combination grown in protected moist woodlands.

Pink turtlehead (*Chelone Lyoni*) has similar flowers with a medium to light pink color and faint purple streaks. The foliage is broader, but the plant does not grow as tall as either. Originally grown only in cultivation.

Mimulus ringens • monkey flower

DESCRIPTION: 20 to 30 inches tall. Opposite lanceolate leaves are attached to square stems. The tubular flowers resemble frilled snapdragons. The colors range from lavender to violet; a white is quite rare.

The lavender species is usually found along stream beds where it is sunny and the soil rarely dries out. It can even tolerate shallow, standing water if it is not stagnant.

PERIOD OF BLOOM: Late June into September, flowering continuously.

SOIL: The monkey flower grows best where soil is fertile, moist, and only slightly acid to neutral. In the nursery we grow it in average garden soil with constant moisture.

LOCATION AND EXPOSURE: Monkey flower grows best in full sun or partial open shade with constant moisture. When planted near a stone, its roots will run underneath to keep cool and seek moisture.

PLANTING TIME: While dormant in spring or fall.

ROOT SYSTEM: New shoots form from the parent plant, which dies in fall. The roots are pure white and fibrous, very similar to lobelias. The rootstocks form dense mats and should be separated every year to bloom well.

PLANTING DEPTH AND SPACING: Space about 1 foot apart. Set the plants ½ to 1 inch deep so that the tip of the new shoot is just at soil level. Spread roots evenly, and mulch if planted in fall.

PLANTING STOCK AND PROPAGATION: Use nursery-grown stock or only the strongest offset of quality collected stock.

Divide clumps, preferably in spring; some stem cuttings I took in early July gave good results.

Sow seeds in late fall or early spring. The seed is dust-fine and should only be scattered on top of the soil and covered with an evergreen bough until germination. Some seedlings will bloom the first year.

COMMENTS: Its long blooming period makes this a useful plant. I find that monkey flower does not need continuous wet as it does in the wild and that it still flourishes with only constant moisture. But drought spells disaster! Both the lavender and rarer white monkey flower are lovely companions for the fiery red lobelia.

Veronicastrum virginicum • Culver's root

DESCRIPTION: 2 to 5 feet tall. Whorls of narrow, toothed leaves encircle the stem at intervals. The terminal white flowers, in spirelike wands, are abundant. Close inspection reveals that the flowers have a faint blue tinge. This species grows more vigorously than cultivated veronicas.

Culver's root is found in meadows and open woods with high shade. In a wooded area along the Menominee River it covers a wide expanse up to the water's edge. Looking across the area on a sunny day gives one the feeling of viewing a calm sea of white, slightly tinged with blue. Here sparsely scattered giant oaks and tall Norway pines offer partial shade.

PERIOD OF BLOOM: June into August.

SOIL: Woods or fertile garden soil of moderate acidity and average moisture. The soil can also be damp.

LOCATION AND EXPOSURE: Excellent for planting in a sunny meadow or in high open woodland shade in large colonies. In the meadow,

Joe-pye and swamp milkweed make good companions. Grow Culver's root at the back of a border or along the edge of a woodland.

PLANTING TIME: While dormant in spring or fall.

ROOT SYSTEM: The rootstock is yellow, fibrous and extensive, each small plant forming a clump.

PLANTING DEPTH AND SPACING: Space 1 foot or more apart. Set the plants with eyes about 1 inch deep, spreading the roots carefully. Mulch in winter or year round.

PLANTING STOCK AND PROPAGATION: Nursery-grown stock has a more compact root system, but also use quality collected stock.

Divide clumps in spring or fall. Sow seeds when they are ripe. Stem cuttings are slow to root and do not bloom until the third year.

COMMENTS: The wild veronica is a good flower to use in bouquets; it lasts a long while after being cut. The dried flower-stalks are excellent for dry floral arrangements.

ACANTHACEAE [Acanthus Family]

Ruellia humilis • wild petunia

DESCRIPTION: The leafy flower stalks are about 2 inches high and tend to spread in mats. The light blue to violet flowers (rarely white), are shaped like cultivated petunias but are much smaller, more slender, and do not flare as much. The flowers are borne on short stems, growing in the axils of the hairy, pointed oval leaves.

Wild petunia is native east and south of Wisconsin, but it has proved hardy in our colder climate. It is usually found in dry sandy soil in open fields or at the edge of a woods.

PERIOD OF BLOOM: June into September.

SOIL: Moderately dry to average sandy garden loam that is fertile and only slightly acid.

LOCATION AND EXPOSURE: Full sun or very light shade. It is a charming plant to grow in the niches of a sunny rock garden.

PLANTING TIME: Spring or fall (spring in cold regions).

ROOT SYSTEM: Fibrous, slowly spreading roots.

PLANTING DEPTH AND SPACING: Space 6 to 12 inches apart. Set crowns at soil level. Potted stock, grown from cuttings, should also be planted at soil level.

PLANTING STOCK AND PROPAGATION: Use nursery-grown stock or quality collected stock (spring planted).

Stem cuttings taken late in June or early July and treated with root hormones give almost perfect results. This is the easiest method. Hold the rooted cuttings in a cold frame until spring. Many will bloom the first year.

Seeds are produced in abundance, but germination is poor.

COMMENTS: This dainty creeper is sure to attract attention. The wild petunia is neat and long-lived and blooms for a long time. It even blooms during dry spells, though not so profusely.

RUBIACEAE [Madder Family]

Mitchella repens • partridgeberry

DESCRIPTION: 4 to 10 inch creeping vine. Small, shiny, dark green leaves with some white veins growing on opposite sides of the stem. Pairs of tiny, fragrant, pink or white flowers are followed by red berries in early fall.

In the woodland you will often find colonies of partridgeberry creeping along over decaying white birch and aspen stumps and fallen logs. Where the earth is moist, the plant establishes itself by sending out roots at the nodes as it forks. In damper evergreen forests it grows in the vicinity of twinflower and bunchberry. In some of these areas the shade may be so dense that small masses cover the forest floor.

PERIOD OF BLOOM: June into July.

SOIL: An almost neutral to acid, humus-rich woods soil is preferable. Add some sharp sand.

LOCATION AND EXPOSURE: A partly shaded nook or an area with light to deep shade is ideal. An excellent spot is under evergreens or deciduous trees where the soil is rich in humus and somewhat moist in spring.

To obtain a natural effect, plant partridgeberry among fallen, decaying logs or around old stumps in the woodland. It is an exceptionally neat groundcover among small plants but spreads slowly.

PLANTING TIME: Spring or fall. Potted stock can be planted anytime.

ROOT SYSTEM: Very small, rather short, fibrous roots form where the nodes touch the damp earth. Potted stock develops strong root systems and can be more easily grown in drier areas.

PLANTING DEPTH AND SPACING: Potted stock should be spaced 8 to 12 inches apart, and planted at soil level. Mulch lightly. When working with bareroot stock, be sure to tuck the tiny roots among the decaying humus; mulch lightly. Any bare stems should be covered with ½ inch of soil or humus, and often new roots will develop, especially if the soil is kept moist. Laying a small stone on a longer vine here and there will often encourage new roots to develop.

PLANTING STOCK AND PROPAGATION: Pot-grown nursery stock is best. While bareroot stock requires considerable care to establish, potted stock grows easily with minimum attention.

Quality collected sods are also preferable to bareroot stock.

Cuttings taken in June will give good results. A rooting hormone aids in root formation. In pots, long-stemmed cuttings develop vigorous roots. A good potting mixture is: equal parts of damp peatmoss, sharp sand, leafmold (or compost), plus fertile woods soil. Plants usually do not bear flowers until the second year.

Sow seeds as soon as they are ripe. The hard-shelled seeds are slow to germinate. Seedlings usually appear in the second year if the soil is kept continuously moist.

COMMENTS: The shiny green vine with its bright red, edible berries (which have an insipid taste) is prized for partridgeberry bowls at Christmas time. It can also be grown in a terrarium with other dainty wildflowers and tiny ferns.

The white-berried form is very rare. It does not have white veining in its foliage.

CAPRIFOLIACEAE [Honeysuckle Family]

Linnaea borealis • twinflower

DESCRIPTION: Crawling vine, 3 to 4 inch stems. A dainty, somewhat woody vine with dull greeen, slightly scalloped opposite leaves. Pairs of fragrant pink or white flowers nod gracefully above the reclining vine.

Twinflower grows on decaying, uprooted stumps or fallen moss-covered logs. It is often found along old logging trails in cut-over evergreen forests.

PERIOD OF BLOOM: June into August.

SOIL: Rich, acid to slightly acid, humus-rich woods soil with high to average moisture content.

LOCATION AND EXPOSURE: A cool damp woods is ideal. Plant among rocks where leafmold and humus are deep. Or prepare a bed in shade. A mixture of woods soil, damp peatmoss, and crumbling, rotted pine wood makes a fine growing medium.

Twinflower is not easy to establish. In my wild garden a vine of twinflower volunteered in the shade of a maidenhair fern among pink creeping phlox. The soil in this spot becomes quite dry in summer, yet the plant maintains its green leaves and even adds a few each year along with an occasional pair of blossoms. One would certainly not expect this to be a good spot when one considers the twinflower's natural habitat.

PLANTING TIME: Plant bareroot stock in spring, potted stock anytime.

ROOT SYSTEM: Very short, fine hairy roots that dry almost immediately when exposed to air. Great care is needed to transplant bareroot stock.

PLANTING DEPTH AND SPACING: Space about 1 foot apart. Plants with soil adhering and potted stock should be planted at soil level.

PLANTING STOCK AND PROPAGATION: Nursery-grown potted stock is best. You can also use quality collected sods.

Seeds are hard to collect and slow to germinate. Seedlings are slow to mature.

Cuttings taken in spring when the plants are still dormant give fair results and have proved to be the best method of propagation.

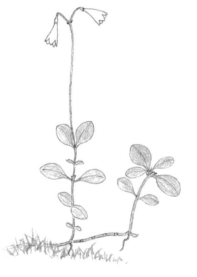

Keep potted stock grown from cuttings in a propagating frame two years before moving to a permanent location.

COMMENTS: This flower from the deep woodland, sometimes called deer vine, is a challenge to grow unless ideal conditions are created for it. Sometimes a volunteer persists against all odds.

Triosteum aurantiacum • horse gentian

DESCRIPTION: 2 to 3 feet tall. A coarse wildflower, resembling the common milkweed at first glance. Observed more closely you will note that, unlike the milkweed, the tip of each leaf is pointed and not blunt, that the plant sends up several stalks from each crown, and that it does not travel beneath the ground. Several small starlike purple flowers are borne in the axils of the leaves. In early fall these are followed by orange fruit, resembling rose hips, but smaller and more oblong.

Though rare in my area, horse gentian is occasionally found growing in moist woods in the company of large white trilliums, hepaticas, and red baneberries. Sometimes it may frequent shaded hillsides of drier woods where aspens grow thick.

PERIOD OF BLOOM: May into June.

SOIL: Slightly acid woods soil or fertile garden soil that does not bake dry in summer. Constant moisture is very important.

LOCATION AND EXPOSURE: An excellent plant in open woodland with filtered sunlight or light shade. It is important to remember that horse gentian must have some moisture at all times to flourish.

PLANTING TIME: Very early in spring before new growth appears, or in fall when dormant.

ROOT SYSTEM: A coarse rootstock with extensive fibrous roots, some of which should be pruned before transplanting.

PLANTING DEPTH AND SPACING: Space 2 feet apart. Set the eyes of the crown about 1 inch deep. With age each plant sends up more shoots and forms a clump.

PLANTING STOCK AND PROPAGATION: Young to medium-sized nursery-grown stock is best. You can use young collected stock, but it is scarce.

Divisions have proved unsuccessful. Of fifty stem cuttings I took one July, only one developed and it did not bloom until the third year.

I know of no easy way to propagate this species, but sowing seeds seems the best.

Remove the seeds from their pulpy hulls and plant them in fall. Germination is slow, often requiring three years. It takes another two years for the plants to bloom. Filing a nick in the hard-shelled seeds sometimes hastens germination by a year.

COMMENTS: Horse gentian is a novelty in the moist wild garden. Once established, it seems to endure forever.

The long-lasting orange fruit is pretty and for some unknown reason does not attract the ambitious chipmunks who claim most of the other seed crops.

CAMPANULACEAE [Bluebell Family]

Campanula glomerata • clustered bluebell

DESCRIPTION: 1 to 2 feet tall. The clusters of intense violet bells are held on erect leafy stems. The basal foliage forms a rosette of ovate leaves. The color of the flowers matches that of Venus's looking-glass.

Originally grown only in cultivation, this bluebell is now found in deserted homestead gardens, along field fence rows, and along open roadsides.

PERIOD OF BLOOM: June into July.

SOIL: Neutral to slightly acid fertile soil. In lean soils bloom is scant.

LOCATION AND EXPOSURE: Full sun or very light shade. Plant blue-bells along the border of the woods or in the perennial flower border. The deep green foliage keeps its color all summer and well into fall.

PLANTING TIME: While dormant in spring or fall. May also be transplanted in late August.

ROOT SYSTEM: A fibrous root system with short rhizomes that do not stray far.

PLANTING DEPTH AND SPACING: Space 12 or more inches apart. Set the plants with the attached rhizomes ½ to 1 inch deep, placing the tips of the rhizomes almost at soil level. Each plant will form a neat, compact mat of green.

PLANTING STOCK AND PROPAGATION: Use nursery-grown stock or quality collected stock.

Divide clumps that become too crowded. To keep the plant blooming vigorously, transplant every third year. Few seeds mature. On rare occasions the plant volunteers.

COMMENTS: The shade of violet-purple of this bluebell is so intense that it always draws favorable comments from anyone who sees the plant bloom.

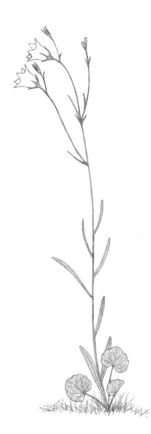

Campanula rotundifolia · harebell

DESCRIPTION: 10 to 15 inches tall. Wiry stems bearing clusters of dainty blue bells grow from a rosette of tiny heart-shaped leaves.

Harebell is found in grassy fields and along sunny roadsides, often where the soil is gravelly. At times I have found it flourishing in pure red sand, especially on roadside shoulders, where other vegetation was extremely sparse.

PERIOD OF BLOOM: June into early August. When the plant is cultivated, the period of bloom often extends into fall.

SOIL: Sandy loam or regular garden soil. Good drainage is very important. Harebells are not demanding otherwise.

LOCATION AND EXPOSURE: Select a sunny spot among grasses, and clear a 12 inch circle. Or select a sunny spot in a rock garden or along the edge of a border.

When the harebell is grown on open ground it is susceptible to rust on the underside of its basal foliage. This does not affect the bloom and is not noticeable until you peek beneath the basal foliage. This problem does not usually arise if the plant is mulched.

PLANTING TIME: Late spring after the basal foliage appears or in late summer into fall. In cultivation or when mulched the plants do not have midsummer dormant spells as they do in grassy areas.

ROOT SYSTEM: A small rootstock with some fibrous roots and many straggly, spreading white rhizomes that are brittle and very easily broken.

PLANTING DEPTH AND SPACING: Space 1 to 2 feet apart. Set the plants with basal foliage at soil level, but any attached offsets should be planted ½ to 1 inch deep. Single-crowned plants will form clumps if not hoed.

PLANTING STOCK AND PROPAGATION: Nursery-grown stock will usually have a more compact root system, especially when grown in sandy soil that is not too fertile. Also use quality collected stock (gather in spring or fall).

Division of clumps in spring gives excellent results. To propagate from seed, scatter the very fine seeds on top of the soil in a flat or in an undisturbed area; germination is variable. Some small seedlings will appear the first year.

COMMENTS: This pretty wildflower is short-lived when grown in cultivation and hoed. I prefer to grow it under mulch.

Harebell is also referred to as the blue bells of Scotland or Scottish bluebells.

Lobelia Cardinalis • Cardinal flower

DESCRIPTION: 15 to 36 inches tall. The lipped flowers are a brilliant fiery red. (There is also a rare white form, *L. Cardialis alba*, which does not grow true from seeds as does the red.) Spikes rise from a neat rosette of lanceolated foliage that becomes smaller as it continues up the leafy stem.

The Cardinal flower is found in wet, sunny meadows and along brooks. Often whole colonies disappear when drainage ditches are dug, only to reappear from seed a few years later.

PERIOD OF BLOOM: July into September, varying with the amount of moisture present and soil fertility.

SOIL: Neutral to slightly acid soil with constant moisture. Soil need not be extremely wet but it must never dry out completely.

LOCATION AND EXPOSURE: Grow the Cardinal flower in full sun or very light shade and mulch to keep the roots moist and cool. It is very much at home growing along a brook with bottle gentians or in a damp meadow among sparse tufts of grasses. It can also grow in a formal border if the soil does not become too dry.

To increase its life span, it is advisable to transplant the Cardinal flower every spring and to cut it back right after it blooms, leaving only a few inches of stalk. As soon as new rosettes form, the parent stalks should be cut back completely.

If you want to collect seed pods, leave only one or two per stalk. Each pod contains an abundance of very fine seed.

PLANTING TIME: Spring planting is best in cold climates. In other areas it can be planted in spring or fall. Potted stock can be planted anytime. In extremely cold regions the plant is best treated as a biennial.

ROOT SYSTEM: The white roots are extensive, coarsely fibrous, and travel far in one year's growth. When transplanting them, cut some of the roots back to about 2½ inches. Potted stock has a more compact root system.

PLANTING DEPTH AND SPACING: Space 8 to 12 inches apart in the garden, or plant at random in a meadow or along a stream.

Set bareroot stock or potgrown stock with crowns at soil level. In fall, before winter mulching, pull a little soil up to the crowns, but do not cover the center.

PLANTING STOCK AND PROPAGATION: Nursery-grown stock is best, though quality collected stock will produce plants also. Stem cuttings taken before the plant blooms can be used too.

Easily grown from seed. Scatter ripe seeds on top of soil in flats and cover with wire mesh. Mulch in the fall and remove mulch in spring. Seedlings should remain in flats until the following spring. For protection, mulch again in the fall using a wire screen to keep from smothering the plants.

COMMENTS: I obtained a specimen of the white variety, *L. Cardinalis alba*, from a New York grower. The plant grew to about 30 inches high and had shiny green, coarsely quilted leaves. A few years later a friend in Missouri gave me a single-crown plant. This lobelia was a division of a lone white plant she had found among many red ones. I was surprised by the difference between the two plants. Hers had narrower, finely quilted dull green leaves. The single crown sent up a lone flower stalk 4½ feet tall; it displayed 74 individual blossoms. What variation within the species!

Lobelia siphilitica • great blue lobelia

DESCRIPTION: 1 to 3 feet tall. The lipped flowers are bright blue with white touches in their throats. Some have a purplish cast, but these do not come true from seed. There is also a pure white form. The entire flower stalk is leafy, with the leaves becoming smaller as they near the top. The basal foliage is a rosette of long, serrated leaves. These are less shiny than those of the Cardinal flower and are not pointed at the tip.

This lobelia is usually found in moist meadows, along stream banks, and often in damp woods at the edge of a swampland.

PERIOD OF BLOOM: August into September; sometimes a few blossoms in October.

SOIL: Neutral to slightly acid fertile soil. Great blue lobelia can be grown in average garden soil if watered during periods of drought. Under such conditions it will not grow as tall. Constant moisture is important if you want to raise ideal specimens.

LOCATION AND EXPOSURE: Full sun or very light shade are equally suitable. This is a good plant to grow with the early white snake-root in an open moist woodland—for contrast, keep all the lobelias together. When the blue lobelia is grown in a wet area it tends to spread.

PLANTING TIME: In cold climates it is best transplanted in spring when new foliage appears. In other areas, fall or spring planting is satisfactory. Mulch in winter in very cold climates.

ROOT SYSTEM: Stringy white fibrous roots.

PLANTING DEPTH AND SPACING: Space 8 to 12 inches apart or plant at random in a meadow. Set the crowns at soil level. A little soil may be pulled toward the crown before mulching and before the ground freezes. This species is more robust than the red one.

Coarse fibrous white roots should be pruned back to 2¼ inches before transplanting. Divide clumps every spring for good healthy growth.

PLANTING STOCK AND PROPAGATION: Nursery-grown stock is best. Also use quality collected stock.

To propagate, divide clumps in spring; also sow seeds.

Seeds sown as soon as they are ripe germinate readily the following spring. Grow the seedlings in a flat for one year and transfer them to pots or to an open field in the spring of the second year. In moist areas, this lobelia self-sows.

The white form of the great blue lobelia does not come true from seed and is best propagated by division of multiple crowns in spring.

COMMENTS: Occasionally a burgundy-colored plant will appear among the blue lobelia seedlings. It does not set seed and can only be propagated by divisions.

COMPOSITAE [Composite Family]

Vernonia noveboracensis • ironweed

DESCRIPTION: 3 to 5 feet tall. This robust plant has loose, terminal clusters of buttonlike, deep lavender to purple flowers. Lanceolated, toothed leaves alternate along the length of the stem.

Ironweed grows naturally in the eastern half of the United States, inhabiting lowlands and banks of lakes and streams.

PERIOD OF BLOOM: Late August into September and October.

SOIL: Ironweed adapts to a variey of soils with constant moisture, although it always grows in wet soil in the wild.

LOCATION AND EXPOSURE: Ironweed is ideal for naturalizing in a moist meadow or along a stream or lake. But do not hesitate to grow it in a tall border where the soil is fertile and has constant moisture. I grew it from seed in regular garden soil in full sun.

PLANTING TIME: While dormant in spring or fall.

ROOT SYSTEM: A stout, fibrous rootstock. It sends out rhizomes that stay nearby.

PLANTING DEPTH AND SPACING: Space 18 inches apart. Or plant at random. Set the plants with the crown at soil level and mulch.

PLANTING STOCK AND PROPAGATION: Use nursery-grown stock of medium size or quality collected stock.

Propagate by divisions, preferably in spring, or sow seeds as soon as they are ripe. Germination may be uneven. Seedlings are slow to develop, and usually do not bloom until the fourth year. Stem cuttings have proved unsatisfactory.

COMMENTS: Ironweed is an interesting specimen for the wild garden and provides some color in late summer.

Eupatorium maculatum • Joe-pye

DESCRIPTION: 4 to 5 feet tall. Dense convex clusters of lavender to mauve flowers top a stout stem that is tinged with purple at the nodes. White flowers are rare. Large, toothed, ovate leaves line the stem in whorls. They are predominately quilted and have a scent like vanilla.

Joe-pye congregates in large colonies in roadside ditches, moist meadows, and open areas not quite so damp. It often grows in the vicinity of tall meadowrue and boneset.

PERIOD OF BLOOM: Late July to September.

SOIL: Any of various soils with reasonably good fertility. In sandy loam soils of only moderate fertility and a minimum of moisture the plant grows much more compactly, not as tall but still pretty and really more refined.

LOCATION AND EXPOSURE: Joe-pye is a bold wildflower best suited for a large moist meadow in full sun. It prefers sunlight, and will tolerate only light shade. Plant in clumps for a more striking display. It contrasts well with Canada goldenrod and tall meadowrue. If the soil has constant moisture it can be grown in a border.

PLANTING TIME: While dormant in spring or fall.

ROOT SYSTEM: A very tough, fibrous rootstock. It is very hard to break up. The purplish eyes are barely visible when the plant is dormant.

PLANTING DEPTH AND SPACING: Space 2 or more feet apart or plant in colonies. Set the rootstock slightly below the soil. Mulch if you wish.

PLANTING STOCK AND PROPAGATION: Medium-sized nursery-grown stock is best, or use quality collected young stock.

Divide the clumps in spring or fall. It is difficult to divide the roots, as they are very intermatted. Trim the wiry roots to a few inches. Vigorous new roots soon develop if ample moisture is available.

The little winged seeds must be covered only lightly when sown. Cover them with an evergreen bough to keep the wind from carrying them away. Joe-pye self-sows.

COMMENTS: Joe-pye is only one of the large group of *Eupatoria*. The white snakeroot is its very charming cousin.

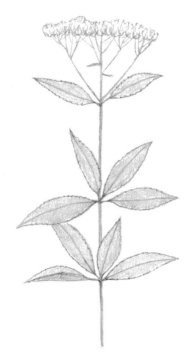

Eupatorium perfoliatum • boneset

DESCRIPTION: 2 to 4 feet tall. Flat-topped dull white flowers, sometimes with a faint bluish cast, form upright clusters. Lance-shaped leaves, prominently veined and heavily quilted, grow opposite each other along the stem. The foliage is quite unusual and very different from any other in this family.

215

Boneset frequents damp ditches, meadows, and river bottoms, often in the company of tall meadowrue and Joe-pye.

PERIOD OF BLOOM: July into August.

SOIL: Any of various soils with very high to average moisture content.

LOCATION AND EXPOSURE: Grow boneset in the meadow with Joe-pye as a companion. An excellent plant for foliage contrast in full sun or light shade.

PLANTING TIME: While dormant in spring or fall.

ROOT SYSTEM: A coarse fibrous rootstock that forms a clump which is difficult to divide.

PLANTING DEPTH AND SPACING: Space about 1 foot apart. When grown in fertile soil each plant forms a clump. Set the crowns at soil level and trim off any excess straggly roots; new roots will grow.

PLANTING STOCK AND PROPAGATION: Use nursery-grown stock of medium size or quality collected young stock.

Divide the clumps in spring or fall. Seed germination has proved poor. Boneset rarely self-sows.

COMMENTS: Boneset is not a pretty flower in itself, but when grown in masses its color and foliage contrast well with other wildflowers.

Eupatorium rugosum • early white snakeroot

DESCRIPTION: 1 to 3 feet tall, often taller in very moist areas. Buttons of dense long-lasting white flowers form showy terminal clusters on rigid leafy stems. The branches have many divisions, giving the plant the appearance of a round bush. The thin petiolate leaves are toothed, tapering to a gradual point. This species is better adapted to cold than the late-flowering *Eupatorium aromaticum*.

Early white snakeroot is found in open damp rocky woods, along streams, and in moist meadows. It grows and blooms profusely in thickets and in the shade of tall hardwoods where the soil is moderately moist and rich in humus.

PERIOD OF BLOOM: July into August, sometimes September.

SOIL: Humus-rich fertile soil that is slightly acid to neutral. Snakeroot needs constant moisture to bloom well. Soil need not be wet, although the plant can tolerate standing water admirably.

216

LOCATION AND EXPOSURE: Grow early white snakeroot in a sunny spot or in a rocky woods where leafmold is deep, or interplant with tall and medium ferns in a shady nook. It is particularly beautiful when reflected in a pool or a slow-running brook, and is also a fine plant for a formal border.

PLANTING TIME: While dormant in spring or fall.

ROOT SYSTEM: A compact, wiry, fibrous rootstock. The eyes of new growth are slow to appear in spring. The roots may seem dead but are very much alive. This is a common trait of the eupatoria.

PLANTING DEPTH AND SPACING: Space 2 to 3 feet apart. Set the eyes of the crowns barely ½ inch below soil level. The late emergence of shoots in spring protects the foliage, which is sensitive to frosts.

PLANTING STOCK AND PROPAGATION: Use nursery-grown stock or quality collected young stock.

Divide clumps in spring or fall; use only the vigorous portions. Seed germination is unreliable. The plant self-sows under ideal conditions.

COMMENTS: A colony of white snakeroot in bloom resembles a blanket of down settling on a meadow. This is my favorite eupatorium.

The juices of the snakeroots are poisonous to man and cattle, and it presented problems to the pioneers.

Liatris scariosa • blazing star

DESCRIPTION: 2 to 3 feet tall. One or two sturdy leafy stalks rise from a rosette of linear basal foliage. Spikes of many buttonlike, feathery flower disks bloom at intervals along the entire length of the stalk. The flower spike blooms from the top downward. This is characteristic of all the liatris. The violet-lavender to rosy-purple variety is the most common. Sometimes a rare white one appears among them.

Blazing star is found in open sandy country, along roadsides, in wastelands, and among sparse prairie grasses—often covering huge areas with splendid color. On wastelands it often grows with early goldenrod, which blooms at the same time.

PERIOD OF BLOOM: August into September, sometimes as early as late July.

SOIL: Blazing star seems to be indifferent to soil pH. Lean soils or

moderately fertile soils encourage the best flowers with the straightest stalks. In rich soil the plant loses its stature and the spikes become limp, bending at odd angles. Good drainage is very important.

LOCATION AND EXPOSURE: Blazing star is a choice plant for sandy problem areas where little else will grow. Once established, the plant endures drought well. Full sun all day and fairly lean soil will ensure straight flower spikes and abundant bloom.

In sandy prairielike areas it is best planted among sparse grasses. Or interperse it with birdfoot violets, butterfly flowers, blue-eyed grass, pussy-toes, goldenrods, and wild asters.

PLANTING TIME: Spring or fall. If the plant is moved during the growing season the flower stalk should be cut off, leaving some of the leafy stem. The top may die, but it will usually appear the next spring.

ROOT SYSTEM: Young seedling corms are cinnamon-colored; they turn dark with age. A black warted corm that increases in size produces many warts when cultivated. In the wild there is rarely more than one stalk.

PLANTING DEPTH AND SPACING: Space about 6 inches apart or scatter. Set the corms 1 inch deep. Deeper planting will encourage the corm to send up extra stalks to form an attractive plant. If the stalks become too crowded the corm should be dug up in the spring and cut into pieces, leaving one or two eyes in each portion.

PLANTING STOCK AND PROPAGATION: Use nursery-grown stock or quality collected stock.

For division of large corms, cut the corm into pieces like potatoes, leaving one or two eyes in each portion. Dry for an hour before planting, or dust with fungicide. Plant 1 inch deep. Mulch in winter only to protect the corm in very cold climates, but remove the mulch in spring.

Seeds are slow to germinate, usually waiting until the second year. One-year-old seedlings can be moved to their permanent home.

COMMENTS: The blazing star is hardy and easy to cultivate. The flowers, opening at the top and working down the stalk, are ideal for floral arrangements. Snip off the wilted flowers and there are no bare stalks to hide.

The blazing star is decidedly a sun lover.

Just a few years ago while hiking in an area where sand dunes and prairie grasses alternated I came upon a colony of liatris—many hundreds of them. In their midst grew a small colony of delicate mauve-pink plants. It is not an easy color to describe, but they were outstanding. My botany books do not list this color phase. Is it a rare form, or a new variety?

Liatris pycnostachya · Kansas gayfeather

DESCRIPTION: 2 to 4 feet tall. Tall wands of closely set florets top sturdy stems with linear foliage. The flowers are violet-lavender to rosy purple, and rarely white. Basal foliage is also linear but broader. It tends to become less prominent as the flowers bloom. This plant is another reserved bloomer.

Kansas gayfeather is found among grasses in damp open prairies, usually in the vicinity of goldenrods.

PERIOD OF BLOOM: August into September.

SOIL: Moderately fertile soils.

LOCATION AND EXPOSURE: Full sun is necessary to grow straight spikes. In shade the plant grows rampantly and produces abundant leaves and crooked, sparsely flowered spikes. Grow Kansas gayfeather in a sunny border or in an open prairielike place.

PLANTING TIME: Spring or fall, preferably spring.

ROOT SYSTEM: A blackish to dark-gray warted corm with many eyes. It increases in size with age.

PLANTING DEPTH AND SPACING: Space about 1 foot apart or plant at random in colonies. Set the corms 1 inch deep. Corms produce more spikes when planted deeper, but require transplanting more often. The first year after transplanting, do not expect well-formed flower spikes. It seems that the plant must adapt itself to its new environment. Mulch in winter only in cold climates.

PLANTING STOCK AND PROPAGATION: Use nursery-grown stock or quality collected medium-sized corms.

The division of large corms is the quickest and surest method of propagation. Cut the corms as one would potatoes for spring planting, leaving one to two eyes in each piece. Dry for an hour or dust with fungicide.

Seeds are slow to germinate, often requiring two years. Seedlings bloom the second and third year.

COMMENTS: Kansas gayfeather is very easy to grow and soon forms large clumps when cultivated. There is a white form but it does not increase as rapidly.

Solidago canadensis • Canada goldenrod

DESCRIPTION: 3 to 4 feet tall. Feathery, rich yellow sprays of florets atop sturdy stems. Narrow medium-green foliage alternates along the entire length of the stem.

This goldenrod is found along roadsides and fence lines, in dry open fields, or in dampish meadows that dry out in summer.

PERIOD OF BLOOM: August into September.

SOIL: Adaptable to most soil conditions. Its height is determined mostly by the fertility and moisture content of the soil.

LOCATION AND EXPOSURE: Goldenrods are sun lovers, but tolerate very light open shade. Lovely for the back of a border and very showy when grown among old fence rails or next to a stone wall with wild blue asters.

PLANTING TIME: Spring or fall.

ROOT SYSTEM: Short slender rhizomes with a touch of rose at the tip. They form large clumps. To produce beautiful plants, the roots must have ample growing room.

PLANTING DEPTH AND SPACING: Space about 2 feet apart. Set rhizomes horizontally about 1 inch deep with the tip leading to the surface. The outer rhizomes produce the strongest plants. Divide clumps and transplant every third year for showy plants that bloom profusely.

PLANTING STOCK AND PROPAGATION: Use nursery-grown stock or quality collected young stock.

Propagate by division of clumps, using only the strong outer rhizomes and discarding the center growth. The plant self-sows readily where soil is open.

COMMENTS: If the goldenrod were not so easily cultivated and not so abundant, perhaps we would prize it more highly. It combines beautifully with many of the late summer and fall flowers, especially in a tall border. The association of goldenrod pollen with hay fever has been discredited.

The galls that form on goldenrods in wastelands are interesting to the dry-flower arranger, and the insects inside the galls provide good bait for the ice fisherman.

220

Solidago rigida • prairie goldenrod

DESCRIPTION: 3 to 4 feet tall. Large flat-topped flower heads of rich golden yellow, atop sturdy stems. Most of the foliage is basal—often 8 inches long and several inches wide, and forming neat, gray-green rosettes. True leaves are scant.

The prairie goldenrod, also called stiff goldenrod, frequents lean meadows, rocky pastures, and hillsides in full sun.

PERIOD OF BLOOM: Late August until frost. The flowers remain yellow for a long time, even after frosts have damaged the leaves.

SOIL: Prairie goldenrod is adaptable. It forms large clumps in the sandy fertile loam of our garden. Good drainage is important.

LOCATION AND EXPOSURE: A showy plant for a large sunny border. Grow it with purple or rose-colored New England asters.

PLANTING TIME: While dormant in spring or fall.

ROOT SYSTEM: A coarse fibrous rootstock with many pinkish to rose-colored shoots. It has long white roots that reach far into the ground for food and moisture.

PLANTING DEPTH AND SPACING: Space 2 or more feet apart since the plants form large clumps. Set the crowns at soil level and spread the roots evenly. Roots should be trimmed back to 3 or 4 inches. Divide the clumps every third year.

PLANTING STOCK AND PROPAGATION: Nursery-grown stock is best; the rhizomes are divided more often, which makes for more vigorous plants. Also use quality collected young stock.

Propagate by division of clumps. Use only the strong outer plants, and discard the center growth. The plant will also volunteer where soil is open.

COMMENTS: "Plume o' gold" is a more fitting name for this lovely plant. It is a good wildflower to grow in colder climates, as early frosts do it no harm.

Prairie goldenrod is very different in appearance from other goldenrods, and I consider it one of the best for late blooming.

Solidago graminifolia • grass-leaved goldenrod

DESCRIPTION: 2 to 4 feet tall. A leafy stalk with many alternate willowlike leaves is topped by a flat open cluster of numerous small yellow flowers.

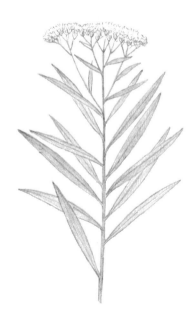

This goldenrod often forms a gold blanket over moist thickets, meadows and roadside ditches.

PERIOD OF BLOOM: Late July into September.

SOIL: A moist, fertile to average garden soil with constant moisture. PH is not important, but the plant is usually found in a somewhat acid soil.

LOCATION AND EXPOSURE: The grass-leaved goldenrod is best suited for naturalizing in a moist open meadow with Joe-pye, swamp milkweed, tall meadowrue and flat-topped white aster. If you prefer a lone specimen in a wild garden, plant it in a bottomless gallon can and bury it at soil level.

PLANTING TIME: While dormant in spring or fall.

ROOT SYSTEM: A slender rhizome that wanders and sends up new shoots at frequent intervals, especially when grown in fertile soil or when mulched.

PLANTING DEPTH AND SPACING: Space 2 feet apart, as rhizomes spread to form colonies. Set rhizomes horizontally 1 inch deep with eye almost at soil level.

PLANTING STOCK AND PROPAGATION: Nursery-grown stock is rarely available. Use quality collected young stock.

Divide rhizome clumps while plant is dormant. It self-sows sparsely.

COMMENTS: Grass-leaved goldenrod is a good plant to grow in the open meadow if you want a mass of yellow to cover a large expanse or to contrast with other wildflowers.

Aster macrophyllus • large-leaved aster

DESCRIPTION: 2 to 3 feet tall. An open cluster of rayed light-blue flowers with darker centers. The basal foliage is large and heart-shaped; the leaves on the stems are smaller and sparse.

Found in dry open woods and moist thickets where the soil is humus-rich, this wildflower rarely blooms in deep shade, but it spreads to make good groundcover.

PERIOD OF BLOOM: August into September.

SOIL: Slightly acid, fertile woods soil, either damp or somewhat dry in midsummer. Constant moisture is important if you want the best foliage.

LOCATION AND EXPOSURE: Grow the large-leaved aster in colonies in high open shade where some sun filters through, or as ground-cover in a more deeply shaded area. The foliage withstands very severe frosts.

PLANTING TIME: While dormant in spring or fall.

ROOT SYSTEM: Many short rhizomes form a large rootstock with fibrous roots.

PLANTING DEPTH AND SPACING: Space 2 to 12 inches apart. Set the crowns at soil level and mulch lightly overall.

PLANTING STOCK AND PROPAGATION: Nursery-grown stock is rarely offered. Use quality collected stock.

To propagate, divide clumps or sow seeds as soon as they are ripe. In barren areas it sometimes self-sows in a moist shady area.

COMMENTS: This particular species of aster is best used as a ground-cover; the foliage is showier than the flowers.

Aster novae-angliae • New England aster

DESCRIPTION: 3 to 4 feet tall. Many fine-rayed terminal clusters of purple-violet flowers. The flowers are usually very uniform in color, but the rose-pink kind has some variation. All have prominent yellow centers. The leaves are long and narrow, somewhat sticky, and cling to the entire length of the hairy stem.

New England aster springs up naturally in open meadows, along roadsides, and in thickets. In central Wisconsin, it blankets road-sides and fields each autumn with splashes of color.

PERIOD OF BLOOM: Late August into October.

SOIL: Neutral to slightly acid fertile soil with constant moisture. The plant grows vigorously under these conditions.

LOCATION AND EXPOSURE: New England aster is an excellent plant to grow in colonies in full sun or very light open shade. Use it in a border with cultivated perennials, or grow it among taller wild-flowers. Mulch this plant heavily to keep the roots cool and the soil moist. When the plant is mulched the leaves grow along the entire length of the stem for the whole season and the flowers are of better quality.

PLANTING TIME: Fall, spring, or late summer after the rhizomes have formed. Late fall is best.

ROOT SYSTEM: Short white rhizomes, often tinged with pink, radiate from the blooming stalk and form a neat clump. Each clump has many fibrous roots that grow extremely long, especially in heavily mulched fertile gardens. Divide the rhizomes often to keep the plant growing vigorously.

PLANTING DEPTH AND SPACING: Space 1 to 2 feet apart, depending on the fertility of the soil and effect wanted. Set the plants horizontally with the roots 1 inch deep and the tips of the rhizomes just below soil level. The extensive fibrous roots should be trimmed back to 3 or 4 inches. Mulch heavily for winter. Remove some of the mulch in spring, then replace it when the new growth has hardened.

PLANTING STOCK AND PROPAGATION: Nursery-grown stock is best and most vigorous. Also use quality collected stock.

Division of rhizomes gives true colors not obtained from seeds. Divide clumps, using only the rhizomes with the strongest tips, and replant often. It self-sows readily in open soils and roadsides.

COMMENTS: For a spectacular color contrast, grow New England aster with late goldenrods and fall sunflowers.

Aster laevis • smooth aster

DESCRIPTION: 2 to 3 feet tall. Violet-blue to deep-sky-blue rayed flowers with large open heads atop smooth stems. The foliage is smooth and lanceolate and the leaves grow along the entire stem.

Smooth aster is found in old hayfields, in open woods, along roadsides where soil is fertile, and at times volunteering in cultivated flower beds. Each autumn it sends a welcome splash of blue across fields and meadows.

PERIOD OF BLOOM: September into October.

SOIL: Smooth aster is not demanding; it will bloom in lean soils as well as fertile ones. When cultivated in fertile soil and mulched, one small plant will grow to the size of a bushel basket within two years. Care, fertile soil, and constant moisture will produce abundant bloom.

LOCATION AND EXPOSURE: Plant this aster at random in an open meadow or along a sunny woodland border for a final splash of blue against the more somber autumn colors. Or grow it in the background of a border of annual or perennial wildflowers. Good air circulation is important to prevent mildew on the foliage.

PLANTING TIME: While dormant in spring or fall; spring is preferable in very cold climates.

ROOT SYSTEM: A compact rootstock with fibrous roots and many pinkish rhizomes. In an open meadow where it competes with other plants or where the soil is lean, the smooth aster rarely sends up more than two stalks. If the roots become crowded cultivated plants quickly die.

PLANTING DEPTH AND SPACING: Space 2 or more feet apart if grown with a heavy mulch in fertile soil. Set the rhizomes horizontally 1 inch deep, with the tip of the rhizome tapering upward.

PLANTING STOCK AND PROPAGATION: Use nursery-grown stock or quality collected stock. Do not divide plants that have only two or more flowering stalks.

Divide large clumps from the garden, using only the stronger outer rhizomes. Seeds scattered in a sparse grassland gave excellent results.

COMMENTS: I have a special fondness for this aster—in my area it is the last splash of blue for the year.

Aster ptarmicoides • frostflower aster

DESCRIPTION: 12 to 18 inches tall. The flat-topped flower heads bear rayed white petals and have yellow centers. When the flowers begin to bloom, the outer petals appear first. The basal as well as the stem foliage is shiny dark green, narrow, and willowlike.

Frostflower aster is usually found scattered in tufts among early yellow goldenrods and blazing stars in dry open fields, wastelands, and prairies.

PERIOD OF BLOOM: July into September.

SOIL: Neutral to slightly acid garden soil or sandy loam. In very fertile soil this aster grows more robust and loses some of its daintiness.

LOCATION AND EXPOSURE: Full sun is preferable, but the plant will tolerate light partial shade. It is best grown in the dry, prairielike garden with early goldenrod, blazing star, harebell, or blue-eyed grass. A neat little plant for edging a perennial border in full sun.

PLANTING TIME: While dormant in spring or fall.

ROOT SYSTEM: Many short rhizomes with fibrous roots form a neat clump. The rootstock becomes woody with age, and the plant loses its vitality.

PLANTING DEPTH AND SPACING: Space 8 to 12 inches apart. Set the rhizome about 1 inch deep with crown at soil level. This aster grows best without mulch. Where the soil is moderately fertile the plant should be separated and transplanted every third year. Otherwise it grows so dense that it chokes itself out.

PLANTING STOCK AND PROPAGATION: Nursery-grown stock is hard to find. Use quality collected young stock.

Divide vigorous young plants in spring or fall, using only the plants with fine fibrous roots. Seeds are slow to germinate, but the plant self-sows under prairie conditions.

COMMENTS: Frostflower aster is a charming wildflower and easy to cultivate. I especially value its shiny, dark green leaves in the wild garden. It is also known as the upland white aster.

Aster umbellatus • flat-topped aster

DESCRIPTION: 3 to 5 feet tall. The flat-topped flower heads consist of many sparsely rayed white flowers with pale yellow centers. The centers fade to a rust color. Many alternating lanceolate leaves grow along the entire length of the stalks.

This aster is usually found in damp meadows growing among Joe-pye, blue vervain, and swamp milkweed. It is also found along fence lines, in thickets, and along the borders of open woods.

PERIOD OF BLOOM: July into October.

SOIL: Neutral to slightly acid soil with constant moisture is preferable, but I find that this plant will grow in wetter or drier soils if it is mulched.

LOCATION AND EXPOSURE: This long-lasting perennial is easily established. Plant it in colonies in sunny moist meadows among other wildflowers. Individual specimens are not so impressive.

PLANTING TIME: While dormant in spring or fall.

ROOT SYSTEM: A coarse rootstock with fibrous roots, usually sending up only one stalk per plant.

PLANTING DEPTH AND SPACING: Space 1 or more feet apart, or plant

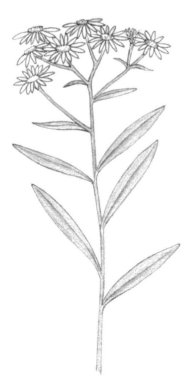

in colonies with other wildflowers. Set the crowns at soil level and spread the roots evenly. If roots are extra long, trim to 3 or 4 inches.

PLANTING STOCK AND PROPAGATION: Use nursery-grown stock if available, or quality collected stock of medium size.

Seeds sown in fall will produce blooms by the second year. The plant self-sows, especially where land is open, and often volunteers in the cultivated border.

COMMENTS: Flat-topped asters look best when planted in masses.

There are many other species of wild asters, though some have unimpressive flowers. Often new species appear in the prairie garden, their seeds evidently carried in on the wind.

Antennaria plantaginifolia · pussytoes

DESCRIPTION: 4 to 6 inches tall. The flower stems bear white woolly flower heads that resemble a kitten's paw. The oblong, round-tipped, gray-green leaves are mostly basal. They have an overall silvery sheen.

Pussytoes is found in most of the eastern half of the United States. In Wisconsin it frequents dry open pastures, wastelands, and sandy roadsides where the soil is very lean. You might find endless stretches of pussytoes carpeting the earth along the edges of reforested prairielands. As the trees mature, they shade the patches, which then get scrawny and gradually disappear. I am sure that some seeds must remain dormant because a year or two after reforested areas are cut over, open areas are again covered with pussytoes.

PERIOD OF BLOOM: May into June.

SOIL: Poor sandy soils to moderately fertile sandy loam soils, all with good drainage. In more fertile soils it grows more robust and is not as pretty.

LOCATION AND EXPOSURE: Give pussytoes a spot in full sun with moderately fertile soil and it will spread, becoming denser each season. It can be used instead of grass in sunny barren sandy areas where nothing else will grow. It makes a remarkable carpet.

Pussytoes is fine for a sandy bank to help hold the soil in place. Also grow it in scattered patches in a prairie garden.

PLANTING TIME: Early spring or late August into fall.

ROOT SYSTEM: Each parent plant with fibrous roots sends out several stolons which take root to form new plants. The stolons divide frequently as they creep, eventually forming dense mats.

PLANTING DEPTH AND SPACING: Space 4 to 8 inches apart, depending on the size of the plants and the desired density. Carefully tuck in the roots and set them with the crown at soil level. Where stolons are attached to the parent plant, carefully cover all small roots with soil, and firm.

PLANTING STOCK AND PROPAGATION: Nursery-grown stock is preferred, but seldom offered. Use quality collected stock that is vigorous. The easiest method of propagation is by stolons from an overcrowded patch in the garden, spring is best. Seeds volunteer on open soils.

COMMENTS: Few other plants can make a more suitable groundcover for a sunny barren area.

Heliopsis helianthoides • ox-eye

DESCRIPTION: 3 to 5 feet tall. A stout stalk with multiple branches bears an abundance of 2 inch flower heads. These heads have many broad-rayed golden-yellow petals, and slightly raised centers peppered with brown. The opposite ovate foliage is toothed and rather coarse. It tends to stick to the skin.

Ox-eye is found in open sunny spots—usually roadsides, railroad beds, and wastelands. The flowers form a maze of yellow so dense that scarcely any of the green foliage shows through.

PERIOD OF BLOOM: Late July into September.

SOIL: Neutral to slightly acid garden soil, or the gritty gravelly soil found along roadsides and railroad crossings. Ox-eye seems to grow in any soil. In very fertile soil it grows rampantly.

LOCATION AND EXPOSURE: Full sun or very open shade along a woodland border. Ox-eye is a fine plant to naturalize in large areas; it is long-lasting and quite drought-resistant.

PLANTING TIME: While dormant in spring or fall.

ROOT SYSTEM: A stout, somewhat rhizomous rootstock with fibrous roots, forming a heavy woody clump with age. Many sturdy stalks arise from the clump, but diminish in size as the roots become crowded.

PLANTING DEPTH AND SPACING: Space 1 to 3 feet apart. Set plants with the eyes just below soil level. Trim back long roots to 3 or 4 inches. Divide cultivated plants every few years; in the wild this does not seem necessary.

PLANTING STOCK AND PROPAGATION: Nursery-grown stock if available, or quality collected stock with strong eyes. Roots may appear dormant and the eyes inconspicuous.

Propagate by division of strong clumps (not easy to divide) and sow seeds in fall or early spring. Ox-eye self-sows, though not abundantly.

COMMENTS: Ox-eye is a coarse wildflower with an exceptionally long blooming period. Cut flowers last long in floral arrangements. This is an excellent plant to use where you want a golden color over a long period of time.

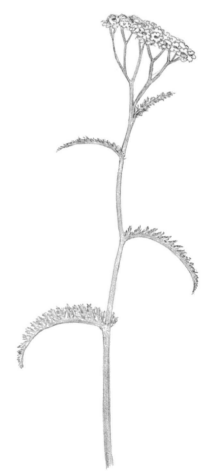

Achillea Millefolium • common yarrow

DESCRIPTION: 1 to 2 feet tall. Each leafy stem divides abruptly at the top to form a flat-topped umbel. The umbel is composed of many small individual white florets with light yellow centers. The fernlike foliage is a lovely shade of dark green.

Originally from Eurasia, this plant has readily adapted to its new environment. It inhabits roadsides and fields, and colonizes in wastelands if the soil is reasonably fertile.

PERIOD OF BLOOM: June into September.

SOIL: Sandy loams, gritty roadside soils, or rich garden soil (where it will grow luxuriantly). The plant is very adaptable.

LOCATION AND EXPOSURE: Common yarrow is best grown in full sun. It is a good plant to grow on slopes, as its extensive rhizomes spread and form mats that hold the soil. It can take more abuse than grass, but do not step on the plants until they are well-established.

PLANTING TIME: Spring, August into fall. The plant will soon make a neat patch of green.

ROOT SYSTEM: Strong white rhizomes. Parent plants produce many rhizomes that fork and make large colonies.

PLANTING DEPTH AND SPACING: Space 6 to 12 inches apart, depending on the desired effect. Set the rhizomes ½ to 1 inch deep with the tip almost at soil level.

PLANTING STOCK AND PROPAGATION: Use nursery-grown stock or quality collected stock.

Divide clumps, using the strong rhizomes. Common yarrow does not readily self-sow.

COMMENTS: To encourage common yarrow to bloom for a longer period of time, the faded blossoms should be picked regularly. Although sometimes called a weed, its cool white blossoms and lush green foliage provide a welcome relief in summer heat. Its cousin, cultivated rose-pink yarrow, makes an interesting companion flower.

In difficult areas where yarrow is grown to hold down the soil or to replace grass, set the lawn mower a little higher than you would for cutting the regular lawn. Yarrow rarely requires more than one cutting after blooming.

Chrysanthemum Leucanthemum • ox-eye daisy

DESCRIPTION: 1 to 2 feet tall. Each stem displays a daisy with single snow-white petals and a compact golden disk. The dainty foliage is dark green and deeply cut. It is sparse on the stem, but forms a neat clump at the base.

Ox-eye daisy is found along roadsides and in abandoned hayfields, where it makes a lovely display.

PERIOD OF BLOOM: June into July.

SOIL: These daisies grow nicely in any soil, though fertility does affect the height of the stem, the size of the flower, and the quality of the foliage. They are pretty in all instances, however. I grow them in sandy loam with superb results.

LOCATION AND EXPOSURE: When grown in full sun and reasonably good soil they bloom luxuriantly. They even bloom well in very light open shade. Ox-eye daisy is a fine and easily grown plant to naturalize in large meadows.

PLANTING TIME: Spring or fall. Clumps may be divided in late August.

ROOT SYSTEM: A compact rootstock with fibrous roots.

PLANTING DEPTH AND SPACING: Space 6 to 12 inches apart, depending on the size of the plants or clumps. Spread the roots evenly and set the crown at soil level. Large clumps should be divided every second or third year, especially when grown in cultivation.

PLANTING STOCK AND PROPAGATION: Use nursery-grown stock or quality collected young stock.

Seeds sown as soon as ripe germinate quickly and make small blooming plants the following year. Ox-eye daisy self-sows readily, but unwanted seedlings soon die when dug under. (Cut back all faded flowers promptly if no seed is wanted.)

COMMENTS: To walk through fields of pure white daisies on a summer's day is to know an indescribable serenity. In some states the ox-eye daisy is classified as a weed—how wonderful that it is so common!

Tanacetum vulgare • common tansy

DESCRIPTION: 18 to 36 inches tall. This plant has a flat-topped umbel composed of many distinct yellow buttons without petals. The stout leafy stems have coarse fernlike foliage.

Common tansy grows vigorously in old pastures, among rocks, and along roadsides. I have seen acres taken over by this somewhat weedy plant.

PERIOD OF BLOOM: July into September.

SOIL: Neutral to slightly acid garden soil, or rocky grit along roadsides and railroad crossings. Common tansy grows readily in most soils, but rampantly in fertile ones.

LOCATION AND EXPOSURE: Full sun is best. Because it is too coarse and large for a small garden, common tansy is suited for naturalizing in large wasteland areas or in unused meadows. If you wish to grow it in the garden, however, you can restrict its growth by planting it in a bottomless gallon container sunk at soil level.

PLANTING TIME: Spring or fall.

ROOT SYSTEM: A creeping rhizome, pinkish at the tip, with many fibrous roots. It forks often.

PLANTING DEPTH AND SPACING: Space 2 feet apart. Set the rhizomes ½ to 1 inch deep with the shoot or eye pointing upward almost to soil level. It spreads to form colonies.

PLANTING STOCK AND PROPAGATION: Nursery-grown stock is rarely offered. Use quality collected young stock.

Tansy self-sows readily. When grown in out of the way places

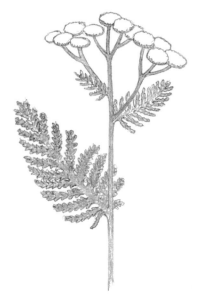

the seeds may be left to ripen—some birds will feast on them.

COMMENTS: Flowers cut just when they are about to bloom are excellent for dried floral arrangements.

Tansy is also used as a tea and as a flavoring in cookies. It has a bitter aftertaste, however. This plant is also called golden buttons and bitter buttons.

The cultivated tansy, *Tanacetum vulgare* (forma *crispum*) is much preferred to the wild species. The foliage is more crinkled and fernlike and the whole plant has a neater appearance.

Senecio aureus • golden ragwort

DESCRIPTION: 10 to 18 inches tall. Several stems rise from a rosette of round, dark green, toothed leaves. The stems bear flat-topped clusters of 1 inch daisylike golden flowers with brown centers. Stem leaves are scant.

Golden ragwort is often found in rocky deciduous woods, along low stream beds in deep shade, and on hummocks in swamplands. In such areas continuous moisture is available. To my surprise it volunteered and flourished in my garden where the soil had only an average moisture content.

PERIOD OF BLOOM: May into June.

SOIL: Slightly acid to neutral soils. The earth may be very damp to wet or only moist. The plant is quite adaptable to average growing conditions.

LOCATION AND EXPOSURE: It is not necessary to duplicate exactly the ragwort's natural environment, since it grows readily both in full sun and in open shade. It is a good plant for a tulip bed. The lovely rosette of dark green leaves remains all season as a groundcover.

PLANTING TIME: Spring or fall.

ROOT SYSTEM: A compact rhizome with short basal offshoots that form a neat compact clump. Roots are white and fibrous.

PLANTING DEPTH AND SPACING: Space 10 to 15 inches apart. Set the crowns at soil level and spread the roots evenly. Each plant forms a neat clump which should be divided every other year. When this flower is cultivated it grows vigorously.

PLANTING STOCK AND PROPAGATION: Nursery-grown stock is much

huskier and stronger than stock from wild plants. But quality collected stock may also be used.

To propagate, divide clumps in spring.

Golden ragwort self-sows under favorable conditions.

COMMENTS: Golden ragwort is rarely offered in wildflower catalogs. It is a good plant to grow in cultivation.

Cichorium Intybus • chicory

DESCRIPTION: 1 to 4 feet tall. The linear basal foliage is much like that of the dandelion. The lanceolate foliage becomes smaller and quite sparse near the top of the much-divided, branching stem. The rayed flower heads of brilliant copen blue (rarely, white or pink), remain open only a few hours in the forenoon and then quickly close to set seed.

Chicory was brought to North America by colonists. On sunny summer mornings the bright blue flowers decorate old meadows, wastelands, and roadsides.

PERIOD OF BLOOM: Flowers continue to open from July into September. Each blossom lasts only a few hours and then quickly fades. Chicory flowers have the shortest life span of any wildflower I know.

SOIL: Chicory grows readily in any of various soils, but it does require good drainage. It even seeds on gravelly shoulders along the highway.

LOCATION AND EXPOSURE: It is best to naturalize chicory in large open spaces; it is too aggressive for a garden. Grow it in full sun in a meadow—its intense blue flower provides a welcome bit of color.

PLANTING TIME: While dormant in spring or fall.

ROOT SYSTEM: A stout, forked, fleshy root with some spreading fibrous roots. It is very resistant to drought.

PLANTING DEPTH AND SPACING: Space 1 to 2 feet apart. Dig quite a deep hole to accommodate the taproot. Set the crown at soil level. It is best to select young plants.

PLANTING STOCK AND PROPAGATION: Use young nursery-grown stock or quality collected young plants.

Chicory self-sows. If you do not wish to have it spread, pick the flowers as they fade.

COMMENTS: In pioneer days the root of the chicory plant was dried, roasted, and ground to use with coffee or as a coffee substitute. I find that ground chicory gives beef gravy a good brown color without altering the taste if used sparingly.

Actinea herbacea • lakeside daisy

DESCRIPTION: The daisylike flowers with rather narrow, showy rays are only a few inches tall. They have very showy butter-yellow petals and large disklike yellow centers. The short-stemmed flowers vary in size according to the growing conditions. The narrow willowlike foliage makes neat mats that remain green all through the summer and into the winter.

Originally found in a very limited area in states bordering the Great Lakes, this rare wildflower was introduced commercially by a Michigan nurseryman and has since spread across the continent. The first stock was rescued from an area which was about to be opened as a limestone pit, and thus lakeside daisy was saved from extinction.

PERIOD OF BLOOM: May into June, but can be extended if the plants are grown in well-drained soil with mulch to conserve moisture.

SOIL: The original stock was found where limestone lay beneath the soil layer, and the soil presumably had a high pH. The nurseryman who introduced them grows the flowers in a well-drained clay soil with wood-shavings mulch, and also under ordinary conditions. He exploded the old supposition that the plant should be left in the wilderness because it was impossible to grow under ordinary garden conditions.

I grow lakeside daisy in full sun in a sandy loam soil with a pH of 6. It usually has constant moisture.

LOCATION AND EXPOSURE: For best bloom, full sun is preferable. Grow the lakeside daisy along the border as an edging or use it in a sunny wildflower garden. It is very versatile indeed.

PLANTING TIME: Spring or fall. I prefer spring planting in very cold climates. When planting in fall, mulch.

ROOT SYSTEM: White, stringy, fibrous roots very much like those of the lobelias. Offsets form around the parent plant to make a neat clump.

PLANTING DEPTH AND SPACING: Plant the crown at soil level and space about 6 to 10 inches apart.

PLANTING STOCK AND PROPAGATION: Use nursery-grown stock.

Propagate by divisions in spring. Sow seeds in fall for spring germination. Blooms appear the second year from seed.

COMMENTS: The lakeside daisy is easy to cultivate, and long-lasting.

Appendix I

Wildflowers to Choose for Special Conditions

Over the years I have found that many wildflowers will grow in environments that differ greatly from their native ones. Some wildflowers from a moist and fertile habitat will grow in lean, dry soils, and vice versa. Some adapt their sun and shade requirements and some do not. Allegheny Mountain gentian is a good example: it is native to moist woods and uplands from Kentucky to Florida, where the climate is mild. Yet this flower has adapted nicely to the climate of northeastern Wisconsin with its extreme winters, and has adapted to lean sandy soil, sandy loam, and fertile garden soil. I have grown it in full sun and in high open shade with equal success.

Other wildflowers, however, must have their native requirements met exactly or they will not flourish. The lady's-slippers are good examples: They must have high open shade and humus-rich woodlands soil that contains mycorhizal fungus or they will soon perish.

The following is a listing of varying conditions of soil, light, and weather, and the wildflowers that are suitable for them—both the wildflowers that grow naturally under such conditions and the wildflowers that can adapt to them. (For detailed growing instructions, see the individual plant.) Plants marked with an asterisk (*) go dormant after blooming—either naturally or under the conditions described.

237

ANNUALS AND BIENNIALS

The wildflowers listed here are very easy to grow in almost any type of soil, and give a quick splash of color.

Wildflowers for Good Garden Soil in Full Sun

These may be grown along a border, in a flower bed, or in a garden row as well as to fill in bare spots until perennial wildflowers take over.

Black-eyed Susan: *Rudbeckia hirta*
California poppy: *Eschscholtzia californica*
Indian mallow: *Abutilon Theophrasti*
Pale corydalis: *Corydalis sempervirens*
Prickly poppy: *Argemone intermedia*
Queen Anne's lace: *Daucus Carota*

Spiked Lobelia: *Lobelia spicata*
Smooth false foxglove: *Gerardia virginica*
Strawberry blite: *Chenopodium capitatum*
Venus's looking-glass: *Specularia perfoliata*
Yellow goatsbeard: *Tragopogon pratensis*

Wildflowers for a Rock Garden in Full Sun

Black-eyed Susan: *Rudbeckia hirta*
California poppy: *Eschscholtzia californica*
Pearly everlasting: *Anaphalis margaritacea*
Spiked lobelia: *Lobelia spicata*

Strawberry blite: *Chenopodium capitatum*
Venus's looking-glass: *Specularia perfoliata*

Wildflowers for High Open Shade in a Rich, Moist Woodland

Allegheny vine: *Adlumia fungosa*
Herb-Robert: *Geranium Robertianum*
Jewelweed: *Impatiens capensis*
Wild cucumber: *Echinocystis lobata*

Wildflowers for Lean Soils in Full Sun

These are usually used to naturalize large areas.

Black-eyed Susan: *Rudbeckia hirta*
Common mullein: *Verbascum Thapsus*
Pearly everlasting: *Anaphalis margaritacea*
Queen Anne's lace: *Daucus Carota*

Wildflowers for Damp, Grassy Meadows in Full Sun

Cow parsnip: *Heracleum maximum*
Fringed gentian: *Gentiana crinita*
Indian paintbrush: *Castilleja coccinea*

Wildflowers for River Bottoms, Damp Thickets, and Along Streams

Cow parsnip: *Heracleum maximum*
Jewelweed: *Impatiens capensis*
Wild cucumber: *Echinocystis lobata*

Weedy Wildflowers

Cut the blossoms before the plants set seed.

Common mullein: *Verbascum Thapsus*
Indian mallow: *Abutilon Theophrasti*
Prickly poppy: *Argemone intermedia*
Queen Anne's lace: *Daucus Carota*
Yellow goatsbeard: *Tragopogon pratensis*

PERENNIALS

Wildflowers for a Very Early Spring Display near the Home

These plants will bloom while snow still lingers in patches in the deep woodland.

Grape hyacinth: *Muscari botryoides*
Purple corydalis: *Corydalis bulbosa*
Snow trillium: *Trillium nivale*

Wildflowers for a Late Fling of Autumn Color

When frost has claimed all the other wildflowers these plants will still boldly display their colorful blooms.

Allegheny Mountain gentian: *Gentiana decora*
Prairie goldenrod: *Solidago rigida*

Wildflowers for a Wild Garden in Full Sun Along a Border or in the Open Yard

Any soil that will grow good vegetables is highly satisfactory.

Amsonia: *Amsonia Tabernaemontana*
Aster, New England: *Aster novae-angliae*
Aster, smooth: *Aster laevis*
Blazing star: *Liatris scariosa*
Blackberry lily: *Belamcanda chinensis*
Blue-eyed grass: *Sisyrinchium angustifolium*
Blue flag: *Iris versicolor*
Blue salvia: *Salvia azurea*
Boneset: *Eupatorium perfoliatum*
Butterfly flower: *Asclepias tuberosa*
*Camass, eastern: *Camassia scilloides*
*Camass, western: *Camassia esculenta*
Celandine poppy: *Stylophorum diphyllum*
Columbine: *Aquilegia canadensis*
Common yarrow: *Achillea Millefolium*
Cranesbill: *Geranium maculatum*
Crested dwarf iris: *Iris cristata*
Culver's root: *Veronicastrum virginicum*
False dragonhead: *Physostegia virginiana*
False blue indigo: *Baptisia australis*
False spikenard: *Smilacina racemosa*
Gentian, Allegheny Mountain: *Gentiana decora*
Gentian, bottle: *Gentiana Andrewsii*
Gentian, soapwort: *Gentiana Saponaria*
Golden ragwort: *Senecio aureus*
Goldenrod, Canada: *Solidago canadensis*
Goldenrod, prairie: *Solidago rigida*
Great blue lobelia: *Lobelia siphilitica*
Greek valerian: *Polemonium reptans*
Harebell: *Campanula rotundifolia*
Hoary puccoon: *Lithospermum canescens*
Joe-pye: *Eupatorium maculatum*

Kansas gayfeather: *Liatris pycnostachya*
Lakeside daisy: *Actinea herbacea*
Meadowrue, early: *Thalictrum dioicum*
Meadowrue, tall: *Thalictrum polygamum*
Monkey flower: *Mimulus ringens*
Musk mallow: *Malva moschata*
Nodding wild onion: *Allium cernuum*
Oswego tea: *Monarda didyma*
Ox-eye: *Heliopsis helianthoides*
Ox-eye daisy: *Chrysanthemum Leucanthemum*
Pasque flower: *Anemone pulsatilla*
Phlox, blue: *Phlox divaricata*
Phlox, prairie: *Phlox pilosa*
Pink bleeding heart: *Dicentra eximia*
Prairie smoke: *Geum triflorum*
*Purple corydalis: *Corydalis bulbosa*
Purple loosestrife: *Lythrum Salicaria*
Pussytoes: *Antennaria plantaginifolia*
Queen of the prairie: *Filipendula rubra*
Rose verbena: *Verbena canadensis*
Shooting star: *Dodecatheon Meadia*
Skullcap, blue heaven: *Scutellaria baicalensis*
Skullcap, downy: *Scutellaria incana*
Skullcap, early blue: *Scutellaria ovata*
Skullcap, mad-dog: *Scutellaria lateriflora*
Skullcap, pink: *Scutellaria integrifolia*
Skullcap, showy: *Scutellaria serrata*
Star-of-Bethlehem: *Ornithogalum umbellatum*
Stoneroot: *Collinsonia canadensis*
Swamp milkweed: *Asclepias incarnata*
Tiger lily: *Lilium tigrinum*
Turtlehead, red: *Chelone obliqua*
Turtlehead, white: *Chelone glabra*
Wild bergamot: *Monarda fistulosa*

Wildflowers for a Wild Garden in Full Sun Along a Border or in the Open Yard (*continued*)

Wild blue lupine: *Lupinus perennis*
Wild petunia: *Ruellia humilis*

Wild senna: *Cassia marilandica*
Woodland strawberry: *Fragaria vesca*

Wildflowers for Groundcover in High Open Shade under Tall Trees

The area should be reasonably free of underbrush. Deciduous woodlands.

Barren strawberry: *Waldsteinia fragarioides*
Bishop's-cap: *Mitella diphylla*
Bloodroot: *Sanguinaria canadensis*
Bluebead lily: *Clintonia borealis*
Bugleflower: *Ajuga reptans*
Canada mayflower: *Maianthemum canadense*
Cranesbill: *Geranium maculatum*
Foamflower: *Tiarella cordifolia*
Ginseng: *Panax quinquefolium*
Golden seal: *Hydrastis canadensis*
Goldthread: *Coptis groenlandica*

Hairy alumroot: *Heuchera villosa*
Hepatica: *Hepatica americana*
Mayapple: *Podophyllum peltatum*
Moneywort: *Lysimachia Nummularia*
Partridgeberry: *Mitchella repens*
Pink bleeding heart: *Dicentra eximia*
Trillium, large white: *Trillium grandiflorum*
Trillium, purple: *Trillium erectum*
Trillium, yellow: *Trillium luteum*
Wild ginger: *Asarum canadense*
Wintergreen: *Gaultheria procumbens*
Woodland strawberry: *Fragaria vesca*

Wildflowers for Sandy Loam Soil (or sandy, gritty soils) as well as for Naturalizing in Lean Prairielike Areas. Full Sun All Day.

In prairielike areas the soil may be lean but there is always a thin layer of humus on top.

Birdfoot violet: *Viola pedata*
Blazing star: *Liatris scariosa*
Blue-eyed grass: *Sisyrinchium angustifolium*
Blue salvia: *Salvia azurea*
Butterfly flower: *Asclepias tuberosa*
Chicory: *Cichorium Intybus*
Common milkweed: *Asclepias syriaca*
Common yarrow: *Achillea Millefolium*
False blue indigo: *Baptisia australis*
Frostflower aster: *Aster ptarmicoides*
Harebell: *Campanula rotundifolia*
Hoary puccoon: *Lithospermum canescens*
Kansas gayfeather: *Liatris pycnostachya*

Ox-eye daisy: *Chrysanthemum Leucanthemum*
Pasque flower: *Anemone pulsatilla*
Prairie goldenrod: *Solidago rigida*
Prairie phlox: *Phlox pilosa*
Prairie smoke: *Geum triflorum*
Pussytoes: *Antennaria plantaginifolia*
Rose verbena: *Verbena canadensis*
Seneca snakeroot: *Polygala Senega*
Shooting star: *Dodecatheon Meadia*
Smooth aster: *Aster laevis*
Wild bergamot: *Monarda fistulosa*
Wine cups: *Callirhoe involucrata*
Wood lily: *Lilium philadelphicum*

241

Wildflowers for a Rock Garden in Full Sun

Reasonably fertile soil that does not get bone dry.

Barren strawberry: *Waldsteinia fragarioides*
Birdfoot violet: *Viola pedata*
Blue-eyed grass: *Sisyrinchium angustifolium*
Blue salvia: *Salvia azurea*
Bugleflower: *Ajuga reptans*
Columbine: *Aquilegia canadensis*
Common cinquefoil: *Potentilla canadensis*
Cypress spurge: *Euphorbia Cyparissias*
*Grape hyacinth: *Muscari botryoides*

Lakeside daisy: *Actinea herbacea*
Pasque flower: *Anemone pulsatilla*
Prairie phlox: *Phlox pilosa*
Prairie smoke: *Geum triflorum*
*Purple corydalis: *Corydalis bulbosa*
Pussytoes: *Antennaria plantaginifolia*
Shooting star: *Dodecatheon Meadia*
Silverweed: *Potentilla anserina*
*Star-of-Bethlehem: *Ornithogalum umbellatum*
Wine cups: *Callirhoe involucrata*

Wildflowers for the Rock Garden in High Open Shade

Humus-rich soil.

Barren strawberry: *Waldsteinia fragarioides*
Bishop's-cap: *Mitella diphylla*
Bloodroot: *Sanguinaria canadensis*
Canada mayflower: *Maianthemum canadense*
Celandine poppy: *Stylophorum diphyllum*
Columbine: *Aquilegia canadensis*
Cranesbill: *Geranium maculatum*
*Dutchman's-breeches: *Dicentra Cucullaria*
Foamflower: *Tiarella cordifolia*
Golden ragwort: *Senecio aureus*
Golden seal: *Hydrastis canadensis*
Goldthread: *Coptis groenlandica*
Greek valerian: *Polemonium reptans*
Hairy alumroot: *Heuchera villosa*
Hepatica: *Hepatica americana*
*Grape hyacinth: *Muscari botryoides*

Moneywort: *Lysimachia Nummularia*
Partridgeberry: *Mitchella repens*
Phlox Laphamii: *Phlox divaricata Laphamii*
Phlox, blue: *Phlox divaricata*
Phlox, mountain: *Phlox ovata*
Pink bleeding heart: *Dicentra eximia*
Rock geranium: *Heuchera americana*
Shooting star: *Dodecatheon Meadia*
*Spring beauty: *Claytonia virginica*
*Squirrel corn: *Dicentra canadensis*
Starflower: *Trientalis borealis*
Violet, American dog: *Viola conspersa*
Violet, downy yellow: *Viola pubescens*
Violet, sweet white: *Viola blanda*
Virginia bluebell: *Mertensia virginica*
Wild ginger: *Asarum canadense*
Woodland strawberry: *Fragaria vesca*
Yellow stargrass: *Hypoxis hirsuta*

Wildflowers to Grow along Lakes and Streams or in High Open Shade or Where There Is Sunshine for Most of the Day

The soil is usually moist and always fertile.

Canada lily: *Lilium canadense*
Cardinal flower: *Lobelia Cardinalis*
Crested dwarf iris: *Iris cristata*
False dragonhead: *Physostegia virginiana*
Forget-me-not: *Myosotis scorpioides*
Gentian, bottle: *Gentiana Andrewsii*
Gentian, soapwort: *Gentiana Saponaria*
Golden ragwort: *Senecio aureus*
Grass of Parnassus: *Parnassia glauca*
Great blue lobelia: *Lobelia siphilitica*
Ironweed: *Vernonia noveboracensis*
Joe-pye: *Eupatorium maculatum*

Lakeside daisy: *Actinea herbacea*
Monkey flower: *Mimulus ringens*
Oswego tea: *Monarda didyma*
Ox-eye: *Heliopsis helianthoides*
Purple loosestrife: *Lythrum Salicaria*
Queen of the prairie: *Filipendula rubra*
Skullcap blue heaven: *Scutellaria baicalensis*
Swamp candles: *Lysimachia terrestris*
Swamp milkweed: *Asclepias incarnata*
Turtlehead, red: *Chelone obliqua*
Turtlehead, white: *Chelone glabra*

Wildflowers for Bogs, Marshes, and Lowlands Where Water Often Stands in Spring

Soil is always fertile. Full sun.

Boneset: *Eupatorium perfoliatum*
Canada lily: *Lilium canadense*
Common cattail: *Typha latifolia*
Flat-topped aster: *Aster umbellatus*
Ironweed: *Vernonia noveboracensis*
Joe-pye: *Eupatorium maculatum*

Marsh marigold: *Caltha palustris*
Skunk cabbage: *Symplocarpus foetidus*
Swamp candles: *Lysimachia terrestris*
Swamp milkweed: *Asclepias incarnata*
Wild calla: *Calla palustris*

Wildflowers for Moist Meadows in Full Sun

The soil is fertile and moisture is always ample, but there is some tolerance to short periods of summer drought.

Blue flag: *Iris versicolor*
Boneset: *Eupatorium perfoliatum*
*Camass, eastern: *Camassia scilloides*
*Camass, western: *Camassia esculenta*
Canada anemone: *Anemone canadensis*

Cardinal flower: *Lobelia Cardinalis*
False dragonhead: *Physostegia virginiana*
Flat-topped aster: *Aster umbellatus*

243

Wildflowers for Moist Meadows in Full Sun (*continued*)

Gentian, bottle: *Gentiana Andrewsii*
Gentian, soapwort: *Gentiana Saponaria*
Goldenrod, Canada: *Solidago canadensis*
Goldenrod, grass-leaved: *Solidago graminifolia*
Grass of Parnassus: *Parnassia glauca*
Great blue lobelia: *Lobelia siphilitica*
Ironweed: *Vernonia noveboracensis*
Joe-pye: *Eupatorium maculatum*
Lily, Canada: *Lilium canadense*

Lily, Michigan: *Lilium michiganense*
Lily, Turk's-cap: *Lilium superbum*
Monkey flower: *Mimulus ringens*
Purple loosestrife: *Lythrum Salicaria*
Queen of the prairie: *Filipendula rubra*
Swamp candles: *Lysimachia terrestris*
Swamp milkweed: *Asclepias incarnata*
Tall meadowrue: *Thalictrum polygamum*
Turtlehead, red: *Chelone obliqua*
Turtlehead, white: *Chelone glabra*

Wildflowers for Cool, Moist Woodlands in Deep Shade

The lower branches of deciduous trees and evergreens are about at head level. Soil is rich, often somewhat acid. This type of woodland usually supports ferns as well as native wildflowers.

Bluebead lily: *Clintonia borealis*
Bunchberry: *Cornus canadensis*
Canada mayflower: *Maianthemum canadense*
Creeping snowberry: *Gaultheria hispidula*
Dwarf ginseng: *Panax trifolium*

Partridgeberry: *Mitchella repens*
Trillium, nodding: *Trillium cernuum*
Trillium, painted: *Trillium undulatum*
Twinflower: *Linnaea borealis*
Violet, sweet white: *Viola blanda*
Wintergreen: *Gaultheria procumbens*

Wildflowers for Sphagnum Bogs and Moss-covered Rotting Logs and Stumps

There is always moisture present except in periods of extreme summer drought. Acid soil.

Creeping snowberry: *Gaultheria hispidula*
Dwarf ginseng: *Panax trifolium*
Goldthread: *Coptis groenlandica*
Partridgeberry: *Mitchella repens*
Pink lady's-slipper: *Cypripedium acaule*
Twinflower: *Linnaea borealis*

Wildflowers for Moist, Rich, Sometimes Rocky Woodlands; Humus-rich Soil in the Shade of Buildings or Trees; Open Deciduous Woodland Where Leafmold Is Plentiful and Existing Shade Is High; Well-drained River Bottoms

Allegheny Mountain gentian: *Gentiana decora*

American bugbane: *Cimicifuga americana*

Amsonia: *Amsonia Tabernaemontana*

Aster, large-leaved: *Aster macrophyllus*

Baneberry, red: *Actaea rubra*

Baneberry, white: *Actaea pachypoda*

Barren strawberry: *Waldsteinia fragarioides*

Black cohosh: *Cimicifuga racemosa*

Bishop's-cap: *Mitella diphylla*

Bloodroot: *Sanguinaria canadensis*

Bluebead lily: *Clintonia borealis*

Blue cohosh: *Caulophyllum thalictroides*

Boneset: *Eupatorium perfoliatum*

Bowman's root: *Gillenia trifoliata*

Bunchberry: *Cornus canadensis*

*Camass, eastern: *Camassia scilloides*

*Camass, western: *Camassia esculenta*

Canada mayflower: *Maianthemum canadense*

Celandine poppy: *Stylophorum diphyllum*

Cranesbill: *Geranium maculatum*

Culver's root: *Veronicastrum virginicum*

*Dutchman's-breeches: *Dicentra Cucullaria*

Dutchman's-pipe: *Aristolochia macrophylla*

Dwarf ginseng: *Panax trifolium*

Early meadowrue: *Thalictrum dioicum*

Early white snakeroot: *Eupatorium rugosum*

Foamflower: *Tiarella cordifolia*

Galax: *Galax aphylla*

Ginseng: *Panax quinquefolium*

Golden ragwort: *Senecio aureus*

Golden seal: *Hydrastis canadensis*

Grass-leaved goldenrod: *Solidago graminifolia*

Greek valerian: *Polemonium reptans*

Green dragon: *Arisaema Dracontium*

Hairy alumroot: *Heuchera villosa*

Hepatica: *Hepatica americana*

Horse gentian: *Triosteum aurantiacum*

Indian cucumber: *Medeola virginiana*

Jack-in-the-pulpit: *Arisaema triphyllum*

Lady's-slipper, mountain: *Cypripedium montanum*

Lady's-slipper, showy: *Cypripedium reginae*

Lady's-slipper, small white: *Cypripedium candidum*

Lady's-slipper, yellow: *Cypripedium Calceolus pubescens*

Lily, Canada: *Lilium canadense*

Lily, Michigan: *Lilium michiganense*

Mayapple: *Podophyllum peltatum*

Nodding mandarin: *Disporum maculatum*

Nodding wild onion: *Allium cernuum*

Oswego tea: *Monarda didyma*

Partridgeberry: *Mitchella repens*

Phlox Laphamii: *Phlox divaricata Laphamii*

Phlox, blue: *Phlox divaricata*

Phlox, mountain: *Phlox ovata*

Pink bleeding heart: *Dicentra eximia*

*Purple corydalis: *Corydalis bulbosa*

Rock geranium: *Heuchera americana*

Rose mandarin: *Streptopus roseus*

Moist, Rich Woodlands; Humus-rich Soil in Shade (*continued*)

Skullcap, downy: *Scutellaria incana*
Skullcap, early blue: *Scutellaria ovata*
Skullcap, mad-dog: *Scutellaria lateriflora*
Skullcap, pink: *Scutellaria integrifolia*
Skullcap, showy: *Scutellaria serrata*
Solomon's seal: *Polygonatum biflorum*
Spikenard: *Aralia racemosa*
*Spring beauty: *Claytonia virginica*
*Squirrel corn: *Dicentra canadensis*
Starflower: *Trientalis borealis*
Stoneroot: *Collinsonia canadensis*
Toothwort, cut-leaved: *Dentaria laciniata*
Toothwort, two-leaved: *Dentaria diphylla*
Trailing arbutus: *Epigaea repens*
Trillium, large white: *Trillium grandiflorum*
Trillium, nodding: *Trillium cernuum*

Trillium, Ozark: *Trillium ozarkanum*
Trillium, prairie: *Trillium recurvatum*
Trillium, purple: *Trillium erectum*
Trillium, rose: *Trillium stylosum*
Trillium, snow: *Trillium nivale*
Trillium, toadshade: *Trillium sessile*
Trillium, yellow: *Trillium luteum*
Trout lily: *Erythronium americanum*
Twinleaf: *Jeffersonia diphylla*
Violet, American dog: *Viola conspersa*
Violet, Canada: *Viola canadensis*
Violet, downy yellow: *Viola pubescens*
Violet, early blue: *Viola palmata*
Violet, smooth yellow: *Viola pensylvanica*
Virginia bluebell: *Mertensia virginica*
Wild ginger: *Asarum canadense*
Wild oats: *Uvularia sessilifolia*
Woodland strawberry: *Fragaria vesca*
Yellow stargrass: *Hypoxis hirsuta*

Wildflowers for Dry, Open Woodlands Where Sunlight Filters Through Leafless Trees in Spring

Leafmold is plentiful and moisture abundant at time of blooming. These wildflowers may also be grown in the shade of tall buildings and trees where soil is humus-rich.

Aster, large-leaved: *Aster macrophyllus*
Aster, New England: *Aster novae-angliae*
Bloodroot: *Sanguinaria canadensis*
Bunchberry: *Cornus canadensis*
Canada mayflower: *Maianthemum canadense*
Cranesbill: *Geranium maculatum*
Culver's root: *Veronicastrum virginicum*
Early meadowrue: *Thalictrum dioicum*
False Solomon's seal: *Smilacina stellata*
False spikenard: *Smilacina racemosa*
Fringed polygala: *Polygala paucifolia*
Hepatica: *Hepatica americana*

Merrybells: *Uvularia grandiflora*
Partridgeberry: *Mitchella repens*
Phlox, blue: *Phlox divaricata*
Pink bleeding heart: *Dicentra eximia*
Pink lady's-slipper: *Cypripedium acaule*
*Purple corydalis: *Corydalis bulbosa*
Rock geranium: *Heuchera americana*
Shinleaf: *Pyrola virens*
Skullcap, downy: *Scutellaria incana*
Solomon's seal: *Polygonatum biflorum*
Trailing arbutus: *Epigaea repens*
Trillium, Ozark: *Trillium ozarkanum*
Trillium, large white: *Trillium grandiflorum*

Dry, Open Woodlands, Filtered Sun (continued)

Trillium, purple: *Trillium erectum*
Trillium, yellow: *Trillium luteum*
Violet, American dog: *Viola conspersa*
Violet, broad-leaved wood: *Viola latiuscula*
Violet, downy yellow: *Viola pubescens*

Wild sarsaparilla: *Aralia nudicaulis*
Wintergreen: *Gaultheria procumbens*
Wood anemone: *Anemone quinquefolia*
Yellow lady's-slipper: *Cypripedium Calceolus pubescens*

Weedy Wildflowers that Have Colorful Blossoms

The spent blossoms of these plants should be cut right after blooming to prevent them from setting seed. Those marked with a dagger (†) also spread by stolons and are best grown in a bottomless gallon can sunk into the earth to within one inch of soil level.

*Bugleflower: *Ajuga reptans*
Canada anemone: *Anemone canadensis*
Chicory: *Cichorium Intybus*
†Clustered bluebell: *Campanula glomerata*
†Cypress spurge: *Euphorbia Cyparissias*

†Gill-over-the-ground: *Glechoma hederacea*
Ox-eye daisy: *Chrysanthemum Leucanthemum*
Queen Anne's lace: *Daucus carota*
*Swamp candles: *Lysimachia terrestris*

Wildflowers for Very Lean Soils or Even Ash Piles

These plants are aggressive and will spread to hide an otherwise ugly site.

*Bugleflower: *Ajuga reptans*
Common cinquefoil: *Potentilla canadensis*
Gill-over-the-ground: *Glechoma hederacea*

Silverweed: *Potentilla anserina*
Toadflax: *Linaria vulgaris*
Violet, common blue: *Viola papilionacea*
Violet, Confederate: *Viola Priceana*

Wildflowers for Soils Containing Some Lime

Soils should be neutral and rarely only slightly acid. Under a high canopy of trees such as maples and birches.

Grass of Parnassus: *Parnassia glauca* (prefers sun)
Green dragon: *Arisaema Dracontium*
Merrybells: *Uvularia grandiflora*
Showy lady's-slipper: *Cypripedium reginae*

Small white lady's-slipper: *Cypripedium candidum*
Twinleaf: *Jeffersonia diphylla*

247

Wildflowers for Acid Soils

Soil is humus-rich and there is a high canopy of shade, usually offered by oaks and evergreens.

Bearberry: *Arctostaphylos Uva-ursi* (prefers sun)
Bunchberry: *Cornus canadensis*
Creeping snowberry: *Gaultheria hispidula*
Dwarf ginseng: *Panax trifolium*

Fringed polygala: *Polygala paucifolia*
Galax: *Galax aphylla*
Pink lady's-slipper: *Cypripedium acaule*
Painted trillium: *Trillium undulatum*
Trailing arbutus: *Epigaea repens*
Wintergreen: *Gaultheria procumbens*

Wildflowers for Climates Where Winters Are Severe and the Soil Freezes

Must have winter mulching.

Butterfly flower: *Asclepias tuberosa*
Early white snakeroot: *Eupatorium rugosum*
Skullcaps: *Scutellariae*
Stoneroot: *Collinsonia canadensis*

Appendix II

Successful Lady's-slipper Cultivation

When you decide to bring lady's-slippers into your garden, be sure that you can provide for their needs. If you start them under the proper conditions, they will take care of themselves thereafter.

Select a woodland spot in open shade; try to arrange the plantings so that filtered sunlight can reach the plants while they are blooming. The steps in cultivation—preparing the soil, planting the wildflower, fertilizing, and mulching—are discussed below.

1. Preparing the Soil

Brought-in soil. If you do not have a spot with suitable soil, you can bring in woodland soil to prepare a bed. Mix the soil with a generous amount of damp peatmoss and add some bonemeal if you wish. First take out about a foot of the old soil and replace it with an equal amount of the new soil and peatmoss mixture, otherwise you will have a high mound and the earth will dry out. Pack the soil down lightly. Mulch it with oats, straw (or leafmold), water thoroughly, and leave it to "mellow" for a year or more.

Virgin soil. When digging up virgin woods soil for a bed, discard the layer that does not contain humus. Remove heavy roots, live plants, and large stones. Do *not* remove small twigs, partly decayed forest litter, and other organic matter. Put the soil in a wheelbarrow and break it up thoroughly. Mix in an equal amount of damp peatmoss.

Peatmoss. Always use damp peatmoss. Dry peatmoss draws moisture out of the surrounding soil, leaving little for the plants' roots to absorb.

pH. The exact pH of the soil is not very important. All our lady's-slippers, even the pink variety, thrive in a soil with a pH of 6.

Mycorhizal fungus. Lady's-slippers, especially the pink variety, require mycorhizal fungus in the soil. This is a threadlike fungus, webbing the woodland earth. You will be able to see the fungus as it forms a lacework on the fine roots of trees and shrubs that penetrate the forest floor. Whenever I find any mycorhizal or other fungus in the woods, I always take some back to my lady's-slipper beds. Fungi can mean the difference between life and death for these plants, which are themselves partially parasitic. (A method for increasing fungi is given in Paragraph 5 below.)

2. Planting

Rake away all the dry forest litter from the selected site and reserve it for future mulching. Dig a hole 1 to 1½ feet wide and from a few inches to a foot deep, depending on the type of lady's-slipper (see individual plant instructions in Perennial Wildflowers for Permanence).

Return at least half of the soil to the hole, and build a shallow mound to within an inch of the top of the hole.

Set the rhizome on the mound of earth, with the roots gradually extending downward until the tips of the roots are 1 to 1½ inches lower than the crown. Cover the roots with the lady's-slippers soil mixture until you have almost filled the hole. The line where the new shoots meet the roots should be about ½ to 1 inch below soil level.

3. Bonemeal

Sprinkle a tablespoonful of bonemeal over the bed as food for future use. Bloodmeal is fine too.

4. Sphagnum moss

Cap the new shoots with a mound of damp-to-wet sphagnum moss. Use just enough to cover the tips and form a 4 inch circle around them. The moss will keep the tips from drying out and will protect them from rodents.

5. Mulch Containing Mycorhizal Fungus

Spread an inch of oak leafmold and old weathered straw or decaying marsh hay (at the stage where it is beginning to turn dark). Make a raised bed of the mixture, about a foot high. If you have a natural woodland setting where there are pockets and depressions in deep shade, try filling them with the mixture. Make a reasonably high mound; the pile will settle as it begins to decompose.

Keep the area moist, but not dripping wet. Introduce some of the mycorhizal fungi on the outer edges and center of the leaf–straw bed. The fungi will gradually run through the entire bed.

Later, portions of this fungi-laden humus can be buried where wanted. Often two years will elapse before the entire bed is filled with fungi.

When you transfer fungi-laden mulch, always cover it with a layer of some other mulch to keep it from drying out.

6. The Top Layer of Mulch

Summer. Fresh lawn clippings used as soon as the grass is cut make a very good mulch in summer. They become part of the soil and provide food for the plant. Dried clippings are useless. Spread 1 inch of clippings over the entire root area. It may be necessary to remove some of the top layer of dry humus, and this can be put aside for reuse in fall. Fresh grass clippings should be added each time the lawn is cut and throughout the entire growing season. Dampen the grass mulch between mulching periods to hasten decay.

Winter. For extra protection during the first winter, mulch with old marsh hay or weathered old straw. Place a twig or small stick as a marker near each plant bud or group of buds so that you will know where to push aside some of the mulch in spring. If the lady's-slippers have too much mulch while they are actively growing, the stalks will be weak and will topple. After the plants bloom, tuck some of the mulch around the stalks.

When lady's-slipper roots are exposed to the air, new roots are stimulated to form at the base of the new root buds so that the plant can survive. The old roots continue to function for a year or two, and then they disappear. If the new roots have not established themselves enough to take over, the plant will die. This is why it is so important to introduce the plant under ideal conditions. Once the plants have grown new roots and established themselves, they grow stronger every year. Do not divide the clumps.

Always keep lady's-slipper beds moist by good mulching. Water deeply when necessary, but do not water them every day. Overwatering may drown the plants; it also washes away valuable nutrients in the soil.

The method I have described has made it possible for lady's-slippers to adapt and grow into beautiful specimens in my gardens. I hope it will work as well for you.

Appendix III

Wildflower Nurseries

All of these nurseries sell wildflower stock through the mail, and most have catalogs worth writing for.

Allgrove
Box 459H
Wilmington, Mass. 01887

Alpenglow Gardens
13328 Trans-Canada Hwy.
North Surrey P.O.
New Westminster, B.C.
Canada

Baldwin Seed Co. of Alaska
Anchorage, Alaska

Claude A. Barr
Prairie Gem Ranch
Smithwick, S.D. 57782

Gardens of the Blue Ridge
Ashford, N.C. 28603

Griffey Nursery
Rt. 3, Box 17A
Marshall, N.C. 28753

Jamieson Valley Gardens
Rt. 3B
Spokane, Wash. 99203

Leslie's Wildflower Nursery
30 Sumner St.
Methuen, Mass. 01844

Lousenberry Gardens
Oakford, Ill. 62673

Midwest Wildflowers
Box 64B
Rockton, Ill. 61072

Mincemoyers
R.D. 5, Box 397-H
Jackson, N.J. 08527

Orchid Gardens
Rt. 3
Grand Rapids, Minn. 55744

The Three Laurels
Marshall, N.C. 28753

Vick's Wildflower Gardens
Box 115
Gladwyne, Pa. 19035

Woodland Acres Nursery
Marie Sperka
Rt. 2
Crivitz, Wis. 54114

Appendix IV

Perennial Wildflowers by Color

The wildflowers listed here are grouped according to the color or colors in which they occur most commonly. For a complete description of a particular flower and its color, the reader can refer to the individual entry for that plant.

Blue to Violet

Allegheny Mountain gentian
American dog violet
Amsonia
Birdfoot violet
Blue-eyed grass
Blue flag
Blue salvia
Bottle gentian
Broad-leaved wood violet
Bugleflower
Chicory
Clustered bluebell
Common blue violet
Crested dwarf iris
Downy skullcap
Early blue skullcap
Early blue violet
Eastern camass
False blue indigo
Forget-me-not
Gill-over-the-ground
Grape hyacinth
Great blue lobelia
Greek valerian
Harebell
Hepatica

Horse gentian
Ironweed
Kansas gayfeather
Large-leaved aster
Mad-dog skullcap
Monkey flower
New England aster
Pasque flower
Prairie phlox
Shooting star
Showy skullcap
Skullcap blue heaven
Smooth aster
Soapwort gentian
Virginia bluebell
Western camass
Wild bergamot
Wild blue phlox
Wild lupine
Wild petunia

Brown

Dutchman's-pipe
Jack-in-the-pulpit
Skunk cabbage
Wild ginger

Green

Bluebead lily
Blue cohosh
Golden seal
Green dragon
Indian cucumber
Jack-in-the-pulpit
Rock geranium
Skunk cabbage
Solomon's seal
Wild sarsaparilla

Orange

Blackberry lily
Butterfly flower
Canada lily
Michigan lily
Tiger lily
Turk's-cap lily
Wild columbine
Wood lily

Pink to Red

Bearberry
Blazing star
Bowman's root

255

Cardinal flower
Common milkweed
False dragonhead
Fringed polygala
Jessie's red violet
Joe-pye
Kansas gayfeather
Mountain phlox
Musk mallow
Nodding wild onion
Oswego tea
Partridgeberry
Pink bleeding heart
Pink lady's-slipper
Pink skullcap
Prairie phlox
Prairie smoke
Prairie trillium
Purple corydalis
Purple trillium
Queen of the Prairie
Red turtlehead
Rose mandarin
Rose trillium
Rose verbena
Rue anemone
Shooting star
Spotted cranesbill
Spring beauty
Swamp milkweed
Toadshade
Trailing arbutus (turns pink
   with age)
Twinflower
Two-leaved toothwort
Western bleeding heart
Wild ginger
Wine cups

White

American bugbane
Bearberry
Bishop's-cap
Black cohosh
Bloodroot
Boneset
Bowman's root
Bunchberry
Canada anemone

Canada mayflower
Canada violet
Common yarrow
Confederate violet
Creeping snowberry
Culver's root
Dutchman's-breeches
Dwarf ginseng
Early white snakeroot
False spikenard
Flat-topped aster
Frostflower aster
Galax
Ginseng
Golden seal
Goldthread
Grass of Parnassus
Hairy alumroot
Hepatica
Large white trillium
Mayapple
Mountain lady's-slipper
Musk mallow
Nodding mandarin
Nodding trillium
Ox-eye daisy
Ozark trillium
Painted trillium
Partridgeberry
Purple loosestrife
Pussytoes
Red baneberry
Rock geranium
Rue anemone
Seneca snakeroot
Shinleaf
Shooting star
Showy lady's-slipper
Small white lady's-slipper
Snow trillium
Spikenard
Spring beauty
Squirrel corn
Starflower
Star-flowered false Solomon's
   seal
Star-of-Bethlehem
Sweet white violet
Tall meadow rue
Trailing arbutus

Twinflower
Twinleaf
Two-leaved toothwort (turns
   pink with age)
White baneberry
White mertensia
White phlox
White turtlehead
Wild calla
Wintergreen
Wood anemone
Woodland strawberry

Yellow

Barren strawberry
Blue cohosh
Bluebead lily
Canada goldenrod
Canada lily
Celandine poppy
Common cinquefoil
Common tansy
Cypress spurge
Downy yellow violet
Ginseng
Golden ragwort
Grass-leaved goldenrod
Hoary puccoon
Indian cucumber
Lady's mantle
Lakeside daisy
Large yellow lady's slipper
Marsh marigold
Merrybells
Moneywort
Nodding mandarin
Ox-eye
Prairie goldenrod
Silverweed
Smooth yellow violet
Solomon's seal
Stoneroot
Swamp candles
Trout lily
Wild oats
Wild senna
Yellow stargrass
Yellow trillium

Glossary

ALTERNATE LEAVES Leaves growing at regular intervals at different levels along the stem, but not opposite each other.

ANTHER The pollen-bearing portion of the stamen.

AXIL The space formed between any two plant parts, usually between the leaf and the stem or between two veins in a leaf.

AXILLARY BUD The bud growing in the axil of a plant.

BRACT A modified or rudimentary leaf growing near the calyx (outer envelope) of a flower or at the base of the flower stalk; bracts may be green and leaflike or colored.

BUD The rudimentary state of a stem or a branch; an unopened flower.

BULB The complete plant at a resting stage of growth; a fleshy leaf-bud with scales or coats formed underground.

BULBIL A small bulb; also a bulblike organ, especially when found on the stem.

CALYX The outer envelope of a flower, usually green, though it can be colored; found below the corolla.

CARUNCLE An outgrowth on the protective outer covering of some seeds.

COROLLA The whorl of colored petals above the calyx.

CORONA The crown of a flower, such as the cup of a narcissus or daffodil.

CORM The fleshy, underground part of a stem, which furnishes reserve material for bud growth; also a solid bulb.

INFLORESCENCE The flowering part of a plant above the last stem leaves; it includes the branch, stem, stalk, bract, and actual flower.

LAYERING A method of inducing a shoot to root before being detached from the parent plant.

NODE A knoblike enlargement on a stem, which normally bears a leaf or whorl of leaves; buds appear at this spot and roots form most readily from it when cuttings are taken.

OFFSET New bulbs, corms, or short runner roots typical of the parent plant which may be detached and used to produce new plants.

OPPOSITE LEAVES Leaves growing directly opposite each other on the stem, usually at regular intervals.

PANICLE A pyramidal, loosely-branched flower cluster; a raceme that branches.

PETIOLE A leaf support; a leaf stalk.

RACEME A simple growth of flowers on short stems on a common, usually elongated, axis.

RADIX A plant root; also its base.

RAY The branch of an umbel or similar inflorescence.

RHIZOME Any horizontal or subterranean stem that produces shoots and roots; it differs from a true root in possessing buds, nodes, and usually scalelike leaves.

ROOT The underground part of a plant that absorbs moisture and carbon dioxide and stores food material; it differs from the stem in that it lacks nodes, buds, and leaves.

ROSETTE A cluster of leaves or other plant parts in a circular pattern.

RUNNER A shoot trailing on the ground which roots at the end to form a new plant.

SCALE LEAF One of the rudimentary leaves which enclose and protect winter buds.

SPADIX A floral spike with a fleshy axis usually enclosed in a type of large bract known as a spathe.

SPATHE A large bract enclosing one or more flowers.

STALK A stem or support of a particular plant organ; for example, a flower stalk.

STEM The plant part that supports the leaves and buds and, in the case of flowering plants, the flowers.

STOLON A horizontal-growing branch, low on the plant, which roots at the tips and nodes; a runner.

SWALE A low-lying stretch of land, such as a small meadow, swamp, or marshy depression.

TAPROOT A primary root that grows directly downward and gives off small lateral roots.

TERMINAL Located at the end of a shoot; not lateral or axillary.

TUBER A swollen underground stem, bearing buds or eyes from which new plants may grow.

UMBEL An umbrellalike growth of stalked flowers rising from a common point.

WHORL A circular arrangement of leaves or flowers on the stem.

Index of Common Names

266

Index of Botanical Names

271

73 74 75 76 77 10 9 8 7 6 5 4 3 2 1